THE YOUNG

The Young Karl Marx is an innovative and important new study of Marx's early writings. These writings provide the fascinating spectacle of a powerful and imaginative intellect wrestling with complex and significant issues, but they also present formidable interpretative obstacles to modern readers. David Leopold shows how an understanding of their intellectual and cultural context can illuminate the political dimension of these works. An erudite yet accessible discussion of Marx's influences and targets frames the author's critical engagement with Marx's account of the emergence, character, and (future) replacement of the modern state. This combination of historical and analytical approaches results in a sympathetic, but not uncritical, exploration of topics including alienation, citizenship, community, antisemitism, and utopianism. *The Young Karl Marx* is a scholarly and original work which provides a radical and persuasive reinterpretation of Marx's complex and often misunderstood views of German philosophy, modern politics, and human flourishing.

DAVID LEOPOLD teaches political theory in the Department of Politics and International Relations, University of Oxford, and is a Fellow of Mansfield College, Oxford. His previous publications include an edition of Max Stirner, *The Ego and Its Own,* for the Cambridge Texts in the History of Political Thought series.

IDEAS IN CONTEXT 81

The Young Karl Marx

IDEAS IN CONTEXT

Edited by Quentin Skinner and James Tully

The books in this series will discuss the emergence of intellectual traditions and of related new disciplines. The procedures, aims and vocabularies that were generated will be set in the context of the alternatives available within the contemporary frameworks of ideas and institutions. Through detailed studies of the evolution of such traditions, and their modification by different audiences, it is hoped that a new picture will form of the development of ideas in their concrete contexts. By this means, artificial distinctions between the history of philosophy, of the various sciences, of society and politics, and of literature may be seen to dissolve.

The series is published with the support of the Exxon Foundation.

A list of books in the series will be found at the end of the volume.

THE YOUNG KARL MARX

German philosophy, modern politics, and human flourishing

DAVID LEOPOLD

Mansfield College, Oxford

CAMBRIDGE
UNIVERSITY PRESS

CAMBRIDGE UNIVERSITY PRESS
Cambridge, New York, Melbourne, Madrid, Cape Town, Singapore, São Paulo, Delhi

Cambridge University Press
The Edinburgh Building, Cambridge CB2 8RU, UK

Published in the United States of America by Cambridge University Press, New York

www.cambridge.org
Information on this title: www.cambridge.org/9780521118262

First published 2007
Reprinted 2009
This digitally printed version 2009

A catalogue record for this publication is available from the British Library

ISBN 978-0-521-87477-9 hardback
ISBN 978-0-521-11826-2 paperback

For Lucinda

Contents

Acknowledgements

This book owes much to the help that I have received from others, and one of the many nice things about its publication is that I am given an opportunity to thank them here.

My longest-standing debt is to Michael Freeden. No-one will believe me, but when I first started visiting his basement office to be educated and inspired, there were empty shelves and I could see the carpet. In the intervening years, and through the accumulating mountain of books and papers, Michael has remained a constant friend and guide. I am hugely grateful for his wise counsel, his enthusiasm for ideas, and his generous support.

I am also immensely grateful for the continuing inspiration and encouragement of G. A. Cohen. Jerry's guidance and support at an earlier stage of this project were especially important. More generally, he has provided both a formidable intellectual example and a striking personal reminder of the value of honesty and humour. I cherish the opportunity that I have had of working with him.

I am also grateful to Stuart White and Jonathan Wolff, who provided welcome reassurance as well as excellent critical comments on an earlier version of what follows. More recently, I was fortunate to receive the generous encouragement of Terrell Carver, whose understanding of, and support for, what I was trying to do here were much appreciated.

I have benefited greatly from the resources of the Bodleian Library, the British Library, and Cambridge University Library. For providing additional materials, I would like to thank the Internationaal Instituut voor Sociale Geschiedenis in Amsterdam, and the Hebrew Union College-Jewish Institute of Religion in Cincinnati.

I would like to record my appreciation to the Warden and Fellows of Merton College, Oxford, who – at a vital moment – helped me find some time to work and (more importantly) think. The assistance of Martin Ceadel and Elizabeth Frazer was crucial in this regard.

A number of friends, colleagues, and complete strangers have kindly provided additional information and support of various sorts. They include: Chris Bertram, David Hine, Douglas Moggach, Hans-Martin Sass, Marc Stears, Lawrence S. Stepelevich, Zoe Waxman, and Jonathan Wright.

I am also grateful to Richard Fisher and the staff of Cambridge University Press for the efficient and professional manner in which they have brought this volume to publication.

Throughout the time I was working on this book, I was fortunate to have the support and example of two clever and loyal friends. Mark Griffith and Matthew Kempshall have very little in common, but that little includes an independence of mind and a commitment to scholarship which have proved a constant source of refreshment to me. I should also like to include Paul Lodge in this esteemed company. Paul arrived too late to suffer the real trauma of association with this project, but his friendship and good sense as it was being completed have been important to me.

Finally, Lucinda Rumsey has been brilliant. It is possible that this book would have been completed without her love and support, but I am unable to imagine how.

A note on language, references, and translation

With some reluctance, I have occasionally followed the convention of using not only masculine pronouns and possessives ('he', 'him', 'his') but also the noun 'man' to denote persons of both sexes. This convention may be grammatically correct but it is also, in certain respects, outmoded. I have used it here in order both to maintain consistency with translations which overwhelmingly adopt that usage and to avoid the appearance of anachronism (since, when he wrote in English, Marx followed this same convention).

I have used short titles for works by Marx and some other authors. Those titles are expanded in the Bibliographical Note that follows the main text. Wherever appropriate and possible – and especially for the writings of Marx and his contemporaries – I have provided references to both a German source and an English translation (although I have not always followed the translation cited).

I have throughout resisted the enthusiasm of some translators of German for capitalising what they consider to be extravagant philosophical entities, not least because that device was not available to the original authors. The one exception concerns Marx's parody of speculative method in *Die heilige Familie*, where capitalisation distinguishes the absolute Fruit from finite fruits in an appropriately exaggerated manner.

CHAPTER I

Introduction

I did not originally set out to write a study of the young Karl Marx. The roots of the present volume lie in a broader, and rather different, project which I subsequently abandoned.[1] When I should really have been reading other things, I found myself returning again and again to Marx's early writings. The allure of these texts may not be immediately apparent. After all, they have been described accurately as 'a number of meagre, obscure, and often unfinished texts which contain some of Marx's most elusive ideas'.[2]

Nevertheless, the writings of the young Marx seemed to me to possess two signal properties: they were *suggestive*, that is, they gave the impression of containing ideas worthy of further consideration; and they were *opaque*, that is, their meaning was far from transparent. It was these characteristics which led eventually to the writing of the present volume. In attempting to understand works which I found interesting but unclear, I hoped to reach a sounder judgement of their worth.

THE 'DISCOVERY' OF THE EARLY WRITINGS

Not everyone has been similarly beguiled by these early writings. They certainly failed to attract much attention from Marx's own contemporaries. Several of the most important of these texts, including the *Kritik* and the *Manuskripte*, were not written for publication, and their existence was discovered only after Marx's death. Other works were published at the time, but in radical periodicals with small and uncertain circulations. Marx's article 'Zur Judenfrage', for example, was published in the *Deutsch-Französische Jahrbücher*, a journal of which only one (double) edition ever appeared, in a print-run of one thousand copies of which some eight hundred seem to

---

[1] A fragment of that earlier project – which was concerned with certain aspects of left-Hegelianism – appears in the introduction and apparatus of Max Stirner, *The Ego and Its Own*, ed. David Leopold (Cambridge, 1995).
[2] John Plamenatz, *Karl Marx's Philosophy of Man* (Oxford, 1975) p. 33.

have been seized by the authorities.[3] At the time, none of these published works attracted either popular or critical acclaim on any scale.

The only writings from the early 1840s which were subsequently reprinted during Marx's lifetime were two pieces of his earliest journalism, which pre-date the early writings as defined here (a somewhat narrow definition elaborated below). These two articles on contemporary German conditions – a comment on the latest Prussian censorship instructions, and a report of the debate concerning freedom of the press in the Sixth Rhineland Diet (both written in 1842) – were reprinted by Hermann Becker under the seemingly inflated title *Gesammelte Aufsätze von Karl Marx* (1851). The rarity of this emaciated 'collection' would be hard to exaggerate. It appears that only a handful of copies were ever printed and that these were never distributed outside of Cologne. (Only recently has the provenance of this exceptionally scarce volume become clearer.[4])

With this lone, partial, and underwhelming exception, neither Marx nor any of his contemporaries showed much interest in rescuing the early writings from the obscurity into which they had almost immediately fallen. Although he preserved his study notebooks from this period, Marx appears to have been less than assiduous in keeping copies of his own published writings. The 1840s were a turbulent, as well as highly formative, period in his life, during which Marx lived in three different countries – Germany, France, and Belgium – before finally settling into (permanent) exile in England (arriving in August 1849). It is, nonetheless, surprising to discover that he had failed to retain a copy of his first book – *Die heilige Familie* (written jointly with Friedrich Engels, and published in February 1845). It was 1867 before he acquired his own copy, presented by Ludwig Kugelmann (a gynaecologist and communist living in Hanover), who, Marx reported to Engels, 'has in his possession a far better collection of our works than the two of us together'.[5] As late as 1892, Engels was having to contact Kugelmann in search of the more recherché of Marx's publications.[6]

[3] These estimates are from Hal Draper, *The Marx–Engels Cyclopedia*, volume 1: *The Marx–Engels Chronicle* (New York, 1985) p. 16. See also Maximilien Rubel and Margaret Manale, *Marx Without Myth: A Chronological Study of His Life and Work* (Oxford, 1975) p. 38.
[4] Evidence now suggests that it was a hastily printed and poorly distributed fascicle, comprising one fifth of the first volume of a projected two-volume set. Police action against Cologne communists prevented the completion of the project. The rest of the first volume was to have included the bulk of Marx's contributions to the *Rheinische Zeitung*. The precise contents of the intended second volume are not certain. See *MEGA②* 1, 1, pp. 976–9.
[5] Marx to Engels, 24 April 1867, *MEW* 31, p. 290; *MECW* 42, p. 360. 'I was pleasantly surprised', Marx continues, 'to find that we have no need to feel ashamed of the piece.'
[6] See Engels to August Bebel, 26 September 1892, *MEW* 38, p. 475; *MECW* 49, p. 543; and Engels to Ludwig Kugelmann, 4 October 1892, *MEW* 38, p. 485; *MECW* 50, p. 3.

A sustained and coordinated effort to publish some of Marx's out-of-print and unpublished writings did take place following his death in 1883. It was directed by Engels, not only Marx's closest collaborator, his literary executor, and a highly respected figure in the burgeoning international socialist movement, but also – in his own estimation – the only 'living soul' who could decipher Marx's notorious handwriting.[7] However, Engels devoted most of his declining editorial energies to the remaining volumes of *Kapital* and to new editions of those (usually previously published) texts which offered clear and relevant practical guidance to the European socialist movement. The works of the young Marx were adjudged not to fulfil those criteria. (The so-called 'Thesen über Feuerbach' were published, but these form part of Marx's preparatory work on *Die deutsche Ideologie*, and so fall outside the 'early writings' as defined here.) Indeed, Engels appears to have considered the early writings to be of rather limited significance.[8] Even where their content was of some interest, he maintained that the 'semi-Hegelian language' of works from this period was 'untranslatable' and – even in the original German – had lost 'the greater part of its meaning'.[9] He resisted proposals for a French translation of the 'Kritik: Einleitung', and dismissed the language of the 'Briefwechsel von 1853' as 'incomprehensible'.[10]

At the beginning of the twentieth century – as a result, in part, of Marx's apparent lack of interest and Engels's considered disapproval – even the most dedicated admirer of Marx's writings would not have known of the existence of, let alone have read, the overwhelming majority of the texts which are considered in the present volume. At most, such an admirer might have heard of *Die heilige Familie*, but never have seen a copy of it.

The first serious effort at unearthing Marx's early writings began with the publication in 1902 of Franz Mehring's collection *Aus dem literarischen Nachlass von Karl Marx, Friedrich Engels, und Ferdinand Lassalle*. However, this edition included only previously published works by the young

---

[7] Marx to Pytor Lavrov, 5 February 1884, *MEW* 36, p. 99; *MECW* 47, p. 93. See also Engels to Karl Kautsky, 28 January 1889, *MEW* 37, p. 144; *MECW* 48, pp. 258–9. Kurt Müller, who learnt graphology in a Nazi prison, subsequently compiled the 'Müller Primer' to help editors decipher Marx's script.

[8] See, for example, Alexis Voden, 'Talks With Engels', Institute of Marxism-Leninism (ed.), *Reminiscences of Marx and Engels* (Moscow, n.d.) pp. 330–2.

[9] Engels to Florence Kelley-Wischnewetzky, 25 February 1886, *MEW* 36, p. 452; *MECW* 47, p. 416. The quoted remarks concern his own *Die Lage der arbeitenden Klasse in England*, but Engels maintained that Marx's early writings suffered the same limitations.

[10] See Engels to Laura Lafargue, 14 October 1893, *MEW* 39, p. 146; *MECW* 50, p. 21; and Engels to Wilhelm Liebknecht, 18 December 1890, *MEW* 37, p. 527; *MECW* 49, pp. 93–4.

Marx (such as *Die heilige Familie* and articles from the *Deutsch-Französische Jahrbücher*).[11]

It was 1927 before the early writings began to appear more fully, as part of the *Marx–Engels Gesamtausgabe* edition (henceforth *MEGA①*) directed by David Ryazanov – a figure of enormous importance in the history of the collection, preservation, and publication of the work of Marx and Engels.[12] Ryazanov published scholarly versions of many of the works of the young Marx discussed here (including the *Kritik*, the *Manuskripte*, and the *Auszüge aus James Mill*). However, in the early 1930s, whilst still in its initial stages, this project was effectively cancelled (and copies of the published volumes subsequently proved difficult to locate). The most important of Marx's early writings were now in print, but they could scarcely be described as widely available.

The wider dissemination of the young Marx's work, and the publication of early writings omitted by *MEGA①*, was a leisurely and uneven process. For example, satisfactory editions of the *Manuskripte* appeared in English only in 1956, and in French in 1962. (Earlier translations existed, but they were either incomplete or problematic in some respect.[13]) A central element in the wider story here is the emergence of a new *Marx–Engels Gesamtausgabe* (henceforth *MEGA②*), whose first volumes appeared in 1975. Not the least important contribution of this new edition was the commitment to include, for the first time, all of his extant study notebooks. It was Marx's lifelong habit to make excerpts from the books that he was reading, occasionally interspersing his own remarks and criticisms. (Some two hundred of these study notebooks have been preserved.) Notwithstanding many difficulties and some significant editorial changes, the *MEGA②* project continues today. It was placed under the 'non-Soviet' managerial auspices of the Internationale Marx-Engels Stiftung (IMES) in 1990, and the first volumes under that new regime were published in 1998. It is scarcely an exaggeration to claim that detailed textual knowledge of the early writings is still in a process of evolution: some interesting texts have only recently been

---

[11] These are the only early writings mentioned in the bibliography attached to Lenin's famous *Granat Encyclopaedia* article 'Karl Marx' (1913). V. I. Lenin, *Collected Works*, volume 21 (Moscow, 1964) pp. 41–91. This article has been identified as the best indicator of the availability of Marx's works before 1914. See Eric J. Hobsbawm, 'The Fortunes of Marx and Engels's Writings', Eric J. Hobsbawm (ed.), *The History of Marxism*, volume 1: *Marxism in Marx's Day* (Bloomington IN, 1982) p. 332.

[12] See Rolf Hecker (ed.), *David Borisovic Rjazanov und die erste MEGA* (Berlin, 1997).

[13] The 1962 French translation by Emile Bottigelli, for example, was preceded by the Molitor translation, which was not based on the *MEGA①* arrangement of the text and omitted the 'first manuscript'. The 1956 English translation by Martin Milligan was preceded by a version by Ria Stone, which – whatever its merits (I have been unable to obtain a copy) – circulated only in mimeographed form.

published;[14] the occasional piece of correspondence is still discovered;[15] some familiar items have been expelled from the corpus;[16] and certain textual disputes remain without definitive resolution.[17]

The main purpose of this abbreviated history is to underline the late appearance of the early writings. It was some fifty years after Marx's death before the bulk of the early writings appeared properly in print. Moreover, the circumstances in which the work of the young Marx was first published and circulated were not entirely propitious. In particular, it occurred at a time when Marxism was increasingly identified with the Soviet experience and with the approved or 'orthodox' body of theory that had begun to solidify around it. That authorised version of Marxism found it difficult to incorporate the language and concerns of the early writings into its systematic world view. The unease of Stalinism with any intellectual work outside of those official parameters was reflected in the fate of the original *MEGA*① project. Following the effective cancellation of this edition, many of its original staff 'disappeared'. Ryazanov himself was first exiled to Saratov, then allowed to return to Moscow after 1934, only to be re-arrested during the great purges, accused of 'Trotskyism', and executed in 1938. This Soviet unease continued in a variety of less dramatic forms. As recently as the 1960s, for example, the collected *Marx Engels Werke* (edited from Moscow and Berlin) posted a symbolic health warning on the early writings by relegating most of them to an unnumbered '*Ergänzungsband*', published outside of the chronological sequence of the other volumes.

Reflecting and reinforcing this hostile reaction, other, less conventional, voices took up the young Marx with enthusiasm, in part as a stick with which to beat that orthodoxy. In such quarters the publication of the early writings was welcomed as a significant event precisely because these works appeared to cast doubt on the authority of Soviet Marxism.

This sharply divided response to the early writings is illustrated by the publication of the *Manuskripte* in 1932. Having lain undisturbed for over

---

[14] For example, the young Marx's notes on Rousseau's *Contrat social* (discussed in Chapter 4) appeared only in 1981.

[15] See, for example, Marx to Wilhelm Saint-Paul, March 1843, *Marx-Engels-Jahrbuch*, volume 1 (Berlin, 1978) pp. 328–9.

[16] For example, the 1843 article 'Luther als Schiedsrichter zwischen Strauss und Feuerbach' is no longer held to be by Marx.

[17] For example, there is a continuing disagreement about the status and editorial arrangement of the *Manuskripte*.

eight decades, the *Manuskripte* now appeared in two competing German editions in the same year. The *MEGA①* version possessed greater textual authority, but the alternative volume had a significant interpretative impact.[18] The editors of the latter – Siegfried Landshut and J. P. Mayer – maintained that the *Manuskripte* revealed the previously hidden thread that ran throughout Marx's entire output, allowing his later work to be understood properly for the first time, and casting doubt on received accounts of its meaning.[19]

This enthusiastic embrace of the apparent heterodoxy of the early writings was repeated in a variety of different contexts. Consider the following two examples, separated by some thirty years and several thousand miles.

Herbert Marcuse would become one of the central figures in the intellectual movement now known as Western Marxism, but it was as an ambitious post-doctoral student of Martin Heidegger, at the University of Freiburg, that he wrote one of the first reviews of the *Manuskripte*. In his review for *Die Gesellschaft* (published in 1932), Marcuse insisted that this newly discovered text could not simply be slotted into existing readings of Marx, but rather required a fundamental revision of those received interpretations. The publication of the *Manuskripte*, Marcuse maintained, was a 'crucial event' precisely because it cast doubt on orthodox accounts of the 'meaning' of Marx's theoretical system, and, in particular, put the entire theory of 'scientific socialism' into question.[20] (The date of this review provides a striking reminder of wider historical events; within twelve months Hitler would be named Chancellor, Heidegger would enter the Nazi Party as Rector of the University, and Marcuse and his family would have abandoned Germany.)

In America in the late fifties and early sixties, the publication of an English translation of the *Manuskripte* generated a similar response, especially amongst those who would form part of the intellectual current subsequently known as the New Left. Marshall Berman has provided an evocative description of his excitement when, as a student at Columbia in 1959, he discovered the '*Kabbalah*' written by Marx 'before he became Karl Marx', and now available in English for the first time.[21] Berman bought twenty

---

[18] See Michael Maidan, 'The *Rezeptionsgeschichte* of the Paris Manuscripts', *History of European Ideas*, volume 12 (1990) pp. 767–81.
[19] See Karl Marx, *Der historische Materialismus*, volume 1: *Die Frühschriften*, ed. Siegfried Landshut and J. P. Mayer (Leipzig, 1932) p. xiii. This edition omitted the 'first manuscript', and its organisation of the remaining text differed from that of *MEGA①*.
[20] Herbert Marcuse, 'Neue Quellen zur Grundlegung des Historischen Materialismus', *Die Gesellschaft*, volume 2 (1932) pp. 136–7.
[21] Marshall Berman, *Adventures in Marxism* (London, 1999) pp. 6–7.

copies of this 'great new product that would change the world' as Hanukkah gifts for friends and family, revelling in the certainty that he had discovered 'something special, something that would both rip up their lives and make them happy'.[22] That 'product' was 'Marx, but not communism'.[23] Berman's reference to Kabbalah is not entirely frivolous. The early writings provided an alternative and esoteric vantage point, with its own sacred literature, which profoundly influenced subsequent generations; the *Manuskripte*, it might be said, became a second Bible to some, at least as venerated as *Kapital*, if not more so.

As the reactions of Marcuse and Berman illustrate, many welcomed the early writings precisely because they appeared to cast doubt on the authority of the orthodox Soviet account of Marx's work. In this way, responses to the early writings became polarised from the very beginning. These texts had to be identified, *either* as rightly abandoned juvenilia, *or* as the long-lost key to a proper interpretation of Marx's entire output. The relative merits of these two sets of disputants is not at issue here. The point is rather to draw attention to the way in which this *Rezeptionsgeschichte* – with its barely concealed political agenda – hampered the study of Marx's intellectual evolution, and distorted the interpretation of the early writings. There are some serious and sophisticated contributions to this interpretative literature, but commentators have found it difficult to get beyond an explanatory framework which offers the impoverished alternative of 'one Marx or two' (the author, either of a coherent body of work whose real achievements are established in its early stages, or of a fractured corpus whose mature accomplishments rest on the abandonment of an earlier false start).[24] This simplistic and suspect dichotomy, together with the historical background which produced it, constitutes an ongoing 'external' obstacle to understanding the early writings which should not be underestimated.

Present circumstances are, of course, rather different. Whilst that 'external' obstacle to understanding undoubtedly still survives, the historical context which created and sustained it has been transformed. I am tempted to offer the optimistic conjecture that our own times might prove comparatively congenial to the serious evaluation of the nature and significance of Marx's thought. (There is, at least, some early and anecdotal evidence

[22] *Ibid.* p. 9.   [23] *Ibid.* p. 15.
[24] Althusser's account, for example, whilst knowledgeable and stimulating, is framed around the implausible notion that a single fundamental division can make sense of Marx's intellectual evolution. Althusser adopts and develops a series of concepts – *lecture symptomale*, *problématique*, and *coupure épistémologique* – whose primary purpose is to justify an 'inventory of possibilities' that he concedes 'may well seem derisory' (namely whether or not the young Marx was 'already and wholly' Marx). See Louis Althusser, *For Marx* (London, 1969) p. 53.

of a normalisation of Marx scholarship within academia.) The existence of
Soviet communism undoubtedly helped distort our knowledge of his work,
and its subsequent collapse might provide an unexpected opportunity, not
to bury Marx, but better to understand him.

ADDITIONAL OBSTACLES

Overcoming the distortions generated by the distinctive history of the
early writings is not the only interpretative difficulty confronting students
of the young Marx. These texts present a formidable variety of additional
obstacles, including problems arising from the form, content, status, and
polemical focus of these texts.

Perhaps the most obvious difficulty for modern readers is the style of
Marx's prose. To adopt a quip made (in a different context) by Engels,
all too often the young Marx wrote like 'a German philosopher', which
is to say he wrote 'very badly'.[25] The language of the early writings can
be difficult, largely because it reflects the intellectual currents and fash-
ions of its time.[26] These wider historical difficulties are compounded by
Marx's occasional enthusiasm for style at the expense of clarity in his own
prose. Consider, for example, his use of chiasmus (the left-Hegelian Szeliga's
talent is said to be 'not that of disclosing what is hidden (*Verborgne zu
enthüllen*), but of hiding what is disclosed (*Enthüllte zu verbergen*)');[27] his
use of paradiastole (the 'perfected Christian state' is said to be 'the atheist
state');[28] and his use of contemporary allusion (a reference to the 'out-
pourings of the heart (*Herzensergießungen*)' of Friedrich Wilhelm IV is
unlikely to remind many modern readers of a collection of essays on art
and music by Ludwig Tieck and Wilhelm Wackenroder).[29] I do not mean
to suggest that Marx was never clear and precise, only that he was not
always so. Indeed, the young Marx can sometimes appear keener to press
such standards on others than he was to adopt them himself. Consider,
for example, his caustic remark about the need to translate Hegel into

---

[25] 'Briefe aus London' 475/386. This comment was directed at Robert Owen, but, elsewhere, Engels
identified 'bad,'abstract, unintelligible and clumsy' forms of expression as a distinctive feature of the
early development of socialist ideas in Germany. 'Fourier' 605/614.

[26] Marx subsequently recognised (some of) these limitations. See, for example, his sarcastic reference
to the use of a term ('*Entfremdung*') which 'will be comprehensible to the philosophers'. *Die deutsche
Ideologie* 34/48.

[27] *Die heilige Familie* 58/56. 'Szeliga' was the pseudonym adopted by the Prussian officer, and sometime
left-Hegelian, Franz Zychlin von Zychlinsky.

[28] 'Zur Judenfrage' 357/156/222.

[29] 'Briefwechsel von 1843' 341/140/204. The book is the wonderfully titled *Herzensergießungen eines
kunstliebenden Klosterbruders*.

'prose';[30] his pointed criticism of Arnold Ruge for making 'every object the occasion for stylistic exercises in public';[31] and his relentless ridiculing of Szeliga's 'dialectical reasoning'.[32]

There are also problems with the content of the early writings. Some of the central ideas with which Marx is preoccupied – of alienation, 'objectification', self-realisation, and so forth – are difficult ones, even considered apart from his occasionally obscuring prose. Moreover, that problem of intrinsic complexity is compounded, for modern readers, at least, by the unfamiliarity of some of those concepts.

The status of many of the early writings also creates problems. These writings include published works, pieces intended for eventual publication but not published, and pieces never intended for publication. The assumption that these various texts should have equal authority is open to doubt. It might seem reasonable to attribute extra weight to those writings which constituted a public statement of Marx's views.[33] However, the wider political context, including the complexities of contemporary censorship, complicates matters here, and published texts certainly cannot be assumed to include all that Marx might have wanted to say. Unpublished texts are no less problematic. Some of the most important of the early writings appear in study notebooks whose primary purpose was the clarification of Marx's own ideas to himself. The problem here is not simply that Marx's prose was never polished for public consumption, but rather that these texts are frequently part of an internal dialogue whose wider meaning is uncertain.

In addition, the polemical focus of these works creates problems for modern readers. It is a striking feature of the early writings that, almost without exception, Marx proceeds by criticising the writings of others. The *Kritik* is a critical commentary on Hegel's *Rechtsphilosophie*; 'Zur Judenfrage' and *Die heilige Familie* are attacks on the work of Bruno Bauer; the 'Kritische Randglossen' is a polemic against Arnold Ruge's journalism; and so on. This adversarial focus may say something about the young Marx's personality and ambition – all of these targets were older and better known than himself – but it also demonstrates his characteristic way of working. Marx tended to develop his own ideas through a critical engagement with the writings of others, and this creates a number of interpretative difficulties for modern readers. In particular, one cannot rely on the young Marx himself

[30] *Kritik* 205/7/61. See also *ibid.* 215/16/72.　　[31] 'Kritische Randglossen' 405/202/416.
[32] *Die heilige Familie* 67/64.
[33] See, for example, Keith Graham, *Karl Marx, Our Contemporary: Social Theory for a Post-Leninist World* (Toronto, 1992) p. 2.

for an accurate account of his critical targets.[34] This is largely the result of
Marx taking the reader's knowledge of those critical targets for granted (and
not, I think, of any systematic or deliberate attempt to mislead). Given his
limited contemporary audience this was not an unreasonable attitude, but
modern readers are obviously a very different matter. As a result, in what
follows I provide (often extensive) accounts of several authors other than
Marx, in particular of G. W. F. Hegel, Bruno Bauer, and Ludwig Feuerbach.[35] Without some knowledge of their work, it is not only impossible to
understand and judge the success of Marx's criticisms, but also difficult to
make sense of his own positive views. The latter have to be reconstructed,
at least in part, from Marx's critical assessment of others.

HUMAN NATURE AND THE MODERN STATE

Thus far it might appear as if the present book were limited only by a
particular – if (as yet) imprecisely specified – time frame. However, my
remit is doubly restricted, bound by both chronology and content. Both
of these constraints require some elaboration.

I have already referred to the first restriction (my limited chronological
remit) noting, for example, the narrow definition of 'the young Marx' and
'the early writings' that is adopted here.[36] To be more precise, I use these
expressions to refer to Marx (who was then in his mid-twenties) and the
work that he produced (beginning with the 'Briefwechsel von 1843' and
ending just before he began writing *Die deutsche Ideologie*) during a two-
and-a-half-year period from March 1843 to September 1845. Of course, in
adopting this nomenclature, I do not mean to deny the existence of perfectly
plausible senses in which Marx was also 'young' in 1846, or his writings still
'early' in 1842. However, this is a close study of a chronologically limited
group of writings and some economical way of referring to those texts and
their author was required.

The second restriction concerns the content or subject matter of those
texts. I am interested, not in all aspects of his early writings, but rather
in the political thought of the young Marx. More precisely (if somewhat

[34] See David McLellan, *The Young Hegelians and Karl Marx* (London, 1969) p. 51; and Allan Megill,
Karl Marx: The Burden of Reason (Why Marx Rejected Politics and the Market) (Lanham MD, 2002)
p. 156.
[35] To avoid confusion, Bauer's brothers – unlike Bruno himself – always appear with their first name
attached.
[36] 'Narrow' since the early writings are often defined more broadly, typically as all of those works
written in and before 1845. See, for example, Jonathan Wolff, *Why Read Marx Today?* (Oxford, 2002)
p. 10.

schematically), the present book is concerned with his account of the emergence, the character, and the (future) replacement of the modern state. In exploring these topics, I have been preoccupied with the close, if sometimes elusive, relation between Marx's account of politics and his conception of human nature.

I conjectured above that present circumstances might provide a comparatively favourable opportunity to improve our understanding of Marx's work. Of course, one might acknowledge the existence of an opportunity, but question the value of pursuing it. It might be thought, for example, that any rationale for being interested in Marx had collapsed with the Soviet Union. However, that some significant percentage of the world's population had his airbrushed portrait on the walls of their government offices was never the best reason for being interested in Marx's *ideas*. Indeed, that ubiquity conspired against a proper appreciation of his work. Marx was a thinker whom there was no need to consult at first hand; everyone already knew what he said, and what they thought about what he said. Yet today, when people can be persuaded to read Marx's writings with care and thought, they are often surprised and excited by what they find. They quickly discover an author who has unexpected and interesting things to say, and whom they no longer feel that they have to swallow (or spew out) whole. The young Marx's discussion of the contemporary fate of individuals in civil society, his account of the achievements and failings of modern political life, and his vision of the (as yet unrealised) possibilities of human flourishing all resonate with this new audience.

There is, of course, a connection between these two dimensions of my remit (the chronology and the content). It is in this period, and in these texts, that the relation between politics, modernity, and human nature forms an especially clear and consistent thread in Marx's work.

Before 1843, although it is always possible to trace more or less plausible adumbrations, Marx neither was committed to the same view of, nor did he have the same interest in, the *modern* state. For example, his *Rheinische Zeitung* articles (on press freedom, wood thefts, the divorce law, and so on) are primarily concerned with the character of Prussian rule in the Rhineland and not with the nature of modern political life.[37] The young Marx would subsequently insist that the modern state was a very different entity from its feudal and other predecessors, and that conditions in politically backward Germany (the subject of his *Rheinische Zeitung*

---

[37] For an interesting attempt to link Marx's earlier journalism with his later work, see Heinz Lubasz, 'Marx's Initial Problematic: The Problem of Poverty', *Political Studies*, volume 24 (1976) pp. 24–42.

articles) could provide little guidance as to its precise character. As a result, the focus of his earlier journalism could reasonably be described as somewhat parochial and limited.

After 1845, although Marx remains interested in the emergence, character, and replacement of the modern state, his account of these matters is less clearly and closely associated with his philosophical anthropology. It is surely not accurate to describe Marx as simply abandoning without trace his concern with this conjunction of subjects, but he does subsequently appear less certain of the relation between politics and human nature. In addition, other, not necessarily related, ideas about the state emerge alongside – indeed come to dominate – these earlier views. It comes as no surprise to discover that many discussions of Marx's work make no reference to the kind of understanding of modern political life which is a central feature of the early writings.[38]

The account of the early writings propounded in the present work does not depend upon, or entail, any particular view about the overall structure of Marx's intellectual development. I hope that readers with widely divergent understandings of that latter issue might accept my reading of the early writings. My characterisation of these texts as 'early' is not meant to be pejorative – no putative lack of development or maturity is intended – nor is it meant to suggest any barrier between the writings of the young Marx and material written before or after my chronological remit. (The comments above, regarding the evolution and fate of this conjunction of concerns in works preceding and postdating the early writings, should not be thought to undermine this claim to bracket any wider interpretation of the evolution of Marx's ideas. My intention was simply to offer some explanation both of the limited chronological span of this study and of the relative neglect of this relation between politics and human nature in the literature on Marxism and the state.)

DOUBTS AND AMBITIONS

The prospect of another study of the young Marx will not fill all potential readers with unbridled enthusiasm. In particular, three reservations about the present study might be broached here.

First, one might consider the early writings to be without merit, and doubt whether the young Marx provides much interesting reflection on

---

[38] See, for example, the 'instrumentalist', 'class balance', and 'abdication' models of the state outlined in Jon Elster, *Making Sense of Marx* (Cambridge, 1985) chapter 7.

topics of importance. In these preliminary remarks, I shall not respond directly to this reservation. I suspect that anyone convinced in advance that the early writings are not of intellectual interest is unlikely to be moved by any brief observations that I might make here. That so many others have been intellectually engaged by these works does not constitute a very powerful rejoinder to this doubt. As one recent critic has observed, many 'brilliant, nutty writers' – such as Henry George in America at the end of the nineteenth century or Alexandre Kojève in post-war France – have been hugely influential for a generation or two without ever establishing a stronger or more lasting claim to our attention.[39] The question whether on reflection, and without the artificial sustenance once provided by the existence of the Soviet Union, Marx might turn out to be 'more like George and Kojève than like Aristotle and Kant' is a serious one.[40] That said, should readers with such doubts venture further, one ambition of this work as a whole is to weaken their scepticism.

Second, one might take the transparency of Marx's early writings for granted, and question the need for any elaborate exegesis. An effective rejoinder to this doubt is easier to provide. I have already raised some of the interpretative difficulties facing modern readers, and it is hard to imagine a persuasive denial of the need for appropriate critical guidance. Indeed, it has become something of a commonplace to remark upon the notorious opacity of the early writings – to bemoan, as one writer has put it, 'the dead formulae and the (by now often meaningless) Hegelian patter that mars some of the most original pages of Marx' – a commonplace, readers will note, that I have not entirely forsworn myself.[41]

Third, one might assume that the existing literature has already covered the pertinent issues, leaving little scope for further discussion; if anything is worth saying about Marx's writings, then surely it must have been said by now. However, whilst there is no shortage of studies of Marx, not all of that work is of a high standard. It may be appropriate to mention three particular features of that secondary material which I have reacted against in my own work. Discussion of Marx's work often takes the form of (more or less convincing) commentary on a small number of familiar passages from well-known works. Careful readings of single works and discussion of less familiar texts are relatively unusual. In what follows, as well as covering some well-trodden ground, I examine many lesser-known passages and texts. I do so, not only better to interpret the Famous Quotations, but

[39] Richard Rorty, *Philosophy and Social Hope* (London, 1999) p. 218.
[40] *Ibid.*, p. 219.   [41] Isaiah Berlin, *The Life and Opinions of Moses Hess* (Cambridge, 1959) p. 38.

also to shift attention away from them.[42] An additional feature of much of the literature is that commentators cluster around two equally implausible evaluative poles. There are those who confuse Marx's endorsement of a claim with that claim's being true, and those who confuse Marx's endorsement of a claim with that claim's being false. I have tried to resist the attractions of both of these poles, pointing out obscurities, omissions, and objections, at the same time as attempting sympathetically to make sense of what Marx wrote. Finally, some of the relevant literature underestimates the degree of 'translation' that Marx's ideas require if they are to be understood. I refer here not to the many literal problems of working from texts written in a language other than English, but to the additional difficulties of understanding works written in an unfamiliar intellectual and cultural context.[43] Indeed, one might reasonably complain that commentators are often rather better at writing in the manner of the young Marx than at helping modern readers understand what he might have meant by what he wrote.[44]

So much for my defensive comments. Corresponding to these (legitimate) doubts, I have three (modest) ambitions for the present volume. I hope that this book provides some support for the claim that the work of the young Marx contains ideas that are worthy of further study, helps clarify some of the arguments and assumptions of the early writings, and adds something of value to an already voluminous existing literature.

It will become apparent that, in addition to these modest aspirations, I seek to revise some established views about particular aspects of Marx's thought. Perhaps the most central of these revisions concerns the widespread assumption that Marx is irredeemably and without qualification opposed to the state and politics. I maintain that Marx's view of the state and politics, at least in the early writings, is both more complex and more positive than this received account would suggest. Other interpretative commonplaces that I challenge, include claims that the *Kritik* simply reproduces the 'transformative criticism' of Feuerbach; that the *Manuskripte* embody a 'return' to Hegel; that the young Marx's comments on the 'Jewish

---

[42] The felicitous capitalisation ('the Famous Quotations') is borrowed from Ben Brewster's translation of 'les Célèbres Citations'. Althusser, *For Marx*, p. 27.
[43] On literal problems, Engels' critical comments on the efforts of 'John Broadhouse' (a pseudonym of H. M. Hyndman) are of interest. See 'How Not to Translate Marx'. These linguistic problems are, of course, compounded by historical distance.
[44] The following 'elucidatory' sentence is taken from a modern commentary (which it might be courteous not to identify here). It purports to explain a passage from the early writings, but could easily pass for an opaque specimen of Marx's contemporary prose: 'In other words, as long as man is political man, that is, an atomistic individual separated from his real social being, religion will continue to be the spirit of civil society, the objectified, alien, social essence; and money will remain the substance of civil society, the objectified, alien, social product.'

question' are antisemitic; that the concept of moral rights is rejected in 'Zur Judenfrage'; and that Marx was relentlessly hostile to utopian socialism. These are just some of the views which I hope do not survive unscathed from what follows.

In addition, I propound some new ways of looking at Marx's contemporaries (notably Bauer and Feuerbach), and at the relation between Marx and some of his precursors (notably Hegel, Rousseau, and Saint-Simon). I hope that these, sometimes extensive, discussions of other authors have a value in addition to the light which they shine on the writings of the young Marx. For example, I seek to cast some significant doubt on the dominant interpretations of both Bauer's antisemitism and Feuerbach's attitude towards politics.

ORGANISATION AND ARGUMENT

Of course, this kind of list – enumerating some of the established views about Marx (and others) that I seek to revise – provides little sense of the structure of the present book. Without pre-empting too much of its substantive content, it may be helpful to close these preliminary remarks with some account of the architecture of what follows. My comments will cover both the overall argument and internal structure of the text.

The present work is organised around three central chapters. These are concerned, broadly speaking, with the emergence, character, and (future) replacement of the modern state, respectively. Each chapter seeks to elaborate and illuminate Marx's account of these topics through an examination of one of the central critical targets of, or formative influences on, the early writings. In Chapter 2, I portray the critical engagement (in the *Kritik* and elsewhere) with Hegel's *Rechtsphilosophie* as providing the frame of reference in which Marx introduces his own understanding of the historical emergence of the modern state. In Chapter 3, I discuss the way in which his rejection (in 'Zur Judenfrage' and elsewhere) of Bauer's antisemitic writings provides the context of Marx's own account of the achievements and failings of 'political emancipation' (the kind of liberation associated with the modern state). Finally, in Chapter 4, from the vantage point provided by an analysis of Feuerbach's philosophical project, I examine Marx's account of the fate of the state and politics in a (future) society based on human flourishing.

These three central chapters are bracketed by two shorter ones. In the first of these (the present chapter), I have provided a brief account of the discovery and reception of Marx's early writings, broached some of the interpretative difficulties that these texts present, and outlined a few of my own ambitions in undertaking this study. In the second of these shorter chapters (which concludes the volume), I summarise some of my findings and attempt to provide some explanation of the (previously identified) weaknesses and omissions in the young Marx's account of future society.

As may already be apparent, this is not a book which propounds a single dominant thesis. It has a number of argumentative threads, not all of which depend upon the others. That said, there is both an intellectual coherence to these various threads and an argumentative structure to the book as a whole. That intellectual coherence is provided by both my subject matter (Marx's account of the emergence, character, and replacement of the modern state) and the distinctive treatment that it receives here (combining analytical and historical concerns). That overall argumentative structure is provided by the contrast between the young Marx's account of the modern state and his vision of what might replace it. Marx's diagnosis of the achievements and failings of the modern state is relatively clear and coherent, whereas his vision of human emancipation remains fragmentary and opaque (not least because its institutional embodiment remains hopelessly underspecified). That latter weakness is identified as flowing, in large part, from Marx's insufficiently motivated rejection of the need to provide 'blueprints' (the various plans, models, and templates) of a possible future society.

So much for the overall structure and argument of the present book. I turn now to address the relation between the young Marx's understanding of the emergence of the modern state and his critical engagement with Hegel's political philosophy.

CHAPTER 2

German philosophy

The extent and nature of his indebtedness to Hegel are perhaps the most fiercely contested issues in Marx scholarship. However, despite widespread and bitter disagreement concerning the *subsequent* development of Marx's thought, the 'Hegelian' character of the early writings is usually treated as incontrovertible. The assumption that it is Hegel who provides the predominant influence on the work of the *young* Marx is shared by proponents of both the 'continuity' and 'discontinuity' accounts of his overall intellectual evolution. Indeed, the purported Hegelianism of Marx's early writings frequently provides the reference point against which these very notions of 'continuity' and 'discontinuity' are defined and defended. The literature typically canvasses only two interpretative possibilities – either Marx ceased to be a Hegelian, or he did not cease to be a Hegelian.[1]

I regard this overwhelming consensus about the Hegelian character of the early writings with a degree of scepticism. Not least, its foundations look problematic. It is typically built on two tempting but contestable interpretative tendencies: the first is to treat German philosophy as the only significant influence on the young Marx; the second is to treat Hegel as if he constituted the entirety (as opposed to a part) of German philosophy. I have tried to resist both of these interpretative temptations in the present work, acknowledging the diversity, not only of German philosophy, but also of other possible influences on the young Marx.

In the present context, it is the second of these contestable interpretative tendencies – identifying as 'Hegelian' ideas whose provenance in German philosophical and cultural thought is much wider than that term would suggest – that is most pertinent. Consider two familiar attempts to establish Marx's Hegelianism by appealing to his use of particular philosophical motifs. Evidence of Hegel's decisive influence on Marx is occasionally found in the latter's use of the term '*Aufhebung*' (sometimes translated, rather

---

[1] See, for example, Jean Hyppolite, *Etudes sur Marx et Hegel* (Paris, 1955) pp. 107ff.

archaically, as 'sublation' in English). The use of *'Aufhebung'* to connote
a distinctive and complex combination of cancellation, preservation, and
elevation, is widely assumed to originate with Hegel. Accordingly, Marx's
use of the term (in anything approaching this sense) is treated as a simple
but effective guarantee of his Hegelianism.[2] However, the term *'Aufhebung'*
is used earlier, and in the same way, by other authors with whose work Marx
was familiar. For example, Friedrich Schiller uses the term in precisely this
sense at several points in his treatise *Über die ästhetische Erziehung des Menschen* (1795). Schiller adopts it, for instance, to characterise the manner in
which certain familiar oppositions (between feeling and thought, passiv-
ity and action, matter and form) are cancelled, preserved, and elevated in
the idea of 'beauty (*Schönheit*)'.[3] The same assumption of Hegelian provenance is made concerning the idea of a dialectical progression from a stage
of undifferentiated unity, through a stage of differentiation without unity,
to a stage of differentiated unity.[4] Where this idea appears in Marx's work
it is presumed to confirm Hegel's influence. Yet it would be a mistake to
identify this dialectical progression with Hegel alone. It constitutes a motif
which was common to a number of writers associated (more or less closely)
with *Frühromantik*, the period of early German romanticism which flourished in Jena and Berlin between 1796 and 1801. For example, this idea of a
dialectical progression forms the organising structure of *Hyperion, oder Der
Eremit in Griechenland* (1799). Through a somewhat sentimental narrative,
Friedrich Hölderlin recounts a story of the loss, and recovery at a higher
level, of humankind's unity with nature and God. (Hölderlin's contribution to German idealism is increasingly recognised, and one commentator
has appositely described *Hyperion* as more 'Hegelian' than anything that
Hegel was himself writing at this time.[5]) I raise these two examples (the
use of *'Aufhebung'* and this idea of dialectical progression), not in order to
substitute the claims of Schiller, Hölderlin, or indeed anyone else for those
of Hegel, but rather to question some familiar ways of trying to establish

[2] See, for example, the (somewhat remorseless) cataloguing of Marx's use of *'Aufhebung'* in order to
demonstrate his Hegelianism, in Shlomo Avineri, *The Social and Political Thought of Karl Marx*
(Cambridge, 1969) pp. 36–8, 84, 99, 105, 150, 160, 179, 186, 202–4, 208–12, 221, 243, 250.

[3] See, for example, Friedrich Schiller, *Über die ästhetische Erziehung des Menschen* (Oxford, 1967)
pp. 123–5, 172–3. Note also the editorial remarks of Wilkinson and Willoughby, *ibid.* pp. 304–5.

[4] See, for example, G. A. Cohen, *History, Labour, and Freedom: Themes From Marx* (Oxford, 1988)
chapter 10.

[5] For *Hyperion*, see Friedrich Hölderlin, *Sämtliche Werke*, volume 3: *Hyperion* (Stuttgart, 1958). For
the apposite description, see Edward Craig, *The Mind of God and the Works of Man* (Oxford, 1987)
p. 163. See also Dieter Henrich, *Hegel im Kontext* (Frankfurt am Main, 1971) pp. 9–40; and Eckart
Förster, 'To Lend Wings to Physics Once Again: Hölderlin and the Oldest System Programme of
German Idealism', *European Journal of Philosophy*, volume 3 (1995) pp. 174–90.

the latter's predominant influence on the young Marx. I do not deny the accuracy and utility of situating Marx in the context of a particular philosophical tradition (in which Hegel undoubtedly plays an important role). However, the tendency to treat German philosophy as the only influence on the young Marx, and the tendency to treat Hegel as if he constituted the entirety (as opposed to an undoubtedly important element) of that tradition, seem to me misguided.

This one-sided emphasis on the Hegelianism of the young Marx has had a number of deleterious consequences. It can be said to have significantly distorted our understanding of both the content of the early writings and the context in which they were produced. In particular, it has encouraged neglect, not only of other influences on Marx's intellectual development, but also of the sustained critique of Hegel and Hegelianism that runs through the early writings.

A wholesale assault on this dominant consensus – concerning the Hegelian character of the early writings – is beyond the remit of the present chapter. My attention here is largely restricted to the young Marx's *own* account of Hegel's achievements and failings, and in particular to his critical assessment of Hegel's political philosophy. In this context, much of the secondary literature is guilty of a double oversight: it has underestimated the critical thrust of Marx's assessment of Hegel's philosophical system; and it has misunderstood the positive elements in Marx's account of Hegel (in particular, failing to recognise Marx's commendation of Hegel's insight into the modern social world). My central aim in the present chapter is to remedy that twofold neglect.

THE 1843 *KRITIK*

The most sustained engagement with Hegel to be found in the early writings is contained in the 1843 *Kritik*. (The *Kritik* was probably written between May and August 1843 at Kreuznach, a spa town in Rhenish Prussia, some 50 miles east of Trier, where the family of Jenny Westphalen, who married Marx in June 1843, had a house.) Whatever one's final evaluation of its content, no serious attempt to understand the thought of the young Marx can afford to neglect this text. It is, however, a notoriously complicated work, which generates a number of interpretative difficulties. Two of those difficulties will preoccupy me in the present chapter.

The first of these difficulties is to identify the rationale behind the significant shift in Marx's intellectual interests that occurs at the beginning of the period with which I am concerned. The best-known summary account

of his intellectual evolution has Marx abandoning German philosophy in
order to pursue more empirical and material subjects. However, on closer
inspection, this famous summary might appear to *invert* the actual chain
of events – whereby the young Marx abandoned a series of empirical studies of German conditions in favour of a critical engagement with Hegel's
political philosophy. After all, it was as a leading contributor to, and subsequently editor of, the *Rheinische Zeitung* that Marx had found himself in
the 'embarrassing position' of having to discuss 'material interests' for the
first time – contributing articles on the latest Prussian censorship instructions, the juridical status of wood thefts in the Moselle, the proceedings of
the regional assembly in the Rhine province (of Prussia), and other topics.[6] Any 'embarrassment' on his part, however, was soon displaced by the
exasperation and anger which was generated by the growing burden of
governmental interference (the 'hypocrisy, stupidity, gross arbitrariness' of
the authorities), together with the editorial restraint that this interference
necessitated (the endless 'bowing and scraping, dodging, and hairsplitting
over words').[7] When the paper was finally closed down (in March 1843), and
notwithstanding his public protestations, Marx confided to Arnold Ruge
that the government had 'given me back my freedom'.[8] One might readily
empathise with this private expression of relief, but the use to which Marx
put his new-found liberty is rather more surprising. Marx 'eagerly grasped'
the opportunity to 'withdraw' to his study, not in order to pursue an examination of contemporary German conditions unhindered by the censor, but
rather to write a marginal commentary on Hegel's *Philosophie des Rechts*.[9]
That is, the young Marx abandoned the concrete and empirical subject
matter of his earlier journalism in favour of a close textual examination
of Hegel's *Rechtsphilosophie*. This apparent shift in his concerns away from
'material interests' and towards 'German philosophy' – the inversion of
the famous summary of Marx's intellectual evolution is deliberate – clearly
requires an explanation.

The second of these two interpretative difficulties is to make sense of
a text which has, with justification, been called 'easily the most complex

---

[6] The (gently ironic) quotations are from Marx's autobiographical reflections in the '1859 Vorwort'
7/261–2.
[7] Marx to Arnold Ruge, 25 January 1843, *MEW* 27, p. 415; *MECW* 1, p. 397.
[8] *Ibid.* For the protestations, see the two petitions – both signed by Marx – supporting the continuation
of the *Rheinische Zeitung*, *MECW* 1, pp. 725–6, 710–11. Political petitions, although officially banned,
were (more or less) tolerated in Rhenish Prussia. For example, lawyers signing the second of these
petitions were informed of the King's displeasure, but no further action was taken. See Jonathan
Sperber, *Rhineland Radicals: The Democratic Movement and the Revolution of 1848–1849* (Princeton,
1991) pp. 103–5.
[9] '1859 Vorwort' 7/262.

and – more to the point – the least read and the most misunderstood' of Marx's writings on politics and the state.[10] This objective is hindered by the obscurity of Marx's prose. Like the text upon which it provides a partial commentary, the *Kritik* cannot be described as a model of transparency.[11] Some familiar difficulties with the almost steganographic character of Marx's language in this period are compounded by both the status and the content of this particular text. Never intended for publication (at least, not in this form), the *Kritik* consists of a series of notes appended to, and interspersed with, extensive excerpts from the section of Hegel's *Rechtsphilosophie* concerned with the state.[12] The primary purpose of Marx's commentary was to clarify his own understanding of Hegel and not to communicate that understanding to others. As a result, it is perhaps not surprising to discover that the meaning of many of his remarks remains obscure. Moreover, the interpretative difficulties that result from these formal complexities are undoubtedly exacerbated by problems with the organisation of his subject matter. In the *Kritik*, Marx tends to identify two distinct issues – the character of speculative thought and the nature of the modern state – in a manner that does not facilitate the comprehension of either. Indeed, he may subsequently have recognised this weakness in the text. Explaining his failure to publish a promised critique of Hegel's *Rechtsphilosophie*, the young Marx notes that his initial attempt 'to combine criticism directed only against speculation with criticism of the various subjects themselves was quite unsuitable; it had hampered the development of the argument and made it difficult to follow'.[13] Few modern readers of the *Kritik* would dissent from that assessment.

The present chapter is intended as a structured response to these two interpretative difficulties. In the first half of the chapter, I explore the apparent shift in the young Marx's concerns away from 'material interests' and towards 'German philosophy'. In particular, I seek to explain how Marx himself could see this renewed preoccupation with philosophy as an expression, rather than as a betrayal, of his developing interest in the modern social world. In the second half of the chapter, I try to clarify the

[10] Lucio Colletti, 'Introduction', Karl Marx, *Early Writings* (London, 1975) p. 47.

[11] For example, Richard Hunt refers to its 'fearsome inscrutability' and describes it as 'written in the murkiest Hegelian jargon'. Richard Hunt, *The Political Ideas of Marx and Engels*, volume I: *Marxism and Totalitarian Democracy, 1818–1850* (Pittsburgh, 1974) p. 50.

[12] In fact, we only have Marx's comments on §§261–313, whereas this section of Hegel's text begins at §257. However, the cover and first four pages are missing from the relevant notebook, and it is reasonable to assume that those absent pages would have contained Marx's remarks on §§257–60. (Marx abandons his commentary at §313, thereby omitting Hegel's discussion of foreign affairs and international law, amongst other topics.)

[13] *Manuskripte* 467/231/280–1.

basic outline of Marx's commentary by disentangling the two threads of his subject matter, that is, separating his discussion of speculative method from his remarks concerning the modern state. This exercise in unravelling reveals a stark and illuminating contrast between, on the one hand, the young Marx's relentless hostility to speculative metaphysics, and, on the other, his insistence that Hegel should be credited with significant insight into the nature of the modern social world.

TRAUMGESCHICHTE AND MODERNITY

In order to disinter the rationale behind his critical engagement with Hegel's *Rechtsphilosophie*, it is helpful to begin with the young Marx's own schematic outline – sketched most clearly in the 'Kritik: Einleitung' – of German historical development.[14] (The 'Kritik: Einleitung' was written in Paris between the end of 1843 and January 1844, and published in the first and only edition of the *Deutsch-Französische Jahrbücher*. It was intended as an introduction, not to the *Kritik*, but rather to a new work on Hegel's political philosophy which Marx subsequently failed to write.) According to this synoptic account, Germany was not a wholehearted participant in the progress of the modern world, but stood rather in an anachronistic relation to more advanced contemporary states. Marx maintained that a fissure had opened up between the historical progress of Germany, on the one hand, and that of America and modern Europe (paradigmatically embodied in France), on the other. Compared to the standard of development established by these other states, German involvement in modernity had been, in some significant respects, limited.

(The accuracy of this account of German historical development is not a primary concern here. However, one might suspect that Marx's observations suffer from the same weakness as many more familiar versions of a Teutonic *'Sonderweg'*; namely, that German exceptionalism is made to depend on characterisations of a 'normal' historical development elsewhere – that is,

---

[14] For suggestions of the *Traumgeschichte* metaphor from elsewhere in the early writings, see, for example, Marx's description of Justus Möser's combination of the eminently bourgeois and entirely fantastical (in his *Patriotische Phantasien*) as having a peculiar affinity with the 'German mind' (*Manuskripte* 527/287/339); and his reference to the 'disparity between the philosophical and political development of Germany' ('Kritische Randglossen' 405/202/416). For a later example, see Marx's claim that in Germany 'mental developments' serve 'as a substitute for the lack of historical development' (*Die deutsche Ideologie* I38). That claim is from a rediscovered six-page section and does not appear in *MEW*. For the German text, see *International Review of Social History*, volume 7, no. 1 (1962) pp. 93–104 (this quotation p. 97).

in countries other than Germany – which is not ultimately sustained by the relevant evidence.[15])

It is important to notice that this idea of German backwardness, which appears in several different contexts and guises in the early writings, is never portrayed as universal, that is, as a characteristic which permeates every aspect of German existence. Rather, the young Marx considered Germany's anachronistic relation to the modern world to be embodied in a distinctive disjuncture between retrogression and advancement, between those areas of life in which the German states had lagged behind their more advanced contemporaries, and those in which they had set the pace. This contrast between German historical backwardness and German historical precocity is described in a variety of terms, perhaps most frequently as an opposition between an 'actual' and an 'ideal' development.

For Marx, like many of his contemporaries, the backwardness of 'actual' German history was beyond dispute. It had several dimensions: economically, German productivity lagged behind the rest of Western Europe;[16] sociologically, an independent bourgeoisie had yet fully to develop;[17] culturally, social life was suffused with philistinism;[18] and so on. However, it was the political element of German backwardness that especially attracted the attention of the young Marx.

The national dimension of this political underdevelopment was not the main object of his interest, although Marx does write scathingly of rulers 'whose greatness is in inverse proportion to their numbers'.[19] (At this time, Germany was divided into what was, by modern standards, an astonishing array of implausibly small and fragmented states with a confusing array of overlapping jurisdictions; the *Staatenbund* established in 1815 consisted of thirty-seven sovereign principalities – twenty-one of which had populations

---

[15] For a critical engagement with some accounts of German exceptionalism, see David Blackbourn and Geoff Eley, *The Peculiarities of German History: Bourgeois Society and History in Nineteenth-Century Germany* (Oxford, 1984).

[16] See 'Kritik: Einleitung' 382/179/248 and 'Kritische Randglossen' 404/201/415.

[17] Marx refers to the 'submission and impotence (*ihre Unterwürfigkeit und ihre Ohnmacht*)' of the German bourgeoisie, and – alluding to the Royal Decree that followed the Düsseldorf banquet – describes Germany as a country where 'the burning desire of the entire liberal bourgeoisie for freedom of the press and a constitution could be suppressed without the aid of a single soldier'. 'Kritische Randglossen' 393/190/403. See also 'Kritik: Einleitung' 389/186/255.

[18] Marx describes Germany as 'the most perfect' embodiment of 'the philistine world (*Philisterwelt*)'. 'Briefwechsel von 1843' 339/137/201. For an English perspective on the German idea of philistinism, see George Eliot's discussion of the historian Wilhelm Heinrich von Riehl in 'The Natural History of German Life', *Westminster Review*, volume 66 (1856) pp. 51–79; and the (later) comments of Matthew Arnold, 'Heinrich Heine', *Essays in Criticism*, first series (London, 1902) p. 178.

[19] 'Kritik: Einleitung' 381/178/246.

of fewer than 100,000 – together with four free cities.[20]) Marx's primary concern was rather with what he characterises as the political *unfreedom* of the German states.

According to the young Marx, the absolutist monarchies, dominant hereditary elites, and traditional modes of (highly restricted and corporativist) representation which characterised most members of the *Staatenbund* placed German political reality 'below the level of history', becalmed somewhere in the 'Middle Ages'.[21] (Generalisations are difficult, but where representative institutions existed, they were typically subordinated to the monarch and nobility, and based on a highly restricted franchise. Voting functioned not as an expression of popular will but as a symbolic affirmation of the established order. Debates within parliaments were carefully controlled, and proceedings rarely public.) In an emphatic and heartfelt comparison, Marx suggests that it was Germany's recent historical distinction to 'have shared the restorations of modern nations without having shared their revolutions'.[22] As a result, measured by the political standards of modernity, the German *'status quo'* was simply 'an anachronism'.[23]

Marx reiterates this claim about the political backwardness of 'actual' German history in a variety of parallel tropes. In two of the most striking of these characterisations, Germany appears as neophyte and laughingstock. In the first of these images, German historical progress is portrayed as 'like some raw recruit', who, unsuited to independence and initiative, is 'restricted to repeating hackneyed routines that belong to the past of other nations'.[24] In the second of these images, Marx depicts Germany as the 'clown' of a world order whose real heroes were already dead, playing the part of buffoon in the process whereby – in order that humankind 'may part *happily* from its past' – history disposes of an established order in stages, beginning with its 'tragic' downfall and closing with a 'comic' funeral procession.[25] (The adumbration of a more famous opening line from a much later work, *Der achtzehnte Brumaire des Louis Bonaparte*, is a striking one.)[26]

---

[20] Note that this plethora of polities was actually the result of an unprecedented period of state-building in the Napoleonic era; at the Imperial Diet of 1781 some 324 principalities had been represented.
[21] 'Kritik: Einleitung' 380/177/246 and *ibid.* 391/187/257.
[22] *Ibid.* 379/176/245.   [23] *Ibid.*   [24] *Ibid.* 383/179/248.
[25] *Ibid.* 381/179/247. See also 'Briefwechsel von 1843' 337/134/200.
[26] See *Der achtzehnte Brumaire* 115/103 (where the thought that historical events occur twice is attributed to Hegel). See also 'Die Taten des Hauses Hohenzollern' 480/421. These adumbrations cast doubt on the occasional suggestion that Marx's addition to Hegel – that the tragedy of the original occurrence is replaced by the farce of the subsequent one – was borrowed from a letter from Engels dated 3 December 1851.

The young Marx appears to have been acutely conscious of the political backwardness of Germany. In one of his contributions to the 'Briefwechsel von 1843' (written from Holland to Arnold Ruge), Marx makes an interesting personal admission. He confides that even individuals who are unable to experience 'national pride' are still capable of feeling 'national shame', explaining that 'in comparison with the greatest Germans even the least Dutchman is still a citizen'.[27]

(In a rather strained aside – the essentials of which are repeated in the 'Kritik: Einleitung' – the young Marx attempts to characterise this national 'shame (*Scham*)' in positive terms. In the first place, he maintains that shame is impossible without knowledge. Thus he describes 'revelation' as amongst its preconditions, and explicitly invokes shame as an antidote to 'self-deception'.[28] In addition, and because it involves 'a kind of anger which is turned inward', Marx suggests that shame might function as a potential motivator of revolutionary agency. In order to gain 'courage', he suggests, the German people must become 'terrified at itself', and that 'if a whole nation really experienced a sense of shame, it would be like a lion, crouching ready to spring'.[29])

Nevertheless, as noted above, this political underdevelopment was crucially not without exception. In particular, it had failed to contaminate the whole of German intellectual life. Whatever the retardations of 'actual' history, Germany *had* managed to keep pace with the progress of the modern world in the 'ideal' sphere of philosophy. Despite having steadfastly avoided 'taking an active part in the real struggles' of modern states, Germany had nonetheless kept company with their progress 'through the abstract activity of thought'.[30] Adopting the familiar metaphor of the body politic, Marx describes modernity as having flourished inside Germany's 'cranium (*Hirnschädel*)'.[31] The significant result of this singular development was that, despite the fact that German institutions stood at the level of the *ancien régime*, the standards of political modernity were embodied in German philosophy. 'We Germans', Marx concludes, 'are the *philosophical* contemporaries of the present, without being its *historical* contemporaries.'[32]

Despite the wording of this particular formulation, Marx is emphatically not claiming that recent history had bypassed the German states entirely. After all, he elaborates, Germany is not Russia; nor – rehearsing the point with a classical (and obscure) allusion to Anacharsis (and Hegel) – is Germany's relation to modernity analogous to the position of the Scythians

---

[27] 'Briefwechsel von 1843' 337/133/199. [28] *Ibid.* 337/133/200 and 'Kritik: Einleitung' 381/178/247.
[29] 'Kritik: Einleitung' 381/178/247 and 'Briefwechsel von 1843' 337/133/200.
[30] 'Kritik: Einleitung' 387/183/252. [31] *Ibid.* 384/181/250. [32] *Ibid.* 383/180/249.

in the ancient world (surviving untouched by the advances of contemporary culture despite their one philosopher).[33] Rather, Germany is a product of a distinctive and asymmetrical involvement in historical progress,
as a result of which, despite its continued absence from German political
reality, the emergence of the modern state is reflected in the verisimilitudes
of German political philosophy.[34] Indeed, Marx claims that one result of
this characteristic disjuncture is that Germany has already 'left behind in
theory' historical stages that 'it has not yet reached in practice'.[35]

In order to encapsulate the resulting contrast between the backwardness
of actual German history and the precocity of German philosophical development, Marx makes a more positive analogy with the intellectual life of
the ancient world: 'Just as the ancient peoples lived their previous history
in the imagination, in *mythology,*' he writes, 'so we Germans have lived our
future history in thought, in *philosophy.*'[36] For the purpose of understanding
the context of the *Kritik*, this is a highly significant claim. On this account,
German philosophy – more precisely, German philosophy of state –
had become the 'ideal prolongation' of actual German history, the one
area of life in which Germany had kept pace with the historical progress
of the modern world (and outpaced philosophy elsewhere).[37] As Marx
insists, the 'dream-history (*Traumgeschichte*)' embodied in German
philosophy is 'the only *German history* which stands on an equal footing
with the *official* modern present'.[38]

HEINE (AND PARIS)

The present section constitutes something of a digression. It provides a
brief foray into the realm of *Quellenforschung*, in pursuit of the provenance
of this notion of a 'dream-history (*Traumgeschichte*)'.

Marx's idea of a '*Traumgeschichte*' is scarcely an unprecedented conceit.
The idea of a characteristically Teutonic preoccupation with '*Innerlichkeit*'
(literally 'inwardness') was already established as a cultural commonplace
by the middle of the nineteenth century.[39] The notion of a characteristic national fragmentation, between an *underdeveloped* sphere of action
and an *overdeveloped* sphere of reflection, was an especially popular varia-
tion on that theme. It can be discerned in the work of a wide variety of
German writers with whom Marx was familiar (or with whom his work

---

[33] *Ibid.*   [34] *Ibid.*   [35] *Ibid.* 386/183/252.
[36] *Ibid.* 383/180/249.   [37] *Ibid.*   [38] *Ibid.*
[39] For its literary expression, see Gordon Craig, *The Politics of the Unpolitical: German Writers and the Problem of Power, 1770–1871* (Oxford, 1995).

shows affinities).[40] Hölderlin, for example, pointedly remarks in 'An die deutschen':

> Spottet ja nicht des Kinds, wenn es mit Peitsch' und Sporn
> Auf dem Rosse von Holz muthig und groß sich dünkt,
> Denn, ihr Deutschen, auch ihr seyd
> Thatenarm und gedankenvoll.

> Never mock the child, when with whip and spurs, he
> Deems himself bold and great on his wooden horse.
> For, Germans, no less than he, you are
> Poor in actions and full of thoughts.[41]

The same theme is echoed elsewhere: in the lament of the German poet in Schiller's 'Die Teilung der Erde' that, since earthly spoils were already distributed, only spiritual rewards remained for historical latecomers;[42] in Hegel's account of the German reception of the idea of freedom as cognitive rather than practical;[43] in Moses Hess's contrast between the effectiveness and clarity of German 'theory' and the ineffectual and opaque nature of German 'praxis';[44] in Ruge's characterisation of 'the split between theory and praxis' as belonging 'to the German spirit in general';[45] in Feuerbach's description of the Germans having 'everything in word but nothing in deed';[46] and so on.

Given such considerations, the attempt to isolate a particular provenance for the *Traumgeschichte* motif may well appear tendentious. That said, Marx's conceit does not simply draw attention to a widely observed asymmetry between material and spiritual development in Germany, but claims further that the political advances of other countries were reflected in the intellectual peregrinations of the Teutonic world. As one striking aphorism, from the 'Kritik: Einleitung', has it: 'In politics the Germans *thought* what other nations *did*.'[47] That particular inflection suggests the work of another German author with whom Marx was familiar, namely Heinrich Heine.

The possibility of Heine's having influenced Marx – let alone the precise nature and extent of that possible influence – was, for many years, neglected

[40] For Marx's literary knowledge and enthusiasms, see S. S. Prawer, *Karl Marx and World Literature* (Oxford, 1976).
[41] Friedrich Hölderlin, *Sämtliche Werke*, volume 1 (Stuttgart, 1953) p. 256; Friedrich Hölderlin, *Poems of Hölderlin* (London, 1943) p. 109.
[42] Friedrich Schiller, *Sämtliche Werke*, volume 1 (Munich, 1960) p. 206.
[43] Hegel, *Vorlesungen über die Geschichte der Philosophie*, iii, 331–2/iii, 425.
[44] Hess, 'Die Tagespresse in Deutschland und Frankreich', *Schriften* p. 181.
[45] Ruge, 'Rechtsphilosophie' 759/220–1. See also Ruge, 'Selbstkritik' 91/246.
[46] Feuerbach, 'Fragmente' 177/292.   [47] 'Kritik: Einleitung' 385/181/250.

by critics.[48] They devoted their efforts instead to the much worked and not obviously fruitful subject of Marx's influence on Heine. (As preserved, Heine's library contained only one work by Marx, a presentation copy of *Die heilige Familie*, which remained uncut beyond its first forty pages.[49]) Amongst Heine scholars that emphasis is happily much changed, although in the Marx literature Heine remains 'an entirely peripheral figure where he is mentioned at all'.[50] In the present context, I should like to stake a modest claim on Heine's behalf, and suggest that he is the most probable source of both the *Traumgeschichte* motif and of the young Marx's enthusiasm for it. Three considerations, in particular, lend support to that suggestion.

In the first place, the *Traumgeschichte* conceit appears clearly and repeatedly in Heine's writings, not only in the form of a broad parallel between modern (that is, French) political progress and German intellectual development, but also in an explicit characterisation of Teutonic political advances as occurring in a sphere of 'dreams'. Its earliest occurrence appears to be in the *Einleitung zu 'Kahldorf über den Adel'* (1831), in which Heine draws a sustained parallel between the political events of the French Revolution and recent developments in German philosophy, insisting that 'our German philosophy is nothing other than the dream (*Traum*) of the French Revolution'.[51] That same parallel between the French Revolution and German philosophy reappears, rather more famously, as a central organising thread in *Zur Geschichte der Religion und Philosophie in Deutschland* (a work with a complicated publication history, but which first appeared in 1834). In that essay, Heine develops a series of inspired satirical comparisons ('a most remarkable parallelism') between the 'great phases' of France's 'political revolution' and the 'philosophical revolution' in Germany – outlining a succession of increasingly provocative parallels between Robespierre and Kant (memorably juxtaposing the storming of the Bastille with the publication of the *Kritik der reinen Vernunft*); between Napoleon and Fichte; and between the restoration of the monarchy and the work of Schelling – insisting to his French audience that 'we had outbreaks in the intellectual world (*geistigen Welt*) just as you had in the material world'.[52] Finally, the

---

[48] On Heine and Marx, see Ludwig Marcuse, 'Heine and Marx', *Germanic Review*, volume 30 (1955) pp. 110–24; William Rose, *Heinrich Heine: Two Studies of His Thought and Feeling* (Oxford, 1956) pp. 68–73; and Ronald Nabrotsky, 'Karl Marx als Heinrich Heines politischer und poetischer Mentor', Gerhard P. Knapp and Wolff A. Schmidt (eds.), *Sprache und Literatur* (Bern, 1981) pp. 129–140.

[49] See Eberhard Galley, 'Heinrich Heines Privatbibliothek', *Heine-Jahrbuch*, volume 1 (1962) pp. 96–116; and Marx to Zacharius Löwenthal, 9 May 1845, *MEW* 27, p. 436; *MECW* 38, p. 31.

[50] Nigel Reeves, 'Heine and the Young Marx', *Oxford German Studies*, volume 7 (1973) p. 45.

[51] *Kahldorf*, p. 134.   [52] *Geschichte*, p. 90.

motif also appears in *Deutschland: Ein Wintermärchen* (published in 1844). As the striking comparison of 'Caput 7' has it:[53]

> Franzosen und Russen gehört das Land,
> Das Meer gehört den Britten,
> Wir aber besitzen im Luftreich' des Traums
> Die Herrschaft unbestritten.
>
> Hier üben wir die Hegemonie
> Hier sind wir unzerstückelt;
> Die andern Völker haben sich
> Auf platter Erde entwickelt.
>
> The land is held by the Russians and French
> The sea's by the British invested,
> But in the airy realm of dreams
> Our sway is uncontested.
>
> Here we exist unfragmented
> And rule without a murmur;
> The other nations of the earth
> Developed on terra firma.[54]

In addition, the young Marx was closely acquainted with Heine's work.[55] Indeed, Heine is one of those authors – along with Cervantes and Shakespeare – who form a constant presence across the chronological range of Marx's work. In Heine's case, that presence is established from Marx's very earliest literary efforts – both Marx's youthful poetry (for example, *'Armida* von Ritter Gluck') and his abandoned novel (*Scorpion und Felix*) can be seen as (not entirely successful) imitations of Heine's anti-bourgeois satire.[56] His continuing engagement with Heine's work is readily apparent from the quotations contained in a wide range of Marx's own writings, including the appearance in *Die deutsche Ideologie* of these last two stanzas from *Deutschland: Ein Wintermärchen*.[57] However, there is also a discernable echo of certain images and ideas from Heine throughout Marx's prose. To give two examples from the early writings: the association of the squabbling in German politics with the cackling of geese that allegedly saved Rome from the Gauls (in 390 BCE) appears in both *Atta Troll* and

---

[53] 'Caput' is the mock-epic designation used by Heine for sections of the poem.
[54] *Deutschland* 106/496.
[55] For Marx's familiarity with Heine's work, see Reeves, 'Heine and the Young Marx'; and Nigel Reeves, *Heinrich Heine: Poetry and Politics* (Oxford, 1974) pp. 151–9.
[56] See Prawer, *Karl Marx and World Literature*, chapter 1.
[57] See *Die deutsche Ideologie* 457/470. For an example of quotation in the early writings, see *Die heilige Familie* 166/157.

Die heilige Familie;[58] whilst the depiction of a crude (and unattractive) form of communism in the *Manuskripte* seems likely to owe something to Heine's apprehension about the radical egalitarian followers of Gracchus Babouf.[59]

Finally, at the time in which the 'Kritik: Einleitung' was written, the two authors were personally close. (Heine and Marx may also have been related, although neither of them appears to have been aware of the possibility.[60]) Marx had met Heine soon after arriving in Paris in November 1843. Heine himself had escaped to the French capital some twelve years earlier, in order, he claimed, 'to breathe fresh air'.[61] Despite the obvious difference in age and status – Marx was a largely unknown twenty-five-year-old radical, whilst Heine, more than twenty years his senior, was an established literary figure with a considerable international reputation – they developed a relationship that has been accurately described as 'warm and friendly to a degree not common in the lives of either man'.[62] For the best part of a year, they met frequently, addressed one another in familial terms, published in the same periodicals, and gave every indication of liking and respecting each other.[63] Although later and anecdotal evidence should always be treated with caution, Marx's daughter Eleanor – in a series of biographical notes made for Karl Kautsky in 1895 – recorded a number of family reminiscences from this period in Paris. They include memories of almost daily visits between Heine and her father, of the two men sitting together revising a poem at inordinate length, and of an incident in which Heine was reputed to

---

[58] Compare *Die heilige Familie* 143/135 with *Atta Troll* 86/480.

[59] See Reeves, 'Heine and the Young Marx', pp. 81ff.

[60] See Heinz Monz, *Karl Marx und Trier* (Trier, 1964) pp. 227ff.

[61] Heine to Varnhagen von Ense, 1 April 1831, *Säkularausgabe* 20, p. 435. On Heine in Paris, see Joseph Dresch, *Heine à Paris, 1831–1856* (Paris, 1956); and Joseph A. Kruse and Michael Werner (eds.), *Heine à Paris: 1831–1856* (Paris, 1981).

[62] Jeffrey Sammons, *Heinrich Heine: A Modern Biography* (Manchester, 1979) p. 262. Their relationship is described as 'increasingly close and friendly' in Auguste Cornu, *Karl Marx et Friedrich Engels: Leur vie et leur œuvre*, volume 3: *Marx à Paris* (Paris, 1962) p. 27. Since Heine was in Germany for three months in 1844 and Marx was expelled from Paris in January 1845, their direct contact probably lasted some ten months. Marx visited Heine again in 1848 and 1849, and also received reports of the poet's declining health and spirits – Heine died in 1856 – from Engels (who visited Heine on Marx's behalf in 1847 and 1848) and Richard Reinhardt (Heine's secretary between 1849 and 1855). Marx continued to refer to 'my friend' Heine. See, for example, *Kapital* 637/605.

[63] Three letters from Marx to Heine survive, including one written as Marx was leaving Paris: 'Of all the people I am leaving behind here, those I leave with the most regret are the Heines. I would gladly include you in my luggage.' Marx to Heine, end of January to 1 February 1845, *MEW* 27, 434; *MECW* 38, p. 21. Only one letter from Heine to 'Liebster Marx' survives, sending proof sheets of *Deutschland* for Marx's 'amusement' and so that he could select 'the best parts' for *Vorwärts!* Heine, *Briefe*, volume 2, pp. 541ff. Heine's warm respect for – if not agreement with – one of 'the most resolute and brilliant (*entschiedenste und geistreichste*)' of his 'fellow countrymen (*Landsleute*)' is well established. *Lutezia* 2, p. 72.

have saved the life of Marx's baby daughter Jenny (by placing her in a warm bath to halt her convulsions). Her father, she recalled, not only admired Heine as a poet, but also had a genuine affection for him: 'He would even make excuses for Heine's political vagaries. Poets [Marx] maintained, were strange fish, not to be judged by ordinary, or even extraordinary, standards of conduct.'[64]

In short, three main considerations suggest Heine as the most likely source of Marx's use of the *Traumgeschichte* motif; namely, the clarity and frequency with which this specific motif appears in Heine's work, Marx's extensive knowledge of Heine's writings, and their significant personal friendship at the time at which the 'Kritik: Einleitung' was written.

I should add that these remarks concerning the possibility of Heine's influence on the early writings are not intended to replace – although they might supplement – other, more familiar, accounts of the considerable impact on Marx's intellectual evolution of his stay in 'the capital of the nineteenth century'.[65] Three significant points of influence might be noted here. It was in Paris that Marx was first directly exposed to French and other socialisms; he made contact with the communist secret societies of 'neo-Babouvists' and 'materialists',[66] with the League of the Just,[67] and (less directly) with Chartism.[68] It was also in Paris that Marx became involved in the nascent German workers' movement; indeed, it has been claimed that the German labour movement was born in Paris, since it was in the French capital that German intellectuals first met workers and that German workers were first introduced to new social theories.[69] Finally, it was

[64] See H. H. Houben (ed.), *Gespräche mit Heine* (Potsdam, 1948) p. 506. See also the letter from Laura Lafargue to John Spargo, 28 September 1909, reproduced in 'Appendix B' of Lewis S. Feuer, 'The Conversion of Karl Marx's Father', *Jewish Journal of Sociology*, volume 14 (1972) pp. 149–66.

[65] Walter Benjamin, *Gesammelte Schriften*, edited by Rolf Tiedemann (Frankfurt am Main, 1982) volume 5, p. 45. Marx called Paris 'the new capital of the new world'. 'Briefwechsel von 1843' 343/142/206. Much later, Engels would remark: 'Paris is no longer the capital of the world (which no longer has a capital).' Engels to Paul Lafargue, 30 October 1882, *MEW* 35, p. 385; *MECW* 46, p. 352.

[66] See Michael Löwy, *La théorie de la révolution chez le jeune Marx* (Paris, 1970) pp. 79–87.

[67] Police reports record Marx's attendance at League meetings; see Cornu, *Karl Marx et Friedrich Engels*, volume 3, p. 7. Marx also knew two of the League's leaders, namely German Mäurer and Hermann Ewerbeck, briefly sharing a house with the former.

[68] Through the writings of Flora Tristan and Eugène Buret (as well as from Engels). For Marx's excerpts from Buret's *De la misère des classes laborieuses en Angleterre et en France* (1840), see *MEGA*② 4, 2, pp. 551–79.

[69] See J. Grandjonc, *Marx et les communistes allemands à Paris* (Paris, 1974) p. 13. Note also the comments on German artisans in Switzerland, London, and Paris, in Marx to Feuerbach, 11 August 1844, *MEW* 27, p. 426; *MECW* 3, p. 355. The population of Paris in 1844 was just over a million, of which 136,000 were foreigners (including 41,700 Germans). For the occupational breakdown of this latter group, see Grandjonc, *Marx et les communistes allemands à Paris*, p. 12; and Löwy, *La théorie de la révolution chez le jeune Marx*, p. 83.

in Paris that Marx was first exposed to a mature bourgeois civilisation;
the unprecedented social, political, and cultural upheaval of Paris perhaps
helping Marx to a more nuanced, and even sympathetic, engagement with
modern life.[70] In short, I am sympathetic to the view that this should be
seen as the most intensely formative of the three exiles – in France, Belgium,
and England – that structured Marx's life.[71] The modest suggestion here
is that the influence of Heine might be seen as one additional and often
neglected element of that sojourn in Paris.

TRAUMGESCHICHTE AND HEGEL'S *RECHTSPHILOSOPHIE*

In the present context, what matters more than its provenance is the way
in which the *Traumgeschichte* motif can facilitate a better understanding of
the early writings. At the beginning of this chapter, I noted two interpretative puzzles that were raised by the *Kritik*. The first of these concerned the
surprising shift in Marx's intellectual concerns, following his enforced retire-
ment from the *Rheinische Zeitung*. That shift comprised two elements: a
(negative) movement away from the empirical study of German conditions;
and a (positive) movement towards a critical engagement with German philosophy. I undertook to explain how those changing intellectual concerns
could be seen as an expression, rather than a betrayal, of Marx's developing
interest in the modern social world. The ingredients of that explanation
are now in place.

 This shift in Marx's concerns was prompted by his growing interest
in the nature of the modern state. Evidence of that growing interest can
be found in the study notebooks which date from the beginning of the
period with which the present work is concerned. As already noted, it was
Marx's lifelong habit to make short excerpts from the books that he was
reading, occasionally interspersing remarks and criticisms of his own. His
growing preoccupation with the modern state is confirmed by the five study
notebooks that have survived from his stay in Kreuznach (between May
and October 1843).[72] The overwhelming majority of the excerpts in these
Kreuznach notebooks are from works of modern French and, to a lesser

[70] On the general cultural significance of the French capital, see Christopher Prendergast, *Paris and the Nineteenth Century* (Oxford, 1992). See also Marshall Berman, *Adventures in Marxism* (London, 1999) chapter 6, and Lloyd S. Kramer, *Threshold of a New World: Intellectuals and the Exile Experience in Paris, 1830–1848* (Ithaca NY, 1988) chapter 3.
[71] Isaiah Berlin, for example, claims: 'The years 1843–5 are the most decisive in his life' (adding, less plausibly, that 'in Paris [Marx] underwent his final intellectual transformation'). Isaiah Berlin, *Karl Marx: His Life and Environment* (Oxford, 1963) p. 80.
[72] The five Kreuznach notebooks are in *MEGA②* 4, 2, pp. 9–278.

extent, British history. (The notebooks also contain notes from historical studies of America, Poland, Sweden, and the Venetian republic, together with some classic works of political thought, notably books by Machiavelli, Montesquieu, and Rousseau.)

The form taken by Marx's growing interest in the nature of the modern state may be unexpected; however, it can be readily explained by his newly formulated conception of German historical development (articulated in the *Traumgeschichte* motif).

Consider first the negative element in Marx's changing intellectual interests, namely his abandoning the empirical study of actual German conditions. Given Marx's growing conviction that the 'political present' of Germany was identical with 'the past of modern nations', it follows that a critical engagement with 'actual' German conditions could only ever reveal 'the *barbaric defects* of the *ancien régime*'.[73] In this way, his new conceptualisation of the limitations of German historical development helps explain the move away from the empirical investigation of 'material interests' in the German states.[74] Marx now concludes that such studies could never disclose anything significant regarding the nature of the *modern* state. Indeed, surveying the recent and inglorious German past, he notes that even a progression to the *next* level of political development would – 'according to the French calendar' – only bring Germany up to the level of 1789.[75]

Consider also the positive element in Marx's shifting concerns, namely his critical turn towards German philosophy. As a result of the distinctive character of German historical development, and despite its 'actual' backwardness, Marx now believed that an examination of the modern state could be accomplished via an investigation of the 'ideal' continuation of that history. In this way, his new conceptualisation of the limitations of German historical development also helps explain the move towards German philosophy. What might, in advanced states, have been a *'practical'* encounter with modern political conditions could in Germany, where such conditions did not yet exist, only take the form of a *'critical'* encounter with their reflection in philosophy.[76]

In short, the *Traumgeschichte* motif identifies both a disjuncture between modernity and German conditions, and a correlation between modernity and German philosophy. Given his growing interest in the specific character of the modern state, that disjuncture explains Marx's retreat from

---

[73] 'Kritik: Einleitung' 381/178/247 and *ibid.* 387/183/253.   [74] '1859 Vorwort' 7/261–2.
[75] 'Kritik: Einleitung' 379/176/245.   [76] *Ibid.* 383/180/249.

the empirical study of German conditions, and that correlation explains his critical turn towards German philosophy. The *Traumgeschichte* motif thereby clarifies what might otherwise remain puzzling, namely how his first attempt to understand the distinctive character of the modern state could consist in a theoretical engagement with contemporary German 'philosophy of state'. In particular, given that German philosophy of state is said to find its 'most consistent, thorough and complete' expression in Hegel, it explains why Marx's earliest attempt to grasp the achievements and limitations of modern political life could take the form of a set of unpublished comments on excerpts from the *Philosophie des Rechts*.[77]

This correlation between German philosophy and modernity also provides an alternative way of characterising Marx's changing intellectual concerns. The shift away from 'material interests' and towards 'German philosophy' could also be described as a movement away from the anachronistic German polity and towards a critical engagement with the modern state. In this way, the turn towards German philosophy can be seen as an expression, and not a betrayal, of Marx's developing interest in the modern social world.

(This discussion of the *Traumgeschichte* motif also helps to explain the chronological starting point of the present study. Since my subject is the young Marx's understanding of the *modern* state, it makes sense to begin with the *Kritik* rather than with his earlier journalism.)

HEGEL'S METAPHYSICS

The second of the two interpretative puzzles which structure this chapter concerns the difficulties faced in attempting to make sense of Marx's commentary on Hegel's *Rechtsphilosophie*. I suggested above that pursuit of this interpretative goal is helped by unravelling the two main threads of Marx's subject matter in the *Kritik* – separating his discussion of speculative method from his remarks concerning the modern state. I begin here with the first, and perhaps more difficult, of those threads.

Not the least of these difficulties concerns the need for some basic understanding of Hegel's speculative method. Unless the reader has a grasp of this difficult and controversial dimension of Hegel's thought, large parts of Marx's commentary are likely to remain unintelligible. In the present section, I attempt to provide an accurate and accessible account of Hegel's speculative method – an aspect of his thought which is notoriously resistant

---

[77] *Ibid.* 384/181/250.

Ge

to any such elucidatory efforts. The phrase 'speculative method' is itself liable to mislead. 'Method', in this context, does not denote an investigative procedure but rather (primarily) refers to Hegel's broad understanding of the structure of reality (and only secondarily to the intellectual approaches or models which might unearth or represent that structure). In short, I am concerned here with Hegel's metaphysics. The adjective 'speculative' is intended to suggest something about the kind of developmental pattern that reality is said to exhibit.

For Hegel, metaphysics (properly understood) is concerned with the attempt to achieve knowledge of the 'absolute', namely that which is independent of, and unrestricted or unconditioned by, anything else. He identifies this absolute with the infinite, although it is important to note that, for Hegel (as for Spinoza), this infinite includes the finite (conveniently providing an example of the speculative ambition to unify apparently opposed concepts). Indeed, the infinite necessarily includes the finite, since the existence of anything outside of the absolute would be a 'limit', and any limit would, by definition, undermine the purported infinitude of the 'absolute'. (Unlike Spinoza) Hegel also identifies the absolute as somehow having the structure of a self (as being potentially a 'subject' as well as 'substance').[78] One way in which Hegel elaborates this opaque claim about the structure of the absolute is through his notorious insistence that this 'absolute' is, in some sense, coextensive with the Christian 'God', at least once the latter has been grasped conceptually rather than anthropomorphically. (In general, Hegel maintains that philosophy and religion have the same subject matter, differing only in their understanding of that shared object – the superiority of philosophy over religion consists in its knowing God through concepts rather than through feeling and intuition.[79]) In what has been called 'perhaps the maddest image in all of Hegel's writings', the task of the 'science of logic' is described as the 'exposition of God as He is in His eternal essence before the creation of nature and a finite world'.[80]

For Hegel, the 'science of logic' is an intellectual discipline as well as the title of one of his own contributions to that discipline. This science of logic involves a certain kind of reflection about thought. More precisely, it involves thinking about abstract and formal thoughts which are (claimed to be) devoid of empirical content and independent of time and space. Hegel

[78] See *Enzyklopädie* §151Z. Spinoza's failure to attain this standpoint is treated as emblematic of his Jewish descent.
[79] See, for example, *ibid.* §1.
[80] The Hegel quotation is from *Logik* 5, 44/50. The striking characterisation of that quotation is from Walter Kaufmann, *Hegel: A Reinterpretation* (New York, 1966) p. 184.

presents a series of categories which purportedly fulfil these criteria, including – and typically failing to distinguish between – those familiar from
formal logic (for example, forms of inference such as the syllogism) and
those applying to things (such as quality and causality). Although his various attempts to distinguish these pure concepts ('*Begriffen*') from empirical
conceptions ('*Vorstellungen*') have been much criticised, it is clear that these
Hegelian categories are supposed to be embodiments of pure thinking and
not derived from empirical experience.[81]

Together these concepts are said to form a categorical system with a
distinctive triadic pattern within which progression is generated by 'contradiction'. Once an appropriate starting point has been found – and glossing over the not inconsiderable difficulties in establishing that satisfactory
beginning – these concepts are seemingly derived from one other. In a
paradigmatic triad, Hegel starts with a particular concept which appears
fixed and distinct. Conceptual analysis reveals that this first concept contains its contrary and that this contrary contains it. Further analysis, of
the relation between these self-contradictory concepts, reveals a third concept which is said to cancel, preserve, and elevate the previous concepts in
a manner which thereby renders them no longer contrary. (This distinctive and complex combination of cancellation, preservation, and elevation
is captured by the concept of '*Aufhebung*' discussed briefly at the beginning of this chapter.[82]) Note that this progression is seen as internal to the
concepts involved rather than as being imposed upon them from outside.
Thought is somehow self-moving, and Hegel, as the paradigmatic speculative philosopher, claims simply to be following and recording the movement
of a self-determining conceptual system. These three developmental stages,
which make up a paradigmatic triad, also correspond to forms of thinking
that are often labelled, respectively, understanding, dialectic, and speculation. Roughly speaking, understanding fixes and separates concepts (and is
associated with deductive argument); dialectic reveals the apparent contradictions that result from such an approach (and is associated with scepticism
and sophistry); and speculation incorporates those apparent contraries into
a positive and stable result which provides clear and profound knowledge.
(Hence the elaboration of 'speculative' suggested above, namely that one
sense in which Hegel's metaphysics is speculative is that it unifies apparently
opposed concepts and entities.)

---

[81] For pertinent criticisms, see M. J. Inwood, *Hegel* (London, 1983) chapter 1. In trying to make sense
of Hegel's metaphysics, I have found Michael Inwood's work enormously helpful.

[82] On '*aufheben*' as exemplifying the speculative spirit of the German language, see *Enzyklopädie* §96,
Z. See also *Logik* 5, 20/32.

Hegel maintains that there is nothing arbitrary in the developmental pattern formed by this categorical system; each particular concept is deemed to have a unique successor. (Although the kind of necessity involved in these progressions is not entirely clear, the notion of contradiction, and hence of dialectic, is undoubtedly central.) The result is what one commentator has judiciously described as a series of 'nested triads' in which later stages are claimed to presuppose or include earlier developments, the progression of stages is described as providing ever more adequate definitions of the absolute, and the beginning and end of the series, in some contested sense, meet up, thereby confirming that a series has been completed.[83] (Feuerbach once offered the brilliant quip that if speculative philosophy had a 'coat of arms' it would be a picture of a circle.[84]) Hegel sometimes refers to the system of concepts as a whole – which is the subject matter of the 'science of logic' – as *the* concept.

Modern readers are liable to think of 'logic', as a study of the necessary relations between concepts, as independent of any study of reality, of what actually exists. On Hegel's account, however, this would be a serious misunderstanding, since logic and metaphysics 'coincide'.[85] The Hegelian logic includes the categories of Kant's transcendental logic, namely the kinds of conceptual structures which enable us to have knowledge of the objects of experience. However, whereas Kant denies that his account commits us to any particular view about the ultimate nature of things, Hegel – who rejects the Kantian distinction between the objects of experience and things as they are in themselves – insists that an account of the necessary relations between concepts is also an account of the necessary structure of reality.[86] In this way, Hegel identifies the necessary relations between the categorical concepts of logic with the necessary structure of reality. In short, the conceptual structure revealed by the 'science of logic' is said to provide the essential structure of the world.

Hegel's developed account of the relation between these logical categories and the world of finite entities – that is, limited entities which cease to exist – is not always clear. However, it certainly involves the claim that the latter (the world of finite entities) is, in some sense, dependent on the former (the system of logical categories). The Hegelian 'concept' is thus not a set of categories formed by humankind in order to make sense of what actually

---

[83] The judicious description is from Inwood, *Hegel*, p. 262. This 'triadicy' is not absolute. See Willem de Vries, 'Hegel's Logic and Philosophy of Mind', Robert C. Solomon and Kathleen M. Higgins (eds.), *The Age of German Idealism* (London, 1993) pp. 216–53.
[84] Feuerbach, 'Zur Kritik' 25/101.   [85] *Enzyklopädie* §24.
[86] See, for example, the remarks on critical philosophy in *Enzyklopädie* §22Z.

exists but is rather to be understood as a non-finite entity on which all finite things depend.[87] Unsurprisingly, the notion of 'dependence' involved here is contentious, but is perhaps best understood as having two component parts. The categorical structure, unearthed by the science of logic, is responsible for both the existence and the development of the sensible world. In order to elucidate his own views, Hegel often appeals to the affinities between absolute idealism and Christianity. In the present case, he explains that absolute idealism, like Christianity, regards 'the sum total of everything that there is' as 'created and governed' by 'God'.[88]

The first element of 'dependence' – the claim that the relation between thought and the sensible world is a relation between thought and its own creation – constitutes a parallel of the divine creation *ex nihilo*. It seems that thought is not only necessarily embodied – that is, requires the existence of the sensible world in order to be what it is – but somehow produces its own embodiment. As a result, the transition from the sphere of logic to the spheres of nature and spirit is not to be understood as a transition to something 'alien' or to a material content that 'stems from outside it'.[89] For Hegel, the natural and social worlds are rather to be seen as a product of the self-realising activity of the concept (whose actualised form Hegel calls the idea).

It is hard to make sense of this suggestion, and commentators are occasionally tempted to treat this relation between thought and the sensible world in terms of the categorical structure of the logic making an impact on some pre-existing or independent material. However, that interpretation of Hegel's position should be resisted. The categories of the logic are formal in the sense of being *a priori* (that is, not derived from experience but rather presupposed in any thinking about the world), but they are not formal in the sense of providing a schema that is subsequently applied to a content obtained from elsewhere.[90] Hegel maintains that thought, or more precisely the concept, is an activity 'that does not need a material at hand outside it in order to realise itself'.[91] As a result, it is a mistake to assert, on the model of the demiurge of the ancients – he presumably has Plato's *Timaeus* in mind – that the world is a product of intelligence in the same way that an artefact is 'created' by a craftsman. Hegel explicitly rejects such an account because it would make God 'not the creator of the world, but

---

[87] See Thomas E. Wartenberg, 'Hegel's Idealism: The Logic of Conceptuality', Frederick C. Beiser (ed.), *The Cambridge Companion to Hegel* (Cambridge, 1993) pp. 102–29.
[88] *Enzyklopädie* §45Z.   [89] *Ibid.* §43Z.
[90] See Michael Rosen, *Hegel's Dialectic and its Criticism* (Cambridge, 1982) chapter 3.
[91] *Enzyklopädie* §163Z(2).

the mere architect of it', and Hegel is not prepared to countenance such a demotion.[92] Hegelian categories, it seems, produce their own content; thereby embracing the 'deeper view' according to which 'God created the world from nothing'.[93]

The second element of 'dependence' concerns the manner in which the Hegelian categories govern (as distinct from create) the finite world. 'Reason', Hegel insists, 'is the soul of the world, inhabits it, and is immanent in it, as its own innermost nature'.[94] The Hegelian categories do not constitute some transcendental entity which uses finite things as a means, nor are they (somewhat caricatured) Platonic archetypes, static entities separated from, and standing behind, the sensible world. The 'concept' does not exist prior to, or apart from, its embodiment in the natural and social worlds. It is rather a developmental plan which is wholly immanent in the sensible world. As Hegel remarks in the *Enzyklopädie*, the concept 'is what truly comes first and things are what they are through the activity of the concept, that dwells in them and reveals itself in them'.[95]

Hegel maintains that this claim – that the essential structure of the sensible world necessarily exists – does not commit him to the view that everything which exists, or which happens, in the world does so of necessity. In this context, he utilises a distinction between, on the one hand, the class of contingent items and events, and, on the other, particular members of that class. Only the former is said to exist necessarily.[96] Thus contingency, as such, exists not as the result of a shortfall of necessity, but in its own right as a category requiring exemplification in the world.[97] However, the existence of sixty rather than fifty-nine species of parrot is a contingent rather than necessary fact about the world.[98] (Allowing what might be called 'full-blown' contingency in this latter context would still seem to create difficulties for Hegel's account of the absolute as something without limit, although probing such difficulties is beyond the remit of the present sketch.)

The precise location of the dividing line between necessary and contingent features is scarcely obvious – 'Herr Krug' is not alone in being puzzled – but Hegel never doubts its existence. (The Kantian philosopher Wilhelm Traugott Krug had famously challenged Schelling to 'deduce' the existence of the pen with which he was writing. Hegel dismisses this challenge to derive 'trivial' entities, but his reasons for doing so are far from

---

[92] *Ibid.* §128Z.   [93] *Ibid.* See also *ibid.* §163.   [94] *Ibid.* §24Z.   [95] *Ibid.* §163Z(2).
[96] See, for example, *Philosophie des Rechts* §214A.   [97] See, for example, *Enzyklopädie* §145.
[98] See *Logik* 6, 375/682. See also *Philosophie des Rechts* §214A.

transparent.[99]) Hegel frequently criticises other philosophers, not only for
failing to extend necessity far enough into the world, but also for the
contrary sin of attempting to extend the realm of necessity – and hence of
philosophy – too far into the world (namely, into the sphere of the properly
contingent). Spinoza is found guilty of the former offence, and chastised
for his reluctance to claim that particular features of the finite world are
required by the nature of God. Plato and Fichte are convicted of the latter charge, and criticised for their treatment of certain contingent claims
as if they were genuinely philosophical recommendations. (Hegel appears
particularly irked by Plato's advice that nurses holding infants should rock
them gently like a boat at sea, and Fichte's suggestion that the passports of
contemporary 'suspect' persons ought to carry their 'painted likeness'.[100])

For Hegel, the immanence of the concept is a question of degree; any
given reality can realise the categories to a greater or lesser extent. He often
makes this point by applying the vocabulary of 'truth' to things (in addition
to judgements, beliefs, and so on). A finite entity is said to be 'true' to the
extent that it adequately expresses (is true to) its essence (the concept).

Hegel characterises an entity which is true to its essence as 'actual (*Wirk-
lich*)'. However, his elaboration of the relation between 'actuality' and the
sensible world is not always clear. According to his dominant account
of these matters, the sensible world includes the actual. For example, the
notorious '*Doppelsatz*' ('double dictum') which appears in the Preface to the
Philosophie des Rechts – claiming that 'what is rational is actual; and what is
actual is rational' – portrays the world as including not only those existents,
referred to as 'appearance (*Erscheinung*)', that are adequate realisations of
the categorical structure of the logic, but also those existents, referred to
as 'semblance (*Schein*)', which are imperfect by virtue of failing to embody
that standard.[101] On this account, the 'actual' makes an appearance in the
sensible world, albeit in a way that does not include either those particular
entities whose existence is wholly contingent or those 'wilted and tran-
sient' entities whose grounding conceptual structure is as yet largely unrealised.[102] (I call this Hegel's dominant account of these matters, because on

---

99 See *Enzyklopädie* §250 and 'Krug'. See also Dieter Henrich, 'Hegels Theorie über den Zufall',
Kantstudien, volume 50 (1958/9) pp. 131–48.

100 See *Logik* 6, 195–6/357 and *Philosophie des Rechts* 'Preface' ¶12. See also Plato, *Laws*, 790d; and
Fichte, *Grundlage des Naturrechts* (1796), *Fichtes Werke*, volume 3 (Berlin, 1971) §21.

101 *Philosophie des Rechts* ¶12. See also *Enzyklopädie* §6A. Dieter Henrich's term '*Doppelsatz*' is rendered
neatly as 'double dictum' by Michael Hardimon. See Dieter Henrich, editorial introduction to
Hegel, *Philosophie des Rechts: Die Vorselung von 1819–20 in einer Nachschrift* (Frankfurt am Main,
1983) p. 14; and Michael O. Hardimon, *Hegel's Social Philosophy: The Project of Reconciliation*
(Cambridge, 1994) p. 24.

102 *Enzyklopädie* §6A.

occasion – and seemingly in tension with that account – Hegel also suggests
that 'actuality' proper is not a feature of the sensible world, and that only
God is genuinely 'actual'.[103])

Hegel's characterisation of the relation between 'actuality' and philosophy would appear to lend support to that dominant account. Speculative
philosophy, he maintains, is properly concerned with the sensible world
only because, and to the extent that, the sensible world is 'actual'. (Since
the relation between 'actuality' and existence parallels that between God
and his creation, this is another way of expressing Hegel's view that, properly speaking, philosophy is theodicy.) Given that Hegel holds that the
essential structure of the natural and social worlds provides an appropriate
subject matter for philosophy, consistency would seem to require that he
also believe that actuality is exemplified in the sensible world (even if only
to some imperfect degree).

For Hegel, both the social and natural worlds should be thought of as
'applied logic, so to speak, for the logic is their animating soul'.[104] However, they embody that categorical structure in a significantly different
manner. The natural world exhibits rationality – not least in the form of
law-governed behaviour – but it does so only in a repetitive and unconscious
way. For Hegel, the natural world embodies no cumulative development, no
'history' proper. It was in this context that he endorsed Schelling's portrayal
of the natural world as 'ossified intelligence (*versteinerte Intelligenz*)'.[105] In
sharp contrast, Hegel portrays the social world as a sphere of genuine
progress. Here the idea – the concept as actualised in the world – functions as a purposeful activity developing through historical stages towards
a goal which is frequently described, in this context, as 'self-consciousness
(*Selbstbewusstsein*)'.

Hegel's account of self-consciousness (or self-knowledge) is suggestive
but fiddly. He rejects any portrayal of self-consciousness as something
immediate, that is, as something given, simple, or direct. Instead self-
consciousness requires the projection of a subject into something other
than itself, and the subsequent recognition of itself in that 'other'. It seems
that self-consciousness results from the recognition of the external world
as, in some sense, the product or embodiment of one's own self. On Hegel's
account, this requirement is paradigmatically exemplified by the relationship between the idea and the finite world. The creation and development of the world is said to constitute the necessary detour by which the

---

[103] See, for example, *ibid.* 24Z(2) and *ibid.* §6A, respectively.
[104] *Ibid.* §42Z(2).   [105] See *ibid.* §24Z (1) and §247Z.

self-consciousness of the absolute is achieved. Note that the relevant 'self' here is not radically distinct from the finite world in which it is realised, not least because it created and governs that 'object'. (As some commentators have noted, Hegel is occasionally tempted by the epistemological claim that thought can know only what it has itself created, that genuine knowledge is always, in some sense, self-knowledge.[106]) There are a number of further complications here. The self-consciousness of the absolute is indirect, in that it requires a vehicle – a role which is happily discharged by humankind. In addition, that role is not a narrowly cognitive one, since self-consciousness requires the establishment of certain social and political arrangements. Moreover, those arrangements appear only as the culmination of a progressive series of (increasingly adequate) dominant cultures. Finally, since self-consciousness is a condition for full-blown selfhood, the absolute is only actually a self at the end, and as a result, of that historical process. (Hence the earlier description of the Hegelian absolute as potentially a 'subject' as well as 'substance'.)

I have already noted Hegel's habit of elucidating his own metaphysics by detailing its affinities with Christianity. This use of religious analogy may have many didactic advantages, but it can also make Hegel's metaphysical views appear rather more conventional than they are. The attempted assimilation of the Christian God and speculative logic can function – whether intentionally or not is hard to judge – to obscure the unorthodox character of certain elements of his thought. For example, Hegel's account of God and the world might be thought to embody the heretical suggestion that the Incarnation should be identified with the Creation. (As others have noted, this reading would seem to place a controversial Christian idea at the very heart of his metaphysics.[107]) It is perhaps not surprising to discover that Hegel offers a (correspondingly) revisionist account of the role of the historical Jesus, who appears not as the Son of God but rather as an important moral teacher (akin but somewhat inferior to Socrates).

Hegel appears to have been genuinely puzzled by certain features of the traditional Christian characterisation of the relation between God and the world. For example, the Christian view that matter – whilst created by,

[106] See Richard Norman, *Hegel's Phenomenology: A Philosophical Introduction* (Brighton, 1976) p. 17; and David-Hillel Ruben, *Marxism and Materialism: A Study in Marxist Theory of Knowledge* (Brighton, 1977) pp. 40ff.
[107] On Hegel's relation to Christianity, see John McTaggart Ellis McTaggart, *Studies in Hegelian Cosmology* (Cambridge, 1901) chapter 7; and Hugo Meynell, *Sense, Nonsense and Christianity: An Essay on the Logical Analysis of Religious Statements* (London, 1964) chapter 4, part 3.

and subordinate to, God – is wholly alien to the divine nature, seems to have suggested a regrettable dualism to Hegel; 'regrettable' in that this insistence on the radical distinctiveness of God and the world risked turning God from the ground of everything into a less than boundless (that is, finite) entity. (On Hegel's account, the existence of anything outside of the absolute would be a limit, and any such limit would undermine God's infinitude.) Hegel thought that this dualistic view had two additional failings. The received Christian view failed to explain why the world exists at all. If God is 'all sufficient and lacks nothing', mused Hegel, 'how does He come to release Himself into something so clearly unequal to Him?'[108] The received Christian view also failed to explain why the world has the particular (historical) shape that it does. Indeed, on that account, God's involvement in the structure and development of the social world might look limited and piecemeal. Hegel considers these shortfalls in this traditional dualistic account to have been made good by his own conception of God's identity with the world.

Of course, the identity of God and the world might be conceptualised in a variety of ways.[109] Hegel considers and rejects two reductive accounts of that identity. The first account that he rejects is an 'atheistic' version of pantheism which downgrades God and asserts that only the world properly exists. The second account that he rejects is the form of pantheism that he calls 'acosmism (*Akosmismus*)', a standpoint which downgrades the world and attributes full-blown existence only to God.[110] Although Hegel deems both of these pantheisms to be ultimately mistaken, he is not neutral between them. His endorsement of Salomon Maimon's 'critical defence' of Spinoza makes it clear that 'acosmism' is the lesser mistake.[111] (Hegel suggests that the popular account of Spinoza as an atheistic pantheist correctly grasps that the latter affirms the identity of God and the world. However, the proponents of that popular account also assume – 'and', Hegel remarks, 'this is certainly not to their credit' – that it is more comprehensible 'that God should be rejected than that the world should be'. On Hegel's own reading, Spinoza takes the more creditable path and downgrades the world rather than God. Against the popular account of Spinoza, Hegel

[108] *Enzyklopädie* §247Z.   [109] See Inwood, *Hegel*, pp. 232ff.

[110] See G. H. R. Parkinson, 'Hegel, Pantheism, and Spinoza', *Journal of the History of Ideas*, volume 38, no. 3 (1977) pp. 449–59.

[111] On the importance of Salomon Maimon for the development of German idealism, see S. Atlas, *From Critical to Speculative Idealism: The Philosophy of Salomon Maimon* (The Hague, 1964); and Frederick C. Beiser, *The Fate of Reason: German Philosophy from Kant to Fichte* (Cambridge MA, 1987) chapter 10.

submits – not unreasonably – that 'a philosophy which maintains that God, and only God, is, should not be passed off as atheism'.[112])

In contrast, Hegel's own account of the relation between God and the world is said to embody a non-reductive identity. Unlike the traditional Christian account – in which God is fully formed before and apart from His creation of, and intervention in, the world – the Hegelian God is no supernatural entity existing apart from its creation. The Hegelian God only exists and grows through the creation and evolution of the world. The generation and development of the finite world is necessary if God is to be, and it seems that God, unlike finite entities, cannot fail to exist. (This claim about God would appear to commit Hegel to some version of what is traditionally called the ontological argument.) God's necessary progression to self-consciousness is reflected in, and depends upon, the structure and development of the finite world. As already noted, Hegel's account of the relation between the idea and the finite world is intended to exemplify the view of self-consciousness as an achievement which requires the projection of a subject into something other than itself, and the subsequent recognition of itself in that 'other'. 'God is God', Hegel insists, 'only insofar as He knows Himself.'[113] And, since He can come to know Himself only in His own creation, Hegel endorses the claim – seemingly heretical by conventional Christian standards – that 'without the world God is not God'.[114]

For the same reason – namely in order not to underestimate the distinctiveness of his basic metaphysical views – it is important not to confuse Hegel's account with more familiar forms of idealism. His claim that a categorical structure, distinct from but immanent in things, explains why they have the character that they do makes Hegel (on most accounts) an idealist. In particular, he is committed to the claim that concepts are the most basic entities in the world, and that finite things have 'actuality' only insofar as they embody the structure of those concepts. For Hegel, this recognition that such finite entities as exist are dependent on some non-finite entity for their essential structure constitutes idealism.[115] However, it is important to note that the Hegelian 'concept' – the non-finite entity which determines the structure of what exists – is not a human product, and, in particular, is not the human mind. Indeed, for Hegel, all finite things, humankind included, are dependent on the 'concept'. Hegel is unsympathetic towards any (supposedly 'post-Cartesian') privileging of the role of the human mind

---

[112] *Enzyklopädie* §50Z.   [113] *Ibid.* §564.   [114] *Vorlesungen über die Philosophie der Religion* 213/308.
[115] The idealism of philosophy, Hegel maintains, 'consists in nothing else than recognising that the finite has no veritable being'. *Logik* 5, 172/154.

in the constitution of objectivity, and he insists accordingly on the superiority of ancient idealism over the 'false idealism (*schlechten Idealismus*)' of the moderns.[116] Whatever their differences, Plato's insistence on the ontological priority of a rational order has an affinity with Hegel's conception of a categorical structure which underlies reality and which that reality strives to actualise. (There is also a possible connection with Aristotle here; the Hegelian concept can be seen as an Aristotelian formal-final cause, in that it provides both the essence of the finite and the goal of its development.[117])

The relation between speculative logic, on the one hand, and the social and natural worlds, on the other, is reflected in the (triadic) organisation of the Hegelian system. The categorical structure of Hegel's logic can be thought of as a developmental plan for all that exists. The 'logic' studies that plan apart from the social and natural worlds in which it is realised; the 'philosophy of nature' studies that plan as it is embedded in the natural world; and the 'philosophy of spirit' studies that plan as it is embedded in the social world.

Given that the knowledge generated by speculative logic is independent of experience, and since, on Hegel's account, that logic can be used to derive (at least) the broad outline of the results of the empirical sciences, the role of the latter might seem uncertain. Apart from cataloguing the various forms of contingency – clarifying the precise number of parrot species, for example – the function of the empirical sciences appears to be to join with, and confirm, the account provided by philosophy proper. They provide empirically known material from which the particular modes of expression of the categorical system can be recognised, thereby illustrating and supporting the claim that reason is in the world.[118] It would seem to follow that a number of distinct approaches to any given subject matter are therefore possible. One might study the conceptual framework that it embodies apart from its embodiment (Hegel's procedure in the science of logic); one might seek to establish the connections between conceptual foundations and empirical embodiment (Hegel's procedure in his philosophies of nature and of spirit); or one might study the empirical embodiment of the absolute in ignorance of its metaphysical foundations (the crude empiricism of many scientific and historical studies of which Hegel is highly critical but whose results he unquestionably appropriates). Applying the

---

[116] *Vorlesungen über die Geschichte der Philosophie* ii, 54/ii, 43.
[117] See Frederick Beiser, *Hegel* (London, 2005) pp. 66–8. For an earlier attempt to elucidate Hegel's work through a discussion of Aristotle, see G. R. G. Mure, *An Introduction to Hegel* (Oxford, 1940).
[118] *Enzyklopädie* §24Z(2).

knowledge generated by the logic to the content of the natural and social sciences – organising their results and making them more systematic, for example – appears to be part of what Hegel portrays as an attempt to give those sciences an *a priori* character.

In this section, I have sought to provide an accessible and accurate account of the broad metaphysical commitments presupposed by Hegel's *Rechtsphilosophie*. However, I should acknowledge that some readers, perhaps especially those familiar with contemporary Hegel scholarship, will have some reservations about that account. Two such doubts might be mentioned here.

In the first place, much recent literature is concerned to deny or minimise the metaphysical dimension of Hegel's work.[119] As a result, some readers might question the seemingly 'extravagant' metaphysics that I have attributed to him. I stand by the accuracy of that account, but note that the present section is intended as a description both of Hegel's thought and of the kind of understanding of Hegel's thought held by the young Marx. Any readers convinced either that Hegel's thought lacks a metaphysical dimension, or that it has a metaphysical dimension radically different from that portrayed here, might deny that happy coincidence. They could then treat this section as accurately describing the kind of – in their view, mistaken – understanding of Hegel's metaphysical commitments broadly presupposed by Marx's *Kritik*.

In addition, much recent Hegel scholarship is concerned to deny or minimise the connections between Hegel's metaphysics and his political philosophy.[120] As a result, readers might question the need for any discussion of the metaphysical dimension of Hegel's work. Much might be said in defence of these connections. Here I simply note that, unlike these commentators, Hegel himself always insisted on the close links between his *Rechtsphilosophie* and the speculative method. It was Hegel's consistent ambition to have provided in his metaphysics a sound foundation for his political philosophy. In the 'Preface' of the *Philosophie des Rechts*, for example, he appeals to the 'nature of speculative knowledge' developed in his *Wissenschaft der Logik* as the 'guiding principle' of his social and political

---

[119] Hartmann, for example, treats the science of logic as a theory of categories, portraying Hegel as concerned not with the nature of the basic entities in the world but with the categories which make our discussion of reality possible. See Klaus Hartmann, 'Hegel: A Non-Metaphysical View', Alasdair MacIntyre (ed.), *Hegel: A Collection of Essays* (Garden City NY, 1971) pp. 101–24; and Klaus Hartmann, 'Die ontologische Option', *Die ontologische Option* (Berlin, 1976) pp. 1–31.

[120] Pelczynski, for example, claims that 'Hegel's political thought can be read, understood, and appreciated without having to come to terms with his metaphysics'. Z. A. Pelczynski, 'Introductory Essay', *Hegel's Political Writings*, ed. Z. A. Pelczynski (Oxford, 1969) p. 136.

thought.[121] Conceding that he had 'omitted to demonstrate and bring out the logical progression in each and every detail', Hegel insists, nonetheless, that it was in this context 'that I would wish this treatise to be understood and judged'.[122] It might be argued that one of the merits of the *Kritik*, in which much of Marx's commentary is taken up with a critical engagement with Hegel's metaphysics, is that it takes Hegel at his word.

WHAT IS DEAD: MARX'S CRITICAL RESPONSE

At this point, the reader might expect an account of the young Marx's metaphysical and epistemological commitments to parallel the outline of Hegel contained in the previous section. Such an account of Marx's *positive* views – whilst acknowledging both the imprecision with which those views are sometimes expressed and the surprising diversity of secondary interpretation to which they have become subject – could have a number of threads.[123] It might note the young Marx's commitment to a 'naturalism' which holds that reality is wholly constituted by the finite world, and accordingly denies the existence of transcendent or 'immaterial' beings (such as the conventional Christian God). It might also examine the links that he saw between those 'naturalistic' views and the truth of certain 'realist' claims; in particular, the claim that the existence of material entities is distinct from, and not dependent upon, the mental activity by virtue of which these entities are conceived or known. In addition, that account might explain that Marx considered knowledge of the world to be empirical – that is, as capable of being disconfirmed by sense experience – and that he often characterises such knowledge as 'reflecting' and 'reproducing' the real. (He resists what might be called the sceptical temptations of such language by insisting that any 'reflection' is part of a broader practical engagement with the world, thereby denying the existence of any problematic gap between our consciousness and the real things that we experience.) It might note that Marx himself does not characterise these epistemological views as 'empiricist' ones, since he associates 'empiricism' with the uncritical recording and organising of the surface appearance of things, an approach which he contrasts with systematic theoretical attempts to capture the underlying

[121] *Philosophie des Rechts* ¶3.   [122] *Ibid.*

[123] For some corroboration of the attribution of these metaphysical and epistemological views to Marx, see Allen Wood, *Karl Marx* (London, 1981) part 4. For some contrasting ('idealist') readings, see Leszek Kolakowski, 'Karl Marx and the Classical Definition of Truth', *Marxism and Beyond* (London, 1969) pp. 58–86; Jean-Yves Calvez, *La Pensée de Karl Marx* (Paris, 1956); and Nathan Rotenstreich, *Basic Problems of Marx's Philosophy* (New York, 1965).

structure of reality.[124] Such an account might, finally, try to make sense of
the affinity that the young Marx identifies between, on the one hand, the
view of scientific knowledge as drawn 'from the world of the senses and the
experience gained in it', and, on the other, the standpoints of materialism
and socialism.[125]

Such an account, especially if developed at any length, could encourage
the impression that the young Marx's positive contribution to metaphysics
and epistemology is a significant or innovative one. That would be regrettable. Marx does, of course, have such commitments, but they are never
developed in anything approaching a systematic or distinctive manner. This
is not, in short, an area in which the early writings have a serious claim to
philosophical attention.

What is of philosophical interest is the young Marx's negative engagement with Hegel's metaphysics. The *Kritik*, in particular, contains a sustained and stimulating attack on speculative method. Marx's criticisms
range over a variety of topics: the epistemological status of the Hegelian
categories, the speculative attitude to the empirical world, the purported
link between the concept and its realisation, the nature of speculative explanation, and the Hegelian identity of God and the world. Despite their range
and power, these criticisms remain sadly neglected in the literature.

At several points in the *Kritik*, Marx rehearses a general account of
speculative method. In developing that account, his aim is not to summarise
Hegel's own understanding of the speculative project, but rather to expose
the flawed nature of that understanding through a demonstration of the
real dynamic of absolute idealism. Marx's remarks are often abbreviated
and imprecise, but they have a consistent focus and follow a recognisable
pattern. He is especially interested in the relation between finite entities and
the categories of speculative philosophy. In that context, he identifies two
central stages in the construction of the Hegelian account of the world.
These two stages – which he characterises as the 'transformation of the
empirical into the speculative and the speculative into the empirical' – are
said to form the systole and diastole of Hegel's speculative method.[126]

The first of these two stages of speculative construction is concerned
with the origins of the Hegelian categories. Marx rejects Hegel's account
of their *a priori* character, and instead maintains that the categories in

[124] For more discussion, see Richard Hudson, 'Marx's Empiricism', *Philosophy of the Social Sciences*,
volume 12 (1982) pp. 241–53; James Farr, 'Marx No Empiricist', *Philosophy of the Social Sciences*,
volume 13 (1983) pp. 465–72; and Daniel Little, *The Scientific Marx* (Minneapolis, 1986) pp. 123–6.
[125] *Die heilige Familie* 138/130. On the plausibility of such affinities, see the balanced remarks in Wood,
Karl Marx, pp. 159–61.
[126] *Kritik* 241/39/98.

question are obtained from empirical experience. Hegel is portrayed as taking concepts which are derived from the finite empirical world and simply (mis)describing them as elements of an *a priori* categorical framework. Marx summarises this first stage of speculative construction as involving 'the transformation of the empirical into the speculative'.[127]

The second of these two stages of speculative construction is concerned with the subsequent fate of the Hegelian categories. In particular, Marx is interested in the actualisation of that categorical framework in the natural and social worlds; interested, that is, in what might be called, somewhat pejoratively, the Neoplatonic dimension of Hegel's account.[128] Marx rejects Hegel's claim that the idea creates and governs the finite, insisting instead that speculative philosophy simply provides an imaginative redescription of the existing empirical world (as an embodiment of the absolute). Marx summarises this second stage of speculative construction as involving the 'transformation' of 'the speculative into the empirical'.[129]

Marx thereby portrays this two-stage process at the heart of absolute idealism in terms of a distinctive and recurring pattern of 'inversion'. Initially, concepts which are themselves derived from the finite empirical world are characterised as elements of an *a priori* categorical framework. Subsequently, that (purportedly) *a priori* categorical framework is characterised as actualising itself in the essential features of the finite world. In this way, the empirical world – from which the categorical framework is in fact derived – becomes transformed into (or, more accurately, is redescribed as) the manifestation of that conceptual system. Marx describes the subject of the 'inversion' here in a variety of ways. At one point, he summarises speculative construction as a process in which 'the fact which serves as a starting point [that is, empirical reality] is not seen as such but as a mystical result'. The same twofold process is characterised in terms of a series of parallel reversals whereby 'the condition is posited as the conditioned, the determinator as the determined, the producer as the product'.[130]

(The young Marx's use of 'inversion' is often identified in the literature as confirming the formative influence of some particular author or other. The candidates proposed include Bauer, Hegel, and Hess.[131] However, contemporary use of this cultural motif was sufficiently widespread as to cast

[127] *Ibid.*
[128] See the suggestive remarks in Edgar Wind, *Pagan Mysteries of the Renaissance*, second edition (London, 1967) pp. 92ff. See also Feuerbach, *Grundsätze* 311/47.
[129] *Kritik* 241/39/98.   [130] *Ibid.* 207/9/63. See also *ibid.* 242/40/99–100.
[131] See Zvi Rosen, *Bruno Bauer and Karl Marx: The Influence of Bruno Bauer on Marx's Thought* (The Hague, 1977) pp. 193ff; Jerrold Seigel, *Marx's Fate: The Shape of a Life* (Princeton, 1978) p. 72; and Shlomo Avineri, *Moses Hess: Prophet of Communism and Zionism* (New York, 1985) p. 113 n. 38, respectively.

doubt – at least, in the absence of further argument – on any strong claims about influence here. For example, visual representations of topsy-turviness were hugely popular, and *Die verkehrte Welt* was the title of both a well-known humorous play by Ludwig Tieck and a brilliant satirical poem by Heine, published in 1844 in *Vorwärts!*[132])

This general pattern of inversion takes a number of forms in Hegel's work. Perhaps the best-known examples involve the speculative hypostatisation of human characteristics. One such case discussed in the *Kritik* concerns the concept of 'subjectivity (*Subjektivität*)' in the *Philosophie des Rechts*. Subjectivity is used by Hegel in a variety of ways, not least to evoke the (distinctively modern) notion of individuals as autonomous sources of moral evaluation – capable of gaining meaning and satisfaction from acting in ways which reflect their own conscience, purposes, and reasoning (in contrast to those actions which are, for example, coerced, habitual, or unthinking).[133] In the *Kritik*, Marx shows little interest in the detail of Hegel's account – for example, in the latter's understanding of moral responsibility as extending to those aspects of an action either that were intended by the individual or that rational reflection might have anticipated (rather than extending, as the ancients had it, to 'the deed in its entirety') – but is concerned instead with the general terms in which the latter often describes the relation between subjectivity and individuals.[134] In particular, he seizes on Hegel's reference to 'subjectivity' being realised in the lives of individual moral subjects.[135] On Marx's account, such formulations are far from arbitrary, but rather illustrate the inversion of subject and predicate which lies at the heart of speculative construction. He finds Hegel guilty of separating attributes ('subjectivity') from their real subjects (finite individuals), and then treating those attributes as if they themselves constituted an independent subject. This is an example of the first stage of speculative transformation in which an empirical predicate is transformed into an ideal subject. The subsequent stage in the speculative transformation occurs when that ideal subject is said to actualise itself, a process which requires its manifestation in the finite world. On closer inspection, the actualised form which the pseudo-subject of 'subjectivity' takes in the 'ordinary empirical

---

[132] For visual representations, see Goethe-Institute (ed.), *Die verkehrte Welt: Moral und Nonsens in der Bildsatire* (Amsterdam, 1985).

[133] For Hegel's view of 'Subjektivität' as a distinctively modern notion, see his account of Plato's *Republic* as 'its own time comprehended in thoughts'. *Philosophie des Rechts* ¶¶12–13. See also *ibid* ¶10, §§ 46A, 185A, and 262Z.

[134] See *ibid*. §§115–18. The travails of Oedipus are said to embody the ancient conception of responsibility.

[135] See, for example, *ibid*. §279A.

world' is nothing other than the actions and attitudes of those individual moral agents with which the speculative construction (in reality) began. This particular hypostatisation of human predicates illustrates the more general pattern whereby, on Marx's account, the categorical framework is realised in the very realm of finite empirical phenomena from which its constituent categories were originally derived.

Marx's first criticism of speculative philosophy, concerning the epistemological status of the categories, may be apparent from the above account. Marx agrees with Hegel that genuine knowledge is possible, but he rejects the speculative claim that knowledge of the essential structure of the world is *a priori*. For Marx, the Hegelian categories, which purport to be products of pure thought 'established and predestined' apart from the spheres of nature and spirit, are nothing other than 'abstractions' from the finite world.[136] Marx typically claims that particular Hegelian categories – 'subjectivity' in the above example – are derived from the ordinary empirical world. On occasion, however, he seems to endorse the stronger, and more contestable, proposition that all knowledge is empirical.

Marx's second criticism of speculative philosophy may also be apparent. He maintains that speculation uncritically reinstates the finite world as it currently exists. Officially, of course, the essential structure of the world is the form taken by the realization of the Hegelian idea. However, Marx insists that 'the existence corresponding to the real idea' is not, as promised, 'a reality generated outside of itself', but is rather 'just the ordinary empirical world'.[137] In short, having first denied its independent status, speculative thought then smuggles the real world back in. In this way, the Hegelian method reverses what Marx considers to be the appropriate analytical procedure, in that empirical reality, which should form 'a starting point' for critical reflection, instead 'becomes a mystical result' of speculative presentation.[138] The contribution of speculation is not to alter the 'content' of the finite but simply to change the 'way in which it is regarded or *talked about*'.[139] Such a redescription leaves finite reality essentially unaltered, and thereby illustrates the uncritical attitude towards the world which is typical of the speculative project; 'empirical reality', he remarks, 'is accepted as it is'.[140] Marx is struck by the bathos of the resulting contrast between the dramatic account of empirical reality as *gesta Dei* and the prosaic familiarity of the natural and social spheres which – outside of that redescription – 'are left just as they were'.[141] On the one hand, it undoubtedly makes a

---

[136] *Kritik* 213/15/70.   [137] *Ibid.* 206/8/62.   [138] *Ibid.* 242/40/100.   [139] *Ibid.* 206/8/62.
[140] *Ibid.* 207/9/63. See also *ibid.* 244/42/102.   [141] *Ibid.* 206/8/62.

'profound impression' to see particular empirical phenomena being singled
out as posited by the idea and thus to encounter the 'incarnation of God
at every stage'.[142] On the other, the finite world is, in reality, left wholly
untouched by this redescription.

Marx's third criticism concerns the arbitrariness of the speculative link
between the categorical structure and its actualisation. Hegel's vocabulary is
intended to suggest that this link is one of 'logical rigour, of deduction and
the development of an argument'.[143] For Marx, however, this impression
is an illusory one. Speculative procedure, at this point, is more accurately
characterised as *allegorical*, as drawing on resemblance in order to make
suggestive connections between the categories and the world. Hegel 'simply holds fast to the *one* category and contents himself with searching for
something corresponding to it in actual existence'.[144] The purpose of that
search is 'to confer on some empirically existing thing or other the *significance* of the realized idea'.[145] Marx's reference to 'some existing thing or
other' is carefully chosen, aimed at conveying what he identifies as the arbitrariness in speculative procedure at this point. As he also remarks, given
its goal of uncovering 'the empirical existence of the truth', speculation
finds it all too easy 'to fasten on what lies nearest to hand and prove that
it is an *actual* moment of the idea'.[146] Once again, the implication is that
almost anything – whatever 'lies nearest to hand' – can be fashioned to
represent 'a determinate incarnation of a moment of the life of the idea'.[147]
In the context of a discussion of the different moments of the concept,
Marx observes that a sufficiently resourceful Hegelian could 'apply these
abstractions to any reality'.[148]

In distinguishing between Hegel's aspiration and his achievement in this
regard, Marx emphasises the gulf between, on the one hand, the suggestive
portrayal of particular existents as instantiations of the various moments
of the idea, and, on the other, a rigorous demonstration that a particular
aspect of the idea could take no other form, or that a particular existent
could instantiate no other aspect of the idea. For Marx, speculation has
no resources to rebut the objection that either 'the same meaning could be
given to a different subject' or 'the same subject could be given a different
meaning'.[149] In this way, Hegel's philosophy fails to fulfil the logical promise
of its own vocabulary. Marx insists that this failure to establish a *necessary*
connection between the concept and the empirical world is not a contingent
failing, which might, for example, be remedied by some subsequent author.

---

[142] *Ibid.* 241/39/98. [143] *Ibid.* 211/12/67. [144] *Ibid.* 250/48/109. [145] *Ibid.* 241/40/99.
[146] *Ibid.* 241/39/98. [147] *Ibid.* 241/40/99. [148] *Ibid.* 214/16/71. [149] *Ibid.* 287/82–3/149.

'Even if we wait to the end of time', Marx writes, 'it will never become possible to construct such a bridge.'[150]

Marx's fourth criticism of Hegel's idealism concerns its failure to satisfy a fundamental criterion of explanatory adequacy, namely that in trying to explain a particular phenomenon, the features that this phenomenon has in common with others cannot be explanatorily sufficient. Marx maintains that in order to understand a particular phenomenon one needs to identify not only those features that it shares with others but also its *differentia specifica*.[151] (Both the substantive claim and Marx's language at this point suggest the influence of Aristotle.[152]) The Hegelian system is said to neglect that explanatory requirement. The starting point of the *Rechtsphilosophie* is, of course, the speculative idea, which develops into and determines the essential structure of the rational state. However, as Hegel admits, this fails to distinguish the state organism from other kinds of organism, since social and political institutions are structured by the same categorical system that determines all (necessary) existents. Commenting on Hegel's account of the structure of the political state (in terms of the nature of the concept), Marx observes that 'if we omit the concrete determinations, which might easily be exchanged for those of another sphere, such as physics, and which are therefore inessential, we find ourselves confronted by a chapter of the *Logik*'.[153] His point here is not that there is an arbitrariness concerning which concrete determination is pinned on to which section of the logic, but rather that the same logical categories are utilised to explain first one phenomenon and then another.

Hegel's account of the transition from family and civil society to the state can provide a pertinent example. According to Marx, this transition is effected, not with reference to the '*particular* nature' of each institution, but rather in terms of the '*universal* relationship of *freedom* and *necessity*'.[154] However, these same categories are pressed into service elsewhere. For example, they are used to account for the progression from 'inorganic nature' to 'life' in Hegel's *Naturphilosophie*, and for the progression from 'essence' to 'concept' in his *Logik*. 'It is always the same categories', Marx comments, 'which are made to supply now one sphere and now another with a soul (*Seele*).'[155] The real priorities of speculative philosophy are said to emerge from these parallelisms. In his enthusiasm to find 'the determinations

---

[150] *Ibid.* 212–13/14/69.   [151] *Ibid.* 210/12/67.
[152] In the *Topics*, Aristotle maintains that a definition – that is, a phrase signifying the essence of a thing – must combine the differentia and the genus. For the Latin, see Boethius, *Aristoteles Latinus* 143a30–35.
[153] *Kritik* 217/18/73–4. (Emphasis amended.)   [154] *Ibid.* 208/10/64.   [155] *Ibid.* 209/10/64–5.

of the concepts of logic at every point', Hegel neglects to investigate 'the particular logic of the particular object'.[156] Marx insists that Hegel's 'sole concern is simply to re-discover "the idea", the "logical idea", in every sphere, whether it is to be the state or nature'.[157] As a result, empirical phenomena 'are and remain uncomprehended because their specific nature has not been grasped'.[158]

In his response to Hegel's characterisation of the state in terms of rationality, Marx rehearses the same complaint. He does not question whether rationality is an appropriate concept by which to judge political life, but rather challenges the appropriateness of Hegel's account of rationality. For Hegel, the internal structure of the state is rational 'in so far as its moments can be resolved into the categories of abstract logic', that is, insofar as its structure reflects the internal differentiation of the concept. But this criterion performs exactly the same function in a variety of other contexts. In short, the weakness of Hegel's conception of rationality is that it fails to grasp the differentia (that is, the distinctive character) of its various objects (here, the political state). It is this failure which marks out the Hegelian account of rationality as an 'alien' standard when it comes to assessing political life. Marx suggests that, in the *Rechtsphilosophie*, Hegel does not pursue a serious investigation into 'the logic of the body politic', but is rather looking to provide his speculative logic 'with a political body'.[159] As a result, speculative method stands accused of failing to satisfy a basic criterion of explanatory adequacy. As Marx puts it: 'An explanation which fails to provide the *differentia specifica* is *no* explanation at all.'[160]

A fifth criticism concerns the speculative identity of God and the world. The young Marx does not simply proffer a brute rejection of speculative premises, but seeks rather to cast doubt on Hegel's own understanding of this identity. As previously explained, on the official speculative account, the identity of God and the world is a non-reductive one which 'downgrades' neither of the entities that it relates (thereby avoiding both atheistic pantheism and Spinozan acosmism). Marx maintains that, whatever Hegel's ambition in this context, speculative philosophy effectively demotes the status of the world. If the relation between God and the world were really one of non-reductive identity, then neither entity would dominate the other. As Marx observes in another context, this kind of 'supposedly two-sided' identity is undermined if one of the relevant entities is revealed to stand in a relation of 'subordination' to, and 'dependence' on, the other.[161] Moreover, there is

[156] *Ibid.* 296/91/159. See also *ibid.* 218/18/73.   [157] *Ibid.* 211/12/67.   [158] *Ibid.*
[159] *Ibid.* 250/48/109.   [160] *Ibid.* 210/12/67.   [161] *Ibid.* 204/6/60.

clearly some sense in which the Hegelian relation between God and the world is unequal in precisely this manner. Since the finite world is created and governed by – that is, owes its 'existence' to and is 'determined' by – the categorical structure, the relation between them is not accurately described as a 'two-sided' one. That relation is better characterised as a reductive one. It is an example of what Marx, at one point, calls a 'specious identity', namely a relation in which the status of one of the entities involved – here, the finite world – is effectively downgraded.[162]

Hegel, of course, maintains that the task of philosophy is to study 'what is', but his insistence that '*what is* is reason' can be said to reduce the empirical world to just so many instantiations of rationality.[163] Since, on Hegel's own account, the categorical structure of speculative logic creates and governs the finite world, Marx denies that the former and the latter have equal standing. Empirical existents are simply the finite phase of the Hegelian idea 'indebted for their existence to a spirit (*Geist*) other than their own; they are not self-determining (*Selbstbestimmungen*) but are instead determined by another'.[164] In the Hegelian narrative of the 'life history' of the idea, human activity necessarily appears as 'the activity and product of something other than itself'.[165]

At this point, it might be objected that since the Hegelian God also needs the world, any dependency is mutual. However, mutual dependency is not enough to dislodge Marx's insistence on the asymmetry that is involved here. The Hegelian categories might need the world for their actualisation, but Marx maintains that it is the concept which is 'the *agens*, the driving force, the determining and differentiating principle'.[166] Particular empirical existents are simply the finite form of this categorical structure, each functioning as 'a mere role' played by the constitutive moments of the logic.[167] The 'fate' of the various powers of the state, for example, is already 'predestined' by the nature of the concept; it lies sealed, as Marx remarks – alluding to the Madrid prison of the Inquisition – 'in the holy archives of the Santa Casa (of the *Logic*)'.[168]

For once, Hegel's terminology is deemed to be entirely apposite. Marx suggests that the speculative characterisation of 'actuality' as an 'appearance (*Erscheinung*)' accurately conveys the manner in which the transformation of the realm of empirical truth into an aspect of the realisation of the idea effectively undercuts the comparative standing of the extant world.[169] 'The soul of an object', Marx maintains, 'is established and predestined prior

[162] *Ibid.*   [163] *Philosophie des Rechts* ¶13.   [164] *Kritik* 207/9/63. See also *ibid.* 206/8/62.
[165] *Ibid.* 241/39/98.   [166] *Ibid.* 213/15/70.   [167] *Ibid.* 267/64/128.
[168] *Ibid.* 213/15/70.   [169] See *ibid.* 206/7–8/61.

to its body which is really just an illusion (*Schein*).'[170] As a result – and notwithstanding his own strictures against Spinoza – Hegel's own thought stands accused of having a strong 'acosmic' cast.

The young Marx's own metaphysical and epistemological commitments are neither fully elaborated nor especially distinctive, but his sustained and wide-ranging critical engagement with speculative method remains of significant interest. The considered assessment of Hegel's metaphysics that results is a relentlessly negative one. Marx propounds five central criticisms of the speculative project. Hegel is judged to have failed to grasp that (at least, some of) the categories are not *a priori* but rather derived from empirical experience, to have embodied an uncritical empiricism in his attitude to the finite world, to have misdescribed the relation between the concept and its realisation as a necessary rather than an allegorical one, to have failed to provide an explanation which engages with the differentia of finite entities, and – despite his own ambitions in this regard – to have endorsed an account of the identity of God and the world which tends towards 'acosmism'.

WHAT HEGEL'S INSIGHT IS NOT

In order to make sense of the *Kritik*, I have already emphasised the value of unravelling the two main threads of Marx's subject matter, separating his discussion of speculative method from his discussion of the modern state. One of the interpretative benefits of this unravelling is that a clear contrast emerges between, on the one hand, the young Marx's unrelenting criticism, and occasional parody, of speculative method, and, on the other, his generous appraisal of Hegel's empirical understanding of the modern social world. In the remainder of this chapter, I will be concerned predominantly with the second of these threads.

That generous appraisal was, of course, heralded by the *Traumgeschichte* motif which credited German philosophy with an important insight into the modern social world. However, before I turn to consider the precise character of that Hegelian insight, some further clearing of the ground may be useful.

The suggestion that Hegel's *Rechtsphilosophie* is to be credited with an important empirical insight is liable to be misunderstood. (Those familiar with the literature are especially susceptible to the relevant misunderstanding.) As I have already emphasised, according to the young Marx the subject

[170] *Ibid.* 213/15/70.

of Hegel's empirical insight is the *modern* state (a polity which does not yet exist in Germany). It is important to notice that this account of Marx's reading of Hegel makes a decisive break with the dominant interpretation of the early writings (and especially of the *Kritik*), according to which the young Marx subscribes to what might be called the Prussian reading of the *Rechtsphilosophie*.

The Prussian reading of Hegel's political philosophy portrays the *Rechtsphilosophie* as providing a (more or less sophisticated) metaphysical justification for contemporary Prussian institutions. On this account, Hegel's empirical acumen would consist not in any insight into modernity but rather in having faithfully smuggled extant German institutions – the very institutions which the young Marx had dismissed as historically outdated – into his account of the rational state.

This reading of Hegel – according to which the rational state embodies the Prussian institutions of his day – has had a lengthy and illustrious career. It was adumbrated in the famous *Staats-Lexikon* edited by Karl Rotteck and Karl Theodor Welcker (published *seriatim* from 1834), but its best-known and most influential statement was probably that of Rudolf Haym (whose *Hegel und seine Zeit* was first published in 1857).[171] Haym's portrayal of Hegel as the official philosopher of the Prussian restoration, not only had a considerable contemporary impact, but has also enjoyed several periods of popularity with subsequent commentators.[172] In particular, the Prussian reading of the *Rechtsphilosophie* had a significant afterlife in twentieth-century English language sources, where it formed one element in a more general hostility towards German philosophy. (Hegel found himself pilloried for his supposedly formative intellectual role in the rise of the twin spectres of German nationalism and Soviet communism.[173]) Hegel was variously described as having 'glorified Prussia',[174] as being 'an apologist for Prussian absolutism',[175] as having presented the constitutional arrangements of the Prussian monarchy 'as the final fruits of the historic

[171] K. H. Scheidler, 'Hegel'sche Philosophie und Schule', Karl von Rotteck and Karl Theodor Welcker (eds.), *Das Staats-Lexikon*, volume 6 (Altona, 1847) p. 608. On Rotteck and Welcker, see Leonard Krieger, *The German Idea of Freedom: History of a Political Tradition* (Chicago, 1972) pp. 229–61. This line of argument was noticed by Bauer, who reported that 'one reads only invective against Hegel' from the 'constitutionalists'. Bauer, *Briefwechsel*, pp. 173–4.

[172] For a survey of interpretations of Hegel's *Rechtsphilosophie*, see Henning Ottmann, *Individuum und Gemeinschaft bei Hegel*, volume 1: *Hegel im Spiegel der Interpretationen* (Berlin, 1977).

[173] See Dominico Losurdo, *Hegel and the Freedom of the Moderns* (Durham NC, 2004) chapter 12.

[174] Bertrand Russell, *Unpopular Essays* (London, 1984) pp. 15, 23.

[175] Karl Popper, *The Open Society and its Enemies*, volume 2: *Hegel and Marx* (London, 1966) pp. 49, 34. See also Gilbert Ryle, 'Critical Notice', *Mind*, volume 56 (1947) pp. 167–72.

development of Spirit',[176] as having converted 'the temporal institutions of the Prussian state into the awesome mansions of the spirit of reason',[177] as having provided 'a philosophical justification for the conservative Prussian monarchy',[178] and so on.

The Prussian reading is of interest here less as a result of its periodic historical popularity with commentators on Hegel than because the young Marx is frequently portrayed as endorsing it. Marx is said to have interpreted the *Philosophie des Rechts* as providing a speculative defence of the social and political arrangements of contemporary Prussia. For example, it is variously claimed that, according to Marx, Hegel misdescribes 'the existing institutions of the Prussian state' as an embodiment of rationality and freedom,[179] that 'Marx argues that by a complicated feint, Hegel gives the impression that his description of the Prussian state is the concrete realisation of the ethical idea',[180] that Marx judges the institutional framework of the *Philosophie des Rechts* 'to be an accurate portrayal of Hegel's own Prussia',[181] that 'Marx treats Hegel's version of the state as summing up German reality at the time',[182] that Marx describes the *Philosophie des Rechts* as 'an apology for the Prussian state of Hegel's day',[183] and so on. An assessment of these various claims requires consideration of the proper interpretation both of Hegel's political philosophy and of the young Marx's account of Hegel's political philosophy. I begin with the former.

Despite its historical longevity and occasional popularity, the Prussian reading of Hegel has little foundation. The most obvious objection to this reading was pointed out by Hegel's first biographer, Karl Rosenkrantz, who observed that the institutional structures of the rational state 'by no means corresponded with the actual conditions of Prussia' at that time.[184] The relevant disparities here are considerable. Even a cursory comparison between the rational state and its contemporary Prussian counterpart reveals that Hegel describes and endorses a constitutional state (rather than

---

[176] J. N. Findlay, *Hegel: A Re-examination* (London, 1958) p. 127.

[177] Sidney Hook, *From Hegel to Marx: Studies in the Intellectual Development of Karl Marx* (London, 1936) p. 20.

[178] Frederick Watkins, *The Political Tradition of the West: A Study in the Development of Modern Liberalism* (Cambridge MA, 1948) p. 199.

[179] H. P. Adams, *Karl Marx in His Earlier Writings* (London, 1940) p. 82.

[180] Louis Dupré, *The Philosophical Foundations of Marxism* (New York, 1966) p. 91.

[181] Joseph O'Malley, 'Editor's Introduction', Karl Marx, *Critique of Hegel's Philosophy of Right* (Cambridge, 1970) p. li.

[182] Andrew Vincent, *Theories of the State* (Oxford, 1987) p. 156.

[183] M. W. Jackson, 'Marx's "Critique of Hegel's *Philosophy of Right*"', *History of European Ideas*, volume 12 (1990) p. 800.

[184] Karl Rosenkranz, *Hegel als deutscher Nationalphilosoph* (Leipzig, 1870) p. 149.

an absolutist one), the rule of law (rather than personal power), central representative institutions (rather than moribund provincial assemblies with restricted memberships and narrowly defined jurisdictions), equality before the law (rather than differential treatment according to status), freedom of the press (rather than extensive censorship), public and oral juridical proceedings (rather than private and written procedures), trial by jury (rather than trial by judiciary), freedom of occupation (rather than reserved occupations in the higher civil service and officer corps for the nobility), civil rights for Jews (rather than elaborate and extensive restrictions), and so on.[185] It is scarcely surprising to discover that modern Hegel scholarship has sided with Rosenkrantz against Haym, and overwhelmingly accepts the clear and substantial gulf between the Hegelian text and the political arrangements of contemporary Prussia.[186] Indeed, the existence of substantial disparities between the rational and Prussian states is beyond serious doubt.

The ramifications of this emphatic rejection of the Prussian reading of Hegel's political philosophy should not be misunderstood. Two clarifications might be helpful.

In the first place, to reject the claim that Hegel's political philosophy enshrines contemporary Prussian institutions as the actualisation of reason is not to deny the existence of *any* connection between Hegel's text and the Prussian context. For example, plausible affinities have been identified between Hegel's rational state and the moderate liberal aspirations of the Prussian reform movement. (The Prussian reform movement – associated, in particular, with Heinrich Karl vom Stein and Karl August von Hardenberg – flourished in the period between 1806 and 1813.[187]) Not least, it is apparent that Hegel and the reform movement shared both broad political enthusiasms (for example, supporting freedom of occupation, and civil and political equality for Jews) and specific institutional commitments (for example, endorsing corporate representation, bicameralism, and a professional bureaucracy).

---

[185] Some of these empirical claims about Prussia are, of course, more complicated than a brute list suggests. For example, jury trials had existed in some regions under Napoleonic rule but were subsequently abolished.

[186] It might be argued that Haym implicitly recognised the existence of this gulf, since he acknowledged a 'liberalistic gloss (*liberalistischen Glanzes*)' to the *Rechtsphilosophie*, and presented Hegel's commitment to Prussian institutions as the authentic meaning of the text, a meaning which required some unearthing. R. Haym, *Hegel und seine Zeit* (Berlin, 1857) pp. 359, 369.

[187] On the Prussian reform movement, see Krieger, *The German Idea of Freedom*, chapter 4; Friedrich Meinecke, *The Age of German Liberation, 1795–1815*, ed. Peter Paret (Berkeley, 1977); and Walter Simon, *The Failure of the Prussian Reform Movement* (Ithaca NY, 1955). On Hegel's affinities with the reform movement, see Jacques d'Hondt, *Hegel en son temps: Berlin, 1818–1831* (Paris, 1968).

In addition, to reject the claim that the rational state embodies contemporary Prussian political institutions does not exhaust the wider and more interesting question of how to characterise Hegel's ideological affinities. (In that context – and despite the implausibility of his Prussian reading of the *Philosophie des Rechts* – Haym makes some pertinent remarks concerning the complex relation between Hegel and conservatism.) I happily accept that Hegel's political philosophy contains some significant liberal elements, but I make no attempt here to broach – still less resolve – some broader issues about his ideological make-up.[188] In particular, I take no stand on the contentious and nuanced dispute amongst those who think that Hegel is best understood as a liberal, or as a conservative, or as something else (perhaps a communitarian), and between all of these commentators and those who maintain that it is misleading to pigeonhole Hegel's thought in this manner (according to categories – liberalism, conservatism, and so on – which he is typically said to have transcended).

So much for the proper interpretation of the relation between Hegel's text and extant German institutions. Simply put, the central institutions of the rational or Hegelian state are not those of contemporary Prussia. However, it is clear that the young Marx cannot be relied upon to reject a claim – here the Prussian reading of the *Philosophie des Rechts* – merely because it is erroneous. Moreover, much of the relevant literature portrays the young Marx as endorsing the interpretation of Hegel's political philosophy which I have described as widely and rightly discredited. As a result, Marx's own understanding of the relation between the Hegelian and Prussian states also needs discussion.

The erroneous character of these accounts of Marx's interpretation of Hegel – according to which Marx understood the *Philosophie des Rechts* as providing a (more or less sophisticated) metaphysical rationale for extant Prussian institutions – should already be apparent. They are undermined by the textual evidence which I discussed earlier and elaborate below. The *Traumgeschichte* motif expressly contrasts the political backwardness of contemporary German institutions with the standards of modernity embodied in contemporary German philosophy. In particular, it contrasts the

---

[188] Hegel lectured on his *Rechtsphilosophie* on seven separate occasions (he died after the second lecture in the seventh series), and student lecture notes have been discovered from six of these series. These notes can appear more liberal in both tone and institutional detail than the published *Philosophie des Rechts*. See, for example, David Leopold, 'Review of Hegel's *First Philosophy of Right*', *History of Political Thought*, volume 18 (1997) pp. 181–2. However, these disparities constitute a difference of emphasis rather than of fundamental standpoint, and the claim that they confirm the existence of an 'exoteric' and 'esoteric' Hegel seems misguided. For such a claim, see Karl-Heinz Ilting's introduction to Hegel, *Vorlesungen über Rechtsphilosophie 1818–1831*, volume 1.

backwardness of German political reality with the reflection in Hegel's *Rechtsphilosophie* of the institutions of 'the modern state'.[189] It seems certain that, for the young Marx, Hegel's empirical insight was not to have delineated the antiquated political institutions of contemporary Prussia, but rather to have grasped the central lineaments of the modern state (distinctive features which were conspicuously absent from German reality). On Marx's account, it is in this sense – and not as an advocate of contemporary Prussian arrangements – that Hegel faithfully embodied his own insistence that philosophy is always 'its own time comprehended in thoughts'.[190] (This remained Marx's view, and he would later rubbish Karl Liebknecht's attempt to revive 'the old Rotteck-Welckler muck (*Dreck*)' concerning Hegel's supposed Prussian sympathies.)[191]

The ramifications of this emphatic rejection – of the attribution to the young Marx of the Prussian reading of Hegel's political philosophy – should not be misunderstood. Two clarifications might be helpful.

In the first place, to reject the claim that Marx endorsed the Prussian reading of Hegel is not to deny that Marx saw *any* connection between Hegel's text and the contemporary Prussian context. For example, in the *Kritik*, Marx observes that the executive committees of senior civil servants that inhabit the Hegelian *Beamtenstaat* (bureaucratic state) are 'unknown in France'.[192] More generally, he diagnoses Hegel's enthusiasm for the civil service as evidence of his intellectual contamination by 'the world of Prussian officialdom'.[193] There is no question of denying or ignoring such remarks here; the issue is rather to determine their proper meaning. In context, I would suggest that these comments are essentially asides, perhaps best thought of as passing jibes at Hegel's parochialism. At most, they might be said to refine rather than displace Marx's account of the fundamental contrast between the backwardness of Prussian reality and Hegel's depiction of the state 'in its *modern* form'.[194]

In addition, to insist that the young Marx identifies an important – if, as yet, unelaborated – affinity between the Hegelian and modern states, is not to suggest that this interpretative claim is without precedent. Marx was not

[189] *Kritik* 289/84/151.
[190] *Philosophie des Rechts* ¶13. Compare this assessment of Hegel with Marx's description of Schelling as 'the thirty-eighth member of the [German] Confederation' and of Schelling's philosophy as 'Prussian policy (*Politik*) sub specie philosophiae'. Marx to Feuerbach, 3 October 1843, *MEW* 27, pp. 419–20; *MECW* 3, pp. 349–50.
[191] Marx to Engels, 10 May 1870, *MEW* 32, p. 503; *MECW* 43, p. 511. See also Engels to Marx, 8 May 1870, *MEW* 32, p. 503; *MECW* 43, p. 509.
[192] *Kritik* 251/49/110. See *Philosophie des Rechts* §289.
[193] *Kritik* 331/127/196.   [194] *Ibid.* 277/73/138.

alone in noticing both affinities between the modern and Hegelian states, and the distance of both of these from German reality. Parallel observations were made by several of his left-Hegelian contemporaries. For example, in Bauer's *Die Posaune des jüngsten Gerichts über Hegel, den Atheisten und Antichristen* (1841), Hegel is said to have despised contemporary German institutions, and to have preferred 'French' political alternatives.[195] (*Die Posaune des jünsten Gerichts* is an interesting but formally complex work. It was published anonymously and implicitly propounded a left-Hegelian account of Hegel under the explicit guise of an unrestrained pietist polemic against the latter's work. Bauer's rhetorical strategy, posing as a dedicated pietist minister, did not prevent the work being proscribed.[196]) Perhaps the clearest of those left-Hegelian precedents comes in Arnold Ruge's article 'Die Hegelshe Rechtphilosophie und die Politik unserer Zeit' (published in the *Deutsche Jahrbücher* in August 1842). Ruge sought to emphasise two points about 'all those great institutions' – he mentions 'national representation, juries, and freedom of the press' – which characterise the *modern* state. In the first place, Ruge maintains, these were institutions which 'we Germans still almost totally lack'. In addition, he notes that Hegel had 'assumed all these institutions into his theory of the state'.[197] This institutional affinity constitutes the main parallel between the modern and Hegelian states. However, Ruge also observes that the identity here is not a perfect one. Whilst Hegel's rational state undoubtedly incorporated the basic institutions of the modern state, it frequently did so in what Ruge describes as a 'somewhat tainted and faded form'.[198] In this way, Ruge's article can be seen to adumbrate both Marx's basic claim (that Hegel's rational state incorporated modern institutional arrangements as yet unknown in Germany) and its subsequent nuance (namely that on occasion the manner in which Hegel accomplished this indicated a certain Teutonic provincialism).

THE LINEAMENTS OF THE MODERN SOCIAL WORLD

Having rejected both the Prussian reading of Hegel's *Rechtsphilosophie* and the claim that the young Marx subscribes to that (erroneous) reading, I now turn to consider the empirical insight that Marx *does* identify in

---

[195] See Bauer, *Die Posaune*, chapters 4–5.
[196] Claims for joint authorship – with Marx and with Ruge – occasionally appear in the literature, but typically without supporting evidence. Bauer's sole authorship is not only suggested by his contemporaneous writings, but also accepted by modern Bauer scholars. See, for example, Bauer, *Briefwechsel*, p. 43; and Rosen, *Bruno Bauer and Karl Marx*, pp. 129ff.
[197] Ruge, 'Rechtsphilosophie' 758/216–17.   [198] *Ibid.*

Hegel's work. It will be readily apparent that if the *Rechtsphilosophie* is to be commended for its insight into modernity, then Marx must have had an understanding of the modern social world against which Hegel's empirical acumen could be judged. It is with this benchmark account of the modern social world that I begin.

The young Marx's first attempt to outline his understanding of modernity is contained in the *Kritik*. That text may not present a transparent or detailed elaboration of Marx's empirical understanding of the modern social world, but the broad contours of his nascent account are nonetheless clearly discernible. There are four main elements in that account. They concern the separation of civil society and state, the relation between these separated spheres, the character of civil society, and the character of the modern state.

The first element in this nascent account of the modern social world concerns the distinctive separation of state and civil society. Marx insists that the modern world is characterised by a separation of state and civil society which is without historical precedent. 'The separation of civil society and the political state', he writes, is a 'modern phenomenon.'[199] In the *Kritik*, this modern phenomenon is most often described in terms of the separation out of two previously conjoined spheres of social activity – the sphere 'of particular interests' and the sphere 'of the general interest' – each of which is then governed by a different principle.[200] The modern social world is said to have been established by a historical process whereby, on the one hand, the world of work and material needs is freed from entanglement with common interests, and, on the other, a distinct sphere of common interests emerges 'alongside the real life of the people'.[201] The young Marx sometimes describes this historical process as involving the separation out (from each other) of economic and political life.

In an attempt to support and dramatise this claim that the separation of state and civil society is without historical precedent, Marx contrasts this modern phenomenon with its pre-modern counterparts. He claims that in both the ancient and the medieval worlds there had existed 'a substantive unity' between economic and political life, between the sphere of particular interests and the sphere of the common good. As a result, these pre-modern societies present a stark contrast with the modern social world in which a political sphere has separated out from the economic sphere to form a new kind of polity standing apart from 'real life'.[202] That is not, of course, to say that the pre-modern substantive unity between economic and political life

[199] *Kritik* 277/73/138. [200] *Ibid.* 203/5/58–9. [201] *Ibid.* 234/32/91. [202] *Ibid.* 321/115/185.

always took the same form. Indeed, Marx recognises historical differences, not only between the ancient and the medieval worlds, but also within the former.

In the ancient world the substantive unity between civil and political life is said to have had a different form in Greece compared to what Marx calls 'Asiatic despotism (*asiatischen Despotie*)', by which he seems to mean 'pre-Classical' societies (such as Sumerian Mesopotamia, Pharaonic Egypt, and Hittite Anatolia). Amongst the ancient Greeks, Marx suggests that the state was identical with the community (at least, the community of citizens). As a result, there was no room for a distinction between a 'political' state and 'the people' (that is, the assembled citizenry). Given the direct participation of Greek citizens in the decision-making of their city state, 'common interests' had no separate life of their own but rather coincided with (aspects of) the real lives of the citizens. 'The *res publica*', Marx claims, 'was the real private concern of the citizens.'[203] However, in the case of 'Asiatic despotism' that substantive unity of particular and common interests took a somewhat different form. In such societies, he suggests, the state was identical with 'the private caprice of a single individual'.[204] (The notion of 'Asiatic despotism' is not, of course, Marx's own invention, but had a lengthy conceptual history in the work of Bodin, Bernier, Montesquieu, and others. The term was typically used to refer to a social and political system characterised by some combination of the state ownership of land, public hydraulic works, political despotism, stifling climatic conditions, a lack of historical development, and so on.[205]) As a result, and despite the significant differences between these two cases, Marx maintains that throughout the ancient world there was no structural separation between particular and common interests.

In the medieval world there was evidence of perhaps an even stronger substantive unity between these two spheres. In the Middle Ages, Marx claims, 'every sphere of private activity had a political character, or was a political sphere'.[206] For example, to be a serf, or to belong to a corporation, or even to own property, was already to have a certain political status. In a society which was organised into particular corporate communities, there was no room for a separate political state. Political and economic spheres, he maintains, were bound tightly together. Thus, instead of social classes, which might or might not lead a political existence, there were only estates, whose 'whole existence' was 'already political'.[207] Even the medieval

[203] *Ibid.* 234/32/91.   [204] *Ibid.*
[205] See Perry Anderson, *Lineages of the Absolutist State* (London, 1974) p. 472.
[206] *Kritik* 233/32/90.

monarch was treated as merely a '*particular* estate' (albeit, of course, one
which enjoyed certain privileges).[208] The unity of 'civil and political' life
embodied in the existence of these estates was simply an expression of a
wider '*identity* of civil and political society'. In the Middle Ages, Marx
writes, 'civil society was political society'.[209]

Since the emergence of the modern social world requires the breaking of
this substantive unity between civil and political life, its birth can be located
at the point where the private sphere 'achieved an independent existence'.
Marx maintains that 'where commerce and landed property are unfree,
where they have not yet asserted their independence [from considerations
of the common good]' the modern social world does not yet exist.[210] In
the *Kritik*, he suggests that the birth of the modern social world can be
dated precisely, since the private sphere finally achieved that independence
in 1789. 'Not until the French revolution', Marx writes, 'was the process
completed in which the estates were transformed into social classes, i.e. the
class distinctions in civil society became merely *social* differences in private
life of no significance in political life. This accomplished the separation of
political life and civil society.'[211]

The second element in Marx's nascent account of the modern social
world concerns the relation between these newly separated spheres. He
maintains that the relation between these two is far from harmonious. In
the *Kritik*, it is treated as a relation between 'the system of particular interests (the family and civil society)' and 'the system of the general interest
(the state)'.[212] Note that these two spheres of social life embody distinct
and conflicting underlying principles: on the one hand, a concern for particular interests, and, on the other, a concern for the common good of
the community. Marx suggests that not only do these spheres 'have nothing in common', but also that they are 'directly opposed' to each other.[213]
In short, civil society and the modern state are not only 'heterogeneous'
(because they embody different principles) but also 'antithetical' (because
those different principles harbour a hostility towards each other).[214] As
a result, Marx claims, there emerges for the first time a characteristically
modern antagonism between civil and political life.

The third element in Marx's nascent account of the modern social world
concerns the character of civil society. He portrays civil society as 'atomistic
(*atomistische*)'.[215] The concept of 'atomism' remains only sketchily elaborated in the *Kritik*. (At the time of writing, Marx may have intended to

[207] *Ibid.* 276/72–3/137–8.   [208] *Ibid.* 276/73/138.   [209] *Ibid.* 275/72/137.   [210] *Ibid.* 233/32/90.
[211] *Ibid.* 284/80/146.   [212] *Ibid.* 203/6/58–9.   [213] *Ibid.* 281/77/143.
[214] *Ibid.* 280/73/142.   [215] See, for example, *ibid.* 283/79/145.

discuss civil society elsewhere in his commentary on the *Rechtsphilosophie*.) Perhaps the best guide to the concept is provided by the stark contrast that Marx draws between, on the one hand, the forms of community available in the ancient and medieval worlds, and, on the other, the 'individualism (*Individualismus*)' of modern civil society. Thus, whereas in the medieval estate, for example, people were motivated by the interests of their community, it is particular and not communal interests which are said to provide the 'ultimate goal' of modern social life.[216] Indeed, Marx maintains that 'the civil society of the present is the principle of *individualism* carried to its logical conclusion'.[217] The result of this unimpeded individualism is a dramatic one. Civil society is judged incapable of supporting a vital dimension of human flourishing – it constitutes a sphere of social life which 'does not sustain the individual as a member of a community, as a communal being (*Gemeinwesen*)'.[218] (This communal aspect of human nature is discussed more fully in Chapter 4.) In short, Marx's characterisation of modern civil society as 'atomistic' is intended to convey an unimpeded individualism, whose effects on the communal dimension of human flourishing are clearly deleterious.

The fourth and final element in Marx's nascent account of the modern social world concerns the character of the state. The modern state originating in Europe is such a historically distinctive phenomenon, by comparison with pre-modern polities, that the young Marx sometimes refers to it as the state *sans* qualification. (This view that the state 'as such', or the state 'proper', is a uniquely modern phenomenon is a familiar one.[219]) In the *Kritik*, Marx is keen to stress that the modern state is distinguished by its 'abstract (*abstrakt*)' character. The 'abstract' character of the state – like the 'atomism' of civil society – is an important but rather elusive notion in the early writings. It is used by Marx in a number of distinct, but never carefully delineated, ways. Two of those senses might usefully be distinguished here.

In places, Marx uses 'abstract' as a synonym of 'separate'. In this sense, he insists that 'the abstraction of the *state as such* was not born until the modern world because the abstraction of private life was not created until modern times. The abstraction of the *political state* is a modern product.'[220] Marx's claim here is simply that the pre-modern unity of economic and political life has ended with the distillation of two separate spheres of civil society and the state (each governed by their own distinct rationale). Here the 'abstraction' of the state is equivalent to the 'abstraction' of civil society – each has separated out from the pre-modern congruence of the economic and political. All this, of course, is simply to rehearse the first of his four claims about the distinctive character of the modern social world.

Elsewhere, however, Marx uses 'abstract' to identify a characteristic of the state that is contrasted with, rather than shared by, civil society.[221] It is this additional connotation which is important here, since it is central to the fourth and final thread in Marx's account of the modern social world. According to this additional connotation, the state is 'abstract' in a sense in which ('concrete' and 'material') civil society is not. In this context, 'abstract' seems intended to suggest the remoteness of the state from the life and influence of ordinary citizens. Marx's vocabulary varies, but he consistently stresses the otherworldly character of the modern state, contrasting the 'real life' of civil society, for example, with the 'transcendental remoteness' and the 'transcendental existence' of the state.[222] To rehearse only a few of the relevant formulations here, modern political life is said to constitute 'the *airy life*', the state is described as an 'ethereal region', and, in a recurring motif, Marx writes of the 'heaven of the political state'.[223] (The association of Christianity and the modern state appears throughout the early writings and is discussed further in Chapter 3.) It seems that modern political life, unlike its civil counterpart, acknowledges the common good of the community, and thereby also the communal dimension of individual human flourishing. However, Marx's characterisation of the modern state as 'abstract' seems intended to suggest that this acknowledgement is accomplished in an inadequate ('transcendental') manner.

From their largely unheralded and unelaborated appearance in the *Kritik*, it would be easy to miss the significance of these last two threads in the young Marx's account of the modern social world. These descriptions, of civil society as 'atomistic' and of the modern state as 'abstract', introduce ideas which are both central to the early writings and have some considerable resonance with modern readers. They embody an early attempt to delineate two main dimensions of *alienation* in the modern social world.

The concept of alienation is a slippery one, discussed, more or less explicitly, at several places in the present work. At the most general level, alienation is a concept used to suggest a kind of dysfunctional relation (for example, an unnatural separation or hostility) between entities.[224] As such, alienation would always seem to involve the loss or lack of something of value (in

---

[221] See, for example, *ibid.* 295/90/158. [222] *Ibid.* 233/31/89.
[223] *Ibid.* 283/79/146 and 303/98/166. [224] See Wood, *Karl Marx*, p. 3.

the present formulation, the loss or lack of the natural connectedness or harmony between the relevant entities).[225]

Alienation, in this sense, is best thought of as a generic concept which can be applied to a wide variety of subjects. Moreover, there seems no good reason to assume either that there is any systematic connection between those varied instances or that those instances have a single underlying explanation.[226] The suggestion that the concept of alienation is always identified by a single locution in Marx's early writings should also be resisted.[227] The received cultural vocabulary of the early 1840s provided a wide variety of words in which this dysfunctional relation between entities could be expressed. Words such as '*Entfremdung*' and '*Entäusserung*' are simply two of the many ways in which the presence of alienation might be indicated. ('*Entfremdung*' corresponds to '*entfremden*', which means 'to estrange' or 'to make alien', and derives from '*fremd*', which means 'alien'.[228] '*Entäusserung*' corresponds to '*entäussern*', which means 'to make outer' or 'to make external', and suggests the idea of surrendering or relinquishing something.[229]) Several other locutions were routinely available to Marx and his contemporaries. (Candidates would include formulations deriving from '*Trennung*', which connotes a divorce or separation, and '*Spaltung*', which indicates a division or rupture.[230]) In short, it is the concept of alienation, rather than the use of particular words to identify it, which is important here. This is not, of course, to deny that the young Marx ever distinguishes between different senses of alienation – or, indeed, between alienation and related phenomena – but rather to suggest that any such distinctions are not marked by the consistent use of a distinct technical vocabulary.

Accounts of this dysfunctional relation are sometimes divided into 'subjective' and 'objective' variants.[231] Alienation is said to be subjective when it consists in the presence (or absence) of certain beliefs or feelings. For example, individuals are sometimes characterised as alienated, either when (negatively) they do not feel 'at home' in the modern social world, or

[225] For a textual justification for attributing the view propounded here to Marx, see *Manuskripte* 588/346/399 (where alienation is equated with 'a flaw, a weakness, something which ought not to be'). For an alternative (neutral) account see Peter Railton, 'Alienation, Consequentialism, and the Demands of Morality', James Rachels (ed.), *Ethical Theory*, volume 2: *Theories About How We Should Live* (Oxford, 1998) p. 222, n. 1.
[226] See Wood, *Karl Marx*, pp. 6ff; and G. A. Cohen, 'Review of Allen Wood, *Karl Marx*', *Mind*, volume 92 (1983) p. 441.
[227] As implied, for example, by Richard Schacht, *Alienation* (London, 1971) pp. 5–7. See Michael Inwood, *A Hegel Dictionary* (Oxford, 1992) pp. 35–8.
[228] See, for example, *Kritik* 283/79/145.   [229] See, for example, *Manuskripte* 577/335/389.
[230] See, for example, *Kritik* 275/71–2/137 and 'Zur Judenfrage' 356/155/222 respectively.
[231] See, for example, Hardimon, *Hegel's Social Philosophy*, pp. 119–22.

when (positively) they do feel estranged from that world. (The use of the label 'subjective' here is not intended to diminish the significance of the alienation thereby identified.[232]) Objective alienation, in contrast, can be discussed in terms which make no reference to the beliefs or feelings of individuals. For example, individuals are sometimes characterised as alienated when they are unable to develop and deploy their essential human capacities (whether or not they experience that lack of self-realisation as a loss). It will be apparent that, as described, these two forms of alienation (subjective and objective) can be exemplified separately or conjointly in the lives of particular individuals.

In characterising civil society as 'atomistic' and the political state as 'abstract', the young Marx can be seen as identifying two central areas of modern social life in which there is objective alienation. He holds that people cannot flourish – at least, not on an extensive scale – in a social world marked by these inappropriate separations between individuals (in civil society), and between individuals and the political community (in the modern state). It seems that Marx is mainly concerned with objective (rather than subjective) alienation. That preoccupation appears to be the result, not of any indifference towards individuals who experience their lives as lacking meaning or fulfilment, but rather of a conviction that such feelings exist – at least, exist on an extensive scale – only in societies scarred by objective alienation. In short, the young Marx seems to assume that widespread subjective alienation is unlikely in a social world which promotes rather than restricts the development and deployment of essential human capacities (that is, in a society which lacks objective alienation).

(It will be obvious that several issues have been glossed over or ignored in these determinedly introductory remarks about the concept of alienation. One of the most significant omissions concerns the criteria which would enable us to identify a particular separation as an 'inappropriate' one. I address that issue in Chapter 4.)

WHAT IS LIVING: HEGEL'S EMPIRICAL INSIGHT

Alongside this embryonic account of the modern social world, the *Kritik* also contains Marx's attempt to assess Hegel's empirical acumen by comparing the *Rechtsphilosophie* with that benchmark. The conclusion of that comparative exercise is an emphatically positive one. Marx maintains that all four of these central elements of modernity – the separation of civil

---

[232] See the helpful remarks in *ibid.* p. 122.

and political life, the antagonistic relation between these two spheres, the atomism of civil society, and the abstract nature of the state – are recognised in the *Rechtsphilosophie*. In short, Marx identifies a happy affinity between 'Hegel's theory and the realities of the modern world'.[233]

The first element in this happy affinity concerns the 'separation of real life from political life'.[234] Marx maintains, not only that the medieval identity of civil and political society had 'disappeared', but also, and to his credit, that 'Hegel presupposes its disappearance'.[235] Indeed, the historically unprecedented separation of civil and political spheres – a separation which 'really does exist' – is said to play a foundational role in Hegel's account of the rational state.[236] Marx describes Hegel as having 'based his argument on the assumption of the *separation* of civil society and the state (a modern phenomenon)'.[237]

This interpretative claim about the *Rechtsphilosophie* has much to recommend it. The separation of civil society and the state is certainly central to Hegel's account of the emergence of the modern social world. Hegel's use of the term 'civil society (*bürgerliche Gesellschaft*)' to refer to a distinct area of social life is increasingly recognised as embodying a significant conceptual innovation, a clear break with the dominant tradition in classical political thought.[238] That tradition, stretching from Aristotle to Kant – via Albertus Magnus, Aquinas, Melanchthon, Bodin, Hobbes, Spinoza, and Locke – had typically identified the state (*polis, civitas*) with civil society (*koinōnia politikē, societas civilis*). Hegel's distinction between civil society and the state not only constituted a conceptual innovation, but also was intended to mark a fundamental historical change – namely the emergence of a sphere of social life in which, for the first time, a distinctive kind of individualism is given 'the right to develop and express itself in all directions'.[239] That social sphere is civil society, and Hegel explicitly identifies its creation as belonging 'to the modern world'.[240] This distinctive individualism – which recognises individuals as both private persons and moral subjects – was unknown in the states of 'classical antiquity' where it 'had not yet been released and set at liberty'.[241] Indeed, on Hegel's account, the inability of the ancient world to cope with the nascent forms of modern individualism – apparent, for example, in Socrates' moral conscience (which broke with, and

[233] *Kritik* 321/115/185.   [234] *Ibid.*   [235] *Ibid.* 275/72/137.
[236] *Ibid.*   [237] *Ibid.* 276–7/73/138.
[238] The work of Riedel has been decisive here. See Manfred Riedel, *Studien zu Hegels Rechtsphilosophie* (Frankfurt am Main, 1969) chapter 6; and Manfred Riedel, 'Gesellschaft, bürgerliche', *Geschichtliche Grundbegriffe: Historisches Lexikon zur politisch-sozialen Sprache in Deutschland*, ed. Otto Brunner, Werner Conze, and Reinhart Koselleck, volume 2 (Stuttgart, 1975) pp. 719–800.
[239] *Philosophie des Rechts* §184.   [240] *Ibid.* §182Z.   [241] *Ibid.* §260Z.

thereby undermined, the unreflective identification with ethical norms that characterised ancient ethical culture) – constituted the central element in its downfall.[242] In contrast, Hegel claims that it is the institutionalised provision, primarily in civil society, of appropriate scope for this individualism to flourish that gives modern states their 'enormous strength and depth'.[243]

The second element in this happy affinity between Hegel's *Rechtsphilosophie* and the modern social world concerns the antagonistic relation between these newly separated spheres. The young Marx maintains that the characteristically modern conflict between civil and political life is recognised by Hegel throughout. That recognition is said to be implicit, for example, in the latter's description of the class distinctions of civil society as non-political. Such a description presupposes that civil and political life are governed by different principles, and is said to reflect Hegel's wider appreciation that 'civil and political life are heterogeneous and even *antithetical*'.[244] The same sensitivity to 'the conflict between the state and civil society' is perhaps more readily apparent in Hegel's frequent contrasting of 'the particular interests and needs of civil society' with 'the absolutely universal interest of the state'. In this way, Hegel is portrayed as drawing attention 'at every point' to 'the conflict between the state and civil society'.[245] Building on these claims, Marx makes a more general observation about Hegel's empirical acumen. The latter's 'profundity', he suggests, is especially evident in his sensitivity to the 'antagonistic character' of social relations.[246]

The young Marx appreciates that, on Hegel's account, what distinguishes civil society and the state is not an institutional separation. After all, in the *Philosophie des Rechts*, the 'external state' is portrayed as extending into civil society; the judicial and 'police' powers, for example, are included as part of '*bürgerliche Gesellschaft*'. (Note that under the category of 'police (*Polizei*)' Hegel includes a much wider range of activities than that word suggests to modern readers: activities including the provision of certain public utilities, the regulation of trade, and the administration of health.[247]) What really distinguishes these two spheres is their '*Bestimmungen*', their differing purposes or underlying rationales – what Marx calls their 'two opposed tempers'.[248] The vocation of civil society is to allow the distinctive individualism of modernity 'to develop and express itself in all directions'.[249]

[242] Hegel also identifies Christianity and Roman Law with this (nascent) modern individualism.
[243] *Philosophie des Rechts* §260.   [244] *Kritik* 280/73/142.   [245] *Ibid.* 277/73/138.
[246] *Ibid.* 257/54/116.   [247] This expansive use of *Polizei* reflects contemporary usage.
[248] *Kritik* 270/67/131. See also Hardimon, *Hegel's Social Philosophy*, pp. 205ff.
[249] *Philosophie des Rechts* §183.

In contrast, the vocation of the state is to promote the common good of the community as a whole, a good that Hegel thinks of as qualitatively distinct from the particular interests of its members (qualitatively distinct even from the particular interests that those individuals may have in common). Indeed, Hegel explicitly censures those writers who view the state as existing solely for 'the security and protection of property and personal freedom, *the interest of individuals (der Einzelnen) as such*'.[250] (In articulating this criticism, Hegel's target is the social-contract tradition, and perhaps especially Fichte's contribution to that tradition.) These writers make the serious mistake of having thereby confused the state with civil society. In this way, Marx concludes that Hegel fully appreciates that the relation between the state and civil society is an antagonistic one, a relation between 'two fixed antitheses, two really different spheres'.[251]

The third element in this happy affinity between Hegel's *Rechtsphilosophie* and the modern social world concerns the 'atomistic' character of civil society. Marx credits Hegel with an acknowledgement of the unrestrained individualism of modern civil society. For example, in his discussion of the role of the executive, Hegel explicitly defines civil society as a 'field of conflict (*Kampfplatz*) in which the interests of each individual comes up against that of everyone else'.[252] Marx describes this portrait of civil society as a '*bellum omnium contra omnes*' as a 'remarkable' one.[253] (Some modern Hegel scholars have followed Marx in seeing the language of the *Rechtsphilosophie*, at this point, as alluding to Hobbes's description of the state of nature in his *Leviathan*.[254])

This reading of Hegel's remarks, whilst it may not do justice to the full scope of his discussion of civil society, does have some textual foundation. For Hegel, the distinctive modern individualism which flourishes in civil society seems to have three main dimensions: modern individuals are aware of having particular interests (distinct from both the particular interests of others and the common good of the community);[255] they are also 'persons' who possess individual rights, not least to property;[256] and they are 'subjects', independent sources of moral evaluation who gain value and understanding from acting in ways which reflect their own private conscience, purposes, and reasoning.[257] The young Marx can be said to focus

---

[250] *Ibid.* §258A.   [251] *Kritik* 275/72/137.
[252] *Philosophie des Rechts* §§288–9.   [253] *Kritik* 243/41–2/101.
[254] See, for example, the editorial note to §289 in G. W. F. Hegel, *Elements of the Philosophy of Right*, ed. Allen W. Wood (Cambridge, 1991) p. 467.
[255] See *Philosophie des Rechts* §182Z.   [256] See *ibid.* §230.
[257] See, for example, *ibid.* §206, and the justification of trial by jury in *ibid.* §228A.

on the first of these threads (at the expense of the other two), and to assume that these particular interests are narrowly egoistic and motivationally dominant. This interpretation of Hegel may run the risk of one-sidedness, but there are undoubtedly passages in the *Philosophie des Rechts* which encourage such a reading. For example, at one point, Hegel describes civil society as a sphere in which 'each individual is his own end, and all else means nothing to him'.[258]

The fourth element in this happy affinity between Hegel's *Rechtsphilosophie* and the modern social world concerns the 'abstract' nature of the state. Hegel is said to have recognised, not only the separation of civil society and the state, but also the otherworldly and remote existence of the latter. At first glance, this seems an improbable claim. After all, Hegel not only insists that the modern social world forms an organic whole but also places a high value on citizenship. Nevertheless, Marx detects a significant parallel between Hegel's *Rechtsphilosophie* and the abstract modern state: namely that, in both cases, 'matters of universal concern' can be decided 'without having become the real concern of the people'.[259]

Marx is perhaps best seen as making two claims about the affinity between the Hegelian (or rational) state and its modern counterpart. In the first place, individuals in the Hegelian state – as opposed to the class of civil servants or the monarch – have only a limited role in determining political outcomes.[260] Indeed, this is one of the key features that are said to distinguish modern from ancient citizenship. 'In our modern states', Hegel insists, 'the citizens have only a limited share in the universal business of the state.'[261] Their political participation is restricted to paying taxes, involvement in public discussion, and (a limited form of) voting (whereby corporations send representatives to an estates-assembly which has only a circumscribed impact on legislation). The self-same suspicion of genuine self-government is, on Marx's account, apparent in the institutional arrangements of the modern state. (This claim about the modern state is discussed more fully in Chapter 3.) In short, both Hegelian and modern states share a lack of enthusiasm for popular participation in political life. In addition, in both Hegelian and modern states, ordinary subjects who have this limited political role live their day-to-day lives in civil society, that is, in a sphere of life dominated by an individualism which is antithetical to the concern for the common good. As a result, their (limited) political participation is likely to be marked by narrowly particularistic concerns.

---

[258] *Ibid.* §182Z.   [259] *Kritik* 265/62/125.   [260] *Ibid.* 321/115/185.
[261] *Philosophie des Rechts* §255Z.

When Marx claims that common affairs in both the Hegelian and modern states are determined 'without the interference of the people', he appears to have two distinct points in mind.[262] Not only do Hegelian and modern citizens have little opportunity to participate, but when they exercise that restricted opportunity they typically do so as individuals motivated by particular interests (and not as members of a community concerned for the common good). The echo of Rousseau here is a striking one. It might be said that, according to the young Marx, citizens of both the Hegelian and the modern state participate in political life as members of a 'multitude' (and not as part of 'the people').[263]

This account of the affinities that exist between Hegel's rational state and the modern social world is a far-ranging and controversial one. I limit myself to two observations.

First, Marx's account of Hegel's empirical acumen is a generous one. The *Rechtsphilosophie* is said to have correctly identified the separation of civil and political life, the antagonistic relation between these two spheres, the atomism of civil society, and the abstract nature of the state. As a result, the young Marx insists that Hegel should be credited with having understood both the basic structure of the modern social world and two central forms of alienation which disfigure it. In Marx's assessment, this empirical insight constitutes a substantial intellectual achievement.

In addition, Marx's account of Hegel's empirical acumen has some affinity with Hegel's own understanding of his project. Hegel maintains that there is a broad correspondence between the rational state outlined in the *Philosophie des Rechts* and what he calls 'the more advanced states of our times'.[264] The breadth of this correspondence is, no doubt, significant. There is certainly no evidence that Hegel saw the *Philosophie des Rechts* as a precise reflection of the social and political arrangements of any particular contemporary state. The young Marx can be said to endorse Hegel's view that German philosophy was 'its own time comprehended in thought'.[265]

THE FAILURE OF HEGELIAN MEDIATION

The young Marx credits Hegel with significant insight into both the basic structure of the modern social world and two central forms of alienation which disfigure it. I have described this as a verdict which is generous and which shares some affinity with Hegel's own understanding of his project

[262] *Kritik* 265/62/125.   [263] See Rousseau, *Contrat social* 380/154.
[264] *Philosophie des Rechts* §258A.   [265] *Ibid.* ¶13.

in the *Philosophie des Rechts*. Of these two claims, it is the latter which will perhaps appear the more improbable. In general, speculative idealism portrays itself as overcoming unnatural separations and antagonistic oppositions. Moreover, in this particular case, Hegel is usually thought to have intended his account of the rational or modern state as a solution to – and not merely a diagnosis of – the problem of alienation. Indeed, the Hegelian state might appear purpose-built to overcome the two dimensions of modern alienation that are identified by Marx: the corporations, for example, mitigating the atomism of civil society, and the estates-assembly bridging the divide between civil and political society. In short, the suggested affinity here – between Marx's assessment of Hegel's empirical acumen and Hegel's own understanding of his project – might be thought to underestimate the extent to which the *Rechtsphilosophie* is offered as a *defence* of the social and political institutions of modernity.

In responding to this concern, there is little reason to challenge this broad account of Hegel's ambition. It is both accurate and helpful to understand Hegel's project as aiming to defend rather than criticise the modern social world. The issue here is whether, and to what extent, the young Marx fails to appreciate that ambition.

In seeking to understand the precise character of Hegel's defence of the modern social world, the distinction between objective and subjective alienation is of some assistance.[266] Hegel maintains that there are both objective and subjective conditions for the overcoming of alienation. That is, alienation will no longer exist when the social world (objectively) facilitates the self-realisation of individuals, and individuals (subjectively) understand that this is the case. Unhappily, this is not quite the situation in which the contemporary audience of the *Philosophie des Rechts* is said to find itself. Adopting the terminology suggested by one modern scholar, the circumstances in which Hegel and his contemporaries find themselves is one of 'pure subjective alienation'.[267] A situation of pure subjective alienation combines the absence of objective alienation with the presence of subjective alienation. Objective alienation is absent because the central institutions of the rational or modern state – the family, civil society, and the political state – are judged to facilitate the actualisation of individuals both as individuals and as members of the community. Subjective alienation is present because individuals either do not feel at home in the modern social world (even though that world does facilitate their self-actualisation) or do feel

---

[266] This account of Hegel's project is indebted to Hardimon, *Hegel's Social Philosophy*.
[267] *Ibid.*, p. 121.

estranged from that world (even though they are not objectively estranged
from it). As a result, Hegel's critical efforts are focused, not on any attempt
to reform the central institutions of the modern social world, but rather
on changing the way in which the latter are understood by members of
that society (or, at least, the way in which they are understood by some
philosophically reflective section of that population).[268]

This account of Hegel's ambition – whereby the *Rechtsphilosophie* is
offered as a defence of the modern social world – is compatible with Marx's
assessment in the *Kritik*. Marx does not question Hegel's insistence that
overcoming objective alienation requires certain social conditions, namely
social conditions which make it possible for people to actualise themselves
as both individuals and as members of the community. (It seems likely, of
course, that Marx's elaboration of those conditions and that actualisation
would differ from Hegel's.) What Marx is concerned to reject is Hegel's
claim that the modern social world embodies those conditions, and thereby
makes it possible for people to actualise themselves as both individuals and
members of the community. The young Marx does not challenge this
account of Hegel's ambition, but protests only against confusing ambition
with achievement.

One element in this denial that objective alienation is overcome in the
modern social world is of particular interest here. Hegel maintains that, in
order to make it possible for individuals to actualise themselves as members
of the community, the rational or modern state must embody a concern with
the common good, and facilitate the life of the *citoyen*. The young Marx –
as I have shown above – denies that the rational or modern state enables
individuals to realise themselves in that regard. Indeed, Marx suggests that
the limited forms of political participation, together with the individualism of civil society, make the actualisation of individuals as members of the
community impossible (or possible only in a weak and inadequate form).
As a result, Marx rejects the claim that the situation faced by Hegel's contemporaries is one of 'pure subjective alienation'. The young Marx is guilty,
in other words, not of failing to understand Hegel's views, but of failing to
share them.

It seems probable that there is a further disagreement here. Marx not only
denies that objective alienation is overcome in the modern social world,
but also appears suspicious of the category of pure subjective alienation. I
suggested above that the young Marx's preoccupation with objective alienation was not the product of a lack of sympathy towards individuals who

[268] For the parenthesised proviso, see *ibid.*, pp. 129ff.

experience subjective alienation, but rather that it reflected his conviction that widespread subjective alienation was likely only in societies which are also scarred by objective alienation. Whilst not denying the very possibility of 'pure subjective alienation', Marx is perhaps sceptical about its being found on any scale. That conviction may colour his response to Hegel's diagnosis of the contemporary situation. For Hegel, the modern social world is characterised by the existence of widespread subjective alienation alongside the absence of objective alienation. Marx is rather less sanguine. He appears to view the widespread existence of subjective alienation in the modern social world as a likely indicator that objective alienation has not yet been vanquished.

In the *Kritik*, Marx does not attempt to provide an overall summary of Hegel's views, but seeks rather to isolate those threads which demonstrate the latter's empirical acumen. In Marx's account of the ways in which the rational state strives to overcome objective alienation, Hegel is judged to demonstrate a keen insight into the improper separations of modernity. It is in these initial diagnoses, rather than in his subsequent solutions, that Hegel's real insight is to be found. For example, Marx acknowledges that Hegel 'hopes to heal the split between "civil and political life"', but it is the implicit recognition of this antagonistic relation (the characteristic modern 'split (*Trennung*)' between civil and political life), and not his subsequent attempt to cure it, that constitutes the latter's real intellectual achievement.[269]

Marx's discussion of the role of the estates-assembly in the *Philosophie des Rechts* can illustrate this assessment. He shows little serious interest in the institutional detail of Hegel's account of the estates-assembly, for example in its bicameral structure or its adoption of corporate representation. What interests Marx is rather Hegel's characterisation of its 'vocation (*Bestimmung*)' as 'a mediating organ'.[270] This concept of 'mediation (*Vermittlung*)' is an important one in Hegel's thought, used in a variety of contexts to suggest the achievement of union between divergent entities. In this case, the divide to be overcome is the separation between civil and political society, between individuals and the common good.

In order to bridge this divide between civil and political life, Hegel claims that the estates-assembly 'should embody in equal measure both the sense and disposition of the state and government and the interests of particular circles and individuals (*Einzelnen*)'.[271] Marx seizes on this description

[269] *Kritik* 275/71–2/137. See also *ibid.* 277/74/139.
[270] *Philosophie des Rechts* §302.   [271] *Ibid.*

as an indication of the inadequacy of Hegel's attempt at mediation. It is one thing, he maintains, to assert that the temper of two different spheres comes together in a single institution, but quite another to show how this achieves their reconciliation. Hegel has provided us with no reason to think that the estates-assembly does anything other than reproduce internally the wider contradiction between civil and political life. 'Far from accomplishing a mediation', Marx observes, the estates-assembly 'is the embodiment of contradiction (*Widerspruch*).'[272] We are therefore left with the same 'unresolved antinomy (*ungelöste Antinomie*)' with which we started.[273] The estates-assembly in its role as mediating institution is simply 'the wooden sword (*das hölzerne Eisen*), the concealed antithesis (*der vertuschte Gegensatz*) between the particular and the universal'.[274]

Marx insists that the difficulty here is no contingent slip, but rather stems from 'within Hegel's own analysis'.[275] Having correctly identified civil and political society as 'real extremes' Hegel cannot easily reconcile their opposed tempers.[276] This concept of a 'real extreme' is an important one. Unlike a single essence in 'a state of differentiation', whose extremes need and complement each other (for example, the north and south poles, or the male and female of the species), 'real extremes' are said to form genuine contraries with 'wholly opposed' natures (for example, pole and non-pole, or human and non-human). Real extremes, Marx claims 'have nothing in common with one another, they have no need for one another, they do not complement one another. The one does not bear within its womb a longing, a need, an anticipation of the other.'[277] As a result, their antipathy, where such obtains, is not easily overcome. (There are echoes here of Friedrich Trendelenburg's attack on Hegel's 'dialectical logic' in *Logische Untersuchungen*, published in 1840. It is not clear whether Marx had read this work, although he was familiar with the Trendelenburg's Aristotle commentaries.[278])

Hegel initially characterises the estates as 'non-political', as unconcerned with the common good. However, if it is to play a mediating role, the estates-assembly needs also to be political, to embody such concerns.[279] As Marx remarks, it is always possible to 'link' the most heterogeneous objects,

---

[272] *Kritik* 290/86/152.   [273] *Ibid.* 204/6/60.   [274] *Ibid.* 288/84/151.
[275] *Ibid.* 300/95/163.   [276] *Ibid.* 293/88/155.
[277] *Ibid.* For an alternative reading, see Laurence Wilde, *Marx and Contradiction* (Aldershot, 1993) pp. 20ff.
[278] See *MEGA②* I, I, p. 25. For a brief account of Trendelenburg, see Klaus Christian Köhnke, *The Rise of Neo-Kantianism: German Academic Philosophy Between Idealism and Positivism* (Cambridge, 1991) chapter I.
[279] *Kritik* 280/76/142.

but what we have here is not a gradual transition but 'a thoroughgoing transubstantiation' of civil into political society, and of the bourgeois into the citizen, which is never satisfactorily explained.[280] He suggests that Hegel's attempt to pretend that the gulf between civil and political life, between bourgeois and citizen, does not exist is confounded 'by the very act of leaping over it'.[281] Hegel's account of the estates appears ambiguously situated between two equally unconvincing alternatives: either the estates of civil society are political (in which case there would be no need for mediation because civil and political life would be governed by shared principles), or the estates of civil society are not political (in which case, although there is now a need for mediation, those estates are ill-suited to play that mediating role, since – on Hegel's own account – satisfying that role requires that they embody common as well as particular concerns).[282]

In short, Marx appreciates that Hegel's treatment of the estates-assembly embodies a concern to bridge the modern divide between civil and political society but he judges that attempt a failure. In an important passage in the *Philosophie des Rechts*, Hegel had conceded that, without the mediating role of the estates-assembly, the separation of state and civil society would remain in place, with political life left 'hanging, so to speak, in the air'.[283] Marx's considered judgement is that this is precisely the result – in both Hegel's work and the modern world – of the failure to overcome the antithesis between these divergent entities.

For Marx, Hegel's treatment of the estates-assembly exemplifies a wider pattern. Hegel's profundity is reflected in his initially experiencing 'the separation of the state from civil society as a *contradiction*'; his subsequent mistake is to confuse 'the semblance of a resolution' with 'the real thing'.[284] More generally, Hegel is judged to be better at drawing attention to 'the *strangeness* (*Befremdliche*)' of situations, than at eliminating 'the *estrangement* (*Entfremdung*)' they contain.[285] In short, Hegel's achievement is to have identified, and not to have overcome, the atomism and abstraction of modern social life.

On this account, there seems little reason to accept the suggestion that Marx misunderstands the nature of Hegel's project. Marx's commentary on the *Rechtsphilosophie* reveals not a misinterpretation of Hegel's ambitions but a critical assessment of his success in fulfilling them. Marx acknowledges that Hegel sets out to overcome the modern separation between individuals, and between individuals and the state; however, he judges

---

[280] *Ibid.* 280/77/143.   [281] *Ibid.* 282/78/145.   [282] *Ibid.* 300/95/163.
[283] *Philosophie des Rechts* §303A.   [284] *Kritik* 279/75/141.   [285] *Ibid.* 283/79/145.

Hegel's attempt to bridge these separations as ultimately a failure. As a result, Hegel's achievement is limited to his having diagnosed, not cured, the main forms of alienation that disfigure the modern social world.

Thus far, I have been tracing the parallel between Marx's account of Hegel's empirical acumen and Hegel's own understanding of his project – in particular, emphasising the broad correspondence, identified by both Marx and Hegel, between the rational state outlined in the *Philosophie des Rechts* and 'the more advanced states of our times'.[286] This can initially seem a surprising claim, but I have tried to show that it can be clarified and made plausible. I end this section with another (initially surprising) parallel which may illuminate Marx's interpretation of Hegel's project.

In the 'Preface' to the *Philosophie des Rechts*, Hegel famously insists that philosophy is always 'its own time comprehended in thought'.[287] In elucidating this remark, he maintains that the proper role of philosophy is a descriptive and not a prescriptive one; that the role of philosophy is not to instruct the world how the state 'ought to be', but rather to 'comprehend what is'.[288] The young Marx can be seen as taking this suggestion seriously, not, I hasten to add, as a recommendation about the proper role of philosophy as such – as Hegel, of course, intended – but rather as an illuminating characterisation of Hegel's own approach.

Hegel illustrates his general dictum about philosophy and the world with a brief discussion of Plato's *Republic*. The example appears an unlikely one. After all, there is something of a scholarly consensus to the effect that Plato is the paradigmatic example of a 'utopian' theoriser, an author whose works show little interest in historical reality.[289] Nor is that consensus of recent origin. Hegel notes that Plato's own contemporaries treated the *Republic* as a 'proverbial example of an empty ideal', a philosophical construction of a 'world beyond' which is unrelated to actuality.[290] Indeed, Hegel is perhaps attracted to this particular example precisely because it seems such a hard case for his general dictum to account for.

Hegel rejects this familiar picture of Plato as engaging in utopian speculation. He suggests that the *Republic* is better understood as a descriptive (not a prescriptive) exercise, which successfully captures the essential values and institutions of Greek society. What initially looks like an empty ideal is, on closer examination, 'the embodiment of nothing other than the nature of Greek ethical life (*Sittlichkeit*)'.[291] ('*Sittlichkeit*' is an important concept

[286] *Philosophie des Rechts* §258A.   [287] *Ibid.* ¶13.   [288] *Ibid.*
[289] See G. E. M. de Ste Croix, *The Class Struggle in the Ancient Greek World* (London, 1981) p. 70.
[290] *Philosophie des Rechts* ¶12.   [291] *Ibid.*

in Hegel's political philosophy. Broadly speaking, it can be thought of as the ethical norms which are embodied in the basic structure and customs of a society.) The claim is a surprising one. It is not easy to swallow the implication that the many and obvious disparities between the ancient Greek city-state and the kind of polity described in the *Republic* concern only inessentials. That said, Hegel's reasoning deserves further scrutiny.

According to Hegel, Greek ethical life is characterised by the existence of an immediate, unreflective, harmony between individuals and society. That harmony was threatened by the nascent forms of subjective freedom – exemplified by Socrates' moral conscience – which were already beginning to emerge in the ancient world. Because ancient *Sittlichkeit* excluded subjective freedom, the latter inevitably manifested itself as 'a hostile element, as a corruption of the social order'.[292] Hegel suggests that Plato's political innovations in the *Republic* were designed to banish subjective freedom; at least, Hegel identifies this as the rationale behind the various Platonic prohibitions on property ownership, family membership, and occupational choice.[293]

Many of Hegel's remarks about the *Republic* seem oddly misdirected. For example, he implies that all members of the polity recommended by Plato are denied private property, family membership, and choice of occupation (whereas these prohibitions, of course, apply only to the rulers).[294] However, it is Hegel's broad assessment of Plato's achievement which is of interest here. Hegel's central claim is that Plato grasps the essential characteristics of both the ancient Greek world and the corrosive force (subjective freedom) that would destroy it. Plato's institutional recommendations in the *Republic* are designed precisely to resist the latter. Of course, there is no question of those recommendations accomplishing that goal. Hegel insists that subjective freedom was 'a deeper principle' which could be neither vanquished from, nor contained by, the ancient world.[295] However, despite the futility of his curative proposals, Plato can nonetheless be credited with considerable insight into both the ancient social world and the forces that would eventually undermine it.

It is perhaps illuminating to read Marx's comments on Hegel's *Philosophie des Rechts* as broadly paralleling Hegel's assessment of Plato's *Republic*. Marx does not mean to suggest that every particular detail of the rational

[292] *Ibid.* §206A.   [293] See *ibid.* §§46A, 185A, 206A, 262Z.
[294] See M. B. Foster, *The Political Philosophies of Plato and Hegel* (Oxford, 1935) chapter 3; M. J. Inwood, 'Hegel, Plato and Greek "Sittlichkeit"', Z. A. Pelczynski (ed.), *The State and Civil Society: Studies in Hegel's Political Philosophy* (Cambridge, 1984) pp. 40–54.
[295] *Philosophie des Rechts* ¶12.

state (corporate representation, for example) can be found in America or France (any more than Hegel meant to claim that ancient Athenian rulers followed Plato's stringent educational regime). Marx's claim is rather that Hegel's institutional proposals reveal a sound understanding of both the essential structure of the modern social world and the forces that threaten it. As a result, the *Rechtsphilosophie*, like the *Republic*, might be said to embody Hegel's dictum that philosophy is 'its own time comprehended in thought'.[296] Marx does not, of course, imagine that Hegel's institutional proposals will succeed in vanquishing, or even containing, the destructive forces – including the unrestricted individualism of civil society – which modernity has unleashed. Yet those proposals confirm Hegel's achievement in having diagnosed, albeit not in having cured, the main forms of alienation that disfigure the modern social world. In this way, whilst accepting that the *Philosophie des Rechts* was intended as a defence of the modern social world, the young Marx might be said to locate Hegel's true legacy as belonging to the critics of that world.

THE CONTINUING RELEVANCE OF THE *KRITIK*

Since its discovery and publication by David Ryazanov, the *Kritik* has received a mixed critical reception.[297] Several scholars have followed Ryazanov's lead in recognising it as an important and interesting text which illuminates both the young Marx's political thought and his relation to Hegel.[298] (It will be apparent that I share this broad judgement of the *Kritik*, and have sought to lend support to it here.) Yet this positive assessment remains something of a minority view. Many well-known accounts of Marx's early writings neglect or even ignore the *Kritik*. It has been dismissed, for example, as of 'limited doctrinal importance' and 'of interest only for Marx's biography and the history of Hegelianism'.[299] This critical resistance strikes me as noteworthy. After all, whatever one's considered assessment of its merits, the *Kritik* remains the young Marx's most sustained engagement with the author who is almost universally acclaimed as his predominant intellectual influence. In these circumstances, the origins and character of this critical resistance may merit further investigation.

[296] *Ibid.* ¶13.
[297] The notebook containing the *Kritik* was unearthed in the Berlin archives of the Sozialdemokratische Partei Deutschlands in 1922, and published in *MEGA*① in 1927. It is now held in the Internationaal Instituut voor Sociale Geschedenis in Amsterdam.
[298] Including, not least, Galvano della Volpe and Lucio Colletti.
[299] Eric Weil, *Hegel et l'état* (Paris, 1950) p. 113.

One feature of this critical resistance to the *Kritik* stands out. A number of what might be called Hegelian enthusiasts for the young Marx appear peculiarly impervious to the charms of this particular text. The origins of that resistance are not easily identified. However, one distinguished such critic dismisses the *Kritik* as a 'partial' analysis which was subsequently made 'superfluous' by the positive appraisal of Hegel in the *Manuskripte*.[300] These two suggestions – namely, that the *Kritik* is in some way limited, and that it was made redundant by the acclamation of Hegel in the *Manuskripte* – have been repeated and developed by other commentators. Thus, the author of a study of the 'extraordinary complexity' of Marx's relationship to Hegel maintains that the *Kritik* is limited because it is 'Feuerbachian through and through', and it is redundant because – following his temporary infatuation with Feuerbach (which encouraged Marx to 'depart' from Hegel) – there is a 'return to Hegel' in the *Manuskripte*.[301] In this latter text, it would seem, we discover not only the authentic birthplace of Marxism, but also a radical reappraisal of Hegel's merits.[302]

I have several doubts about this account. These Hegelian enthusiasts for the young Marx offer a storyline which is both familiar and attractive – in which a tawdry suitor (Feuerbach) disrupts but does not derail the path of true love (between Marx and Hegel) – but whose detail is not entirely convincing. Three elements in this questionable romance require further comment: the characterisation of the *Kritik* as a 'Feuerbachian' text, the wholly negative assessment of Feuerbach's influence, and the theoretical gulf that is posited between the *Kritik* and other writings of the young Marx (especially the *Manuskripte*).

The characterisation of the *Kritik* as a 'Feuerbachian' text (the first element in this account) is presumably intended to indicate and underline the predominant influence on its contents. I have some reservations about the accuracy and utility of that characterisation, but the doubts that I raise here concern only the manner in which this characterisation is usually defended. The justification for using this label ('Feuerbachian') typically proceeds in two stages: first, the argument of the *Kritik* is reduced to the so-called 'transformative criticism' (whereby Hegel is accused of reversing the correct relation of subject and predicate); and second, that notion of 'transformative

[300] See István Mészáros, *Marx's Theory of Alienation* (London, 1970) pp. 18–19.
[301] See Arthur, *Dialectics of Labour*, pp. 109–10, 126. See also C. J. Arthur, 'Editor's Introduction', Karl Marx and Friedrich Engels, *The German Ideology*, ed. C. J. Arthur (London, 1970) p. 4.
[302] See also Georg Lukács, 'Zur philosophischen Entwicklung des jungen Marx', *Deutsche Zeitschrift für Philosophie*, volume 2 (1954) pp. 288–343, and Herbert Marcuse, 'Neue Quellen zur Grundlegung des historischen Materialismus', *Die Gesellschaft*, volume 2 (1932) pp. 136–7.

criticism' is identified wholly with Feuerbach.[303] Both of these steps are open to criticism. It is clear that Marx's characterisation and criticism of Hegel's idealism incorporate the notion of 'transformative criticism'; that is, it echoes Feuerbach's insistence that speculation (like Christianity) had reversed the correct relation of subject and predicate. However, it is far from obvious that this thread in Marx's account exhausts the content of the *Kritik*. As I have sought to demonstrate above, the *Kritik* contains a number of additional and independent elements. These include not only further criticisms of Hegel's metaphysical vision (such as Marx's complaint about its acosmic cast), but also an account of Hegel's empirical acumen and of some limitations of his political philosophy. It is neither helpful nor accurate to subsume all of these additional threads under the notion of 'transformative criticism'. The second of these interpretative moves – that is, the portrayal of transformative criticism as synonymous with Feuerbach – can also be challenged. This identification (of transformative criticism with Feuerbach) might be thought to obscure the extensive philosophical history that is attached to this particular critical motif (namely the reversal of the correct relation of subject and predicate).[304] The work of the Italian scholar Galvano della Volpe is of relevance here. Della Volpe has represented the young Marx's 'methodological' critique of speculative inversion as rehearsing a series of philosophical arguments which were developed by a variety of previous thinkers. He has identified pertinent affinities with Aristotle's critique of Plato's diairesis, with Galileo's criticisms of the scholastics (especially his responses to Christoph Scheiner and the interlocutor known as 'Simplicio'), and with Kant's (incomplete) criticisms of Leibniz.[305] Della Volpe's work was concerned only with issues of intellectual affinity, and not with the possibility of intellectual influence. However, it is certain that Marx was aware of at least some of this adumbratory literature. For example, a familiarity with Aristotle's criticisms of Plato's metaphysics is apparent in the preliminary studies that Marx undertook when working towards his doctoral dissertation (which examined the differences between the Democritean and Epicurean philosophies of nature).[306]

The negative assessment of Feuerbach's influence (the second element in the account of these Hegelian enthusiasts for the young Marx) is also

[303] See Arthur, *Dialectics of Labour*, p. 110. See also David McLellan, *Marx Before Marxism* (London, 1970) pp. 108–9; and Shlomo Avineri, 'The Hegelian Origins of Marx's Political Thought', Shlomo Avineri (ed.), *Marx's Socialism* (New York, 1973) p. 3.
[304] For Feuerbach's 'reformatory critique', see 'Vorläufige Thesen' 244/157.
[305] See Galvano della Volpe, *Logic as a Positive Science* (London, 1980).
[306] See, for example, *Hefte zur epikureischen, stoischen und skeptischen Philosophie* 87/439ff.

worthy of comment. The adjective 'Feuerbachian' seems to function in this literature, not only in a descriptive manner to indicate intellectual influence, but also as a critical term designating intellectual weakness. The *Kritik* is deemed limited *because* it is 'Feuerbachian'. As before, my remarks will focus less on the claim itself – here that Feuerbach's influence on Marx is regrettable – than on the manner in which it is typically defended. It can easily appear as if the malign character of Feuerbach's influence is simply to be assumed without further argument. (In general, Feuerbach's philosophical stock is not currently high; amongst these Hegelian enthusiasts for the young Marx, it is at rock bottom.) Where there is a clear line of reasoning in support of this claim, it usually appeals to the fact that Marx subsequently criticised Feuerbach's writings.[307] (Towards the end of 1845 – provoked by Max Stirner's anti-Feuerbachian polemic in *Der Einzige und sein Eigentum* – Marx re-examined his own view of Feuerbach's work.) However, no shadow is cast over the intellectual standing of the *Kritik* by the mere existence of these later criticisms of the author who, for the sake of argument, we can allow to have constituted an important influence on that earlier text. Before Feuerbach's influence could be judged malign, one would need to establish both the soundness of those subsequent objections to Feuerbach's work and their precise relevance to the *Kritik*. It might be that a plausible case could be assembled in support of the claim that, whilst the *Kritik* was influenced by Feuerbach's negative critique of speculative philosophy, Marx's later complaints focused largely on (elements of) Feuerbach's positive project, the so-called 'new philosophy' of 'sensationalism'. On this account, even if Marx's later criticisms of Feuerbach were sound (again, something that would need to be established), they would cast no significant doubt on the main elements of the *Kritik*. (A more detailed discussion of both Feuerbach's work and Marx's relation to it appears in Chapter 4.)

The theoretical gulf that is posited between the *Kritik* and other early writings (the third element in the account of these Hegelian enthusiasts for the young Marx) is also open to question. The crucial suggestion here is that the 'Feuerbachian' account of Hegel contained in the *Kritik* is made redundant by subsequent developments in Marx's early writings, in particular by the alleged 'return' to Hegel (and concomitant 'departure' from Feuerbach) embodied in the *Manuskripte*. The remainder of the present section will examine that suggestion.

There is, of course, an apparent irony in Hegelian enthusiasts for the *Manuskripte* lambasting the *Kritik* for being written under the influence

---

[307] See, for example, Mészáros, *Marx's Theory of Alienation*, pp. 235ff.

of an infatuation with Feuerbach. After all, the transformative critique attributed to Feuerbach – the claim that speculation (like Christianity) had reversed the correct relation of subject and predicate – appears clearly and repeatedly in the *Manuskripte*.[308] Moreover, the *Manuskripte* overflow with fulsome praise for Feuerbach, an author who is not even mentioned in the *Kritik*. It is in the *Manuskripte* – and not the *Kritik* – that Marx commends Feuerbach, not only for the 'magnitude of his achievement', but also for 'the quiet simplicity' with which he presents his analysis to the world.[309] Marx justifies this recommendation that Feuerbach be hailed as the 'true conqueror of the Hegelian philosophy' on the grounds that his most recent writings had 'destroyed the foundations of the old dialectic'.[310]

Of course, authors can be mistaken about the character of their own work. Marx might simply have failed to notice that in the very text in which he (explicitly) praised Feuerbach for having overthrown Hegel, he had himself (implicitly) returned to the standpoint of this ostensibly vanquished author (and thereby departed from that of Hegel's ostensibly victorious challenger). What matters here is the textual evidence, and, in particular, whether in his subsequent writings (and especially the *Manuskripte*) the young Marx broke with the critical account of Hegel's views that was outlined in the *Kritik*.

This issue is addressed in two stages here. First, I consider whether the central criticisms of Hegel's metaphysics found in the *Kritik* are echoed and endorsed elsewhere in the early writings. I will assume that the continued appearance of those criticisms constitutes *prima facie* evidence that the young Marx did not abandon his earlier account of Hegel.[311] Second, I consider whether the young Marx's subsequent remarks about Hegel contain any additional account of his achievement; more precisely, whether they contain any additional account of Hegel's achievement which is incompatible with the analysis provided in the *Kritik*. I will assume that the continued absence of any such account casts doubt on the alleged redundancy of the latter text.

Apart from the *Kritik*, the only writings of the young Marx which contain significant discussions of Hegel and of speculative idealism are the *Manuskripte* and *Die heilige Familie*. Both of these texts contain clear echoes and endorsements of the account propounded in the *Kritik*.

---

[308] See, for example, *Manuskripte* 575/334/387.   [309] *Ibid.* 569/328/381.   [310] *Ibid.*
[311] In the 'Postface' (1873) to the second edition of *Kapital*, Marx refers to having criticised the 'mystificatory side of the Hegelian dialectic' in his earlier writings, without seeking to distance himself from those criticisms. *Kapital* 27/19.

In the *Manuskripte*, Marx offers a 'few remarks' concerning the character of the 'Hegelian dialectic'.[312] The description that follows is rather abbreviated, but clearly recalls the two stages of speculative construction familiar from the *Kritik*.[313] The stages that Marx had previously characterised as involving the 'transformation of the empirical into the speculative and the speculative into the empirical', are described in the *Manuskripte* as involving 'the philosophical dissolution and restoration of the empirical world'.[314] The first of these two stages – which concerns the origin of the Hegelian categories – is said to demonstrate Hegel's 'uncritical idealism'. The second of these stages – which concerns the actualisation of those categories in the natural and social world – is said to demonstrate Hegel's 'uncritical empiricism'.[315]

The *Manuskripte* also contain clear evidence of all five of the criticisms of Hegel's metaphysics that were identified in the *Kritik*. Marx's first complaint was that Hegel had failed to understand that his own categories were not *a priori*, but were instead derived from empirical experience. The same objection is advanced in the *Manuskripte*, where Marx describes the categories which the speculative idealist 'thought to create from nothing' (from pure conceptual activity) as 'nothing else but *abstractions* from *characteristics of nature*'.[316] Marx's second complaint in the *Kritik* was that Hegel's philosophy embodied an uncritical attitude to the finite world. That charge of 'uncritical empiricism' is also repeated in the *Manuskripte*, not least in a discussion of the speculative transition from logic to nature (a transition 'which has caused the Hegelians such terrible headaches').[317] Having initially created the absolute by abstracting from the natural world, that absolute can subsequently do no better than to 'let *nature*, which it concealed within itself... *issue freely from itself*'.[318] Once again, Marx bemoans the fact that the empirical world is treated by speculative philosophy as a result of, rather than as a starting point for, critical activity. The third and fourth of Marx's complaints from the *Kritik* are also alluded to in the *Manuskripte*. The comment that the Hegelian categories are 'indifferent to all content' can be read as suggesting that the relation between the

[312] *Manuskripte* 568/326/379.
[313] Given the content of these remarks – as well as their brevity and opacity – it is surprising to find commentators claiming that the *Manuskripte* contain 'a criticism of Hegel which is more profound and more systematic than anything which Marx had yet written', and that Marx's position in relation to Hegel is 'spelled out more explicitly and systematically [in the *Manuskripte*] than elsewhere in his early (and later) writings'. John Maguire, *Marx's Paris Writings* (Dublin, 1972) p. 9; and Richard Schacht, *Hegel and After* (Pittsburgh, 1975) p. 97, respectively.
[314] *Kritik* 241/39/98 and *Manuskripte* 573/332/385.   [315] *Manuskripte* 573/332/385.
[316] *Ibid.* 587/345/399.   [317] *Ibid.* 586/344/397.   [318] *Ibid.*

concept and its realisation in particular empirical phenomena is not a necessary one.[319] And Marx's remark that the Hegelian categories are 'forms of
abstraction which fit every content' might be seen to imply that Hegel has
failed to capture the differentiae of particular finite entities.[320] Marx's fifth
complaint in the *Kritik* – that Hegel, despite himself, ends up endorsing an
acosmic account of the identity of God and the world – is also echoed in the
Manuskripte. Hegel is judged to have turned the finite world into a product
of consciousness, and Marx insists that such an entity can never be 'a *real*
thing'; the best it can manage is what he calls 'thingness (*Dingheit*)', the
appearance of objectivity.[321] Whereas real objective entities are '*external*' to,
and independent of, consciousness, the Hegelian finite is 'a mere creature,
a *postulate* of self-consciousness'.[322] As a result, the Hegelian finite, for all
its appearance of objectivity, is not an 'independent, real being' at all.[323]

    Die heilige Familie also contains a sustained, albeit indirect, discussion
of speculative method. (Since *Die heilige Familie* was written by Engels
and Marx, the present discussion might be thought to raise some thorny
problems of attribution. However, in the first edition of the book, the
author of each section was clearly identified. This division of labour – in
which, to his evident embarrassment, Engels wrote 'barely one-and-a-half'
of the twenty-two printer's sheets – is confirmed both by textual evidence
and by their surviving correspondence.[324] In the present chapter, I refer
only to those parts of the book written by Marx. Note that I do not adopt
this strategy in order to lend support to any of the standard claims about
possible differences between these two authors, but rather in order to avoid
having to address that important and complex issue here.)

    The discussion of speculative method occurs in the course of a remorse-
less attack on Szeliga's review of *Les mystères de Paris* – Eugène Sue's hugely
popular (and highly moralistic) novel of Parisian underworld life. In this
context, Marx addresses the contribution made by Hegel's epigones to the
development of the speculative method. He suggests that Szeliga provides a
peculiarly informative *reductio ad absurdum* of Hegelian metaphysics, since
the pupil had managed to reproduce all of the problems contained in the
work of his master, without either the grasp of 'real content' or the 'masterly
sophistry' that are also found in the latter.[325]

    Once again, Marx rehearses the two-stage characterisation of absolute
idealism familiar from the *Kritik*. However, as befits the changed context –
his remarks appear as part of a critical examination of the journalistic efforts

[319] *Ibid.* 585/343/397.   [320] *Ibid.* 583/343/397.   [321] *Ibid.* 577/335/389.   [322] *Ibid.*
[323] *Ibid.*   [324] Engels to Marx, c. 20 January 1845, *MEW* 27, p. 16; *MECW* 38, p. 18.
[325] *Die heilige Familie* 63/61.

of one of Hegel's less distinguished disciples – this version of 'the secret of speculative construction' proceeds largely by parody.[326] Marx announces that the first step in speculative construction (the stage of 'uncritical idealism') is to imagine that an abstract idea – in this case, he suggests the 'Fruit' (an abstract idea derived from real particular apples, pears, and so on) – is 'an entity existing outside me'.[327] However, and here the second step in speculative construction (the stage of 'uncritical empiricism') unfolds, reason then has to relinquish its abstraction, to 'find its way back' from 'the Fruit' to the empirical diversity of 'ordinary real fruits'.[328] 'The Fruit', we are accordingly informed, is 'a living, self-differentiating, moving essence', whose differentiated unity is developed in, and realised by, particular earthly fruits.[329] The process by which the 'incarnation' of 'the Fruit' takes place is portrayed, not as the activity of the speculative philosopher, but as the '*self-activity*' of the absolute subject ('the Fruit').[330] Particular apples, pears, and almonds are unveiled as 'crystallisations' (*sic*) of '"*the* Fruit" itself'.[331] Echoing his earlier remarks in the *Kritik*, Marx observes that, no matter how great our familiarity with matters fructiparous, this portrayal of 'natural objects' as the 'unreal *creation*' of the absolute gives the impression of 'something *extraordinary*', an 'act of creation', a 'miracle'.[332] Indeed, Hegelian theodicy is said to put its Christian counterpart to shame. Whereas the latter knows only one earthly incarnation of the divine, 'speculative philosophy has as many incarnations as there are things'.[333]

The five complaints found in the *Kritik* are also rehearsed in *Die heilige Familie*. First, the absolute ('the Fruit'), which pretends to be an *a priori* construction, is simply an abstraction derived from the empirical world (of apples, pears, and so on). In short, the 'metaphysical categories' of the Hegelians are judged to be 'abstractions extracted out of *reality*'.[334] Second, the object in which the self-activity of the absolute (the Fruit) is realised turns out to be nothing other than the familiar empirical world (those same apples, pears, and so on), albeit imaginatively redescribed. In this way, despite having initially denied the empirical world, speculative philosophy ends up in the 'most irrational and unnatural bondage' to the 'most accidental and most individual attributes' of the finite.[335] Nor are the

---

[326] For a suggestive discussion of the function of parody in the early writings, see Margaret Rose, *Reading the Young Marx and Engels: Poetry, Parody and the Censor* (London, 1978) part 2.

[327] *Die heilige Familie* 60/57. This analogy may have been suggested by *Enzyklopädie* §13A.

[328] *Die heilige Familie* 60/58.   [329] *Ibid.* 61/58–9.

[330] *Ibid.* 61/59–60.   [331] *Ibid.* 61/59.   [332] *Ibid.* 62/60.

[333] *Ibid.* 61/59. Marx repeats this wry observation, in a different context, in *Misère de la philosophie* 127/163.

[334] *Die heilige Familie* 145/137.   [335] *Ibid.* 63/61.

other criticisms from the *Kritik* ignored in *Die heilige Familie*. The third complaint is reflected in the observation that verbal sleight of hand rather than logical necessity provides 'the magic hooks (*die magischen Haken*) which hold together the links of the chain of speculative reasoning'.[336] The fourth complaint, concerning Hegel's failure to identify the differentia, is suggested by Marx's description of categories being 'foisted' on particular finite entities.[337] The fifth complaint, about Hegel's acosmism, is implied by Marx's insistence that it is 'the "Fruit"' which constitutes 'the *true* essence of the pear, the apple, etc.'.[338] As a result, the view that the 'real existence' of the apples, pears, and so on consists in what is 'perceptible to the senses' is rejected in favour of a characterisation of those particular comestibles as 'mere forms of existence, *modi*, of "Fruit"'.[339] Real fruits are merely '*Schein*früchte', semblances whose true essence speculative reason locates elsewhere.[340] (Marx is so pleased with this parody of speculative method that he cannot resist repeating it later in a marginally different – and mercifully briefer – form. This alternative version – involving the abstraction of 'the "Animal"' which is subsequently incarnated in the lion, the snake, the bull, the horse, and the pug dog – does not require separate treatment here.[341])

The purpose of this somewhat compressed textual survey is to confirm that the account of Hegel's metaphysics first propounded in the *Kritik* is repeated throughout the early writings. In particular, both the twofold characterisation of speculative method and the five criticisms of Hegel are subsequently echoed (and endorsed) in the *Manuskripte* and *Die heilige Familie*. This constitutes *prima facie* evidence against the suggestion – advanced by these Hegelian enthusiasts for the early writings – that the young Marx subsequently abandoned the standpoint adopted in the *Kritik*.

It still remains to discuss the second possibility that was broached above, namely that one or more of the early writings which postdate the *Kritik* might contain an additional account of Hegel's achievement which is incompatible with the position adopted in that earlier text. An additional and incompatible account of Hegel's achievement might lend support to the portrayal of the *Kritik* as having been made redundant by those subsequent early writings. (Of course, that redundancy would still need to be demonstrated, but the existence of such an alternative account would be a start.) The only serious candidate for such an account consists of a much-quoted passage in the *Manuskripte* in which Marx comments on Hegel's *Phänomenologie*.

[336] *Ibid.* 73/69–70.   [337] *Ibid.* 60/58.   [338] *Ibid.* 60/57.   [339] *Ibid.* 60/58.
[340] *Ibid.*   [341] *Ibid.* 79–80/75–6. This analogy may have been suggested by *Enzyklopädie* §24Z.

The passage in question is quoted frequently but its meaning remains obscure. Marx asserts that the 'importance' of the *Phänomenologie* consists in its author's appreciation that 'the self-creation of humankind (*Selbsterzeugung des Menschen*)' is a process whose initial stages take 'the form of estrangement (*Entäusserung*)' and whose completion requires the 'transcendence (*Aufhebung*)' of that estrangement.[342] Some guide as to the meaning of these remarks is provided by their immediate context. At this point in the *Manuskripte*, it would appear that Marx is concerned with the concept of self-realisation. (As used here, 'self-realisation' connotes the development and deployment of the essential capacities of an individual.) In the relevant passage, Marx can be seen as making two distinct claims. The first of these concerns self-realisation. He insists that individual self-realisation – at least, on an extensive social scale – is an achievement that can be accomplished only after a (historical) detour in which individuals are alienated from those essential human capacities.[343] (Marx's account of human flourishing, of which these remarks form a part, is discussed further in Chapter 4.) The second claim concerns Hegel's work. He insists that this view about self-realisation can be found in the *Phänomenologie*. In short, in this somewhat opaque passage, Marx commends Hegel for appreciating that the development and deployment of essential human powers – at least, on an extensive scale – require a (historical) detour though a stage of alienation.[344]

In the *Manuskripte*, Marx immediately qualifies this commendation. He suggests that Hegel's appreciation of this truth about self-realisation is limited by the context in which it is elaborated. In particular, he claims that Hegel's insight into this struggle for the development and deployment of essential human potentialities is concealed within an '*abstract, logical, speculative*' form.[345] The suggested insight here – that the process of self-realisation requires a detour through a stage of alienation – is contained in the general model of selfhood (and its conditions) to which Hegel subscribes. According to this model, to be a (fully developed) self requires self-consciousness (or self-knowledge). Self-consciousness, in turn, requires the projection of a subject into something other than itself, and the subsequent recognition of itself in that 'other'. As Marx notes, this account of the process by which one becomes a full-blown subject involves a narrative of alienation and its transcendence as successive conditions for self-realisation. However, Marx insists that, in Hegel's work, the paradigmatic location of this process concerns the relation between the idea and the finite world.

---

[342] *Manuskripte* 574/332–3/385.   [343] See *ibid.* 574/333/386.
[344] *Ibid.* 574/332/385.   [345] *Ibid.* 570/329/382.

That is, the primary subject of alienation in Hegel's work is 'absolute' self-consciousness, not humankind but 'God'.[346] This constitutes the limitation of Hegel's insight. The estrangement of *this* subject from the world is an estrangement of thought from its own creation, and not from something which is genuinely 'other'. As a result, estrangement can be overcome by 'absolute knowledge', by the recognition that the seemingly 'other' is really the subject's own creation, and this is a solution which allows the alienated object (here, the finite world) to remain 'in existence in reality'.[347] The 'one-sidedness' of Hegel's account stems from the fact that in this paradigmatic case – the estrangement of thought from its own creation – both the source of, and solution to, alienation are characterised in terms of consciousness.[348]

This account of the young Marx's opaque comments about the *Phänomenologie* is likely to provoke a number of exegetical misgivings. Two of these warrant some response.

The first of these exegetical misgivings concerns my reading of the *Manuskripte*. That reading might appear to understate the young Marx's view of Hegel's achievement. In particular, I have thus far made no reference to the point at which, in a moment of enigmatic clarity, Marx describes Hegel as grasping that the achievement of self-realisation is a product of 'labour'. My initial account made no reference to that passing remark because I am reluctant to read much into it. As before, Marx immediately moves to clarify his comment. He explains that by 'labour' Hegel understands thought, that is, 'abstract mental labour'.[349] Note, in particular, that, in these opaque and passing remarks, Marx is not announcing that Hegel has identified the fundamental role of productive activity in human history.[350] (If Marx had subscribed to that surprising and false claim about Hegel, he would surely have repeated it elsewhere.) Rather Marx is to be understood as rehearsing his view that, whilst appreciating that self-realisation requires a historical detour through alienation, for Hegel it is ultimately the activity of thought which mediates the relation between consciousness and its products.

The second of these exegetical misgivings concerns Marx's reading of Hegel. It might seem that these remarks in the *Manuskripte* understate the historical and social dimensions of Hegel's text.[351] The *Phänomenologie* resists easy summary but it certainly contains an account (albeit complexly

---

[346] *Ibid.* 584/342/396.   [347] *Ibid.* 582/340/393.   [348] *Ibid.* 574/333/386.   [349] *Ibid.*

[350] For a dissenting view, see Heinrich Popitz, *Der entfremdete Mensch. Zeitkritik und Geschichtsphilosophie des jungen Marx* (Basel, 1953) pp. 111ff.

[351] See Michael Forster, *Hegel's Idea of a Phenomenology of Spirit* (Chicago, 1998) pp. 464 n. 1, 471 n. 13, 486–7.

ordered) of historical epochs (which are typically presented as embodiments of particular stages of thought and culture), together with a diagnosis of the ills of modernity (ills which include a series of unfortunate divisions between individuals, and between individuals and the community). Moreover, there is no suggestion in Hegel's work that these separations might be overcome by humankind in a purely 'subjective' manner. Hegel does not imagine that individuals can escape alienation by accommodating themselves to whatever social and political arrangements happen to obtain (by self-deception, for example), but rather insists that individuals are properly 'at home' only when those social and political arrangements are of the right kind (and are recognised as such). In short, the existence of a historical and social dimension to the *Phänomenologie* is not in doubt. The question here is whether the young Marx's remarks deny this. The intended target of Marx's comments is surely relevant. In these *Manuskripte* remarks, he appears primarily concerned with Hegel's basic metaphysical vision, and not with the details of the historical narrative contained in the *Phänomenologie*. It is in this metaphysical context that Marx contends that historical and social alienation, on Hegel's account, is ultimately nothing 'but the *semblance*, the *cloak*, the exoteric shape of these oppositions which alone matter, and, which constitute the *meaning* of these other profane oppositions'.[352] Of course, if the speculative account of a categorical structure which creates and governs the world is disregarded, then the young Marx is keen to credit Hegel with considerable social and historical insight. (That avidity is amply evidenced by the account of Hegel's empirical acumen outlined above.) Nor is that enthusiasm limited to the account of the *Philosophie des Rechts* that appears in the *Kritik*. In *Die heilige Familie*, for example, Marx insists that 'in many instances', and provided that – an important qualifier this – we ignore the 'speculative original sin', Hegel's *Phänomenologie* also contains 'the elements of a true description of human relations'.[353]

The second possibility broached above was whether the early writings contained an additional account of Hegel's achievement which was incompatible with the assessment propounded in the *Kritik*. (It was suggested that the existence of such an account might lend some support to those who would portray the *Kritik* as having been made redundant by subsequent early writings.) On the interpretation offered here, the *Manuskripte* discussion of the *Phänomenologie* is an unsuitable candidate for this role. The account of Hegel contained in the *Manuskripte* does not conflict with, still less displace, Marx's earlier assessment in the *Kritik*. In particular, the

---

[352] *Manuskripte* 572/331/384.   [353] *Die heilige Familie* 205/193.

The Young Karl Marx

suggestion that Hegel appreciates that self-realisation requires a detour in alienation is entirely consistent with the claim that Hegel recognises two central forms that such a detour takes in the modern social world (namely the atomism of civil society and the abstraction of the state).

(The relationship between Hegel's *Phänomenologie* and his later work – that is, between the *Phänomenologie* and the system to which it officially constitutes an introduction – is a controversial and difficult one. The issues raised by that relationship fall well outside the remit of the present study. However, note that the young Marx does not attribute any exceptional status to Hegel's *Phänomenologie* compared with his subsequent work. Not least, Marx insists that all the central failings of Hegel's later writings are already to be found 'in latent form, in embryo', in his earlier introduction to the system.[354] It seems that the same might be said for Hegel's achievements, not least his empirical insight into the forms of contemporary alienation.)

Thus far my remarks have been aimed primarily at casting some doubt on the position of those Hegelian enthusiasts for the young Marx who would diminish the standing of the *Kritik* in favour of the *Manuskripte*. I have sought, in particular, to undermine the view of these texts as having *competing* claims to our attention. I conclude this section with some broader, and rather more heretical, observations concerning what might be called the exaggerated standing of the *Manuskripte*.

The first of these iconoclastic observations concerns the degree of importance that is typically ascribed to the *Manuskripte*. In both the general and the more specialist literature, they are heralded as by far the most valuable of Marx's early writings. The *Manuskripte* are said to constitute the 'most significant work of the young Marx';[355] 'the most important early work of Marx';[356] 'the first important document of Marx's thought';[357] and so on. Yet the rationale that underpins these affirmations of their relative value is far from transparent. Those verdicts are certainly not grounded in Marx's own assessment, since he makes no extant reference to the *Manuskripte*. But nor do these judgements rest – at least, non-controversially – on the intrinsic worth of the relevant texts. I do not mean to suggest that the contents of the *Manuskripte* are uninteresting or unimportant. For instance, it would be hard to reconstruct the young Marx's view of alienated labour if the *Manuskripte* had not survived (although the *Auszüge aus James Mill*

[354] *Manuskripte* 573/332/384. On the introductory functions of the *Phänomenologie*, see Forster, *Hegel's Idea of a Phenomenology of Spirit*.
[355] Popitz, *Der entfremdete Mensch*, p. 3.
[356] Perry Anderson, *Considerations on Western Marxism* (London, 1976) p. 50.
[357] James D. White, *Karl Marx and the Intellectual Origins of Dialectical Materialism* (London, 1996) p. 1.

would provide considerable assistance in this regard). However, I do question whether their intrinsic merits alone can justify the relative importance which is routinely attributed to them. It could, of course, be thought that their privileged status derives from their claim to be Marx's earliest discussion of political economy. However, not only might one have reservations about the privileging of that particular subject matter, but also that chronological claim is far from certain. Some research suggests that the *Auszüge aus James Mill* pre-dated and provided material for (at least parts of) the *Manuskripte*.[358] (The fact that the respective *MEGA②* editors of these two texts appear not to agree about the chronology here might cause those of us who are not manuscript scholars to be wary of trying to bolster the standing of the *Manuskripte* in this way.) My own suspicion is that the privileging of the *Manuskripte* is to a large extent the product, not of their intrinsic importance or place in Marx's intellectual evolution (still less, of Marx's own assessment of their merits), but rather of their publication history, and, in particular, of their role in provoking a (highly political) debate about the development and character of Marx's thought. (Some aspects of that history were outlined in Chapter 1.)

The second of these iconoclastic observations concerns the textual integrity of the *Manuskripte*. It is standardly assumed that the *Manuskripte* is a single work, namely the (incomplete) draft of an early critique of political economy. However, the textual issues here are far more complicated than that standard view suggests. The raw material of the *Manuskripte* is typically provided by three surviving manuscripts, which have different (non-contiguous) pagination, which are incomplete (for example, both the first and the second manuscripts break off in mid thought), and which have a complex internal structure (for example, part of the first manuscript is divided into three columns with headings, which Marx variously follows closely, deviates from, and wholly ignores).[359] Those who would treat the *Manuskripte* as a single work have to decide how to order material written in different manuscripts and different columns, how (if at all) to subdivide and caption material, whether to collect together material from different places on the same topic, and so on. (There is also the issue of the so-called 'fourth manuscript' – a summary of the last chapter of Hegel's

---

[358] The editors of *MEGA②* 4, 2, suggest that Marx made excerpts from Mill before writing the 'second manuscript', whereas the editors of *MEGA②* 1, 2, suggest that Marx made excerpts after writing the 'third manuscript'.

[359] *MEGA②* contains two versions of the *Manuskripte*, one edited more heavily than the other. See *MEGA②* 1, 2, pp. 187–322, 323–438. See also the illustrations of the 'first manuscript' in *ibid.* pp. 711–739, and the critical account of Jürgen Rojahn, 'Die Marxschen Manuskripte aus dem Jahre 1844 in der neuen Marx-Engels-Gesamtausgabe', *Archiv für Sozialgeschichte*, volume 25 (1985) pp. 647–63.

Phänomenologie – which appeared as an appendix to the *MEGA*① edition of the *Manuskripte* but promptly disappeared from view in most subsequent publications and discussion of the text.[360]) However, these editorial difficulties also hint at a more fundamental problem, namely that on philological grounds it is not easy to distinguish the excerpts, notes, and commentary that were collated to form the *Manuskripte* from other contemporaneous notebooks.[361] The grounds for treating these manuscript materials together, as if they constituted the (incomplete) draft of a single work, are far from obvious. The main textual reason that is advanced for treating these pages as the draft of a single work is the so-called 'Preface (*Vorrede*)' to the *Manuskripte*. However, the 'Preface' in question – which appears unannounced in the third of the relevant manuscripts (although it is placed at the very beginning of the text of most published editions) – contains nothing which would justify the selection of these particular pages as a single work. (I do not mean to suggest that this 'Preface' was intended as anything other than an introduction to a single work, only to claim that it contains nothing to demonstrate that the single work in question is constituted by this particular collection of manuscript notes.[362]) Indeed, it is hard to resist the conclusion that the isolation and reorganisation of the *Manuskripte* as a separate text, complete with its own introductory 'Preface', is an editorial presumption. This editorial presumption receives scant support from the form of the relevant manuscripts, the content of the manuscripts, or any subsequent remark by Marx. I note with interest that the very first publication of any part of the relevant manuscripts was in a Russian translation of 1927.[363] The title under which those excerpts were presented – 'Preparatory materials for *Die heilige Familie*' – made no assumption that these materials formed (part of) a separate and self-contained work.

A (BRIEF) DIGEST

In conclusion, it might be helpful to rehearse some of the ground covered in this chapter. I have been concerned with the critical engagement

[360] *MEGA*② I, 2, pp. 439–444.
[361] The work of Jürgen Rojahn is crucial here. See, Jürgen Rojahn 'Marxismus-Marx-Geschichtswissenschaft: Der Fall der sogenannten Ökonomisch-Philosophischen Manuskripte aus dem Jahre 1844', *International Review of Social History*, volume 28 (1983) pp. 2–49.
[362] Marx certainly intended to write a work on political economy; signing a contract (dated 1 February 1845) with the publisher Karl Leske for a book provisionally entitled *Kritik der Politik und Nationalökonomie*.
[363] See Michael Maidan, 'The *Rezeptionsgeschichte* of the Paris Manuscripts', *History of European Ideas*, volume 12 (1990) p. 770.

with Hegel contained in the early writings, and, in particular, with the way in which that critical engagement illuminates the young Marx's nascent understanding of the modern social world. The resulting discussion has been organised around identifying a solution to two interpretative puzzles.

The first of these interpretative puzzles was to understand the rationale behind the shift in Marx's intellectual interests that occurred at the very beginning of the period under discussion. The young Marx took advantage of the personal freedom occasioned by the closure of the *Rheinische Zeitung* in order to write a marginal commentary on (part of) Hegel's *Philosophie des Rechts*. At first glance, this retreat to his study might be thought to embody a surprising shift away from a concern with 'material interests' (the hard empirical subject matter of his earlier journalism) and towards the study of 'German philosophy' (culminating in the work of Hegel). This initial characterisation is 'surprising' because it reverses the standard summary account of Marx's intellectual evolution. However, on reflection, that apparent reversal is misleading. The real shift in Marx's interests is indicated by the notion of a *Traumgeschichte*, according to which the standards of political modernity are reflected in German philosophy. (It was suggested that the most likely source of this conceit was Heine – not only one of Marx's favourite authors, but also one of his closest friends during his Parisian exile.) The young Marx's shifting intellectual interests are thereby revealed as embodying a movement away from a concern with the extant and anachronistic German polity (the subject of his *Rheinische Zeitung* articles), and towards the modern state, whose essential contours he saw reflected in German philosophy (as perfected in the *Philosophie des Rechts*).

The second of these interpretative puzzles was to make sense of the *Kritik*, a work which contains the young Marx's most sustained engagement with Hegel, but which remains fiendishly difficult to understand. Some of the familiar difficulties of comprehension that confront any reader of the early writings are compounded by the form and organisation of this particular text. The *Kritik* takes the form of a marginal commentary on the *Philosophie des Rechts*, a commentary whose purpose was to clarify Marx's own understanding of Hegel (and not to communicate that understanding to anyone else). Moreover, in developing his thoughts, the young Marx tends to identify two distinct subject matters – the character of speculative thought and the nature of the modern social world – in a manner which does not facilitate the comprehension of either. In order to understand the *Kritik* it is necessary to disentangle the contrasting verdicts that the young Marx delivers on speculative metaphysics and on Hegel's empirical acumen.

Hegel's metaphysical views are heavily criticised in the *Kritik*. Marx sought to expose the real dynamic of absolute idealism in terms of a recurring pattern of inversion whereby the empirical world (from which the Hegelian categorical framework is, in reality, derived) becomes transformed into (or, more accurately, is redescribed as) the manifestation of that conceptual system. In developing this account, Marx identifies five central criticisms of the speculative method. He accuses Hegel of failing to grasp that the speculative categories are derived from empirical experience, of maintaining an uncritical attitude towards the empirical world, of misdescribing the relation between the concept and its realisation as a necessary rather than allegorical relation, of failing to grasp the differentia, the distinctive character, of finite entities, and of having – despite himself – endorsed an 'acosmic' account of the identity of God and the world.

In contrast, the young Marx provides a generous account of Hegel's empirical acumen, and, in particular, of the latter's insight into the main contours of the modern social world. Hegel is commended for having understood that modernity is characterised by a distinctive separation between civil society and the state, that the relation between these civil and political spheres is an antagonistic one, that civil society is 'atomistic', and that the modern state is 'abstract'. More generally, Hegel is credited with having appreciated that the development and actualisation of the essential powers of humankind require a historical detour in alienation (albeit that this appreciation occurs within a misguided speculative framework), and that alienation, in the modern social world, contaminates both the relation between individuals and the relation between individuals and the state. In his account of the empirical acumen embodied in the *Philosophie des Rechts*, Marx remains determinedly unconvinced by Hegel's attempt to show how alienation is overcome in the rational or modern state.

I have maintained that these contrasting judgements concerning Hegel's metaphysics and his empirical acumen, contrasting judgments which appear first in the *Kritik*, are repeated, developed, and defended elsewhere in the early writings. Those other works contain no significant alternative account of Hegel's achievement. As a result, the claim – made by some Hegelian enthusiasts for the young Marx – that the *Manuskripte* embody a 'return' to Hegel which makes Marx's earlier 'Feuerbachian' commentary on the *Rechtsphilosophie* redundant is deemed unconvincing. Indeed, having insisted that the *Kritik* deserves to be recognised more widely as an important and interesting text which illuminates both the young Marx's political thought and his relation to Hegel, I ventured some heretical doubts about the (comparatively inflated) status of the *Manuskripte*.

So much for the emergence of the modern state and the young Marx's account of Hegel. In the next chapter, I turn to address the relation between Marx's understanding of the character of the modern state and his critical engagement with Bauer's political philosophy.

CHAPTER 3

Modern politics

In the *Kritik*, Marx not only commends Hegel's empirical acumen, he also articulates his own nascent understanding of the 'atomism' and 'abstraction' of the modern social world. Marx's characterisation of modernity in terms of this double separation – of individuals from each other, and of individuals from the state – is elaborated and developed throughout the early writings. In this chapter, I am interested primarily in the second of those separations, that is, the abstraction of modern political life. More precisely, I examine the young Marx's portrayal of the modern state, outlining his understanding of the achievements and limitations of what he calls political emancipation.

The focus of the present chapter is provided by the young Marx's polemical attacks on Bruno Bauer. In particular, it is Marx's two-part article 'Zur Judenfrage' that forms its textual centre of gravity. (The article was written in the autumn of 1843. It was probably started at Kreuznach but may have been completed in Paris. It was published in the first and only edition of the *Deutsch-Französische Jahrbücher* in February 1844.) 'Zur Judenfrage' is a briefer, more polished work than the *Kritik*, and has occasioned a considerable volume of comment and criticism.[1] Yet whilst there is little need to press its claims to the attention of commentators, there remains considerable room for clarification and questioning of both the central argument and dominant interpretation of this short, rich, and 'notoriously obscure' text.[2]

---

[1] Carlebach maintains that there 'can be little doubt that the volume of literature inspired by Marx's review-essays on the Jewish question is out of all proportion to their substantive content'. Julius Carlebach, *Karl Marx and the Radical Critique of Judaism* (London, 1978) p. 187. (There appears to be no conscious irony in this remark appearing less than midway through a 466-page book dominated by that very text.)

[2] Brian Barry, *Culture and Equality: An Egalitarian Critique of Multiculturalism* (Cambridge, 2002) p. 330 n. 21.

INTRODUCTION TO BAUER

One immediate barrier to an adequate understanding of 'Zur Judenfrage' is that its critical target is neither a familiar nor an accessible one. Like several of his contemporaries, Bauer has suffered the ignominious fate of being best known to modern readers as one of the targets of the young Marx's polemic.[3]

This obscurity, however merited it might be, is problematic. In the absence of some familiarity with Bauer's works, much of Marx's discussion proves hard to understand. For example, both the character and purpose of the much-quoted critical examination of rights in 'Zur Judenfrage' (discussed below) are illuminated by an understanding of Bauer's rationale for excluding Jews from the protection that rights afford. In addition, without some familiarity with Bauer's ideas it is impossible to assess the validity both of Marx's criticisms of his work and of the many comparisons between the two authors which appear in the scholarly literature. For example, I would maintain that the elision of the differences between Bauer and Marx – a move which has often featured in characterisations of 'Zur Judenfrage' as antisemitic – is harder to sustain in the light of a fuller understanding of the nature of Bauer's writings on Jews and Judaism.

In order to mitigate such difficulties, I begin this chapter with a brief description of Bauer's life and work, followed by an account of those of his writings which are criticised by Marx in 'Zur Judenfrage'.

To describe Bauer as a prolific writer might understate the case; a recent bibliography identifies him as publishing some twenty-two books and pamphlets, fifty-nine articles, and one edition, between 1838 and 1845.[4] (Marx caustically remarked that 'Herr Bruno is known to make a bulky work out of the tiniest semblance of a thought'.[5]) Bauer's literary career can conveniently be divided into three biographical periods, a tripartation which oversimplifies but does not seriously misrepresent his intellectual development.

In the first of these biographical periods (between 1837 and 1841), Bauer pursued a conventional academic career, and was usually identified as belonging to the Hegelian right (not least by David Friedrich Strauss, with

[3] The standard biographical work remains Ernst Barnikol, *Bruno Bauer: Studien und Materialien* (Assen, 1972). (This published volume represents only part of a much larger manuscript on Bauer – the product of forty years of research – held at the Internationaal Instituut voor Sociale Geschiedenis in Amsterdam.) For Bauer's writings before 1848, see also Douglas Moggach, *The Philosophy and Politics of Bruno Bauer* (Cambridge, 2003).
[4] See the bibliography compiled by Lawrence S. Stepelevich in Bruno Bauer, *The Trumpet of the Last Judgement Against Hegel the Atheist and Antichrist: An Ultimatum* (Lewiston NY, 1989) pp. 209–15.
[5] *Die heilige Familie* 159/151.

whom the influential differentiation of a Hegelian left, centre, and right originated).[6] Bauer initially attracted academic attention as the author of a prize-winning essay examining Kant's aesthetics from a Hegelian perspective (the judges of the competition included Hegel himself).[7] However, Bauer was perhaps best known for his editorial work on Hegel's *Vorlesungen über die Philosophie der Religion*, and for a two-volume study of the 'Old Testament'.[8] Bauer's orthodox credentials were confirmed and consolidated by his selection as the reviewer of Strauss's heretical *Das Leben Jesu* for the *Jahrbücher für wissenschaftliche Kritik* (the flagship journal of the Hegelian establishment). Originally a *Privatdozent* at Berlin, Bauer moved to the University of Bonn, where his appointment was increasingly resented by a theology faculty largely hostile to Hegelianism.[9] From 1839, growing academic and financial difficulties accompanied Bauer's movement away from the Hegelian right.[10] At this time, until 1842, he became something of a friend and mentor to the student Marx, dispensing career advice and divulging the increasingly apocalyptic dimension of his own thought to his younger acquaintance.[11]

In the second of these biographical periods (between 1841 and the mid-1840s), Bauer was forced to abandon his academic employment and moved rapidly to a leading position on the Hegelian left. His initial break with the Hegelian right was detailed in *Kritik der evangelischen Geschichte der Synoptiker* (1841–2), the work which led to his dismissal from the University of Bonn. Bauer's new allegiances were announced in the anonymous parody *Die Posaune des jüngsten Gerichts*, in which he sought to demonstrate the incompatibility of Hegelianism with both Christianity and the absolutist German status quo. Academic frustration and political radicalisation went hand in hand, with Bauer emerging as a leading figure in two informal left-Hegelian groups in Berlin – the *'Doktorklub'* and *'Die Freien'*.[12]

[6] See Strauss, *Streitschriften*, part 3, pp. 95ff. For the location of Bauer, and a response to his review of *Das Leben Jesu*, see *ibid.* pp. 101–20.
[7] Bauer's long-lost Latin text was rediscovered in 1992. See Bauer, *Über die Prinzipien des Schönen*.
[8] On Bauer's editorial labours, see Peter Hodgson's remarks in Hegel, *Lectures on the Philosophy of Religion*, volume 1, pp. 24–30. Bauer's lecture notes were also utilised in Heinrich Hotho's edition of Hegel's *Vorlesungen über die Ästhetik*.
[9] See John Edward Toews, *Hegelianism: The Path Towards Dialectical Humanism, 1805–41* (Cambridge, 1980) chapter 9; and Bauer to Edgar Bauer, 6 May 1841, in Bauer, *Briefwechsel*, p. 136.
[10] See Bauer to Edgar Bauer, 15 March 1840, Bauer, *Briefwechsel*, p. 51.
[11] For Bauer's surviving letters to Marx, see *MEGA②* 3, 1, pp. 335–6, 340–6, 349–50, 352–9, 369, 371, 386–7.
[12] Little is known about the '*Doktorklub*', a discussion group attended by students and academic staff. See Marx to Heinrich Marx, 10–11 November 1837, *MEW Erg. I*, p. 10; *MECW* 1, p. 19. On '*Die Freien*', see Gustav Mayer, 'Die Anfänge des politischen Radikalismus im vormärzlichen Preußen', *Zeitschrift für Politik*, volume 6 (1913) pp. 1–113.; and Robert J. Hellman, *Berlin – The Red Room and White Beer: The 'Free' Hegelian Radicals in the 1840s* (Washington DC, 1990).

His developing 'terrorism of pure theory' was promoted in a series of books, pamphlets, and short-lived journals, most importantly the *Allgemeine Literatur-Zeitung* (which was published between December 1843 and October 1844).[13] In several of these works, Bauer sought to chronicle and justify his own intellectual and professional struggles in a manner which equated those personal travails with imminent historical upheavals of a monumental scale.[14]

An impressionistic, but not inaccurate, account of both Bauer's reputation and the bohemian atmosphere of these left-Hegelian circles in Berlin, is provided in the contemporary mock-epic poem written by Engels and Edgar Bauer (Bruno's younger brother).[15] *Der Triumph des Glaubens* provides a revealing and satirical sketch of Bauer's climactic ascent from the theology faculty at the University of Bonn to Hippel's Weinstube on the Friedrichstrasse (one of the regular haunts of '*Die Freien*'). Bauer's fanatical temperament – Ruge called him the 'Robespierre of Theology' – and his hostility to religion are emphasised repeatedly.[16] The description of his lectures at the University of Bonn, for example, does not suggest much effort, on Bauer's part, at any accommodation with his more conventional academic colleagues:

> Auf dem Katheder, wo nur Fromme sich gesetzt,
> Lehrt durch des Teufels List der tolle *Bauer* jetzt.
> Da steht er, schäumt vor Wut, ein Teufelchen im Nacken,
> Ihn lehrend, wie er soll die Theologen packen.
> Da heult er auf voll Grimm, ein wasserscheuer Hund . . .

> Upon that Chair of erstwhile pious reputation
> Mad *Bauer* lectures through the Devil's ministration.
> He stands and foams with rage; a demon on his back
> Goads him and sets him on the Theologians' track.
> Just like a hydrophobic dog, he howls and bays . . .[17]

The same temperamental fanaticism and uncompromising hostility to religion appear in the account of Bauer's subsequent arrival at a gathering of

[13] The phrase appears in a letter from Bauer to Marx, 28 March 1841, *MEGA②* 3, 1, p. 353.
[14] Most famously in *Die gute Sache der Freiheit und meine eigene Angelegenheit* (1842). For a modern anthology of Bauer's second-period writings, see Bruno Bauer, *Feldzüge der reinen Kritik* (Frankfurt am Main, 1968).
[15] On Edgar Bauer, see Erik Gamby, *Edgar Bauer: Junghegelianer, Publizist, und Polizeiagent: mit Bibliographie der E. Bauer – Texte und Dokumentenanhang* (Trier, 1985); and Eric v. d. Luft, 'Edgar Bauer and the Origins of the Theory of Terrorism', Douglas Moggach (ed.), *The New Hegelians: Politics and Philosophy in the Hegelian School* (Cambridge, 2006).
[16] Arnold Ruge to Ludwig Ruge, 26 September 1842, *Briefwechsel*, p. 281. See also Bauer, 'Letter to Arnold Ruge (19 October 1841)'.
[17] *Triumph* 292/327.

left-Hegelians in Berlin, at which his intellectual leadership was confirmed and celebrated:

> Kaum sind zur Stelle sie, da tost heran der *Bauer*,
> Gehüllt in Qualm und Dampf und Höllenregenschauer.
> Er rast im grünen Rock, ein schmaler Bösewicht,
> Den Höllensohn verrät das lauernde Gesicht.
> Er schwingt die Fahne hoch, daß rings die Funken flogen
> Von seiner Schmachkritik der Bibel einem Bogen.

> As soon as they arrive, in bursts the frantic *Bauer*,
> Engulfed in smoke and steam and Hell-rain's deadly shower.
> He raves, a lanky villain in a coat of green;
> Behind the leering face Hell's offspring can be seen.
> He hoists his flag aloft, and in an arc up high
> The sparks of his rude Bible criticisms fly.[18]

Finally, in the third and longest of the biographical periods that I want to distinguish (stretching from the mid-1840s until his death in 1882), Bauer's influence waned and he moved to a position on the political right. Following the rapid disintegration of the Hegelian left and the failure of the 1848 Revolution, Bauer's writings became increasingly pessimistic.[19] Several pamphlets, including *Russland und das Germanentum* (1853), foreshadowed what might be called 'Spenglerian' themes in the context of the emerging 'Eastern Question', portraying Germany as the endangered and unappreciated hope of a stagnating and decadent European civilisation which was about to be swept away by an energetic and emergent Russia.[20] Between 1859 and 1866, Bauer also acted as an assistant to the reactionary Hermann Wagener – editor of both the *Berliner Revue* and a multi-volume *Staats- und Gesellschafts-Lexikon* – thereby contributing to the newly developing vocabulary of racial antisemitism (the latter term first appeared in the late 1870s).[21] Towards the end of this third period, Bauer also wrote some historical studies of early Christianity, in which, whilst acknowledging that the

---

[18] *Ibid.* 301/336.
[19] In 1855, Marx met up with Bauer – who was visiting his brother Edgar in London – and was struck by his 'gloom and despondency over the "present"'. See Marx to Engels, 14 December 1855, *MEW* 28, pp. 466–7; *MECW* 39, pp. 562–4; and Marx to Engels, 18 January 1856 and 12 February 1856, in *MEW* 29, pp. 5–7, 11–15; *MECW* 40, pp. 3–5, 8–12.
[20] See *Russland und das Germanentum*, pp. 75–122. An unfinished manuscript by Marx, written in January 1857, discusses two of Bauer's other pamphlets on the 'Eastern Question'. See 'Bauer's Pamphlets'. Marx judged them 'feeble and pretentious'. Marx to Engels, 10 January 1856, *MEW* 29, p. 93; *MECW* 40, p. 90.
[21] See Jacob Katz, *From Prejudice to Destruction: Anti-Semitism 1700–1933* (Cambridge, 1980) pp. 210ff.; and Ivan Hannaford, *Race: The History of an Idea in the West* (Baltimore, 1996) chapter 9. On Bauer's work with Wagener, see Barnikol, *Bruno Bauer*, pp. 347ff.

gospel history reflected the experience of early Christian communities, he claimed that the representation of this experience was the work of a single person.[22] He insisted variously that there was no non-literary evidence for the life of Jesus, that the gospels had a single source, and that the writings of the *Urevangelist* (the creator of this original account) were fictional. He also emphasised the role of several Greek and Roman authors – in particular, Philo of Alexandria and Seneca – in the intellectual formation of certain Christian doctrines.[23] Increasingly forgotten, although with something of a local reputation for eccentricity, the 'hermit (*Einsiedler*) of Rixdorf' died in austere and impecunious circumstances in April 1882.[24]

The young Marx's critical engagement with Bauer is concerned with writings from the second of these three periods, especially those published between 1843 and 1845. In this chapter, I do not attempt to discuss all aspects of Marx's critical engagement with these texts, but rather focus on his response to Bauer's discussion of 'the Jewish question'. I am concerned, in particular, with those aspects of Marx's response which illuminate his own views of the modern state.

Prompted by the complex and overwhelming impact of modernisation, both Jews and Gentiles had, under the heading of 'the Jewish question', raised a series of related questions about the traditional legal status, occupational structure, and religious behaviour of European Jewry.[25] Perhaps the most important of these questions concerned 'Jewish emancipation', that is, the issue of whether, and under what conditions, states should remove the discriminatory legal constraints to which Jews, but not the majority Christian population, were subject.[26] The German debate on Jewish

[22] See Albert Schweitzer, *The Quest of the Historical Jesus: A Critical Study of Its Progress from Reimarus to Wrede* (Baltimore, 1998) pp. 141ff.
[23] See, for example, Bauer, *Christus und die Cäsaren*. For Engels' interest in these studies, see Engels, 'Bruno Bauer und das Urchristentum', and Alexis Voden, 'Talks With Engels', Institute of Marxism-Leninism (ed.), *Reminiscences of Marx and Engels* (Moscow, n.d.) p. 331.
[24] Bauer lived frugally – trying to provide for the orphaned children of his brother Egbert – on a smallholding in Rixdorf (then a village outside Berlin), with a study in an outbuilding. See Marx's (predictably unsympathetic) letter to Engels, 12 February 1856, *MEW* 29, pp. 11–15; *MECW* 40, pp. 89–91.
[25] See Jacob Toury, '"The Jewish Question": A Semantic Approach', *Leo Baeck Institute Year Book*, volume 11 (1966) pp. 85–106, and Peter Pulzer, *Jews and the German State: The Political History of a Minority, 1848–1933* (Oxford, 1992) p. 29.
[26] See Jacob Katz, 'The Term "Jewish Emancipation": Its Origin and Historical Impact', Jacob Katz, *Emancipation and Assimilation: Studies in Modern Jewish History* (Farnborough, 1972) pp. 21–45; David Sorkin, 'Emancipation and Assimilation: Two Concepts and Their Application to German-Jewish History', *Leo Baeck Institute Year Book*, volume 35 (1990) pp. 17–33; and Karl Martin Grass and Reinhart Koselleck, 'Emanzipation', *Geschichtliche Grundbegriffe: Historisches Lexikon zur politisch-sozialen Sprache in Deutschland*, ed. Otto Brunner, Werner Conze, and Reinhart Koselleck, volume 2 (Stuttgart, 1975) pp. 153–97.

emancipation is frequently dated from the publication of Christian Wilhelm Dohm's *Über die bürgerliche Verbesserung der Juden* (1781), but interest in this issue, especially in Prussia, intensified in the early 1840s (see below).

It is important that readers do not underestimate the extent and diversity of discriminatory restrictions to which German Jews were subject, although (as ever) the variety of social and political arrangements in nineteenth-century Germany make generalisations difficult. (In Prussia alone, it has been estimated that Jews were governed by some two dozen different regional jurisdictions.[27]) The emancipation of German Jewry did not consist in a stable progression to formal legal equality (achieved in 1871) but rather took an uncertain and circuitous route.[28] In the eighteenth century, Jewish settlement had been prohibited in some German territories and encouraged in others. Where Jews had been permitted to settle, they were typically treated not as native subjects but as protected aliens whose areas of residency and overall numbers were tightly controlled and who might be expelled at any moment. Jews were subject to heavy and discriminatory taxes, and systematically excluded from certain economic activities.[29] Subsequently, some German states, including those affected by Napoleonic rule and influence (such as parts of Prussia), had seen a degree of emancipatory legislation, although such advances were neither uniform nor consistent. In Prussia, the most significant measure was probably the '1812 Edict', which granted a degree of civil equality, for example, by removing special taxes and giving Prussian Jews the status of 'native residents (*Einländer*)' in return for their adoption of German surnames and business records. (It is significant that a decision on access to 'public service and state offices' was

[27] For this estimate, see Christopher M. Clark, 'German Jews', Rainer Liedtke and Stephen Wenderhorst (eds.), *The Emancipation of Catholics, Jews and Protestants. Minorities and the Nation State in Nineteenth-Century Europe* (Manchester, 1999) p. 128. On the social and political lives of nineteenth-century German Jews, see Jacob Toury, *Soziale und politische Geschichte der Juden in Deutschland, 1847–1871* (Düsseldorf, 1977), and Michael A. Meyer (ed.), *German-Jewish History in Modern Times*, volume 2: *Emancipation and Acculturation: 1780–1871* (New York, 1997).

[28] Difficult routes seem to be the metaphor of choice amongst historians. See Reinhard Rürup, 'The Tortuous and Thorny Path to Legal Equality: "Jew Laws" and Emancipatory Legislation in Germany from the Late Eighteenth Century', *Leo Baeck Institute Year Book*, volume 31 (1986) pp. 3–33; and Werner E. Mosse, 'From "*Schutzjuden*" to "*Deutsche Staatsbürger Jüdischen Glaubens*": The Long and Bumpy Road of Jewish Emancipation in Germany', Pierre Birnbaum and Ira Katznelson (eds.), *Paths of Emancipation: Jews, States, and Citizenship* (Princeton, 1995) pp. 59–93. Bauman has remarked in a related context that 'there were few, if any, straight roads in modern Jewish history'. Zygmunt Bauman, 'Exit Visas and Entry Tickets', *Telos*, volume 77 (1988) p. 45.

[29] For the eighteenth century and earlier, see Jacob Katz, *Out of the Ghetto: The Social Background of Jewish Emancipation, 1770–1870* (Cambridge MA, 1973); Herman Pollack, *Jewish Folkways in Germanic Lands (1648–1806). Studies in Aspects of Daily Life* (Cambridge MA, 1971); and R. Po-Chia Hsia and Hartmut Lehmann (eds.), *In and Out of the Ghetto: Jewish–Gentile Relations in Late Medieval and Early Modern Germany* (Cambridge, 1995).

deferred to a later, and unspecified, date.) However, following the Wars of Liberation, there was evidence of a significant, albeit slow and uneven, retreat from these earlier advances.

In Prussia, an extensive and diverse set of discriminatory constraints on the small Jewish population remained in force between 1815 and 1848.[30] Perhaps most obviously, Jews continued to be subject to restrictions on political activity and public service; they were, for example, excluded both from the electorate of the provincial diets and from holding an extensive range of 'public' offices. Jews could not practise as lawyers or serve on juries, and there was a continued presumption, codified in law, that they could not bear witness in certain criminal cases (the 'Jew's Oath', which implied that Jews were pecularly inclined to perjury, was also widely used). Jews could serve as soldiers but could not be promoted to the officer corps. Jews were also subject to continued restrictions in economic life and discriminatory intervention in their communal affairs.[31] In some of the partially integrated enclaves within Prussia, restrictions were even greater: in Cologne, for example, the older residency constraints, which treated Jews as resident aliens, remained in force. In short, in a state which was (in general) politically backward, Jews continued to suffer significant discrimination.[32]

Bauer's *Die Judenfrage* (1843) had a considerable, albeit short-lived, impact on the wider German debate about Jewish emancipation. It provoked responses from well-known opponents and supporters of emancipation, such as Friedrich Wilhelm Ghillany and Karl Grün, respectively. Less predictably, it also elicited a series of contributions from a large and diverse group of distinguished German Jews, including Abraham Geiger, Mendel Hess, Samuel Hirsch, Gustav Phillipson, Gabriel Riesser, and Gotthold Salomon.[33] Explaining this impact is beyond the remit of this chapter; however, the form, content, and timing of Bauer's pamphlet would all appear to be relevant factors. Bauer was an accomplished polemicist and

[30] Jews made up 1.2 per cent of the Prussian population in 1816, and 1.4 per cent in 1861. See the estimates of Henry Wasserman quoted by David Sorkin, 'The Impact of Emancipation on German Jewry: A Reconsideration', Jonathan Frankel and Steven J. Zipperstein (eds.), *Assimilation and Community: The Jews in Nineteenth-Century Europe* (Cambridge, 1992) p. 180.
[31] See Herbert Strauss, 'Pre-emancipation Prussian Policies Towards the Jews 1815–1847', *Leo Baeck Institute Year Book*, volume 11 (1966) pp. 107–36; and Michael A. Meyer, *Response to Modernity: A History of the Reform Movement in Judaism* (Oxford, 1988) pp. 30–46. The Prussian state offered incentives to conversion, including a royal 'christening present' of 30 marks for converts naming the king as their 'godfather'. See Christopher M. Clark, *The Politics of Conversion: Missionary Protestantism and the Jews in Prussia 1728–1941* (Oxford, 1995) pp. 99–100.
[32] See Mosse, 'From "*Schutzjuden*" to "*Deutsche Staatsbürger Jüdischen Glaubens*"', p. 71.
[33] See Nathan Rotenstreich, 'For and Against Emancipation: The Bruno Bauer Controversy', *Leo Baeck Institute Year Book*, volume 4 (1959) pp. 3–36.

Die Judenfrage was a deliberately provocative text. Consider, for example, his dismissive characterisation of Moses Mendelssohn as having helped 'neither humanity nor his own people'.[34] (Mendelssohn was the hero and embodiment of the Haskalah, a writer whose life was credited with having demonstrated 'that even a Jew could be a philosopher and a man of high personal virtue'.[35]) In addition, the distinctive intellectual position that Bauer occupied was potentially threatening to proponents of emancipation. It was not simply that Bauer was an ostensible radical who rejected Jewish emancipation, but that he rejected emancipation despite his willingness to think of Jews in religious rather than, for example, national terms. (Several responses to *Die Judenfrage* came from those sympathetic to the Reform movement, which shared this religious definition of Jewish identity.[36]) Finally, Bauer's intervention came at a time when a series of events had combined to provoke renewed interest, especially in Prussia, in the question of Jewish emancipation. (Several events reflected and reinforced this intensification of interest. Those events included Friedrich Wilhelm IV's – subsequently abandoned – proposal to organise Prussian Jews into separate corporations apart from the duties and rewards of political life,[37] the resurgence of Jew-hatred which followed the Damascus blood libel,[38] and a vote in the Provincial Diet of the Rhine province supporting the removal of local civil and political restrictions on Jews.[39])

My concern here is not with this wider debate, but rather with those threads in Marx's response to Bauer which illuminate the account of political emancipation contained in the early writings. As early as August 1842 (when he had contacted Dagobert Oppenheimer requesting copies of K. H. Hermes' *Kölnische Zeitung* articles 'against the Jews'), Marx had been thinking about writing on 'the Jewish question', but it was Bauer who provoked him into print.[40] In 'Zur Judenfrage', Marx responded to both Bauer's original *Die Judenfrage* and his subsequent article 'Die Fähigkeit

[34] *Die Judenfrage* 83/87.
[35] Michael A. Meyer, *The Origins of the Modern Jew: Jewish Identity and European Culture in Germany 1749–1824* (Detroit, 1967) p. 58. Graetz describes Mendelssohn as turning the name 'Jew' almost into 'a title of honour'. Heinrich Graetz, *History of the Jews*, volume 5 (Philadelphia, 1895) p. 292. On the Haskalah, see David Sorkin, *The Transformation of German Jewry, 1780–1840* (Oxford, 1987).
[36] On the Reform movement, see Meyer, *Response to Modernity*.
[37] See Meyer (ed.), *Emancipation and Acculturation*, pp. 46ff.
[38] See Jonathan Frankel, *The Damascus Affair: 'Ritual Murder', Politics, and the Jews in 1840* (Cambridge, 1997).
[39] See Dieter Kastner (ed.), *Der Rheinische Provinziallandtag und die Emanzipation der Juden im Rheinland, 1825–1845. Ein Dokumentation*, part 1 (Cologne, 1989) pp. 55–6.
[40] Marx to Oppenheimer, approximately 25 August 1842, *MEW* 27, pp. 409–10; *MECW* 1, pp. 391–2. On Hermes and the *Kölnische Zeitung*, see Shulamit S. Magnus, *Jewish Emancipation in a German City: Cologne, 1798–1871* (Stanford CA, 1997) pp. 130ff.

der heutigen Juden und Christen, frei zu werden', which had been published in Georg Herwegh's important collection *Einundzwanzig Bogen aus der Schweiz* (1843). (The title of the latter alluded to the restriction whereby books of over twenty 'printer's sheets' – that is, 'signatures' of eight pages each – were exempt from preliminary censorship in many German states. As Marx elsewhere observed, 'books of more than twenty printed sheets are not books for the people'.[41]) Some months later – provoked by some of Bauer's replies to his critics – Marx briefly reprised his views on 'the Jewish question' in *Die heilige Familie*, a book-length polemic against 'critical criticism' (Marx's name for the strand of left-Hegelian thought that he identified with Bauer and his entourage).[42] (Note that, as before and for the same reason, I refer here only to those parts of *Die heilige Familie* which were written by Marx.) Since there seems to be no significant movement in the young Marx's views between these two texts, I treat them together.

BAUER AND JUDAISM

The next three sections of this chapter are concerned with Bauer's middle-period writings on 'the Jewish question', especially *Die Judenfrage* and 'Die Fähigkeit der heutigen Juden und Christen, frei zu werden'. In the present section, I outline Bauer's hostile account of the nature and historical role of Judaism and of Jews. In the two sections that follow, I consider his emphatic denial that meaningful liberty is possible for Jews.

Given Bauer's infamous atheist reputation, his own introductory remarks, and some later commentary, one would expect *Die Judenfrage* to be dominated by the denunciation of religion in general.[43] However, Bauer's discussion is dominated less by a hostility to religion and to religious believers in general than by a strident and deeply held contempt for Judaism and Jews in particular. Bauer portrays Judaism as a religion which 'does not teach universal truths', but rather gives only 'positive' commandments, which are, in turn, interpreted casuistically.[44] In short, Judaism is said to be an exclusive, positive, and hypocritical religion.

[41] Marx to Arnold Ruge, 13 March 1843, *MEW* 27, p. 416; *MECW* I, p. 398.
[42] Bauer responded to Gustav Phillipson, Samuel Hirsch, and Mendel Hess in 'Neueste Schriften über die Judenfrage', in *Allgemeine Literatur-Zeitung*, no. 1, December 1843; to Gabriel Reisser in a second article (confusingly) with the same title in *Allgemeine Literatur-Zeitung*, no. 4, March 1844; and to Marx in 'Was ist jetzt der Gegenstand der Kritik?', in *Allgemeine Literatur-Zeitung*, no. 8, July 1844.
[43] For example, Peled maintains that 'Christianity did not fare any better than Judaism in Bauer's two essays'. Yoav Peled, 'From Theology to Sociology: Bruno Bauer and Karl Marx on the Question of Jewish Emancipation', *History of Political Thought*, volume 13 (1992) p. 469.
[44] *Die Judenfrage* 12/14.

First, and perhaps most importantly, Bauer endorses the claim that Judaism is an exclusive or particularistic religion in a sense that Christianity is not.[45] He appeals to his earlier 'Old Testament' studies – especially *Herr Dr. Hengstenberg. Kritische Briefe über den Gegensatz des Gesetzes und des Evangeliums* (1839) – as demonstrating conclusively that biblical Judaism does not teach 'universal love for one's fellow human being'.[46] Bauer insists that 'to the Jew only another Jew is his brother and neighbour'.[47] He reluctantly concedes that biblical Judaism promotes charity towards strangers, but maintains that, for Jews, strangers always remain precisely that – an unfamiliar and foreign element.[48] Bauer's dubious strategy for dealing with further counter-examples, such as the messianic belief that 'Jehovah' (*sic*) will ultimately reveal himself as 'the God of all nations and receive them into his community', is simply to characterise them as 'inconsistencies (*Inkonsequenzen*)' whose only effect is to illuminate and emphasise the characteristic exclusiveness of Judaism.[49] Occasionally, Bauer even suggests that Judaism is actively hostile to universality, that it advocates a 'war against humanity'.[50] The contrast here is with the purported universality of Christianity. The Christian 'God of Love', Bauer claims, 'does not discriminate among the nations but accepts into his kingdom everyone who accepts the true faith'.[51] (It will be apparent that Bauer glosses over the significance of faith in Christianity. The universality of Christianity may not appear so unqualified when one considers that the individual salvation it promises is dependent on a revelation which has been bestowed on only a minority of humankind. At the same time, Bauer ignores the historical openness of Judaism to conversion, albeit not to proselytising.[52])

Second, Bauer claims that Judaism is a 'positive' religion, in the pejorative Hegelian sense that it lays down rituals and rules which are to be accepted purely on authority and not because they are either rational or coherent with the life of its adherents.[53] Judaism, he maintains, regards its own laws as arbitrary, 'as something alien, inexplicable, as the will of "Jehovah", an order which is not connected at all with the nature of the circumstances

[45] Nachman Krochmal may be the lone Hegelian dissenter from this claim, portraying Jews as the bearers of universality in his Hebrew treatise *Moreh Nevuchei Ha-zman*. On Krochmal, see Jay M. Harris, *Nachman Krochmal: Guiding the Perplexed of the Modern Age* (New York, 1991).

[46] *Die Judenfrage* 30/33.

[47] *Ibid.* 31/34. For a spirited contemporaneous rejection of such claims, see Heinrich Graetz, *The Structure of Jewish History and Other Essays*, translated and edited by Ismar Schorsch (New York, 1975) p. 155. The title essay, 'Die Construction der jüdischen Geschichte', was first published in 1846 as a kind of prolegomenon to Graetz's monumental *Geschichte der Juden*.

[48] *Die Judenfrage* 31/34.   [49] *Ibid.* 32/35.   [50] *Ibid.* 79/83.   [51] *Ibid.* 17/19.

[52] See Michael Walzer, Menachem Lorberbaum, and Noam J. Zohar (eds.), *The Jewish Political Tradition*, volume 2: *Membership* (New Haven, 2003) chapter 14.

[53] See *Die Judenfrage* 42/45.

in which it was given'.[54] Critical reflection on the nature of religious claims, Bauer continues, is discouraged by Judaism; the origin of particular dietary laws, for example, is never to be questioned. All that is required of adherents is an unthinking obedience to 'unintelligible and arbitrary commands'.[55]

Third, Judaism is said to have a 'chimerical' and 'hypocritical' character. Bauer suggests that, because its laws cannot be obeyed literally (this is the sense in which they are deemed 'chimerical'), its adherents develop strategies for maintaining the appearance of obedience alone. This concern for the appearance of obedience, in the absence of literal compliance, is characterised as 'hypocritical'. (Bauer equivocates over whether this supposed hypocrisy is a foundational characteristic which was present in the Hebrew Bible, or a later accretion reflected only in the post-biblical literature, which he treats as coextensive with the Talmud.[56]) Bauer gives as an example of such 'hypocrisy' the employment by Jewish families of Christian servants to work on the Sabbath.[57] He designates such practices as 'Jewish Jesuitism', a 'Jesuitism' which, in explicit contradistinction to its Christian counterpart, he characterises as 'clumsy and repulsive', as demonstrating only an unsophisticated 'animal cunning'.[58]

This account of Judaism reveals not only a lack of sympathy on Bauer's part but also a lack of knowledge. Bauer's biblical scholarship may have been considerable but his understanding of post-biblical Judaism was limited and flawed. In particular, he was highly dependent on Johann Andreas Eisenmenger's vast, influential, and irredeemably hostile compendium *Entdecktes Judenthum* (1700), which Bauer judged to be a 'work of solid theological scholarship'.[59] (In this assessment Bauer was mistaken. Eisenmenger was a skilled linguist and had consulted a wide variety of relevant source materials, but he carefully selects passages – shorn of their wider textual, intellectual, and historical, context – in order to substantiate a series of familiar Christian charges against the theology of Judaism and the morality of Jews.[60])

[54] *Ibid.* 36/39.   [55] *Ibid.* 37/40.
[56] See David Leopold, 'The Hegelian Antisemitism of Bruno Bauer', *History of European Ideas*, volume 25 (1999) pp. 183–4.
[57] *Die Judenfrage* 43/46 and 'Fähigkeit' 181/139.   [58] 'Fähigkeit' 180–1/139.
[59] *Die Judenfrage* 86/90. The title of Bauer's *Das entdeckte Christenthum* alludes to Eisenmenger's compendium.
[60] See J. A. Eisenmenger, *Entdecktes Judenthum*, 2 volumes (Königsburg [Berlin], 1710). See also Katz, *From Prejudice to Destruction*, chapter 1; and Frank E. Manuel, *The Broken Staff: Judaism Through Christian Eyes* (Cambridge MA, 1992) pp. 151–4. In an abridged and expurgated English translation – *The Traditions of the Jews, or, the Doctrines and Expositions Contain'd in the Talmud and Other Rabbinical Writings* (London, 1743) – the editor, one Reverend John Peter Stehelin, suggests (implausibly) that the veracity of its content is not compromised by Eisenmenger's personal hostility.

Bauer's understanding of the historical role of Judaism is revealed in his account of the relation between Judaism and Christianity. Bauer characterises his own account of this relation as illustrating the 'orthodox' view, according to which Judaism and Christianity stand in a relation of 'cause' and 'consequent'.[61] However, some care is needed here. Bauer is not simply claiming that Christianity arose out of, and was chronologically subsequent to, Judaism, but rather suggests that 'Judaism was the preparation for Christianity and Christianity the completion and perfection of Judaism'.[62] Judaism and Christianity are thereby placed in a developmental framework of preparatory ground and completion. As a result, Bauer calls Judaism 'an uncompleted, unfinished Christianity', and characterises Christianity as 'a Judaism which has effected its own completion'.[63]

At one point, Bauer describes the relation between Judaism and Christianity as analogous to that between mother and daughter. The point of this analogy is not only to make vivid the conflict between the two religions – thus, as the daughter is 'ungrateful' to her mother, so, in turn, the mother refuses to 'acknowledge' her daughter – but also to suggest the notion of a historical progression between generations.[64] This historical progression has two striking features. Bauer maintains that the daughter (Christianity) has 'the higher right', has 'progress' on her side,[65] and that the mother (Judaism) and daughter (Christianity) cannot both survive ('the new', he insists, 'cannot be if the old endures').[66] Both of these claims require some elaboration.

Ever the good Hegelian, Bauer associates historical development with the progressive realisation of 'universality'. Moreover, he maintains that the superiority of Christianity over Judaism consists in the purportedly more 'embracing conception of humankind' of the former.[67] For Bauer, it is this recognition of 'universal love' which establishes both the superiority of Christianity over Judaism and the affinity of Christianity with historical progress.[68] (In order to leave a historical role for Bauer's own atheism, Christianity is said only to recognise universality and not to realise it; at least, not to realise it adequately.[69])

Bauer's explanation of the purported necessity of the demise of Judaism appears to rest on this account of a historical progression from less adequate to more adequate embodiments of universality (exemplified by the relation between Judaism and Christianity).[70] In this historical progression, anything of value in the less adequate entity (Judaism) is supposedly incorporated in the more adequate entity (Christianity). Finally, it is assumed

[61] *Die Judenfrage* 15/17.   [62] *Ibid.* 45/48.   [63] *Ibid.*   [64] *Ibid.* 16/18.
[65] *Ibid.*   [66] *Ibid.* 15–16/18.   [67] 'Fähigkeit' 184/141.   [68] *Ibid.*
[69] *Ibid.* 191/146–7.   [70] See *Die Judenfrage* 45/48.

that the rationale for the existence of an entity is whether it has anything of independent value to contribute to historical progress. As a result, less perfect entities have no rational licence for continued existence once more perfect entities have arrived on the historical scene. It is Bauer's commitment to something like this Hegelian narrative which provides one justification for his hostility to contemporary Judaism. Having contributed to historical progress by giving rise to Christianity, there no longer remains any rationale for the continued survival of Judaism. Indeed, Bauer is prepared to characterise the continued existence of Jews as constituting a historical 'wrong (*Unrecht*)'.[71]

This account of the historical relation of Judaism to Christianity provides the context in which to understand Bauer's account of the nature of Jews in these middle-period writings. For Bauer, Jews are defined as such by their religious commitments.[72] Not only is a baptised Jew no longer a Jew, but even a sufficiently heretical Jew, such as Spinoza, is not to be considered a Jew.[73] (As a result of his 'abominable heresies', the precise nature of which is still disputed, Spinoza was in 1656 made the subject of an unusually fierce order of *cherem* whereby he was expelled from, and cursed by, the Jewish community of Amsterdam.[74])

In particular, it is the 'exclusiveness' of Jews – their commitment to the claim that 'they were the chosen people' – which Bauer judges to be their most foundational characteristic.[75] He equates the doctrine of the election of Israel with a spurious belief in superiority, with 'the idea of special destiny, the kingdom, in short the chimera of the most enormous privilege'.[76] As a result, Bauer concludes, the idea of privilege and the nature of the Jew are irremediably 'intertwined'.[77]

Not least, this belief in their own 'exclusivity' is used to explain other characteristics that Jews are said to possess. These include their 'conceit and arrogance',[78] their tendency towards cruelty (what has been called

---

[71] *Ibid.* 34/37.
[72] See *ibid.* 74/78. This religious definition of membership – accepted by the Reform movement – was not uncontroversial. Graetz, for example, insisted on the national dimension of Jewish identity, and even denied that Judaism was a religion at all (since religions necessarily made claims about the relation between the *individual* and God).
[73] *Ibid.* 9/11.
[74] See Steven Nadler, *Spinoza: A Life* (Cambridge, 1999) chapter 6; and Steven Nadler, *Spinoza's Heresy: Immortality and the Jewish Mind* (Oxford, 2001).
[75] *Die Judenfrage* 14/16.
[76] *Ibid.* 29–30/32. On election see David Novak, *The Election of Israel: The Idea of the Chosen People* (Cambridge, 1995); and Walzer, Lorberbaum, and Zohar (eds.), *The Jewish Political Tradition*, volume 2, chapter 11.
[77] *Die Judenfrage* 30/32.   [78] *Ibid.* 39/42.

Jewish courage turns out to be evidence of 'bestiality', of an animal 'rage to annihilate' an adversary which is judged to have 'no right to exist'),[79] and especially their 'tenacity', their 'stubbornness' in clinging to their nationality and resisting 'the movements and changes of history'.[80] (Bauer refers to the 'oriental nature' of Jews, using the convenient and pejorative Hegelian shorthand for 'unchangeableness' and even resistance to progress.[81]) Confronted with a conflict between the continued existence of Jews and a philosophy of history which predicts their demise, Bauer never seriously questions the latter. Rather, it is the tenacity of Jews which he denounces as contrary to 'the first law of history', namely the human tendency to evolution and progress.[82]

At one point, Bauer propounds the striking claim that since the completion of the Talmud 'the Jews have had no history'.[83] This assertion is not intended to suggest that Jews have been unaffected by change, but rather that they no longer contribute to historical progress (indeed, since the Middle Ages, they are said to have opposed it). Bauer finds confirmation of the radically non-historical nature of Jews in the purported absence of any specifically Jewish contribution to the progress of Western civilisation. In elaborating this extraordinary suggestion, he claims that Jews have failed to make any significant contribution to either political or scientific advancement in Europe.

In defence of the claim that Jews have never had 'a very beneficial influence on the life of states', Bauer makes much of the contemporary fact that what he calls the 'most imperfect state of Europe' (namely Poland) had a Jewish population equal to that of the rest of Europe put together.[84] That Jews chose overwhelmingly to make a home for themselves in 'a state which to a great extent is no state' is said to confirm their inability to become members of a 'real state'.[85]

In defence of the claim that Jews have never contributed to scientific progress, Bauer adopts a twofold strategy against obvious counter-examples: either he fiercely denies the merit of the contribution, or he simply rejects the inclusion of the potential contributor. Moses Maimonides is a victim of the first strategy; his 'unclear, confused and servile sophistry' is contrasted unfavourably with the rigour and insight of the late medieval Christian

---

[79] *Ibid.* 39/42–3.   [80] *Ibid.* 4–5/5.   [81] *Ibid.* 11/12.   [82] *Ibid.* 5/5.   [83] *Ibid.* 82/87.
[84] *Ibid.* 7/7. At the turn of the eighteenth century, just over one million of 1.75 million European Jews lived in Poland (where they enjoyed a significant degree of communal autonomy). On pre-emancipation Polish Jewry, see Artur Eisenbach, *The Emancipation of the Jews in Poland, 1780–1870* (Oxford, 1991) chapter 2.
[85] *Die Judenfrage* 7/7–8.

scholastics.[86] Spinoza is a victim of the second strategy; whilst his philosophical contribution is adjudged significant, Spinoza himself is said to
have been 'no longer a Jew when he created his system'.[87]

(Spinoza provides a revealing illustration of an important development
in Bauer's views. In both his middle-period and late-period writings, Bauer
maintains that Jews are incapable of serious intellectual insight. What alters
is his definition of what it is to be a Jew, and, as a result, his assessment of
intellectual merit in particular cases. In Bauer's middle-period writings –
when he is operating with a religious definition of what it is to be a Jew –
Spinoza is judged to be an original and important thinker but not Jewish. However, in his late-period writings, reflecting and contributing to the
newly emerging literature of racial antisemitism, Bauer adopts a biologi-
cal definition according to which Jews possess a 'different kind of blood'
from the peoples of Christian Europe, a kind of blood which makes their
assimilation impossible and justifies their exclusion from political life. On
this racial definition, Spinoza has to be categorised as Jewish, but – in
order to maintain the claim that Jews are incapable of intellectual insight –
Bauer now judges him to be an entirely unoriginal and inconsequential
thinker.[88])

Given this alleged failure to contribute to political or scientific advancement, Bauer warns against admiring the tenacity of the Jews. There is, he
insists, no dishonour in contributing, and then succumbing, to progress.
We do not, he observes, admire Greek mountains above ancient Greek culture just because the former have survived unchanged whereas the world
of Homer, Sophocles, Pericles, and Aristotle has disappeared.[89] Jewish tenacity, Bauer concludes, far from being admirable, is a 'selfish tenacity' which
attempts to deny 'the true consequences of historical development'.[90]

BAUER AND REAL FREEDOM

Nineteenth-century examples of Germans who held derogatory views about
Judaism or Jewry and yet were prepared to support the removal of the
various discriminatory social and political obstacles to which Jews were
subject are easy to find. (It is a much more difficult task to locate German
Gentiles who supported emancipation but did not hold derogatory views
about Jews or about Judaism.) Hegel provides a well-known and relevant

[86] *Ibid.* 83/88.   [87] *Ibid.* 9/11.
[88] See Bauer, *Das Judenthum in der Fremde*, p. 7. See also Bauer, 'The Present Position of the Jews',
p. 5.
[89] *Die Judenfrage* 12/14.   [90] *Ibid.* 33/36.

example – relevant not least because some of the negative threads from his writings reappear, albeit in a less tempered and nuanced form, in Bauer's own work. Throughout his writings, Hegel expressed derogatory views about both Judaism and Jews. For example, in the so-called *Theologische Jugendschriften*, he characterises the religious culture of Jews as overwhelmingly 'servile' in character, and repeatedly portrays Judaism as the paradigm of a 'positive' – that is, authoritarian and irrational – religion, whose single jealous God is alienated from both the natural and social worlds.[91] Although there is some evidence of development in Hegel's views on these topics – in later works, for example, such remarks are tempered by a more positive account of the contribution to historical progress made by pre-Christian Judaism – he never left such characterisations entirely behind.[92] However, Hegel remained willing to endorse Jewish emancipation. In the *Philosophie des Rechts*, for example, he insists that, since Jews are human beings, they must be given equal rights and social acceptance in a rational state.[93]

In short, that Bauer has a derogatory view of both the (exclusive and tenacious) nature of Jews and their (exclusive, positive, and hypocritical) religion does not fully explain his rejection of their claim to share the same civil and political rights as Christian subjects. His arguments to that end require further examination.

It is apparent that Bauer holds that it is not possible for Jews to possess meaningful liberty. The exegetical difficulty is to make sense of the bewildering variety of distinct, and often opaque, considerations that he puts forward in support of that claim. (Bauer was never a careful or consistent thinker, and at times in these middle-period works he appears to revel in that lack, as if it somehow betokened a more emphatic radicalism.) Some structure can be given to that variety by recognising a distinction that Bauer makes between the inadequate forms of liberty (mere 'emancipation (*Emanzipation*)') that were being sought for German Jews by his contemporaries, and the meaningful liberty ('real freedom (*wahre Freiheit*)') which Bauer had himself identified.[94] The remainder of the present section is concerned with Bauer's conception of 'real

---

[91] See especially 'Der Geist des Christentums'. 'So-called' because of objections to this title (chosen by the editor Hermann Nohl). See, for example, Georg Lukács, *The Young Hegel* (London, 1975) pp. 3–18.

[92] See, for example, Hegel's portrayal of Judaism as the religion of 'sublimity', expressing a necessary stage in the development of the ideal. *Vorlesungen über die Philosophie der Religion*, 233–4/331–2. See also Peter Hodgson, 'The Metamorphosis of Judaism in Hegel's Philosophy of Religion', *The Owl of Minerva*, volume 19, no. 1 (1987) pp. 41–52, and Yirmiyahu Yovel, *Dark Riddle: Hegel, Nietzsche, and the Jews* (Cambridge, 1998) part 1.

[93] See *Philosophie des Rechts* §270A.   [94] *Die Judenfrage* 87/92.

freedom'. (His criticisms of 'emancipation' are discussed in the following section.)

For Bauer, 'real freedom' is not simply one valuable good amongst others; it can be said to form the goal and impulse of human history.[95] Moreover, since human nature is fully and authentically actualised only in circumstances of real freedom, that historical process can be seen as a process of human self-realisation. Real freedom requires that individuals both (cognitively) understand and (practically) acknowledge their common humanity. A society which embodied real freedom would be one in which the 'universality' of human nature was not only understood intellectually, but also fully realised in social and political arrangements. Such a society may not yet exist, but – at least in his more apocalyptic moments (moments which occurred rather often in this period) – Bauer thought of that future, and thereby the end of history, as tantalisingly close. Humankind is said to stand at a historical juncture where a 'sweeping revolution' which could cure 'all ills' is possible.[96] In the present context, three further Bauerian claims about the nature of real freedom are significant.

The first of these three claims is that real freedom is incompatible with religious belief. For Bauer, religion is an interim and inadequate stage in the development of human self-consciousness. The inadequacy of religion consists in its cognitive and practical failings, which prevent the realisation of real freedom. The relevant cognitive failing of religion is that it misidentifies human nature with some sectional characteristic, for example with circumcision or baptism.[97] The practical failing is that religious commitments encourage sectional identifications, which, in turn, generate social conflict; more emphatically, religion is said at one point to form the 'basis' of all civil and political 'prejudice'.[98] In short, religion conflicts with the cognitive and practical conditions for real freedom, namely that we both understand and acknowledge our common humanity. Religion fails to recognise our common humanity (because it embodies sectional, and therefore false, views of human nature), and it sets individuals against one another (because the sectional identification on which religion is based is socially divisive).

This account of the failings of religion helps to flesh out Bauer's account of a society in which our common humanity would be understood and acknowledged. The political condition for the realisation of real freedom

---

[95] See 'Fähigkeit' 175/135.   [96] *Ibid.* 192/147.
[97] See *ibid.* 175/135. For his alternative ('Feuerbachian') account of the cognitive failing of religion, see Leopold, 'The Hegelian Antisemitism of Bruno Bauer', p. 191.
[98] *Die Judenfrage* 95–6/101.

is the replacement of the existing 'Christian state' by the 'higher state-idea (*höhern Staats-Idee*)' which Bauer sometimes calls a 'commonwealth'.[99] On Bauer's account, the 'Christian state' is a state which 'confesses its Christian character and where the Christian religion is designated as the state religion'.[100] As such, it is a state based on sectional privileges. In contrast, the Bauerian 'commonwealth' is a state in which there are 'rights' rather than 'privileges', and in which politics is 'a common affair of all'.[101] For Bauer, it is only in a state which contains no religion that any of this is possible.

It is important to realise that, on Bauer's account, it is not enough that religious privileges be removed from the state, since there are individual as well as political conditions for the establishment of a 'commonwealth'. Real freedom also requires that individuals adopt what might be called Bauerian atheism. There are two elements to this Bauerian atheism. Its negative requirement is that individuals abandon their religious beliefs. Its positive requirement is that individuals replace those abandoned religious beliefs with (a rather under-described) identification with humankind. In short, the Bauerian atheist not only has to abandon his previous religious convictions but also has 'to make the cause of humanity his own'.[102]

(Note that this first claim about real freedom constitutes the only significant point, in either of the two main texts under examination, at which Bauer develops a criticism which applies to both Christianity and Judaism without obvious distinction.[103] Indeed, there is a significant tension between the overall trend of these middle-period writings, in which the universality of Christianity is contrasted with the exclusiveness of Judaism, and this particular thread in Bauer's argument, in which Christianity falls foul of the sectional identification at the heart of all religions. The context of these claims is perhaps relevant here. That dominant account, emphasising the universality of Christianity, seems to prevail when Bauer is attacking Judaism. However, when he turns to consider the advantages of Bauerian atheism, he introduces this subordinate claim dismissing religion in general.)

The second of these three claims (about the nature of real freedom) is that Christianity has a greater conceptual affinity with real freedom than

[99] *Ibid.* 20/23. See also Douglas Moggach, 'Republican Rigorism and Emancipation in Bruno Bauer', in Moggach, *The New Hegelians*, pp. 114–35.
[100] *Die Judenfrage* 68/70.   [101] *Ibid.* 88/93.
[102] *Ibid.* 92/97. See also *ibid.* 60/62 and 'Fähigkeit' 177/137.
[103] See *Die Judenfrage* 19/22. As Marx paraphrases Bauer, both Jew and Christian have to recognise their respective religions 'as nothing more than *different stages in the development of the human spirit*, as snake-skins cast off by *history*, and *man* as the snake which wore them'. 'Zur Judenfrage' 348–9/148/213.

does Judaism. Given the link between real freedom and universality – and the dominant claim of these middle-period writings that, unlike Judaism, Christianity, with its 'boundless (*schrankenlos*) idea of humankind', recognises the universality of humankind – Bauer can now rehearse the purported superiority of Christianity in terms of its conceptual affinity with real freedom.[104] He does not hesitate to describe this conceptual affinity in evaluative terms. In short, Bauer insists that, in standing closer to real freedom, 'Christianity stands far above Judaism, the Christian far above the Jew'.[105]

The third and last of these claims (about the nature of real freedom) is that Christianity is somehow more germane than Judaism to the achievement of real freedom. This greater relevance is elaborated in two directions.

Bauer suggests that, relative to Christians, Jews have greater difficulty in making the break with religion that is required by real freedom. His reasoning here draws on the conceptual affinity between Christianity and real freedom, which seemingly makes it easier for Christians to adopt Bauerian atheism. Ever the good Hegelian, Bauer expresses this comparative ease in terms of the conceptual progression which is embodied in both historical progress and individual development. Just as humankind, in order to reach real freedom, has to pass through Judaism and Christianity in turn, so also the individual Jew 'has to break not only with his Jewish essence, but also with . . . the completion of his religion, with a development which has remained for him foreign and towards which he has not acceded'.[106] Bauer concludes that 'the Christian has only one stage; namely to surmount his religion in order to abandon religion in general', whereas 'the Jew has it harder if he wants to raise himself to freedom'.[107] Bauer does not maintain that such a (twofold) leap is impossible, but there is every suggestion that he considers it highly unlikely.

In addition, Bauer distinguishes between the historical consequences of Jewish and Christian apostasy. Appealing to the two elements of Bauerian atheism – the (negative) absence of religious beliefs and the (positive) identification with humankind – Bauer suggests that Jewish, unlike Christian, faithlessness can fulfil only the first of these conditions. For the purposes of this comparison, Bauer treats both religions as embodying concerns the pursuit of which is somehow constrained and compromised by their religious kernel. When individuals abandon their religious commitments, they are portrayed as releasing the pursuit of those concerns from the constraint of religion. The difference between Judaism and Christianity, in this context,

---

[104] 'Fähigkeit' 183/140. See also *ibid.* 192/147.   [105] *Ibid.* 192/147.   [106] *Ibid.* 195/149.   [107] *Ibid.*

rests on the different concerns that they are said to contain. Judaism, for Bauer, embodies only particularistic interests. Thus, when Jews abandon their religious law, he maintains that it results only in the existence of a few more egoists who can now furnish their particularistic interests unhindered by, for example, dietary laws.[108] There is, it appears, no wider result. Christianity, in contrast, embodies universal concerns. Bauer concludes that if Christianity, particularly Christianity in its highest (Protestant) form, were to be 'dissolved', it would give us 'complete' and 'free' men capable of the 'highest creations'.[109] It appears that the supposed Christian concern for universal interests, freed from its religious shell, would automatically reappear in the form of full-blown Bauerian atheism with its positive concern for the whole of humankind. Whereas the irreligious Jew 'gives nothing to humankind if he disregards his restricted law for himself', the Christian apostate, in striking contrast, 'gives humankind everything there is to take if he dissolves his Christian essence'.[110]

Left-Hegelians are often (and correctly) characterised as believing that religious alienation has a foundational status. That is, left-Hegelians typically believe that once religious unfreedom is overthrown, all other constraints, including social and political restrictions, will easily and automatically be removed. However, for Bauer, it would appear that it is only the overthrow of *Christian* religious alienation which has that effect. Humanity may be on the verge of a sweeping revolution which can cure all ills, but it appears that Jews can do little to hasten its progress. Only the *Christian* apostate, Bauer maintains, contributes to 'a struggle which is against unfreedom in general', whereas the Jew who rejects Judaism simply 'lifts a restricted law for his own best interests'.[111] Judaism, as a result, stands not only 'far below' Christianity in Bauer's conceptual hierarchy, but also 'far below the possibility of freedom and a revolution which decides the fate of the whole of humankind'.[112]

BAUER AND EMANCIPATION

Bauer presents a bewildering variety of objections to the forms of emancipation that were sought by, and on behalf of, German Jews. Making sense of those various objections is far from easy. However, some structure can be lent to Bauer's argument by identifying the three main emancipatory strategies to which his contemporaries were attached. According to what I will call the 'conversion strategy', meaningful liberty for German Jews

[108] *Ibid.* 186/143.   [109] *Ibid.*   [110] *Ibid.*   [111] *Ibid.*   [112] *Ibid.* 192/147.

would follow from their conversion to Christianity. According to what I will call the 'extension strategy', meaningful liberty for German Jews would follow from the extension to them – by the existing Christian state – of the contemporary privileges enjoyed by the majority population. According to what I will call the 'French strategy', meaningful liberty for German Jews would follow from the establishment of a religiously neutral state in which civil and political rights were distributed irrespective of religious beliefs.

Bauer has a rather blunt knock-down argument against all of these strategies. Since they each leave either the religious nature of the state and/or the religious nature of the individual untouched, all three strategies fall short of the demands of meaningful liberty ('real freedom'). However, the most striking feature of these middle-period writings is the additional considerations that Bauer uses to bolster his conclusion that meaningful liberty for Jews, in particular, is not possible. It is these additional considerations, rather than his knock-down argument, which most provoked Bauer's contemporaries, and which form the primary subject matter of this section.

According to the 'conversion' strategy, meaningful liberty for German Jews would follow from their conversion to Christianity. Bauer rejects the view that a Jew could become a 'free human being' through baptism as a 'fantasy and self-deception (*Einbildung und Selbsttäuschung*)'.[113] Apart from its failure to fulfil the conditions for meaningful liberty – since it leaves the religiosity of both individual and state intact – Bauer puts forward two additional objections to the strategy.

Bauer's first (additional) objection is that conversion to Christianity is always insincere. Conversion purports to be concerned with promoting liberty but is, in reality, always motivated by a prudential desire for personal advantage. Accordingly, judged as an attempt to gain liberty 'it can no longer be sincere (*aufrichtig*)'.[114] (Bauer offers no evidence to support this empirical, and contestable, claim that conversion is always motivated by the instrumental calculation that it will promote self-interest.[115])

Bauer's second (additional) objection is that, considered in these prudential terms, conversion fails. Both Christians and Jews, he maintains, are 'servants and bondsmen', and conversion 'only exchanges the one

[113] *Ibid.* 193/148.   [114] *Ibid.*
[115] On the sincerity of conversion, see Carl Cohen, 'The Road to Conversion', *Leo Baeck Institute Year Book*, volume 6 (1961) pp. 259–79; Steven M. Lowenstein, *The Berlin Jewish Community. Enlightenment, Family, and Crisis, 1770–1830* (Oxford, 1994) pp. 168ff; and Deborah Hertz, *Jewish High Society in Old Regime Berlin* (New Haven, 1988) chapter 7. Well-known counter-examples to Bauer's claim include Andreas Gottschalk, who – as a doctor, he was already in an occupation open to Jews – converted only after sincere study on the (contestable) ground that Christianity provided a better foundation for socialism.

privileged class for the other, the one which is allied with more drudgery for the other which appears more profitable'.[116] The reference here to an 'apparent' advantage is deliberate. Despite the overwhelming mass of evidence to the contrary (some of which I surveyed earlier in this chapter), Bauer denies that German Jews are peculiarly disadvantaged relative to the majority population. He insists that the possession of civil rights by the majority population in a state which is not yet a 'commonwealth' is wholly ineffective and non-advantageous.[117] Indeed, Bauer goes on to propound the extraordinary view that the situation of those subjects of the Christian state who possess civil rights is 'even worse' than those who do not have them.[118] He maintains that the unvarnished discrimination to which German Jews are subject is preferable to the 'coating of glamour' which surrounds the lives of Christian rights bearers.[119] (The implausibility of this extraordinary view does not need belabouring here.)

(Since it is premised on the possibility of an individual escaping classification as a member of a discriminated-against minority, rather than on the removal of that discrimination, some may baulk at my description of conversion as an 'emancipatory' strategy. However, conversion was a route that a significant number of German Jews took in the first half of the nineteenth century, especially in order to free themselves from occupational restrictions.[120] The importance of occupational freedom should not be underestimated. Whilst not necessarily liberating anyone from popular prejudice, or indeed self-doubt, conversion did, for example, enable Eduard Gans to teach at the University of Berlin, and Marx's father to practise law in Trier.[121])

---

[116] 'Fähigkeit' 193/147–8.   [117] *Die Judenfrage* 88/93.   [118] *Ibid.*   [119] *Ibid.*

[120] Jacob Toury estimates that in Germany between 1800 and 1870 there were some 11,000 conversions – a statistic which scarcely supports the picture of an 'epidemic'. The visibility and significance of conversion resulted from its occurring predominately amongst elite groups in urban areas, and, to an extent, in waves (for example, after the failure of reform in 1815). See Toury, *Soziale und politische Geschichte der Juden in Deutschland*, p. 53. For a stark individual case study, see Warren I. Cohn, 'The Moses Isaacs Family Trust – Its History and Significance', *Leo Baeck Institute Year Book*, volume 18 (1973) pp. 267–80.

[121] On Gans, see Hanns Günther Reissner, 'Rebellious Dilemmas: The Case Histories of Eduard Gans and Some of His Partisans', *Leo Baeck Institute Year Book*, volume 2 (1957) pp. 179–93; Hans Günther Reissner, *Eduard Gans: Ein Leben im Vormärz* (Tübingen, 1965); and Norbert Waszek, *Eduard Gans (1797–1839): Hegelianer–Jude–Europäer: Texte und Dokumente* (Frankfurt am Main, 1991). It was 1847 before an unconverted Jew (the physiologist Robert Remak) was appointed at a Prussian university. See Pulzer, *Jews and the German State*, pp. 92–3. On Heinrich Marx, see Heinz Monz, *Karl Marx: Grundlagen der Entwicklung zu Leben und Werk* (Trier, 1973) chapters 17–19; Lewis S. Feuer, 'The Conversion of Karl Marx's Father', *Jewish Journal of Sociology*, volume 14 (1972) pp. 149–66; and Saul K. Padover, 'The Baptism of Karl Marx's Family', *Midstream*, volume 34 (1978) pp. 36–44. The description of Heinrich Marx's conversion as exemplifying 'ambition in its gross form' seems unjustified. David Vital, *A People Apart: The Jews in Europe, 1789–1939* (Oxford, 1999) p. 125.

According to the 'extension' strategy, meaningful liberty for German Jews would follow from the extension to them of the existing privileges enjoyed by the majority population. This strategy accepted the existence of a Christian state in which civil rights functioned as sectional privileges (granted by 'birth or grace') rather than universal moral entitlements.[122] However, its proponents – objecting to the inequality in the existing distribution of those privileges – maintained that, without any fundamental alteration in the nature of the state, liberty would result from the extension to non-Christians of the civil and political rights held by the Christian majority. Apart from its failure to fulfil the conditions for meaningful liberty (since it left the religiosity of the individual and the state intact), Bauer advances four additional objections to the 'extension' strategy.

Bauer's first (additional) objection is that a strategy which involves a Christian state extending privilege to non-Christians is somehow inconsistent. A Christian state, he maintains, is a state which 'confesses its Christian character and where the Christian religion is designated as the state religion'.[123] Moreover, since Christianity and Judaism are 'mutually exclusive', Bauer concludes that a Christian state must, by its very nature, discriminate against Jews.[124] Since the Christian state is defined by its commitment to sectional privilege, any extension of the existing privileges of the Christian majority to the minority Jewish population would undermine its essential nature. (This claim, that a Christian state could not extend privilege to Jews *and* remain a Christian state, was a popular one amongst contemporary conservative opponents of emancipation.[125])

To its proponents, of course, 'extension' was a strategy that had already been tentatively introduced, and subsequently reversed, when several German states extended 'full civil rights' to Jews during the Wars of Liberation.[126] Bauer, however, reinterprets this extension of privilege as a temporary product of 'tempestuous times' in which the Christian state was on the verge of disintegration.[127] He insists that the experience of the Wars of Liberation had not demonstrated that the extension strategy was a stable or permanent solution, but only that, during 'periods of stress', the Christian state – 'in need and in danger of its life' – may make momentary concessions to a 'higher state-idea'.[128]

Bauer's second (additional) objection challenges the claim, to which he believes advocates of the 'extension' strategy are committed, that in

---

[122] *Die Judenfrage* 88/92.   [123] *Ibid.* 68/70.   [124] *Ibid.* 53/56.
[125] See, for example, the *Kölnische Zeitung* editorial, dated 6 July 1842, quoted in Magnus, *Jewish Emancipation in a German City*, p. 102.
[126] *Die Judenfrage* 59/62.   [127] *Ibid.*   [128] *Ibid.* 20/23.

discriminating against Jews the Christian state behaves improperly. He maintains that in a Christian state 'the oppression of the Jews is no wrong'.[129] The rationale for this remarkable view rests on two significant assumptions: that it is in the nature of the Christian state to discriminate against Jews (the Christian state is a state 'which denied and had to deny liberty to the Jews');[130] and that improper behaviour is behaviour which is not in accordance with the nature of the relevant agent. (The highly counter-intuitive consequences of this second assumption should be apparent.) The Christian state, Bauer concludes, does not behave improperly when it discriminates against Jews, because such actions embody no 'inconsistency', no 'repudiation of its basic principles'.[131]

Bauer's third (additional) objection is that the 'extension' strategy is not aimed at achieving meaningful liberty for all, but rather at increasing the material benefits received by the minority population. Moreover, he denies that this prudential goal would be achieved by extending the privileges of the Christian majority to the Jewish minority. As already seen, Bauer maintains that German subjects who possess civil rights, whether by birth or by grace, not only have no advantages, but may even be disadvantaged, in comparison with German Jews. Even if Jews were somehow to achieve the same civil rights as the majority population, they would not thereby be materially benefited. Indeed, on Bauer's account, it appears that they would be worse off as a result.

Bauer's fourth (additional) objection is that the strategy of extending, rather than overthrowing, privilege is misguided from the perspective of those who genuinely seek liberty. The only meaningful liberty for Bauer is real freedom, and the extension of privilege is portrayed as delaying rather than facilitating its achievement. In order to motivate support for this claim, Bauer suggests that privilege in general will only fall as a result of a direct assault, and that such a direct assault would be delayed if, and to the extent that, the 'extension' strategy came to monopolise the agenda for social change. Pressing for Jewish emancipation, he maintains, distracts attention from other kinds of suffering. As a result, the 'advocates of the Jews' are guilty of neglecting their 'fellow sufferers' in the absolutist state. (These 'fellow sufferers' include, of course, those Christian subjects who possess civil rights, and are thereby said to be worse off than the Jewish minority.[132])

According to the 'French' strategy, meaningful liberty for German Jews would follow from the establishment of a religiously neutral state in which

[129] *Ibid.* 68/70. See also *ibid.* 101/107.   [130] *Ibid.* 3/3.   [131] *Ibid.* 92/97.   [132] See *ibid.* 87/92.

civil and political rights were distributed irrespective of religious beliefs (which would thereby be relegated to the status of a private concern). Amongst Bauer's contemporaries, of course, there were many German admirers of French solutions to political questions. (Arnold Ruge, for example, had insisted that in political affairs 'the French have set the example'.[133]) Bauer claims that to these enthusiastic observers of French politics the July Revolution had appeared to 'abolish the state religion as such, liberated it [the state] from every clerical influence, and made participation in all political and civil rights independent of religious and church affiliation'.[134] Bauer characterises this as a 'juste milieu' solution, that is, as a solution which 'stops half-way', removing religion from the state without removing it from civil society.[135] (It is in the context of criticising such 'half-way' solutions that Bauer describes Judaism as 'an evil (*Übel*)', and insists that an evil is thoroughly 'abolished' only if it is 'torn out by the roots'.)[136]

(Some commentators have identified this 'French' solution – abandoning religious differences to the private sphere, and granting equal civil and political freedoms to all individuals – as Bauer's own.[137] In its elementary variant, this interpretation makes the mistake of ignoring the second of his two conditions for meaningful liberty, namely that individuals must abandon their religious belief in favour of Bauerian atheism. However, a sophisticated version of this interpretation does not ignore this second condition, but rather portrays it as the automatic result of establishing the first condition – that is, a state which privileges no religion – for meaningful liberty.[138] However, although one or two passages in *Die Judenfrage* might suggest something like this account, it lacks widespread or unambiguous textual support.[139] Moreover, the suggested interpretation sits uneasily with Bauer's fierce hostility to the 'juste milieu' solution. It is hard to understand why Bauer would have objected so vehemently to the half-heartedness of the 'French' strategy, if he had really believed that creating a secular state would automatically lead to individuals abandoning their religious beliefs.)

Apart from its failure to fulfil the conditions for meaningful liberty (since it leaves individual religiosity intact), Bauer offers an additional objection

---

[133] Ruge, 'Selbstkritik' 101/256.   [134] *Die Judenfrage* 64–5/67.   [135] *Ibid.* 72/75.   [136] *Ibid.* 3/4.
[137] See, for example, Sander L. Gilman, *Jewish Self-Hatred: Anti-Semitism and the Hidden Language of the Jews* (Baltimore, 1986) p. 191.
[138] See Daniel Brudney, *Marx's Attempt to Leave Philosophy* (Cambridge MA, 1998) p. 125.
[139] For such a suggestion, see Bauer's remark that there 'is no religion anymore as soon as there is no privileged religion'. *Die Judenfrage* 66/69. Significantly, this comment is quoted in 'Zur Judenfrage' 350/149/215.

to the 'French' strategy. Proponents of this strategy are said to rely on an assumption that is false, namely that Jews are capable of being good citizens. Bauer maintains that that there exists a 'basic contradiction' between the religious commitments of Jews and membership of this liberal state. Jews are, by their very nature, unsuited to citizenship.[140] Bauer identifies three necessary conditions for citizenship in a 'juste milieu' state which Jews cannot 'sincerely' fulfil.[141]

The first of these conditions is that citizens must recognise a distinction between religion and politics. Bauer insists that Jews are incapable of doing this. He maintains that politics 'is nothing but religion' for Jews, and that religion, as a result, cannot ever be treated as a private matter.[142] Indeed, Bauer maintains that nothing has a purely secular significance for Jews. 'Everything in Judaism', he claims, 'is divine, nothing human. Everything is religion'; even the washing up, he remarks mockingly, is regarded as a religious rite.[143] (The disdainful allusion is to the cleaning of cooking vessels and cutlery on the eve of Passover.) For Bauer, a Jew who subscribes to a distinction 'between civil and religious laws and still believes himself to be a Jew is under an illusion'.[144]

The second of these conditions is that citizens must place the demands of politics above those of religion. Bauer insists that, even if Jews were able to recognise the distinction between religion and politics, historical evidence shows that, whenever these two spheres conflict, they are unable to put political above religious commands.[145] Bauer appeals to the evidence provided by the so-called 'Great Sanhedrin', where the most important speeches were delivered in Hebrew and then translated into French. He suggests that this ordering reflects the low status attached to citizenship by French Jews.[146] For the Jew, Bauer remarks, 'the Hebrew is the original, the real, the true, the kernel; the French is the translation, the unreal, the offprint, the illusion, the shell'.[147] (The so-called 'Great Sanhedrin' was called by Napoleon in 1807 to provide the rabbinically sanctioned answers to a series of official questions about the relationship between French Jews and the majority population, and especially about the willingness of the former to participate fully as citizens and patriots.) The same meagre evaluation

---

[140] *Die Judenfrage* 107/115. Most German liberals believed that German Jews currently (but not inevitably) lacked the requisite *Bildung* for citizenship. They disagreed about whether such 'education' was a consequence of, or a prior condition for, the removal of legal discrimination.

[141] *Ibid.* 106/113.   [142] *Ibid.* 108/115. See also *ibid.* 113/122.   [143] *Ibid.* 108/115–6.

[144] *Ibid.* 109/117.   [145] *Ibid.* 112–13/121.

[146] On the 'Great Sanhedrin', see Simon Schwarzfuchs, *Napoleon, the Jews and the Sanhedrin* (London, 1979). Marx's uncle, Samuel Marx, was a member of the Sanhedrin.

[147] *Die Judenfrage* 111/119.

of citizenship is reflected, Bauer suggests, in the enlistment of German Jews in the Wars of Liberation. He insists that enlistment in the army occurred only after Jews had been given permission by their 'Synagogues and Rabbis'. The real attitude of Jews towards their religious and political duties was demonstrated by such examples. For the Jew, Bauer insists, the religious law always stands in principle above the state 'which receives only a precarious privilege'.[148] (The Wars of Liberation were the first occasion on which German Jews had performed military service on any scale; some fifty-five Jews died at Waterloo, and between 1813 and 1815 seventy-two Jews were awarded the Iron Cross.[149])

Bauer's argumentative strategy is, as ever, noteworthy. The judgement of the so-called 'Great Sanhedrin' regarding the attitude of Judaism towards the state, and the enthusiastic participation of German Jews in the Wars of Liberation, were examples which were widely used by advocates of emancipation to support the claim that Jews could be good citizens. Bauer appeals to these same historical examples in order to draw the opposite conclusion. As long as the Jew remains Jewish, Bauer insists that his 'Jewish and restricted (*beschränktes*) essence always and at last carries away the victory over his human and political duties'.[150]

The third of these conditions is that citizens must believe in the fundamental moral equality of all citizens. Bauer claims that this is a belief which Jews cannot accept with sincerity. He maintains that the endorsement of such universalist views by contemporary Jews is disingenuous. The religious actions of the Jew, Bauer suggests, 'refute his prettiest speeches about equality and humanity'.[151] Bauer notes that dietary laws presuppose that all Gentiles are unclean, and claims that they thereby constitute proof that the Jew 'regards non-Jews not as his equals, not as fellow men'.[152]

The failure of Jews to fulfil these three conditions for citizenship is not, on Bauer's account, a contingent one. Those Jews who appeal to the excellence of their religious morality as proof of their capacity to be good citizens have, he suggests, misunderstood the nature of, and qualifications for, citizenship in the 'juste milieu' state.[153] Since emancipation on the 'French' model presupposes these qualifications for citizenship, anyone

---

[148] 'Fähigkeit' 177/136.
[149] The symbolic importance of these events is vividly portrayed in Moritz Oppenheim's well-known painting 'The Homecoming of a Jewish Volunteer from the Wars of Liberation to His Traditionally Observant Family'. On Oppenheim ('the first Jewish painter'), see Ismar Schorsch, *From Text to Context: The Turn to History in Modern Judaism* (Hanover NH, 1994) chapter 5.
[150] 'Fähigkeit' 176/136.   [151] *Die Judenfrage* 30/32.   [152] *Ibid.* 30/33.   [153] 'Fähigkeit' 176/136.

seeking in this way to emancipate German Jewry is in the same position
as someone who 'wanted to wash the Moor white'.[154] The 'emancipated
Jew', Bauer concludes, is a contradiction in terms. Jews are capable only of
counterfeit citizenship.

(Note that what I am calling the 'French' strategy had not, according
to Bauer, been fully implemented in France. He maintains that the July
Revolution had failed to abolish completely the legal protection of religious
privilege, because some laws – such as the 'Luneau amendment' to child
labour legislation making Sunday a compulsory day of rest – still protected
the advantages of a 'privileged majority'.[155] Nonetheless, I consider my
adopted terminology appropriate, because the attempt, as yet not wholly
successful, to realise this strategy was widely associated with France, not
least by Bauer himself.)

For Bauer, the estrangement of Jews from the modern world would
appear to be fairly comprehensive. Their clannish and tenacious nature,
which reflects their exclusive, positive, and hypocritical religion, is not
only incompatible with the real freedom which forms the subject and end
of human history – an end which Jews have neither an affinity with nor an
effect upon – but also makes them unsuitable recipients of more mundane
forms of contemporary emancipation. Bauer maintains that baptism does
not offer German Jews the possibility of escape from disadvantage, that
the exclusion of Jews from the privileges of the majority in the Christian
state is no wrong, and that Jews are incapable of fulfilling the conditions
of citizenship in a modern constitutional polity.

Bauer dismisses the idea that this comprehensive estrangement from the
modern world might be regretted. Regret, he suggests, is an appropriate
response towards those who find themselves in an unwelcome situation
only if two further conditions are satisfied. First, some more welcome alternative situation must be possible. Second, the individuals in question must
not be responsible for their own predicament. In the case of Jews, neither of
these further conditions is deemed to obtain. First, Bauer insists that Jews
could never feel properly at home in a world 'which they did not make, did
not help to make, which is contrary to their unchanged nature'.[156] Jews, he
maintains, are 'of necessity oppressed and their suffering is incurable'.[157] Second, Bauer insists that the discrimination and opprobrium which Jews have
received is wholly a result of their own behaviour. For example, he rejects
the suggestion that the exploitation of Gentiles by Jews through usury
was the result of the exclusion of the latter from other forms of economic

---

[154] *Ibid.*   [155] *Die Judenfrage* 70/72. See also *ibid.* 72/75.   [156] *Ibid.* 2/3.   [157] *Ibid.* 14/16.

activity.[158] Bauer asks (rhetorically) whether it is possible for Jews to have been excluded from the structure of estates and corporations if they 'had not excluded themselves' (by regarding themselves 'as a nation').[159] Indeed, Bauer suggests that those (such as Dohm) who, whilst admitting that 'the attitude, the character, and the condition of the Jews' are deplorable, would seek to blame those factors on the oppression that Jews have suffered are guilty of special pleading.[160] On Bauer's account, Jews were themselves to blame for the oppression they suffered 'because they provoked it by their adherence to their law, their language, to their whole way of life'.[161]

In another provocative rhetorical reversal, Bauer suggests that subscribing to a view of their historical innocence does Jews a serious injustice (namely the 'injustice' of positing as an effect what was actually a cause). The Jews were the first to practise exclusiveness, and what they did to others, he remarks ominously, they are now getting back in 'full measure'.[162] Indeed, at one point, Bauer suggests that discrimination against Jews is merited, not only because it is provoked by their own actions, but also because that discrimination reflects the Jew's 'own wishes'.[163] Since the Jew 'regards himself as something special compared with the Christian', the Christian state is only respecting that claim when, in turn, it treats the Jew 'as something special' by discriminating against him.[164]

Bauer does briefly consider one further source of possible regret at the fate of modern Jewry. He appears willing to bemoan the fact that the oppression which they have suffered has never had a salutary effect on Jews. Unlike the early Christian communities, for example, who were improved by discrimination, Bauer notes that Jews 'have never discovered a moral principle which might renew the shape of the world or of their own nation'.[165] However, he cautions that although this failure might be regretted it can scarcely occasion surprise. Oppression, Bauer notes, can improve only those groups which embody the principles of historical progress.[166]

In short, Bauer's overall conclusion is that some familiar claims about prejudice and discrimination need to be rethought. Jews, he insists, are the instigators, and not the victims, of discrimination, and, accordingly, no real compunction should be felt at their estrangement from the modern world.

RECONSTRUCTING BAUER'S CONCERNS

Whereas Bauer's middle-period writings discuss the nature of Jews and Judaism, in 'Zur Judenfrage' Marx provides an account of the characteristic

---

[158] *Ibid.* 8–9/10. [159] *Ibid.* 9–10/10–11. [160] *Ibid.* 4/4. [161] *Ibid.* 4/5.
[162] *Ibid.* 53/56. [163] *Ibid.* 57/60. [164] *Ibid.* 57/59. [165] *Ibid.* 13/15. [166] *Ibid.* 23–4/27.

achievements and limitations of what he calls political emancipation. Despite the obvious connection here – namely that political emancipation was the kind of liberty being sought by, and on behalf of, German Jews – any comparison of the two authors is complicated by these divergent subject matters. Whereas in the *Kritik* Marx stays close to Hegel's text, in 'Zur Judenfrage' he tends rather to use Bauer's comments as a starting point for more wide-ranging reflections of his own.

Marx identifies two claims as central to Bauer's rejection of Jewish emancipation: that 'the Jew by his very nature cannot be emancipated', and that 'the Christian state is by its very *nature* incapable of emancipating the Jew'.[167] Although Marx rejects both these claims, he considers them worth examining because they raise wider issues about the nature of the modern state.[168] Marx can make this assertion only because he interprets these two claims in a distinctive manner, thereby shifting the focus of attention away from Bauer's express concerns (the character of Jews and of Judaism) and towards the issue in which he is himself primarily interested (the nature of political emancipation). I will start by considering Marx's rejection of the first of these Bauerian claims. (Marx's rejection of the second Bauerian claim is discussed in the section that follows.)

Marx begins by restating Bauer's first claim – that 'the Jew by his very nature cannot be emancipated' – in a more general form, that is, as asserting that religious individuals cannot (by virtue of their religious nature) be the recipients of meaningful liberty.[169] There are three notable elements to this reformulation: Marx treats Bauer's reference to emancipation as a reference to meaningful liberty (that is, Marx neither acknowledges nor utilises Bauer's distinction between 'real freedom' and 'emancipation'); Marx assumes that political emancipation is a form of meaningful liberty (that is, he treats Bauer as making a claim about the kind of political freedom available in the modern social world); and Marx treats Bauer's claim about the nature of Jews as a particular variant of a more general claim about religion (namely that religious individuals cannot, by virtue of their religious nature, be emancipated).

This last point is worth emphasising, not least because of the close attention and extensive comment that Marx's observations regarding Judaism and Jewry have received. In the first part of 'Zur Judenfrage', Marx treats Judaism as representative of '*religion* in general', and not, like Bauer, as the embodiment of a particularly retrograde and abhorrent form of belief.[170]

---

[167] 'Zur Judenfrage' 347–8/147/212.   [168] See *ibid.* 349/148/214.
[169] *Ibid.* 347–8/147/212.   [170] *Ibid.* 353/151/218.

Similarly, Marx treats Jews as representative of 'the *religious* human being in general', and not, like Bauer, as the embodiment of a particularly retrograde and abhorrent form of humanity.[171] (Many readers have found Marx's remarks in the second part of 'Zur Judenfrage' to be very different in character, and those comments are examined separately towards the end of this chapter.)

According to the initial reformulation of Bauer's first claim, religious individuals cannot, by virtue of their religious natures, experience meaningful liberty. Since Marx assumes that political emancipation is a form of meaningful liberty, he portrays Bauer as claiming that political emancipation is incompatible with individual religious commitment, that modern citizenship requires that 'the Jew give up Judaism and that humankind in general give up religion'.[172]

Marx denies that atheism, in this familiar negative sense, is a condition for modern citizenship.[173] Indeed, he maintains that the political state does not have 'the right (*das Recht*)' to demand that Jews, or indeed any individuals, abandon their religion.[174] (The young Marx's much misunderstood attitude towards rights is discussed later in this chapter.)

Since political emancipation is a defining feature of the modern social world, Marx appeals to empirical examples to substantiate this rejection of Bauer's account of its conditions. Germany, of course, cannot provide such evidence, because the modern state is absent from German historical reality, if not its philosophical *Traumgeschichte* (see Chapter 2).[175] However, whereas in the *Kritik* France and America had been treated together as exemplars of political modernity, Marx now accepts that France may be an inappropriate example of political emancipation, not because, as in Germany, political emancipation is unknown, but rather because of the 'incompleteness' of its political emancipation.[176] That is, at least, for the purposes of argument, Marx accepts Bauer's claim that political modernisation in France is significantly compromised by the legislative protection of the religion of the majority. Instead, Marx appeals to the 'free states' of North America – there are subsequent references to New England, New Hampshire, and Pennsylvania – as evidence of the relationship between religion and the modern state in 'its characteristic and pure form'.[177] Only in these American states, Marx suggests, does 'the political state' exist in its 'fully developed form'.[178]

[171] *Ibid.*   [172] *Ibid.* 350/149/215.   [173] See *ibid.*   [174] *Ibid.* 351/150/216.
[175] See *ibid.* 348/147/213.   [176] *Ibid.* 351/150/216. See also *Die heilige Familie* 122/115.
[177] 'Zur Judenfrage' 351/150/216.   [178] *Ibid.*

Marx utilises empirical evidence from three published sources (two French and one English): *Marie ou l'esclavage aux Etats-Unis*, a novel by Gustave de Beaumont; the work of Beaumont's eminent friend Alexis de Tocqueville, *De la démocratie en Amérique* (of which Marx used only the first volume, published in 1835);[179] and Thomas Hamilton's *Men and Manners in America*, which Marx read in German translation.[180] (One modern scholar has expressed surprise at Marx's failure to indicate that Beaumont's work was different in 'kind' to the others.[181] However, the fictional element of *Marie*, as Beaumont happily acknowledged, was a largely transparent pretext for an unremittingly empirical account of American society. Nearly half of the book consists of purely descriptive notes and appendixes.)

On Marx's reading, these three authorities all concur in identifying a striking contrast between the political and the civil fate of religion in America. On the one hand, in many American states, there is no established religion, and there are no religious conditions for the exercise of political privileges; on the other, these sources reliably inform us that North America is the land of 'religiosity *par excellence*'.[182] According to Beaumont, for example, people in the United States do not believe that an atheist could ever be 'an honest man'.[183]

It is the civil element of this contrast between the political and civil fate of religion which casts doubt on the alleged incompatibility of religious commitment and political emancipation. Marx contends that the empirical evidence from the land of '*complete* political emancipation' reveals not merely that religion still exists, but that it exists 'in a *fresh* and *vigorous* form'.[184] The point is an important one. He concludes that 'the existence of religion does not contradict the perfection of the state', and that Bauer's insistence on the incompatibility of religious commitment and political emancipation is mistaken.[185]

Indeed, this American evidence is said to reveal the characteristic 'form and manner' of political emancipation.[186] On Marx's account, political emancipation 'neither abolishes nor tries to abolish man's *real* religiosity'.[187]

[179] That Marx read only the first volume might be regretted, since Tocqueville's second volume (published in 1840) is, in some respects, more interesting; it is both more general (less about America) and somewhat bleaker (more pessimistic about the fate of continental Europe).
[180] Marx read and took notes from a translation by L. Hout, published in 1834. See *MEGA②* 4, 2, pp. 266–75.
[181] S. S. Prawer, *Karl Marx and World Literature* (Oxford, 1976) p. 62.
[182] 'Zur Judenfrage' 352/151/217.
[183] Gustave de Beaumont, *Marie ou l'esclavage aux Etats-Unis, tableau de mœurs Américaines*, volume 2 (Brussels, 1835) p. 217. Marx refers to this claim in 'Zur Judenfrage' 352/151/217.
[184] 'Zur Judenfrage' 352/151/217.   [185] *Ibid.*   [186] *Ibid.* 353/151/218.   [187] *Ibid.* 357/155/222.

Rather, the political emancipation of Jews, Christians, and 'religious man in general', consists in 'the *emancipation of the state* from Judaism, from Christianity, from *religion* in general'.[188] There are, on this account, two elements in the achievement of political emancipation: society separates out into a political and civil realm, and religion is 'exiled' to the sphere of civil society.[189] A parallel transformation is effected in each individual. The separation of the civil and political is accomplished by the 'splitting (*Spaltung*)' of man into his *public* and his *private* self (each individual is separated into 'Jew and citizen, Protestant and citizen, religious man and citizen'), and religion is 'exiled' to the sphere of personal belief.[190] As Marx elaborates in *Die heilige Familie*, the state emancipates itself politically from religion 'by emancipating itself from *state religion* and leaving religion to itself within civil society', whilst individuals emancipate themselves polit-ically from religion 'by regarding it no longer as a *public* matter but as a *private matter*'.[191]

Although much of 'Zur Judenfrage' is ostensibly concerned with religion, it is readily apparent that the young Marx's real interests lie elsewhere. Not all of his references to religion are to be understood literally, and, even when dealing with religion as such, his concern is often with religion as the representative 'spiritual' precondition of the modern state. Moreover, Marx holds that the modern state has 'material' as well as 'spiritual' preconditions, and that these two different kinds of precondition behave in analogous ways. The representative 'material' precondition of the modern state is private property, and its fate broadly parallels that of religion.

In the first place, as confirmed by the experience of free states in North America, 'the political annulment of private property does not mean the abolition of private property', but rather its relegation to the non-political sphere.[192] Once again, political emancipation is characterised as involving a twofold process: society separates out into a political and civil realm, and private property is relegated to the sphere of civil society.

In addition, Marx maintains that the empirical evidence confirms the same striking contrast, between the civil and political fate of the state's material preconditions, as was the case with its spiritual preconditions. The modern state has been liberated from private property, in that the property qualification for both 'active and passive election rights' – that is, for both standing and voting for political office – has been abolished. At the same time, however, its relegation to the civil sphere leads not only to

---

[188] *Ibid.* 353/151/218. [189] *Ibid.* 356/155/222. [190] *Ibid.*
[191] *Die heilige Familie* 118/111. [192] 'Zur Judenfrage' 354/153/219.

the continued existence but also to the *burgeoning* of private property (and the individualism which accompanies it).

In this way, Marx effects a second reformulation of Bauer's complaints about the antipathy between Judaism and modernity. Having initially treated Bauer's discussion as raising the issue of the relation between the modern state and religion, Marx now treats it as raising the issue of the relation between the modern state and its preconditions. This is the 'secular conflict' to which 'the Jewish question' is ultimately reduced, namely 'the relationship of the political state to its preconditions (*Voraussetzungen*)', preconditions which divide into 'material elements' (whose paradigmatic example is property) and 'spiritual ones' (whose paradigmatic example is religion).[193]

THE PRECONDITIONS OF THE MODERN STATE

In describing the (reinvigorated) existence of religion and property as two central 'preconditions' of the modern state, Marx is suggesting that the political state somehow depends on modern civil society.[194] There are two dimensions to this dependence. In a historical sense, it was only as a result of the separation out of civil and political life that the modern state could come into existence. In a constitutive sense, the 'universality' of modern political life continues to depend on, and define itself against, the individualism of civil society. Both of these claims require some elaboration.

The historical sense is most evident in Marx's schematic account of the emergence of the modern social world. He identifies two central features of 'feudal' society. These, in turn, form a structured contrast with the modern social world.

In feudal society, civil and political life form a unity. That is, under feudalism there existed no separation of civil and political spheres, in that the various elements of the old civil society – property, family, and work in the forms of seigniory, estate, and guild – all 'had a *directly political* character'.[195] This much, of course, is familiar from the *Kritik*. However, Marx now emphasises a second feature of the Middle Ages, namely that it contained no common political life, no political community to which all subjects belonged (directly). The relationship of the individual to the state as a whole, which Marx identifies as the individual's '*political relationship*', was typically an indirect one, taking place through the various

---

[193] *Ibid.* 355/154–5/221.   [194] *Ibid.* 355/154/221.   [195] *Ibid.* 367–8/165/232.

corporate structures to which each individual belonged.[196] These corporate structures, for all that they might have provided pockets of solidarity and mutual support – that is, have constituted meaningful communities for the individuals involved – established 'barriers between the different sections of the people'.[197] The segmented character of feudal society ensured that, as far as what might be called inter-corporate relations were concerned, individuals stood in a 'relationship of separation and exclusion' towards each other.[198] Marx maintains that since there was no common political life in the medieval world, the various 'estates, corporations, guilds and privileges' could be seen as embodying 'the separation of the people from its community'.[199] To the extent that there existed general political concerns – for example, concerning the unity of the state – they were deemed to be 'the *special* concern' of one part of that community, namely of the ruler and his officers 'separated from the people'.[200]

In short, feudal society combined the presence of a unified civil and political life with the absence of a political community to which all belonged. In contrast, the modern social world is characterised by the development of a political sphere which constitutes a concern of the whole community, but which has separated out from everyday life in civil society.

In 'Zur Judenfrage', the young Marx develops the account of the modern social world which first appeared in the *Kritik*. He emphasises not only the fact of separation (between civil and political life) but also the effect of that separation on the character of each of its component parts. The modern divide between civil and political life does not involve the separation out of two otherwise unaltered elements, but rather a significant transformation of these previously conjoined spheres. Marx describes this transformation as involving the 'perfection (*Vollendung*) of the idealism of the state', and the 'perfection of the materialism of civil society'.[201]

The 'perfection of the idealism of the state' consisted in the transformation of political life which had resulted from the overthrow of the corporate structure of feudalism.[202] In the Middle Ages, the 'political spirit' of society had been in what Marx calls a 'state of dispersion', that is to say it was 'dissolved, dissected and dispersed in the various cul-de-sacs of feudal society'.[203] The political revolution which inaugurated the modern social world gathered up that spirit, not only 'liberating it from the adulteration of civil life' but also concentrating it into a single 'sphere of community' to which all belonged.[204] The rule of one part of feudal society over all the

---

[196] *Ibid.* 368/165/232.   [197] *Ibid.* 366/164/230.
[198] *Ibid.* 368/165/232.   [199] *Ibid.* 368/166/232.   [200] *Ibid.*
[201] *Ibid.* 369/166/233.   [202] *Ibid.*   [203] *Ibid.* 368/166/233.   [204] *Ibid.*

others was thus overthrown in favour of turning 'the affairs of the state into the affairs of the people'.[205] For the first time, political life had become 'a concern of the whole people (*als allgemeine Angelegenheit*)'.[206]

The 'perfection of the materialism of civil society' consisted in the transformation of civil life which resulted from the separation out of the political state. For Marx, feudal society, with its unity of civil and political concerns, had always tempered any nascent individualism with a concern for collective interests. However, the political revolution which inaugurated the modern social world '*abolished* the *political character of civil society*'.[207] This 'emancipation of civil society from politics' had serious consequences for the component parts of civil life.[208] Not least, these were now 'unbridled', that is to say they were liberated from even the '*appearance*' of a concern for the common good.[209] In shaking off its political constraints, modern civil life was 'shaking off the bonds which had held in check the egoistic spirit'.[210]

Marx's account of the intensified individualism that results has a number of threads, not all of which are characterised clearly or carefully in 'Zur Judenfrage'. He describes civil society as 'the sphere of egoism and of the *bellum omnium contra omnes*', a description which – echoing Hobbes's account of the state of nature – suggests that this intensified individualism affects both individual motivation and social relationships.[211]

As far as the motivations and character of individuals are concerned, Marx characterises the members of modern civil society as driven by 'private' rather than 'communal' interests.[212] He maintains that they regard themselves and others in a wholly instrumental way; that is, private persons think of, and treat, themselves and others as merely 'means' to individual ends.[213]

As far as the relations between these narrowly self-interested individuals are concerned, Marx does not claim that modern individuals are wholly unconnected but rather that the social bonds between them are of a peculiarly competitive and antagonistic kind. Civil society, Marx suggests, in substituting 'egoism and selfish need' for communal bonds, generates a world of narrowly self-interested individuals 'confronting each other in enmity (*feindlich*)'.[214]

There are a number of other threads and emphases in Marx's rather unstructured account of modern individualism in 'Zur Judenfrage'. In an adumbration of his later concept of fetishism – whereby social products

[205] *Ibid.* 368/166/232.   [206] *Ibid.*   [207] *Ibid.*
[208] *Ibid.* 369/166/233. See also *Die heilige Familie* 123/116.   [209] 'Zur Judenfrage' 369/166/233.
[210] *Ibid.*   [211] *Ibid.* 356/155/221.   [212] *Ibid.* 355/154/220.   [213] *Ibid.*   [214] *Ibid.* 376/173/240.

are endowed with an independent power which in truth they lack – Marx describes the individual in civil society as becoming increasingly powerless, increasingly the 'plaything of alien powers'.[215] And in one of several echoes of Tocqueville, Marx portrays the member of civil society as an atomised individual, as 'an isolated monad' increasingly 'withdrawn into himself, his private interests and his private desires'.[216]

Marx also utilises an extraordinary series of striking and overlapping images, inspired by Hamilton's *Men and Manners in America*, in order to convey the distinctive character of modern individualism. On Marx's account, Hamilton accurately portrays the member of modern civil society as spiritually bedevilled, as coldly calculating, and as irrationally acquiescent. The spiritual bedevilment appears in the account of the American citizen as an individual 'possessed' by the spirit of bargaining, whose 'idol' is 'Mammon', a deity which he worships with all the power of 'his body and soul'.[217] The cold calculation appears in the characterisation of the emancipated citizen of New England as viewing the world as nothing but a 'Stock Exchange', as being an individual who can relax only 'by exchanging objects', and who understands his 'sole vocation here on earth' as being 'to get richer than his neighbours'.[218] The irrational acquiescence appears in the picture of the citizen of the United States – in what is perhaps the most extravagant of these images – as a kind of willing Laocoon, choked by the snakes of commerce but not making 'even the slightest effort to free himself'.[219] (The ancient statue of Laocoon and his two sons trapped by the coils of a serpent, excavated at Rome in 1506, was of extraordinary importance in the contemporary German debate about the achievements of Greek culture.[220])

On Marx's account, the 'perfection' of the 'idealism' of the state (the formation of a political community to which all belonged) and the 'perfection' of the 'materialism' of civil society (the intensification of the individualism of everyday life) were not separate historical transformations. 'The

---

[215] *Ibid.* 355/154/220. For Marx's later account of fetishism, see G. A. Cohen, *Karl Marx's Theory of History: A Defence* (Oxford, 1978) chapter 5.

[216] 'Zur Judenfrage' 364/162/229 and 366/164/230. See also Marx's remarks about atomism in *Die heilige Familie* 127–8/120–1.

[217] 'Zur Judenfrage' 373/170/237. [218] *Ibid.* 373/170–1/237. [219] *Ibid.* 373/170/237.

[220] On the German reception of Laocoon, see H. B. Nisbet, 'Laocöon in Germany: The Reception of the Group since Winckelmann', *Oxford German Studies*, volume 10 (1979) pp. 22–63; and E. M. Butler, *The Tyranny of Greece Over Germany: A Study of the Influence Exercised by Greek Art and Poetry Over the Great German Writers of the Eighteenth, Nineteenth, and Twentieth Centuries* (Cambridge, 1935) especially chapters 2–3. J. J. Winckelmann had famously contrasted the stoical bearing of the statue with the cries that Laocoon is made to utter in Virgil's account of his death (see *The Aeneid*, book 2, lines 199–224).

constitution of the *political state* and the dissolution of civil society into independent *individuals*, Marx writes, were achieved 'in *one and the same act*'.[221]

It is not only their historical origins, but also the continued existence of state and civil society, which are said to be bound up with each other. (This is what was earlier called the constitutive sense of dependency.) Marx wants to claim, not only that the political state and modern civil society share an origin, but also that their fates continue to be intertwined. In particular, although political life imagines itself to be independent of civil society, the modern state is actually dependent on the continuation of civil society 'in order to exist'.[222]

In the 'Kritische Randglossen', having reprised the distinction between state and civil society as involving 'antitheses' between 'public and private life' and between 'universal and particular interests', Marx draws an illuminating analogy between the ancient and modern worlds. He suggests that, in both cases, the existence of the state is 'inseparable' from the existence of slavery.[223] The city-state and the slavery of antiquity, he maintains, 'were not more closely *welded* together than the modern state and the cut-throat world of modern business'.[224]

This image of the state and civil society being 'closely *welded* together' clearly implies an interrelationship between these two elements.[225] However, this is not an interrelationship of equal partners but of dominant and subordinate elements. It is the sphere of 'private life' and 'particular interests' which is deemed to have some kind of primacy over political life and the sphere of the common good.

In the early writings, the primacy of civil society over the state is characterised in a variety of ways. In the *Kritik*, Marx characterises the political state as 'supported impotence', and insists that greater power lies in the 'supports' of the state than in the state itself.[226] In 'Zur Judenfrage', he maintains that it is civil society which exercises supreme power, and subsequently characterises the 'sovereignty' of the state as 'fictitious (*eingebildeten*)'.[227] In the 'Kritische Randglossen', Marx claims that 'the fragmentation, the depravity and *slavery of civil society* is the natural foundation of the modern state, just as the civil society of slavery was the natural foundation of the state in *antiquity*'.[228] And in *Die heilige Familie*, he portrays civil society as the 'natural basis' of the state.[229]

---

[221] 'Zur Judenfrage' 369/167/233.   [222] *Ibid.* 354/153/219.
[223] 'Kritische Randglossen' 401/198/412.   [224] *Ibid.*   [225] *Ibid.*
[226] *Kritik* 320/114/184.   [227] 'Zur Judenfrage' 355/154/220.
[228] 'Kritische Randglossen' 401/198/412. See also *Die heilige Familie* 120/113.
[229] *Die heilige Familie* 120/113.

However, it is less the fact of continuing dependence than the effect of this continuing dependence on the nature of the modern state that Marx is keen to examine in 'Zur Judenfrage'. In particular, he suggests that the dependence of the political state on civil society has significant consequences for the kind of public life that is available in the modern social world. (In order to elucidate this suggestion, it is helpful to consider Marx's rejection of the second of the two Bauerian claims identified above.)

CHRISTIANITY AND THE MODERN STATE: THE POSITIVE ANALOGY

The second of the two claims that Marx identifies as central to Bauer's *Die Judenfrage* is that 'the Christian state is by its very *nature* incapable of emancipating the Jew'.[230] Marx's response to this familiar claim is initially puzzling. He proceeds by rejecting Bauer's account of what constitutes a 'Christian' state and proposing an alternative candidate for such an appellation.

The rejection of this definition of a Christian state is initially puzzling because Bauer's usage is entirely conventional. For Bauer, the Christian state is the state whose 'foundation and essential characteristic' is religious privilege, the state which bases itself on the Christian Bible, the state whose very nature is to discriminate against other religions, and so on.[231] Indeed, in referring to the 'so-called (*sogenannte*) Christian state' Marx appears – at least, implicitly – to recognise the conventional nature of such usage. Moreover, this conventional usage is one that Marx had previously adopted himself.[232] For example, in an article for the *Rheinische Zeitung*, he had described the states of the ancien régime as 'the most Christian states of all'.[233] Now, however, Marx maintains that we should abandon this conventional usage on the grounds that 'the perfected Christian state is not the so-called *Christian* state which recognises Christianity as its foundation, as the state religion'.[234]

Marx's alternative definition of the Christian state is also initially puzzling since he recommends a usage of the appellation 'Christian' which is idiosyncratic and whose advantages over the conventional sense are unclear. Marx suggests that 'the perfected Christian state' is 'the *atheist* state, the *democratic* state, the state which relegates religion to the level of other elements of civil society'.[235] According to this alternative usage, the 'final form

---

[230] 'Zur Judenfrage' 347/147/212.   [231] *Die Judenfrage* 55/57.   [232] 'Zur Judenfrage' 357/156/222.
[233] 'Der leitende Artikel' 102/200.   [234] 'Zur Judenfrage' 357/156/222.   [235] *Ibid.*

of the Christian state' is the modern state which 'disregards the religion of its members'.[236]

Given this revisionist definition of the Christian state, the reasoning behind Marx's rejection of the second Bauerian claim – that the Christian state, by its very nature, is incapable of emancipating the Jews – is straightforward enough. As the relevant American evidence confirms, the emancipation of Jews is compatible with, indeed is required by, the modern democratic state. Accordingly, if the Christian state just *is* the modern democratic state, then Bauer is clearly mistaken in suggesting that the Christian state cannot emancipate the Jews.

The difficulty here lies not in following Marx's argument, but rather in understanding why one might want to adopt this idiosyncratic definition of the Christian state. In part, Marx was perhaps tempted by this revisionist definition for formal (and unconvincing) reasons, namely that it allows him to indulge his enthusiasm for paradiastolary figures of speech. On the revisionist definition, Marx can insist that the true Christian state is the atheist state, the state that disregards the religion of its members, and so on.[237] Fortunately, a more substantive and persuasive reason for adopting this alternative usage can be identified. He is also attracted to this revisionist definition because of a number of (unstructured and overlapping) analogies between the nature of Christianity and the nature of the modern state. For Marx, two particular parallels (between Christianity and the state) convey some significant truth about the character of modern political life, and thereby justify this revisionist definition of what constitutes a Christian state.

In order to make sense of these parallels, some understanding of the young Marx's conception of Christianity is required. (In the early writings, Marx often, and unhelpfully, uses the terms 'Christianity' and 'religion' interchangeably.) Although attracting the attention of numerous commentators who have dissected his remarks at considerable length, much of what Marx says on the topic of Christianity is indirect and derivative.[238] It is indirect, in that his comments typically appear as introductory, passing, or metaphorical remarks, in the context of a discussion of non-religious subjects. It is derivative in that much of the little that Marx says on this subject can also be found elsewhere in the works of the Hegelian left, and especially

---

[236] *Ibid.* 361/160/226. See also *Die heilige Familie* 118/111.

[237] See, for example, 'Zur Judenfrage' 357/156/222.

[238] See, for example, Alasdair MacIntyre, *Marxism and Christianity*, revised edition (London, 1968); Werner Post, *Kritik der Religion bei Karl Marx* (Munich, 1969); and David McLellan, *Marxism and Religion: A Description and Assessment of the Marxist Critique of Christianity* (London, 1987).

in the writings of Ludwig Feuerbach (discussed in Chapter 4).[239] As a result, only those aspects of Marx's account which are needed to make sense of the parallel between Christianity and the modern state are broached here.

The 'Kritik: Einleitung' contains a much-quoted section on Christianity (which includes a famous analogy, whose provenance is fiercely contested, between the character of religion and the use of opiates).[240] In the course of his discussion, Marx advances the claim that Christianity 'is the *fantastic realisation* of the human essence since the human essence has not acquired any true reality'.[241] There are three elements to this account. Marx insists that human nature is reflected in Christianity, that this reflection is somehow 'fantastic' (that is, human nature is acknowledged not in 'reality' but in a secondary world of religious illusion), and that a connection exists between the sphere of 'reality' and the sphere of 'illusion' (namely that where human nature has not yet been adequately actualised in the former, it finds expression in the latter). 'Religion', Marx observes – in one of his more elliptical remarks – 'is only the illusory sun which revolves around man as long as he does not revolve around himself'.[242] (It is in this context that the young Marx suggests that the fantastical expression of human nature provides a consolation, albeit an inadequate one, for its lack of earthly realisation. It is this suggestion – that religion provides a deficient consolation for earthly suffering – which prompts the famous drug analogy. Like opium, religion is said to provide an 'illusory happiness', a 'halo' in the 'vale of tears' that constitutes our material lot.[243])

The affinity between this account of religion and the historical model of self-realisation which is contained in the *Kritik* and the *Manuskripte* (discussed in Chapter 2) should be apparent. The latter provided a model according to which the development and actualisation of essential human powers requires a detour through alienation, and Marx now endorses the view that religion is one of the forms that this detour takes. It seems that as long as human nature is not fully actualised in individual lives, it will find an indirect expression in the form of religious ideas.

---

[239] For Bauer's possible influence, see Zvi Rosen, *Karl Marx and Bruno Bauer: The Influence of Bruno Bauer on Marx's Thought* (The Hague, 1977) pp. 133–47; and K. L. Clarkson and D. J. Hawkin, 'Karl Marx on Religion: The Influence of Bruno Bauer and Ludwig Feuerbach on His Thought and the Implications for the Christian Marxist Dialogue', *Scottish Journal of Theology*, volume 31 (1978) pp. 533–55.

[240] On the disputed origins of the opium analogy, see Helmut Gollwitzer, *The Christian Faith and the Marxist Criticism of Religion* (Edinburgh, 1970) pp. 15–23.

[241] 'Kritik: Einleitung' 378/175/244.   [242] *Ibid.* 379/176/244.

[243] *Ibid.* See also G. A. Cohen, *If You're An Egalitarian, How Come You're So Rich?* (Cambridge MA, 2000) pp. 79–83; and Jonathan Wolff, *Why Read Marx Today?* (Oxford, 2002) pp. 19–20.

There is much that might be said about this account. The significant point to note here is that this is not a wholly negative or dismissive understanding of Christianity. In 'Zur Judenfrage', Marx portrays Christianity as embodying both an achievement and a limitation. Simply put, the achievement of Christianity is that it embodies an acknowledgement of human nature, and the limitation of Christianity is that this acknowledgement is an inadequate one (situated as it is in a secondary world of illusion).

This account of the achievement and limitation of Christianity provides the framework of the two sustained parallels that Marx develops between the nature of Christianity and the nature of the modern state. The first (positive) parallel concerns the achievement of Christianity and of the modern state (and forms the subject of the remainder of this section). The second (negative) parallel concerns the limitation of Christianity and of the modern state (and forms the subject of the following section).

The positive parallel rests on the claim that both Christianity and the modern state embody an 'acknowledgement (*Anerkennung*)' of human nature.[244] This claim is made directly and reinforced in other analogies that Marx draws. For example, he maintains that both religion and politics are characterised by a dualism between heaven and earth, on the one hand, and between state and civil society, on the other. In both of these cases the divide is said to run between a sphere in which human nature is recognised (the sphere of 'species life') and a sphere in which it is not (the sphere of 'individual life'). 'The members of the political state are religious', Marx writes, 'because of the dualism (*Dualismus*) between individual life and species life, between the life of civil society and political life'.[245] It is clear that this division between two spheres (in both the political and religious cases) is one which cuts across each individual (and not simply between different groups of individuals). In both cases, Marx claims that each 'man leads a double life, a life in heaven and a life on earth'; a life in which his human nature is recognised and a life in which it is not. As Marx elaborates, in the political, unlike the religious, instance, this division occurs not merely in 'consciousness, but in *reality*'.[246]

Marx appeals to this positive parallel – between the recognition of human nature in the modern state and the recognition of human nature in Christianity – in an attempt to justify both the rejection of Bauer's conventional definition of the Christian state and the promotion of his own apparently idiosyncratic alternative. Marx appeals to the distinction between Christianity as such (by which he means the explicit doctrinal

[244] 'Zur Judenfrage' 353/152/218.   [245] *Ibid.* 360/159/225.   [246] *Ibid.* 355/154/220.

and religious content of Christianity) and what he refers to as 'the human foundation of Christianity' (by which he means the human nature of which Christianity is, properly understood, the alienated expression).[247] Marx suggests that the conventional definition of the Christian state – a definition which is, of course, endorsed and utilised by Bauer – applies the appellation 'Christian' to a state which is ostensibly founded on a commitment to the doctrinal content of Christianity. In contrast, Marx's alternative usage applies to a state which is based, not on the religious views of Christianity, but on its anthropological foundations, that is, on the human nature which underpins and is reflected in Christianity. It is because Marx sees a parallel between the reflection of human nature in Christianity and the reflection of human nature in the modern state that he identifies the latter – and not, for example, the pre-modern state based on the doctrinal content of Christianity – as 'Christian'.

Indeed, at one point, Marx suggests that it is because it 'realises' the model of human nature embodied in Christianity, that the *'perfected'* modern state can 'discard' Christianity as such, relegating it to the sphere of civil society.[248] On this account, it would appear that it is the progressive actualisation of human nature in the state which makes Christianity as such increasingly unnecessary in political life. In contrast, Marx suggests that 'the *imperfect* state' of the *ancien régime* – a state which does not embody the model of human nature reflected in Christianity – required the *'supplement* and *sanctification'* of the Christian religion, as a 'means' to bolster its continued survival.[249] Religion in this latter case is a political 'cover' beneath which the pre-modern state pursued 'the infamy of its *secular* ends'.[250]

The suggestion that the modern state resembles Christianity in its recognition of human nature is scarcely self-explanatory. Marx is perhaps best understood as making two different kinds of claim. The first is a descriptive claim about the goods which are reflected in both Christianity and the modern state. The second is an explanatory claim which, assuming that human nature actualises itself in religious and political life, links those goods to essential human attributes.

The primary good which Marx identifies as reflected in both Christianity and the modern state is community. He suggests that community is reflected in Christianity, not least in its conception of 'heaven', where the individual is regarded as a member of a collectivity.[251] It is also reflected in the modern state, which Marx variously identifies as 'the sphere of the community',[252]

---

[247] *Ibid.* 360/159/225.   [248] *Ibid.* 358/156–7/223.   [249] *Ibid.*
[250] *Ibid.* 360/158/225.   [251] *Ibid.* 355/154/220.   [252] *Ibid.* 368/166/233.

the area of life in which the individual exists 'in community with other men',[253] and so on.

However, the young Marx's understanding of community is scarcely precise or transparent. One significant problem is that, although he rarely discusses the nature of community directly, what he does say tends to overwhelm the concept with associations. (One modern scholar has noted that Marx's 'was a fertile rather than a tidy mind', adding, rather generously one might think, that 'had it been tidier' it 'might have been less fertile'.[254]) For example, community is often linked with some rather imprecisely specified notion of equality. Thus Marx characterises the political community as 'Christian' inasmuch 'as it regards man – not just one man but all men – as a *sovereign* and supreme being'.[255] (The contrast with the inequality of the 'so-called Christian state' is made explicitly; in states based on the idea of divine right, Marx observes, 'the only man who carries weight, the *king*, is specifically different from other men' by virtue, not least, of his direct communion with heaven.[256]) In addition, community is linked with the idea of individuals operating with a specific kind of concern for others.[257] Marx thinks of community as a sphere of common, rather than particular, interests, in which individuals behave as 'communal' rather than partial beings.[258] This notion of behaving as a 'communal being (*Gemeinwesen*)' is an important one in the early writings. For individuals to behave as 'communal beings' means not only that they co-operate with others, but also that they possess a genuine, and not merely instrumental or self-regarding, concern for others.[259] (I discuss Marx's account of community further in Chapter 4.)

As well as elaborating a thread in the young Marx's understanding of community, the notion of a 'communal being' provides a link to the explanatory claim mentioned above. The good of community is not only reflected in Christianity and the modern state, but is also connected with the realisation of essential human attributes. The explanation for this acknowledgement of community in religious and political life is that both Christianity and the modern state reflect our essential human nature. It is the actualisation of the human capacity to be 'a *communal being*' which underpins the affinity between Christianity and the modern state.[260]

Marx's emphasis in 'Zur Judenfrage', reinforced by the content of much subsequent commentary, has tended to obscure his view that the modern

[253] *Ibid.* 356/155/221.   [254] John Plamenatz, *Karl Marx's Philosophy of Man* (Oxford, 1975) p. 103.
[255] 'Zur Judenfrage' 360/159/225–6.   [256] *Ibid.* 360/158/225.
[257] See 'Kritische Randglossen' 402–3/198/412.   [258] See, for example, 'Zur Judenfrage' 366/164/231.
[259] See, for example, *ibid.* 366/164/230.   [260] *Ibid.* 355/154/220.

state embodies a positive achievement. However, this appreciation of political emancipation runs throughout the early writings. In the *Kritik*, Marx describes the modern state as 'a definite advance in history'.[261] In 'Zur Judenfrage', Marx acknowledges political emancipation as 'a big step forward', and as the most developed form of 'practical' emancipation possible '*within* the prevailing scheme of things'.[262] And in *Die heilige Familie*, Marx describes the state which does not emancipate Jews as 'underdeveloped' in comparison with the modern state which gives them equal civil and political rights.[263]

However, the basis of Marx's assessment, that political emancipation embodies a positive achievement, is usually less clear. The suggestion made here is that a central achievement of the modern state is its acknowledgement of the value of community. In this way, modern political life (like Christianity) also acknowledges an essential aspect of human nature.

CHRISTIANITY AND THE MODERN STATE: THE NEGATIVE ANALOGY

The second parallel that Marx draws between Christianity and the modern state is between their negative elements, that is, their shared limitations. His suggestion, in 'Zur Judenfrage', is that, although the modern state (like Christianity) acknowledges community, it does so (like Christianity) in an inadequate manner.

Marx's account of the parallel limitations of political and religious life requires a considerable amount of unravelling. The relation between Christianity and politics, on the one hand, and what he calls their preconditions, on the other, is central to this account. Marx maintains that the modern state presupposes the defects of civil society, just as the Christian heaven presupposes our earthly 'vale of tears'.[264]

Marx identifies three main limitations as affecting the relation between Christianity and its preconditions. Each of these limitations elaborates the failure of Christianity to overcome the defects which it presupposes.

The first limitation is that the defects of our everyday life continue, because in Christianity those defects are overcome 'only deviously, through a medium'.[265] That is, the failings of this world are overcome not in this world but in another. For example, the good of community is recognised in

---

[261] *Kritik* 283/79/146.   [262] 'Zur Judenfrage' 356/155/221.   [263] *Die heilige Familie* 117/110.
[264] 'Kritik: Einleitung' 379/176/244.   [265] 'Zur Judenfrage' 353/152/218.

the Christian heaven at the same time as the individualism of our everyday lives continues as before.

The second limitation is that Christianity actually intensifies the defects of our everyday lives. Religious alienation involves the transfer of all our 'divinity' to 'Christ', and Marx maintains that our own everyday lives are impoverished as a result.[266] The suggestion here seems to be that the human goods which find reflection in heaven are accordingly, and to that extent, unavailable in this world. This claim is echoed elsewhere in the early writings. In the *Manuskripte*, for example, Marx maintains that 'the more the man puts into God the less he retains in himself';[267] and in the *Auszüge aus James Mill*, having characterised God as a mediator between humankind and human nature, Marx notes that 'man . . . becomes poorer . . . in proportion as the mediator becomes richer'.[268]

The third limitation is a little more elusive. It is suggested by Marx's characterisation of Christianity as embodying an 'unreal universality (*unwirklichen Allgemeinheit*)'.[269] These are both slippery words. '*Allgemeinheit*' literally means 'common to all', and appears to be used here to connote the idea of community which finds reflection in Christianity. The suggestion that the kind of community which is embodied in religious forms is somehow 'unreal (*unwirklich*)' seems readily intelligible. After all, on Marx's account, this Christian community is achieved, not in this world, but in a secondary world of illusion. There is, however, an additional connotation here, one which makes better sense of Marx's extended analogy between religion and the modern state. The term '*unwirklich*' can suggest not only illusoriness and fantasy, but also the failure to have an effect or make an impression (the etymological connection here is with '*wirken*').[270] Marx maintains that the Christian heaven is ineffective in overcoming the 'restrictions of the profane world', and ends up having to 'acknowledge', 'reinstate', and 'allow itself to be dominated by' those restrictions.[271] On this account, the third limitation of the religious embodiment of community is that it is not simply illusory but also ineffectual. In particular, Christianity ends up being governed by, and bearing the imprint of, the profane limitations which it presupposes.

In short, on Marx's account, the profane preconditions of religion first continue, secondly are intensified and thirdly come to shape and dominate the sacred. These broad claims are repeated in Marx's parallel account of the relation between political life and its preconditions.

[266] *Ibid.* 353/152/219.   [267] *Manuskripte* 512/272/324.   [268] *Auszüge aus James Mill* 416/212/261.
[269] 'Zur Judenfrage' 355/154/220.
[270] Note that this is a conventional – not a peculiarly Hegelian – usage.
[271] 'Zur Judenfrage' 355/154/220.

In this context, a useful starting point is provided by Marx's summary characterisation of political emancipation as not the most 'complete (*durchgeführte*) and consistent (*widerspruchslose*)' form of emancipation.[272] The suggestion here is that these limitations, the 'incompleteness and inconsistency' of political emancipation, can be broken down into three elements.

The first limitation is that political emancipation does not overcome the spiritual and material defects of the modern social world. The state is freed from these defects without individuals being liberated from them. Political emancipation, as Marx has already noted, 'neither abolishes nor tries to abolish' the defects of civil society.[273] For example, the modern state can emancipate itself from religion even though the overwhelming majority of its population is still religious, and, as Marx pointedly remarks, one 'does not cease to be religious by being religious *in private*'.[274] More generally, it is clear that, on Marx's account of political emancipation, 'the *state* can liberate itself from a restriction without man himself being *truly* free of it, that a state can be a *free state* without man himself being *a free man*'.[275]

The second limitation is that political emancipation effectively intensifies the spiritual and material defects of society. The inverse relationship that Marx locates between the sacred and profane is paralleled in his account of the modern social world. As Marx's historical account of its emergence had already sought to establish, the perfected 'idealism' of the state is inversely related to the perfected 'materialism' of civil society. The relegation of religion and private property to civil society had, at the same time, released them from any constraints of commonality. As a result, and for the first time, the defects of civil society were allowed to 'assert their *particular* nature in *their* own way'.[276] As Marx's examination of the American example had confirmed, religion and property (the representative defects of civil society) not only continue to exist but do so in '*fresh* and *vigorous*' forms.[277]

The third limitation concerns not the restricted extent of community so much as the effect of that limited remit on the actualisation of community. The modern conflict between the competing principles embodied in civil and political life is typically resolved in favour of the former. That is, the intensified individualism of civil society comes to dominate and contaminate the political community. The significant assumption here is that civil society has a primacy in its interrelationship with political life. 'Ideally speaking', Marx observes, the modern state 'is superior to' the individualistic world of civil society, 'but in actual fact' it is 'in thrall (*Leibeignen*)

---

[272] *Ibid.* 353/152/218.   [273] *Ibid.* 357/155/222.   [274] *Ibid.* 353/152/218.
[275] *Ibid.*   [276] *Ibid.* 354/153/219.   [277] *Ibid.* 352/151/217.

to it'.[278] As a result of this primacy, Marx maintains that even where the modern state attempts to overcome the defects of the profane world, those defects continue to intrude and dominate. The reinvigorated existence of material and social defects in civil society comes to eclipse and shape the concerns of the state. In our political as well as our religious lives, Marx suggests, we are forced to 'acknowledge', 'reinstate', and allow ourselves to be 'dominated' by the defects of the profane world. In the modern social world, the attempt to achieve community does not take the form of over-coming the defects of 'the profane world', but rather of standing above and apart from them.[279] However, since these defects have a degree of primacy, this strategy for establishing community is an ineffective one. Not only does the sphere of community fail to extend into the rest of society, but its already limited remit becomes contaminated by the individualism which obtains elsewhere.

In short, there are three elements in Marx's suggestive account of the limitations of political emancipation: first, the various material and spiritual defects of civil society carry on in private; second, as a result of being freed from the constraints of commonality, these defects are intensified; and third, as a result of the primacy of civil society, they come to shape and dominate the state. Marx summarises this account of the limitations of political emancipation in his claim that it suffers from 'incompleteness and contradiction'.[280]

I have already noted that *Quellenforschung* is not a primary aim of the present work. It is nonetheless worth remarking that this association of Christianity with an ineffective realisation of community has a rich con-ceptual prehistory. Not least, it appears in the writings of Machiavelli and Rousseau.

One reason for singling out these two authors is that both Machiavelli's *Discorsi sopra la prima deca di Tito Livio* and Rousseau's *Contrat social* appear amongst the works that Marx read during his stay at Kreuznach. The second Kreuznach notebook includes fairly extensive notes from the *Contrat social* (see Chapter 4), and the fifth Kreuznach notebook contains a shorter set of passages from a German translation of the *Discorsi*.[281] (Marx may have completed 'Zur Judenfrage' in Paris, but he probably began the article in Kreuznach.)

In the *Discorsi* – alongside a conception of history according to which no polity can escape the cycle of growth and decay – Machiavelli insists that the

[278] *Ibid.* 374/172/238.   [279] *Ibid.* 355/154/220.   [280] *Ibid.* 361/160/226.
[281] Marx made some twenty short excerpts from a translation by Joh. Ziegler published in 1832. See *MEGA②* 4, 2, pp. 276–8.

ancients were fonder of republican liberty than the moderns. He explicitly blames the waning of that earlier attachment to collective self-rule on the deleterious effect that Christianity has on civic virtue. On this account, religion is a prerequisite of civic virtue, but modern religion does not favour republican freedom. The incompatibility between Christianity and civic virtue is said to result from both the otherworldliness of Christianity (it is a religion which 'makes us esteem less the honour of the world'), and its encouragement of an inappropriate set of virtues (Christianity glorifies 'humble and contemplative men' over 'fierce and vigorous' ones).[282] It is clear that, on this account, individuals who care for their souls above their city are ill suited to the responsibilities of citizenship.

Rousseau also offers both an officially cyclical view of history and a narrative of progressive decline, whereby the local and particularistic societies of the ancient world give way to the cosmopolitan or 'general' kingdom of Christianity. In the *Contrat social*, Rousseau argues both that religion is a necessary support for a virtuous city, and that Christianity is peculiarly unsuited to this role. (Both Pierre Bayle and Bishop Warburton are mistaken: the former for famously imagining that a community of atheists was possible, the latter for claiming that Christianity formed the strongest support of the body politic.[283]) Its otherworldliness (the 'Christian's fatherland', Rousseau claims, 'is not of this world') and its preferred virtues ('Christianity preaches nothing but servitude and dependence') ensure that Christianity is unable to sustain the freedom of the ancients, which is embodied in specific communities and bound by a particularistic 'patriotic' spirit.[284] Of Christianity and a real republic, Rousseau writes, 'each of these words excludes the other (*chacun de ces deux mots exclud l'autre*)'.[285] A society of true Christians, he goes on to suggest, might be 'the most perfect community (*la plus parfaite société*)' but it 'would not be a community of men (*ne seroit plus une société d'hommes*)'.[286]

Not the least of the affinities between the *Discorsi* and the *Contrat social* is that Christianity is portrayed as antithetical to the effective realisation of community. That 'Zur Judenfrage' was, in some sense, written under the immediate influence of Machiavelli and Rousseau perhaps helps to explain Marx's enthusiasm for a parallel between religion and politics which might otherwise appear strained and unfamiliar.

---

[282] *Niccolò Machiavelli Opera: I primi scritti politici* (Turin, 1997) p. 333; and Machiavelli, *The Chief Works and Others* (Durham NC, 1989) volume I, p. 331.
[283] Rousseau, *Contrat social* 464/219.   [284] *Ibid.* 466–7/220–1.   [285] *Ibid.* 467/221.
[286] *Ibid.* 465/220. See also Rousseau, 'Lettres à Usteri'.

MARX AND RIGHTS

The claim that Marx is hostile to the very idea of rights has become an interpretative commonplace. In particular, he is widely portrayed as hostile to the concept of moral rights, the rights that individuals have on moral, and not merely legal, grounds. The nature of this purported hostility is not easily summarised, both because it is characterised in a variety of ways and because of the slippery nature of much rights talk.

'Zur Judenfrage' is usually adduced in support of this general hostility. As a result, the young Marx's discussion of rights in the first part of this article has become one of the best-known – or, at least, most often quoted – sections of the early writings.

Despite the frequency with which 'Zur Judenfrage' is characterised as a piece of supporting evidence, I can find little sign of this purported hostility to moral rights either in this text or elsewhere in the early writings. To those familiar with the relevant literature this may well appear an astonishing claim, and I begin with some ground-clearing.

The concept of rights is a notoriously ambiguous one. Perhaps the broadest sense in which it might be said that some entity has rights is simply to say that it has some independent (that is, non-derivative) 'moral standing'.[287] Most readers of this sentence, for example, probably hold that, morally speaking, people count in a way that filing cabinets do not. To say that something has rights, in this broad sense, is to say that the way in which we treat it is of non-derivative moral significance.

It seems clear that the young Marx believes in rights in this broad sense. It is readily apparent, for example, that he identifies people as having an intrinsic moral relevance that other objects lack. What may be less obvious is the importance of this claim in his early writings.

Not least, it plays a central role in his use of a rather imprecise notion which is unfortunately most familiar to modern readers under the name of 'objectification'. This label is unfortunate because, in the context of Marx's work, the term objectification is more usually used to denote something else, namely the process which he calls '*Vergegenständlichung*'. In order to help distinguish these two ideas I shall refer to the notion at issue here as 'objectification' (with quotation marks), and the notion (of '*Vergegenständlichung*') with which it might unfortunately be confused as objectification (without quotation marks).

---

[287] Shelly Kagan, *Normative Ethics* (Boulder CO, 1998) p. 170.

Objectification concerns the relation between human beings and external objects. The term is used by Marx to characterise the historical process whereby the capacities and character of humankind become embodied in, and reflected by, the material world.[288] Marx is, of course, keen to emphasise the extent to which that world is transformed by human purposes, not least as a result of our working on it in production.

It is, however, 'objectification' which is at issue here. 'Objectification' involves the idea of inappropriately treating one type of thing as if it were another type of thing. More precisely, 'objectification' connotes the moral impropriety of systematically treating a human being as if he or she were an object, thing, or commodity. (Such treatment might take a number of forms, not all of which are to be considered equally pernicious.[289]) Since the relevant impropriety consists in the systematic treatment of an entity with high independent 'moral standing' as if it were an entity without such standing, 'objectification' clearly presupposes this distinction between entities.

The young Marx frequently appeals to something like this idea of 'objectification'. In the *Manuskripte*, for example, he complains that modern social conditions have 'depressed' workers 'to the level of a machine'.[290] By requiring only simple 'mechanical movement' from them, the development of contemporary industry is said to have stunted the intellectual and physical development of workers.[291] As the worker sinks to the level of a commodity, Marx suggests that wages now have the same meaning 'as the *maintenance and upkeep* of any other productive instrument'.[292] He clearly bemoans the impropriety involved in treating human beings as if they were an object or commodity, namely the impropriety of treating an entity with high independent moral standing as if it were an entity without such standing.

The same basic view appears elsewhere. In the 'Kritik: Einleitung', for example, Marx ventures a joke about the 'debased' conditions in which the members of modern civil society are typically sunk. He observes that these conditions were acknowledged by the anonymous Frenchman who, when it was proposed that a tax be placed on dogs, exclaimed: 'Poor dogs! They want to treat you like human beings!'[293] This joke – such as it is – relies on reversing, for humorous effect, the claim (which Marx

[288] See, for example, *Manuskripte* 512/273/325.
[289] See the interesting typology in Martha C. Nussbaum, 'Objectification', *Sex and Social Justice* (Oxford, 1999) p. 218.
[290] *Manuskripte* 474/237–8/285.   [291] *Ibid.* 562/322/374–5.
[292] *Ibid.* 524/284/335.   [293] 'Kritik: Einleitung' 385/182/251.

clearly endorses) that human beings have a high moral standing that makes it inappropriate to treat them like dogs (which, on this account, lack comparable standing). That is, the joke presupposes the distinction between those entities which possess high 'moral standing' (and so have rights in this expansive sense) and those entities which lack such status (and so lack rights in this expansive sense).

That the young Marx believes in moral rights in this broad sense may well appear unremarkable. In this sense, nearly all normative theories would seem to believe in the existence of rights. No doubt, when commentators claim that Marx is hostile to moral rights, they have a less expansive notion of rights in mind.

Since less expansive conceptions of moral rights vary considerably, it seems necessary to offer some minimal outline of the conception that will be used here. However, I should stress that my concern here is not to advance a particular account of the nature of rights at the expense of some other particular account, but rather to examine the purported tension between Marx's early writings and a representative and less expansive notion of rights.

To say that a person has rights in a less expansive sense is typically to recognise that there are constraints on how we are permitted to treat them. We can think of these rights as entailing duties, in that others have a duty to perform (or refrain from performing) some action in respect of that to which the person is said to have a right. On many accounts, it is some fact about the right-holder which is held to constitute a reason for holding others to have such a duty. For example, the duties which correlate to rights claims are sometimes grounded in the well-being of individuals.[294] We can think of rights, in this case, as protecting and promoting the fundamental interests of individuals, a function that they discharge by establishing constraints on others.

Rights, in this narrower sense, are often described as recognising prohibitions on the performance of certain actions, even when those actions would result in the best overall outcome. That is, rights are thought of as paradigmatically deontological considerations in the sense that they acknowledge the moral relevance of factors other than the goodness of outcomes, and, indeed, invest those factors with sufficient significance that they might outweigh those good results.[295]

---

[294] See, for example, Joseph Raz, *The Morality of Freedom* (Oxford, 1986) pp. 180–3. For a contrasting account, see H. L. A. Hart, 'Are There Any Natural Rights?', *Philosophical Review*, volume 64 (1955) pp. 175–91.

[295] That is, rights can be described as deontological without claiming that they are absolute, that they always trump those other considerations.

Note that the young Marx's account of 'objectification' also appears consistent with this less expansive account of rights. Consider a further example of 'objectification' from the *Auszüge aus James Mill*. In the course of an examination of the credit relation, Marx considers what he sarcastically refers to as the 'romantic possibility' of a rich man extending credit to an impecunious man, on account of the relevant virtues (industriousness, sobriety, and so on) possessed by the latter.[296] Marx urges us to contemplate the 'immorality' implicit in this transaction, and in particular the way in which it involves the '*evaluation* of a man in terms of *money*'.[297] He identifies a number of ways in which 'the poor man's life, his talent and his labours' count only in so far as they function as a guarantee on the loan.[298] For example, when the poor man is judged a 'good' man by his creditor, it does not mean, as it might in another context, that he is 'not a scoundrel', but only that he is thought to have sufficient resources and energy to repay the loan.[299] Our familiarity with such language should not prevent us from appreciating the distinctiveness of the moral viewpoint that it encapsulates. Marx condemns as 'vile' the manner in which 'morality itself' thereby becomes an object of commerce.[300]

However we judge these remarks as insights into the credit relation, their present significance is that they clarify Marx's claim that the evaluation of 'a man in terms of money' is morally wrong.[301] Marx is not simply saying that humans have a 'moral standing' which dollar bills lack; he is claiming that humans have a moral standing which we have a duty to respect, and which we fail to respect if we treat them (at least, treat them systematically) in certain ways, namely as if they were objects. I would suggest that his meaning is not significantly distorted – as distinct from being expressed in less familiar language – if we claim that, for the young Marx, individuals have a moral right not to be systematically treated as things, and that, if we do treat them in this manner, we violate their right not to be so treated. Moreover, this injunction to avoid treating people as objects broaches a deontological consideration, in that it asserts the existence of a moral consideration other than the goodness of outcomes (and a moral consideration that may outweigh those outcomes).

'Objectification' is not the only notion found in the early writings which is consistent with this narrower conception of rights. Consider an idea with which 'objectification' might easily be confused, namely the idea of treating

---

[296] *Auszüge aus James Mill* 449/215/263.   [297] *Ibid.*
[298] *Ibid.*   [299] *Ibid.*   [300] *Ibid.*   [301] *Ibid.*

people simply as a means (as opposed to treating them also as an end, as required by the well-known Kantian principle).

One of the threads in Marx's account of civil society in 'Zur Juden-frage' (discussed briefly above) involved criticising the way in which the members of modern civil society treated 'other men as a means'.[302] There seems little reason to think that Marx is committed to all the details of Kant's account, and he certainly shows no serious *theoretical* interest in Kant's ethical writings. That said, it is scarcely plausible to think of Marx's choice of language here as coincidental. The apparent allusion to Kant is, for example, reinforced by Marx's reference, at the same point, to treating oneself also as a means, and by a subsequent description of the ethos of civil society as demonstrating a contempt 'for man as an end in himself'.[303]

The Kantian principle that individuals should be treated not merely as a means but also as an end is sufficiently ambiguous as to have been subject to a number of different interpretations. The second part of the principle would seem to be the more relevant one here. The first element of the principle tells us that if we treat people merely as a means we are failing to treat them in some more appropriate way; only the second element of the principle tells us what that more appropriate treatment is (namely that we must also treat them as an end).

For Kant, to treat someone as an end means to respect their 'dignity (*Würde*)', that is their 'unconditional, incomparable worth'; in other words, to treat them as having a value which is not dependent on contingent facts (such as whether or not they are actually valued by anyone), and which trumps any other sorts of value.[304] (Kant himself seems to have held, not only that entities which possess dignity cannot be legitimately traded off against entities which lacked dignity, but also, and perhaps less plausibly, that there are no legitimate trade-offs in the treatment of entities possessing dignity.[305])

The broad implication of Marx's language seems clear enough. Human beings have a value which we fail to recognise by systematically treating them only as a means, as happens, for example, in the routine functioning

---

[302] 'Zur Judenfrage' 355/154/220.
[303] *Ibid.* 375/172/239. Kant's principle says that you must act in such a way that you treat humanity 'whether in your own person or in the person of any other, always at the same time as an end, never merely as a means'. Immanuel Kant, *Grundlegung zur Metaphysic der Sitten, Gesammelte Schriften*, volume 4 (Berlin, 1902) p. 429; and Immanuel Kant, *Groundwork of the Metaphysics of Morals, Practical Philosophy* (Cambridge, 1996) p. 80.
[304] *Grundlegung zur Metaphysik der Sitten*, p. 436; *Groundwork of the Metaphysics of Morals*, p. 85.
[305] See Thomas E. Hill Jr, *Dignity and Practical Reason in Kant's Moral Theory* (Ithaca NY, 1992) chapter 2.

of modern civil society. I can see no obvious reason for Marx's use of this language – language which would certainly be familiar to his intended audience – other than to encourage us to think of the individual as having a value which others have a duty to respect, and which is independent of the goodness of outcomes.

Consider, in this context, another example of the young Marx's self-consciously Kantian vocabulary. In the 'Kritik: Einleitung', Marx refers to the existence of a 'categorical imperative (*kategorischen Imperativ*)'.[306] To speak rather generally, we can say that to call a normative judgement an imperative is to claim that it is a rational requirement; that is, a judgement which expresses what Kant would call an 'objective' principle, a principle which all rational persons would adopt if acting rationally. To call an imperative 'categorical' is to say that the constraints or ends that it prescribes are required by reason whether or not we happen to desire them (or desire something to which they might be means). The particular categorical imperative which Marx invokes here appears to cover both the impermissibility of systematically treating people as if they were objects and the impermissibility of failing to treat people as ends. The young Marx insists that the starting point for social criticism is 'the *categorical imperative to overthrow all conditions* in which man is a debased, enslaved, neglected and contemptible being (*ein erniedrigtes, ein geknechtetes, ein verlassenes, ein verächtliches Wesen*)'.[307] In short, he insists that we have a duty to overthrow any conditions in which individuals are not treated as ends or in which they are systematically treated as objects (conditions such as those embodied in modern civil society). Again, I would suggest that his meaning is not significantly distorted, as opposed to being expressed in less familiar language, if we state that, for the young Marx, individuals have both a right to be treated as ends and a right not to be treated (systematically) as objects.

At this point, some readers will be close to exasperation. Thus far I have sought to show how certain threads in the early writings, namely Marx's hostility to 'objectification' and his endorsement of the Kantian principle, suggest no hostility to the notion of rights (constituted both broadly and more narrowly). But to some this will seem to miss the point. The young Marx's view of rights, it will be said, is not to be reconstructed from what he says about the moral standing of individuals or even regarding the moral constraints on the treatment of individuals. Marx's view is rather to be found in his explicit discussion of rights, especially in 'Zur Judenfrage'. An

---

[306] 'Kritik: Einleitung' 385/182/251.   [307] *Ibid.*

examination of these remarks, it is claimed, will readily confirm that he was 'scathingly contemptuous' of any reference to moral rights.[308]

This approach seems misguided. In the first place, it seems possible to talk about rights without using that term; that is, it seems possible to translate rights talk into some other vocabulary (about moral standing, constraints, and so on). (There is also a translation problem here: sifting Marx's texts for the appearance of a particular term is made harder because the most obvious candidate here is a slippery word with a number of meanings. As an adjective, *'recht'* can mean 'correct, lawful, and just'; as a noun, *'(das) Recht'* can mean 'a right', 'justice', or 'the system of legal norms and institutions'.) In addition, this approach seems to privilege what we might call Marx's own view of his own views in an inappropriate way, inappropriate because it is possible for someone to reject explicitly a view that they endorse implicitly. Indeed this is a familiar phenomenon. In particular, a deficient self-understanding can lead people to misdescribe their own beliefs. It might be – to paraphrase a locution from recent discussions of Marx's views concerning the injustice of capitalism – that Marx did believe in moral rights although he did not think that he did so.[309]

Nonetheless, for the purposes of argument, it is worth examining the explicit references to rights contained in the early writings. It soon emerges that doing so offers little comfort to those who insist on the young Marx's hostility to rights. In particular, 'Zur Judenfrage' is not the attack on rights which it is widely supposed to be.

One difficulty in establishing this last claim is that accounts of Marx's hostility to rights vary considerably. However, some progress can be made by attending to two relevant distinctions. The first of these differentiates between rights claims in general and particular categories of rights (such as legal, natural, human, civil, political, special, general, and so on). The second of these differentiates between the formal character of rights claims and their 'content', that is, the interests that particular rights seek to promote and protect.

A survey of the relevant literature reveals an overwhelming tendency to characterise Marx's complaints in 'Zur Judenfrage' as both general and formal. First, Marx is portrayed as discussing rights in general rather than any particular category of rights. We are told, for example, that he does not merely object to *'bourgeois rights'*, but rather provides 'a more radical

[308] Kai Nielsen, *Marxism and the Moral Point of View: Morality, Ideology, and Historical Materialism* (Boulder CO, 1989) p. 245.
[309] See G. A. Cohen, 'Review of Allen Wood, *Karl Marx'*, *Mind*, volume 92 (1983) p. 443; and Norman Geras, 'The Controversy about Marx and Justice', *New Left Review*, no. 150 (1985) p. 70.

critique in which all rights are to be rejected'.[310] Second, Marx is portrayed as concerned with the formal character of rights claims rather than with their 'content'. 'Zur Judenfrage' is portrayed, for example, as an attack on 'the concept of rights'.[311]

It is my contention that these characterisations of the subject matter of 'Zur Judenfrage' are mistaken. In the first place, the young Marx is concerned, not with rights in general, but with two particular categories of rights. He does not discuss rights claims in general, and I doubt whether his remarks about particular rights can be extrapolated to cover such claims. In the second place, Marx's interest is in the content and not the form of rights. He is concerned with the values and interests which are protected and promoted by particular rights and not with an analysis of the form of these rights claims. In order to substantiate this reading, I now turn to examine the relevant passages.

The context of Marx's discussion is of considerable significance. It is provided by Bauer's insistence that the religious and egoistic nature of Jews disqualifies them from the possession of human rights.[312] It is this claim that Marx is concerned to reject and which forms the focus of his discussion.[313]

In order to assess Bauer's claim, Marx again appeals to empirical evidence, examining what he calls 'human rights (*Menschenrechte*)' as they are understood in modern states – and especially as they are elaborated in various French and American constitutional documents.[314] 'Human rights', in this context, appear to be understood best as a variety of moral rights, namely those moral rights for which individuals qualify by virtue of being human, rather than, for example, by virtue of having made some contract or performed some action. After all, the constitutional documents in question were not lists of legal rights *simpliciter* but rather sought to embody the basic normative principles of the political community, principles which were intended to guide the subsequent actions of legislature and executive.[315] Marx notes that these 'human rights' are conventionally divided (by contemporaries) into the '*droits de l'homme*' and the '*droits du citoyen*' – as

[310] R. G. Peffer, *Marxism, Morality and Social Justice* (Princeton, 1990) p. 324. Elsewhere, 'Zur Judenfrage' is described as a text in which 'Marx rejects rights' as such. Philip J. Kain, *Marx and Ethics* (Oxford, 1988) p. 75.

[311] William A. Edmundson, *An Introduction to Rights* (Cambridge, 2004) p. 79. Elsewhere, 'Zur Judenfrage' is described as an attack on 'the very concepts' of civil and political rights. Allen E. Buchanan, *Marx and Justice: The Radical Critique of Liberalism* (London, 1982) pp. 67–8.

[312] See Marx's quotation from Bauer in 'Zur Judenfrage' 362/160/227.

[313] 'Zur Judenfrage' 361/160/227.   [314] *Ibid.* 362/160/227.

[315] The preambles to these various French declarations vary, but typically invoke – as the 1789 version has it – the 'natural, inalienable, and sacred' nature of the rights to be respected by subsequent laws and political actions.

evidenced by the famous 'Declarations' of the French revolution – and indicates that he will also adopt this distinction.[316]

(Unhelpfully, in 'Zur Judenfrage', Marx occasionally uses the label '*Menschenrechte*' to refer to the general category of 'human rights', as well as to the sub-category which he also refers to as the '*droits de l'homme*'.[317] There is no serious danger of confusion here since the context makes clear which of the two he is referring to at any one point. However, some translators render what we might call '*Menschenrechte*' in general as 'human rights', and '*Menschenrechte*' proper as 'rights of man'. For clarity, I will follow that convention here, referring to the 'rights of man', like the 'rights of the citizen', as a sub-category of what I shall call 'human rights'.)

Marx begins his discussion with the 'rights of the citizen', which he also calls 'civil rights'.[318] He makes it clear that he is primarily interested in the 'content' of these rights. 'What constitutes their content', writes Marx, 'is *participation* in the *community*, in the *political* community or *state*'.[319] In particular, such rights include the right to active and passive suffrage (to stand and to vote in elections). Civil rights, in short, acknowledge and protect the 'political freedom' whose achievements and limitations Marx has been considering throughout the article.[320]

Marx insists that, as a result, Bauer is mistaken in thinking that Jews can be legitimately excluded from civil rights. Marx has already demonstrated that political emancipation does not presuppose 'the consistent and positive abolition' of religion.[321] Indeed, as we have seen, the empirical evidence confirms that religion not only survives but even flourishes in modern civil society. Accordingly, the claim that Jews are religious cannot provide a reason for excluding them from the '*droits du citoyen*'. Indeed, religious individuals, as the American evidence demonstrates, are among the archetypal beneficiaries of political emancipation. Marx suggests that Bauer is simply mistaken in claiming that the religious nature of Jews (or indeed of anyone else) disqualifies them from possessing these political rights.

At this point, Marx turns to consider 'the *droits de l'homme* as distinct from the *droits du citoyen*'.[322] His primary concern, once again, is to examine whether Bauer is correct to insist that the possession of a religious or egoistic nature provides a reason for excluding an individual from the protection that such rights offer.[323]

---

[316] 'Zur Judenfrage' 362/160–1/227–8.   [317] See *ibid.* 362/160/227.
[318] *Ibid.* 362/160–1/227.   [319] *Ibid.* 362/161/227.   [320] *Ibid.*   [321] *Ibid.* 362/161/227–8.
[322] *Ibid.* 362/161/228.   [323] *Ibid.*

That individuals are religious, Marx insists, provides no licence to exclude them from the 'rights of man'. Again he appeals to empirical evidence, insisting that in the most advanced political states the *'privilege of faith'* is acknowledged explicitly as one of the 'rights of man'.[324] The 'rights of man', as Marx elaborates, typically assert a core right to freedom which has, as one of its derivative rights, freedom of conscience, that is, 'the right to practise one's own religion'.[325] That Marx is concerned with the content (in this case, whether the religious commitments of individuals are protected) of particular rights (in this case, the 'rights of man' enumerated by modern states) is confirmed by his argumentative procedure at this point. He parades a series of quotations from his chosen constitutional examples which demonstrate that Jews, as religious individuals, are entitled to the protection variously offered by Article 10 of the 1791 version of the French 'Déclaration des droits de l'homme et du citoyen', by Title I of the 1791 French Constitution, by Article 7 of the 1793 version of the French 'Déclaration', by Title XIV, Article 354, of the 1795 French Constitution, by Article 9, section 3, of the Constitution of Pennsylvania, and by Articles 5 and 6 of the Constitution of New Hampshire. Marx concludes that the supposed incompatibility which Bauer identifies, between religious commitment and the rights of man, is in reality 'so alien to the concept of the rights of man that the *right to be religious* – to be religious in whatever way one chooses and to practise one's chosen religion – is expressly enumerated amongst the rights of man'.[326]

(Earlier in the article, Marx had asked: 'Does the standpoint of *political* emancipation have the right (*das Recht*) to demand from the Jews the abolition of Judaism and from man the abolition of religion?'[327] His subsequent reply is, of course, an emphatically negative one, namely that the modern state has no right to require atheism as a condition of citizenship. It will be apparent that Marx uses, without comment, qualification, or criticism, the concept of rights to formulate this question. On the present account of his views there is nothing surprising about this fact. However, if 'Zur Judenfrage' were intended to demonstrate Marx's hostility to the very concept of rights, it would certainly be careless of him to have utilised in this way the very notion to which he is supposed to have objected so strongly.)

Marx also addresses Bauer's claim that the egoistic nature of Jews makes them ineligible as bearers of human rights. Marx insists that Bauer is mistaken in suggesting that egoism provides any licence for excluding individuals from the protection of the rights of man. Indeed, he suggests that

[324] *Ibid.*   [325] *Ibid.*   [326] *Ibid.* 363/162/228.   [327] *Ibid.* 351/150/216.

egoism, far from disqualifying an individual from the protection offered
by the rights of man, is subtly acknowledged and safeguarded by those
very rights. Once again, Marx proceeds by reviewing and quoting from his
chosen empirical examples, examining a series of goods (liberty, property,
equality, and security) which are explicitly promoted and protected in the
constitutional documents of advanced political states. Note that in each of
these cases, Marx does not reject the value of the relevant good as such,
nor does he reject the idea of individuals having a right to these goods.
Instead, he critically examines the particular way in which these goods are
understood and protected by modern states.

A right to liberty, Marx notes, is explicitly protected by both Articles 2
and 6 of the 1793 French 'Déclaration' and by Article 6 of the 1791 French
'Déclaration'. However, the liberty that is promoted in, and protected by,
these documents is characterised by Marx as 'the right to do and perform
everything which does not harm others'.[328] The individual, on this account,
is treated as 'an isolated monad who is withdrawn into himself', who thinks
of others as 'boundary' posts circumscribing his freedom.[329] The liberty that
these constitutional declarations defend, he suggests, is founded not on the
'association of man with man but rather on the separation of man from
man'.[330] In short, Marx maintains that the relevant documents presuppose
both an individualistic account of humankind and a conception of liberty
which treats other individuals as undesirable constraints.

A right to property, Marx notes, is explicitly protected by Article 16 of
the French Constitution of 1793. However, this right is interpreted as giving each individual licence to 'enjoy and dispose *at will* of his goods, his
revenues and the fruit of his work and industry'.[331] In particular, Marx elaborates, individuals are given complete licence to use their resources 'without
regard for other men and independently of society'.[332] Like the account of
liberty embodied in the same document, this understanding of property
encourages us to think of the claims of others as undesirable constraints on
our own actions. That is, such rights embody and reinforce the view that
each individual should see other individuals not as 'the *realisation*' but as
the '*limitation*' of his own freedom.[333]

Marx makes comparable claims concerning the content of the remaining
rights of man, namely the right to equality and to security. Thus he interprets Article 3 of the 1795 Constitution as defining civil rather than political
equality, and suggests that this civil equality consists in equal access to the

[328] *Ibid.* 364/162/229.   [329] *Ibid.*   [330] *Ibid.*   [331] *Ibid.* 365/163/229.
[332] *Ibid.*   [333] *Ibid.* 365/163/230.

individualistic liberty described above. The equality of humankind which is defended in these constitutional documents is said to consist in nothing more than considering every individual 'to be a self-sufficient monad'.[334] Nor does the concept of security, as defended in Article 8 of the 1793 Constitution, offer any respite from this remorselessly individualistic vision of the world. Indeed, security is interpreted in these documents as 'the *guarantee*' of the egoism of modern civil society, in that the role of the political community is reduced to that of 'a mere *means*' to defend and promote the narrow self-interest of the 'partial', 'egoistic', and '*bourgeois*' individual of modern civil society.[335] The community, on this account, 'appears as a framework extraneous to the individuals, as a limitation of their original independence'.[336]

In short, the focus of Marx's discussion of rights in 'Zur Judenfrage' is provided by Bauer's insistence that the religious and egoistic nature of Jews makes them ineligible as bearers of human rights. From his examination of the '*droits de l'homme*' and the '*droits du citoyen*', as embodied in recent French and American constitutions, Marx argues that the contemporary understanding of human rights, far from being incompatible with the religion and egoism that flourishes in modern civil society, actually protects and promotes it. As a result, he can claim that Bauer has failed in his attempt to provide a justification for continuing discrimination. Marx's own argumentative strategy in this discussion is not to attack the very concept of rights, but rather to reject this contemporary justification for excluding Jews from the possession of human rights.

This account is confirmed by the (less well-known) remarks in *Die heilige Familie*, where Marx has occasion to remind Bauer of the position taken in 'Zur Judenfrage'. Marx summarises his earlier conclusion as being that the human rights embodied in the constitutional understanding of modern states 'recognise and sanction' the individualism and religiosity of 'modern bourgeois society'.[337] Human rights, he maintains, as outlined in the relevant documents, embody an implicit acknowledgement by the modern state of its interrelationship with, and domination by, civil society.[338] The egoistic and religious nature of individuals can, as a result, scarcely disqualify them from being bearers of such rights, and Bauer's attempted justification of continued discrimination against Jews fails. (In *Die deutsche Ideologie*, Marx would also refer back to this discussion in 'Zur Judenfrage',

---

[334] *Ibid.*   [335] *Ibid.* 366/164/230–1.   [336] *Ibid.* 366/164/230.
[337] *Die heilige Familie* 129/122.   [338] *Ibid.* 120/113.

explaining that he had therein sought to expose illusions 'only in relation to the human rights proclaimed by the French Revolution'.[339])

On this account, Marx's real concern is less with the nature of rights than with what might be called the conditions for citizenship – that is, with the requirements and responsibilities attached to membership – in the modern political state. Bauer had insisted that the Jew was disqualified from modern citizenship because 'his Jewish and restricted nature always triumphs in the long run over his human and political obligations'.[340] For Marx, the error embodied in this claim is both basic (because egoism and religion flourish in modern states) and illuminating (because contemporary citizenship emerges as entirely compatible with egoism and religion).

Indeed, egoism and religiosity, rather than disqualifying individuals from modern citizenship, are said to be characteristics which modern citizenship is designed to promote and protect. Even in its most idealistic moments – and it is, Marx reminds us, 'the ardour of its youth' which is reflected in the founding constitutional documents under consideration – modern political life can raise no more inspiring ideal than that of being 'the servant of egoistic man'.[341] The constitutional self-understanding of these advanced states, announced in these various declarations, reveals modern political life to be 'a mere means whose goal is the life of civil society'.[342] Marx concludes that, in the modern social world, 'the sphere in which man behaves as a communal being (*Gemeinwesen*) is thereby degraded to a level below the sphere in which he behaves as a partial being'.[343] The source of his disapproval is clear. This model of political life underestimates the value of community and citizenship, treating the 'partial being' of civil society as the '*real* and *authentic* man', and reducing citizenship, in turn, to a celebration of 'man as *bourgeois*'.[344] Not only are modern citizens liable to let their narrow and particularistic interests corrupt their understanding of the common good, but this state of affairs is implicitly condoned by the constitutional self-understanding of the political state.

(Finally, I should mention an argument often attributed to Marx, and offered as evidence that he regarded rights as superfluous under socialism. In broad outline, the argument runs as follows: the protective function of rights is required only where individual interests are liable to be seriously infringed; serious infringements of individual interests are a product of class society; socialism is not a class society; therefore, under socialism there will

---

[339] *Die deutsche Ideologie* 181/197.
[340] 'Fähigkeit' 176/136. This passage is quoted in 'Zur Judenfrage' 349/148/214.
[341] 'Zur Judenfrage' 366/164/231.   [342] *Ibid.*   [343] *Ibid.*   [344] *Ibid.*

be no need for rights.[345] This argument, as will be readily apparent, is not a persuasive one. Not least, its second premise, concerning the source of significant interpersonal conflict, looks implausible. However, despite the literature, and making due allowance for formulations whose vocabulary belongs more properly to Marx's later work, I can find little trace of this argument in 'Zur Judenfrage'. Moreover, efforts to 'reconstruct' such an argument from what Marx does say there remain unconvincing. That said, this line of reasoning does indirectly broach a number of important issues about the nature of the polity that might replace the modern state, some of which are discussed further in Chapter 4.[346])

ANTISEMITISM AND JEWISH SELF-HATRED

I begin this section with a disclaimer. It is important to understand the limitations of what I am trying to establish here. In particular, I do not attempt to reach a considered judgement regarding either Marx's overall attitude towards Jews and Judaism (including his purported 'antisemitism') or his overall reaction towards his own Jewish identity (including his purported Jewish 'self-hatred'). I am concerned here only with a particular piece of textual evidence, albeit one that anyone holding an informed view on those wider issues must engage with, namely Marx's remarks in the second part of 'Zur Judenfrage'.

(Somewhat reluctantly, I use 'antisemitism' here in an expansive way to refer to all forms of Judeophobia, and 'racial antisemitism' to refer to its late nineteenth-century racial variant – 'somewhat reluctantly' because the original hyphenated term 'anti-Semitism' and its various correlates were a late nineteenth-century invention of Judeophobes. In using the term to refer to all forms of Judeophobia – from the xenophobic Judeophobia of the ancient world, through Christian anti-Judaism, to the racial anti-Semitism of the Nazis – there is a danger, not only of exaggerating or prejudging the similarities between very different historical phenonema, but also of lending credibility to the racial concept of Semitic languages and peoples.)

In the first part of 'Zur Judenfrage' – as was noted above – Marx typically treats Judaism as a representative religion, and Jews as representative of individuals with religious commitments. That is, unlike Bauer, he does not treat Judaism as a distinctly retrograde and abhorrent kind of belief, and

---

[345] See, for example, Buchanan, *Marx and Justice*, pp. 66–7; and Steven Lukes, 'Can a Marxist Believe in Human Rights?', *Praxis International*, volume 1 (1982) p. 342.

[346] For some adjacent doubts about Buchanan's account, see Jeremy Waldron (ed.), *Nonsense Upon Stilts: Bentham, Burke and Marx on the Rights of Man* (London, 1987) pp. 126ff.

Jews as a distinctly retrograde and abhorrent kind of humanity. However, in the second part of the article, Marx makes a series of derogatory remarks about 'Judaism' and about 'Jews' which have appeared to many readers to embody precisely the kind of hostility that he had earlier avoided. These remarks have occasioned an extraordinary volume of commentary.[347] The overwhelming majority of that literature portrays Marx as crudely reproducing some platitudes of contemporary Jew-hatred, and his remarks are typically interpreted as largely incontrovertible evidence of either his anti-semitism or his Jewish 'self-hatred'.

The content of the remarks in question is easily enumerated. In the course of four or five pages, Marx variously (and repetitively) associates Jews and Judaism with 'practical need',[348] 'self-interest',[349] 'haggling' (Marx uses the derogatory word '*Schacher*', which was often adopted by contemporaries for the business transactions of Jews),[350] the worship of 'money',[351] 'anti-social' activities,[352] 'egoism',[353] the worship of 'exchange',[354] contempt for 'man as an end in himself',[355] the rootless nature of 'money in general',[356] and 'selfish need'.[357] These characteristics are, broadly speaking, familiar from his portrayal of modern civil society, not least in the first part of the article. Marx now takes those negative characteristics of civil society and associates them with Jews and with Judaism. This much is largely uncontroversial. Rather less certain, however, is the wider context, and accordingly the meaning, of these remarks.

Marx opens the second part of 'Zur Judenfrage' by characterising Bauer's approach as a theological one. Marx notes, in particular, that on Bauer's account a Jew is a religious individual committed to Judaism. Marx refers to this religious individual as 'the *Sabbath* Jew (*den Sabbatsjuden*)'.[358] However, Marx announces that he intends to consider not this religious individual but rather 'the *everyday* Jew (*den Alltagsjuden*)', or what he also refers to as 'the real secular Jew (*den wirklichen weltlichen Juden*)'.[359] Since it is the 'everyday' Jew and not the 'Sabbath' Jew who is the target of

[347] For an annotated bibliography, see Carlebach, *Karl Marx and the Radical Critique of Judaism*, pp. 438–49. Subsequent discussions include Helmut Hirsch, *Marx und Moses: Karl Marx zur 'Judenfrage' und zu Juden* (Frankfurt am Main, 1980); Paul Lawrence Rose, *German Question/Jewish Question: Revolutionary Antisemitism from Kant to Wagner* (Princeton, 1992); and Gilman, *Jewish Self-Hatred*.
[348] 'Zur Judenfrage' 372/169/236.   [349] *Ibid.*
[350] *Ibid.* 372/170/236. See also Michael Schmidt, 'Schacher und Wucher', *Menora: Jahrbuch für deutsch-jüdische Geschichte*, volume 1 (1990) pp. 235–77.
[351] 'Zur Judenfrage' 372/170/236.   [352] *Ibid.* 372/170/237.
[353] *Ibid.* 374/171/238.   [354] *Ibid.* 375/172/239.
[355] *Ibid.* (Consequently, Marx claims, contempt for 'theory', 'art', and 'history'.)
[356] *Ibid.*   [357] *Ibid.* 376/173/240.   [358] *Ibid.* 372/169/236.   [359] *Ibid.*

Marx's derogatory remarks, it is essential to identify this subject with some precision.

The significance of this issue is easily missed, and the subject of Marx's remarks in the second part of 'Zur Judenfrage' is often misidentified as a result. Many readers take it for granted that any mention of Jews in this article has a perfectly familiar and literal sense.[360] However, what this literal sense could be is not obvious. Consider two literal senses in which the 'everyday Jew' might be considered as a Jew. One possibility is that the 'everyday Jew' is simply what liberal contemporaries might have called a German subject of the Mosaic faith. However, in this case, the contrast with Bauer's usage would look completely empty. Both 'everyday' and 'Sabbath' Jew would share, and be defined by, their religious commitments. An alternative possibility is that the 'everyday' Jew is defined, not by religion, but by some alternative yet still literal criteria (such as nationality, ethnicity, or race). However, whilst this would enable the contrast with Bauer's 'Sabbath' Jew to be established, there is no plausible evidence – either in 'Zur Judenfrage' or elsewhere in the early writings – of Marx employing such a definition. Indeed, all of that textual evidence suggests that the young Marx shares with Bauer the religious definition of what it is to be a Jew.[361]

The interpretative suggestion advanced here is that Marx's 'everyday' Jew is not in any *literal* sense a Jew at all, but is rather to be understood as the modern egoistic member of civil society *whatever* his religious commitments and *whatever* his national, ethnic, or racial, background. In short, Marx's distinction between the 'Sabbath' Jew and the 'everyday' Jew distinguishes between, on the one hand, the members of a specific religious minority and, on the other, the members of civil society whatever their religious commitments (or indeed national, ethnic, or racial, identity).

This reading, which might be labelled metaphorical, not only makes sense of Marx's distinction between 'Sabbath' and 'everyday' Jew, but also clarifies several of his subsequent remarks (which would otherwise appear highly puzzling). For example, Marx states that in the modern social world 'the Christians have become Jews'.[362] On a literal reading, he would appear to be making a bizarre and inaccurate empirical claim about a pattern of religious conversion. On the metaphorical reading, however, Marx is claiming rather that all modern citizens (whatever their religious commitments) are marked by the egoism of civil society. Similarly, when he characterises

---

[360] See, for example, the explanation that Marx's focus is not the 'Sabbath Jew' of Bauer, but rather 'contemporary Jewry'. Robert S. Wistrich, *Revolutionary Jews: From Marx to Trotsky* (London, 1976) p. 33.

[361] See, for example, 'Zur Judenfrage' 353/151/218.   [362] *Ibid.* 373/170/237.

Christian teaching in America as reflecting the 'domination of Judaism over the Christian world', Marx is not making an implausible theological remark about the doctrinal content of American evangelising, but rather emphasising that in America the very proclamation of the Christian Gospel has become a commercial matter.[363] Finally, when he claims that 'Judaism' reached the 'peak' of its development under 'the rule of Christianity', Marx is not making the literal suggestion that the achievements of Jewish communities, or of rabbinical Judaism, were at their greatest under the Christian states of the Middle Ages, but rather combining the current motif (associating Judaism and commercial activity) with the motif examined earlier (associating Christianity with the modern state).[364] The claim that Judaism 'not only managed to survive in Christian society' but in fact 'reached its highest level of development there', is Marx's metaphorical way of rehearsing his view that commercial activity not only survived the separation out of political state and civil society but flourished in the modern social world as never before.[365]

The metaphorical reading removes another interpretative difficulty. Many commentators have been puzzled by Marx's failure to reproduce the derogatory vocabulary with which he characterises the 'everyday' Jew in the second part of 'Zur Judenfrage' – at least, to anything like the same degree – elsewhere in the early writings (perhaps especially in the first part of the same article and in the reprise of his views on the Jewish question in *Die heilige Familie*).[366] However, if, in the second part of 'Zur Judenfrage', the young Marx is not directly abusing (literal) Jews as distinct from the Christian majority, it is no longer surprising to discover that, when he is (elsewhere) directly discussing (literal) Jews as distinct from the Christian majority, he largely refrains from the derogatory language in question.

The metaphorical reading also clarifies Marx's argumentative strategy in the second part of 'Zur Judenfrage'. Marx identifies Bauer as endorsing what was undoubtedly a widespread derogatory association between Jewry and 'egoism'.[367] (This derogatory association between Jewry and egoism is sufficiently widespread in nineteenth-century German culture that the search for Marx's original 'philosophical' source seems to me misguided. Those who disagree usually find that philosophical origin in the work

[363] *Ibid.* 373/171/238.   [364] *Ibid.* 376/173/240.   [365] *Ibid.* 374/171/238.
[366] See, for example, Marshall Berman, *Adventures in Marxism* (London, 1999) p. 94, and Carlebach, *Karl Marx and the Radical Critique of Judaism*, pp. 174ff.
[367] See 'Zur Judenfrage' 347/146/212. See also D. S. Landes, 'The Jewish Merchant: Typology and Stereotypology in Germany', *Leo Baeck Institute Year Book*, volume 19 (1974) pp. 11–23; and Ernest K. Bramsted, *Aristocracy and the Middle Classes in Germany: Social Types in German Literature, 1830–1900*, revised edition (Chicago, 1964) pp. 134–41.

of either Spinoza or Feuerbach.[368]) Marx's argumentative strategy is to expand that association to apply to the 'everyday' Jew, that is, to all the individuals (whatever their religious commitments) who make up modern civil society. This metaphorical usage was undoubtedly facilitated by the contemporary usage of '*Jude*', and its cognates, to indicate a variety of disreputable forms of the pursuit of profit.[369] (The derogatory associations of *Jude* and of *jüdisch* were sufficiently widespread that many German Jews referred to themselves rather as *Israelit*, or as being of *mosaisch* faith. Indeed, some, including David Friedländer, sought a linguistic reform of public documents along these lines, in the hope that it would discourage prejudice.[370]) Marx, in other words, adopts a linguistic extension here. Whereas Bauer took the received language in which the Christian majority abused the Jewish minority (as egoistic individuals who worshipped money) and repeated it, Marx took that language and extended it so as to include the majority Christian population (as egoistic individuals who worshipped money).

In short, the metaphorical reading has a number of advantages over its literal alternative: it can account for the contrast of 'Sabbath' and 'everyday' Jew; it helps make sense of Marx's subsequent, and otherwise puzzling, remarks about the relation between Judaism and Christianity; it makes the contrast with the rest of the early writings less problematic; and it elucidates the argumentative strategy of 'Zur Judenfrage'.

This interpretation also provides a justification for rejecting the plethora of secondary accounts which assume that all of Marx's derogatory remarks refer to Jews and Judaism in some literal sense. Not least, the extraordinary suggestion that Marx's remarks concerning 'the emancipation of society from Judaism' should be interpreted in an annihilationist manner, as if Marx were talking literally of ridding contemporary society of Jews, can be rejected.[371] Such an extraordinary suggestion can be dismissed on textual as well as contextual grounds. Marx is envisaging, not, as one such commentator has it, 'a world without Jews', but rather a future without the egoism of civil society.[372] This is not only clear from the text of 'Zur

---

[368] For links to Spinoza, see, for example, Joel Schwartz, 'Liberalism and the Jewish Connection: A Study of Spinoza and the Young Marx', *Political Theory*, volume 13 (1985) pp. 58–84; and Steven B. Smith, *Spinoza, Liberalism, and the Question of Jewish Identity* (New Haven, 1997) p. 109. For attributions to Feuerbach, see, for example, Carlebach, *Karl Marx and the Radical Critique of Judaism*, pp. 152–3; and Rose, *German Question/Jewish Question*, p. 300.

[369] See, for example, Keith Spalding, *A Historical Dictionary of German Figurative Usage*, with the assistance of Kenneth Brooke and Gerhard Müller-Schwefe, 6 volumes (Oxford, 1952–2002) pp. 1413ff.

[370] See Meyer, *The Origins of the Modern Jew*, p. 69.   [371] 'Zur Judenfrage' 377/174/241.

[372] *A World Without Jews* is the title given by Dagobert Runes to his edition of 'Zur Judenfrage'.

Judenfrage', but also confirmed by Marx's gloss in *Die heilige Familie* where he describes his earlier comments on 'the task of abolishing the essence of Jewry' as equivalent to 'the task of abolishing the *Jewish character of civil society*, abolishing the inhumanity of the present-day practice of life, the most extreme expression of which is the *money system*'.[373] (References in the more wayward literature to the 'Marx-Hitler brand' of malevolent Jew-hatred are tendentious and absurd.[374])

However, in rejecting the literal reading of the second part of 'Zur Juden-frage', I certainly do not intend to suggest that Marx's comments are either unproblematic or inoffensive. His remarks make many of us uneasy, and it is important to locate the source of that discomfort.

The widespread derogatory association was an exclusive one, in that it suggested that Jews were 'egoistic' in a way that the Christian majority were not. This exclusive association was endorsed by Bauer and rejected by Marx. However, the form of Marx's rejection is significant. That exclusive association could be challenged in two ways: either one might question the association as such, or one might question the exclusivity of that association. Marx's linguistic extension adopts the latter strategy. That is, he does not question the characterisation of contemporary Jews as 'egoistic' but rather rejects the exclusivity of that association, extending the charge to include the Christian majority. For example, in *Die Judenfrage*, Bauer refers to the circumvention of (religious) law for reasons of self-interest by Jews as 'Jewish Jesuitry'. Marx does not challenge this initial association but simply extends it to the Christian majority. The very same 'Jewish Jesuitry', he suggests, is found in the modern relation between individuals and (political) law; given sufficient opportunity, all members of civil society tend to circumvent legislation when it is in their narrow self-interest to do so.[375]

As a result, although Marx denies their exclusive nature, his linguistic extension reproduces some of the derogatory associations of 'Jew' created and popularised by Gentile abuse. Not surprisingly, this approach fails to respect many of our own sensibilities regarding these issues. Less anachron-istically, I would suggest that Marx's argumentative strategy also has sub-stantive weaknesses of its own. In particular, it has what might be called strategic and critical failings.

The strategic failing of Marx's linguistic extension is that it risks reinfor-cing rather than challenging contemporary prejudice. There is at least some

---

[373] *Die heilige Familie* 116/110.
[374] Dagobert D. Runes, 'Introduction', Karl Marx, *A World Without Jews*, ed. Dagobert D. Runes (New York, 1959) pp.x–xi.
[375] 'Zur Judenfrage' 375/172–3/240.

evidence from its subsequent publication history that 'Zur Judenfrage' did not entirely avoid this fate.[376] (It appears, for example, that selections from Marx's article were later reprinted by Wilhelm Hasselmann as part of his antisemitic editorial activities for the Lassallean ADAV.[377])

The critical failing of Marx's linguistic extension is that it reproduces, in an apparently unthinking manner, associations which he might well have questioned. For example, Judaism does not strike all of us as the most obvious religion to link metaphorically with 'egoism', perhaps especially when compared with Christianity, a religion which appears to place individual salvation at its very core.[378]

Despite these significant failings, it remains important not to lose sight of, or to underestimate, the differences between Bauer and Marx on 'the Jewish question'. On this issue, the existing literature is not always a reliable guide. Commentators typically characterise Marx's remarks in (the second part of) 'Zur Judenfrage' as evidence of, either his antisemitism, or his Jewish self-hatred. In order to assess the propriety of such characterisations, a working definition of the relevant concepts is required. I begin with the concept of antisemitism.

According to what might be characterised as a historically promiscuous definition, antisemitism consists in holding or expressing derogatory views about Jews (as distinct from other social groups) or about Judaism (as distinct from other religions). I call this a historically promiscuous definition because in the context of nineteenth-century Germany some would judge it rather too effective in identifying antisemites. In particular, it would label nearly all Gentiles (and not a few Jews) who expressed an opinion on these issues antisemitic. Even eminent so-called 'philosemites' would fall within its compass. For example, at the heart of Dohm's controversial proposal to grant to Jews civil rights and obligations equal to those of the Christian majority was the idea of exchanging civil equality for moral improvement.[379] Dohm sought to alter the social environment – for instance, by offering incentives to restructure Jewish economic life – which he held responsible for the 'degenerate' character of the Jews. About the

---

[376] See the pertinent remarks in Paul W. Massing, *Rehearsal for Destruction: A Study of Political Anti-Semitism in Imperial Germany* (New York, 1949) p. 159.

[377] See Eduard Bernstein, 'Di yidn un di daytshe sotsial-demokratie', *Tsukunft*, volume 26 (1921) pp. 145–7; and Jack Jacobs, *On Socialists and 'The Jewish Question' After Marx* (New York, 1992) chapter 2.

[378] See, for example, Graetz, *The Structure of Jewish History*, p. 70; and Hess, *Rom und Jerusalem* 5/19.

[379] On Dohm, see Jonathan M. Hess, *Germans, Jews and the Claims of Modernity* (New Haven, 2002) chapter 1; and Robert Liberles, 'Dohm's Treatise on the Jews: A Defence of the Enlightenment', *Leo Baeck Institute Year Book*, volume 33 (1988) pp. 29–42.

latter, however, Dohm had few doubts, maintaining that Jews 'are guilty of a proportionately greater number of crimes than the Christians; that their character in general inclines more towards usury and fraud in commerce; that their religious prejudice is more antisocial and clannish' and so on.[380] In short, not only would this definition include the overwhelming majority of nineteenth-century Germans who expressed a view on this matter; it would seem also to risk glossing over the (significant) differences between them.

According to what might be characterised as a less historically promiscuous definition, in order to qualify as antisemitism the hostility shown towards Jews as a group is required to have a practical or political dimension. Making what might be called 'persecution' an essential element of antisemitism is compatible with the expansive use of the latter term, since persecution can take a wide variety of forms (including expulsion, pogroms, legal discrimination, and extermination). However, by comparison with the promiscuous definition, it might seem to promise a standard which is historically more discriminating, a standard which can identify, and engage with, important divides and disagreements. In nineteenth-century Germany, for example, it has been suggested that the appropriate benchmark of antisemitism is not whether an individual expresses derogatory views about Jews or about Judaism, but rather whether – those derogatory views apart – an individual was in favour of, or opposed to, emancipation.[381]

Note that according to either of these definitions, 'Zur Judenfrage' is not an antisemitic text. It might initially appear that Marx's remarks qualify according to the historically promiscuous definition. However, if my account of Marx's metaphorical usage is correct, that judgement would seem mistaken. In the relevant parts of his article, Marx does not apply the derogatory language in question to Jews (as opposed to other groups) or to Judaism (as opposed to other religions). His strategy of linguistic extension is aimed precisely at denying that Jews have any characteristics that are not shared by other members of civil society *whatever* their religious commitments and *whatever* their national, ethnic, or racial, background. Using the less historically promiscuous definition, 'Zur Judenfrage' is similarly innocent of antisemitism.[382] In both parts of the article, Marx is primarily concerned to demonstrate that there are no differences between Jews and Christians which could justify excluding the former from citizenship in the modern state. This support for Jewish emancipation is voiced throughout

---

[380] Dohm, *Über die bürgerliche Verbesserung der Juden*, p. 18.
[381] See, in this context, Yovel, *Dark Riddle*, pp. 98, 89.
[382] As Seigel remarks: 'If his language makes us squirm, his actions do not justify putting him in the camp of the racists'. Jerrold Seigel, *Marx's Fate: The Shape of a Life* (Princeton, 1978) p. 114.

the early writings.[383] It is also reflected in what we know of his political practice in this period. Thus, Marx responded positively, despite what he described as his 'dislike' for the Jewish religion, to a request from the head of the Jewish community in Cologne to sign a petition to the provincial assembly in favour of Jewish emancipation.[384] Moreover, this remains his most immediate political difference with Bauer.[385] As Marx observes: 'We do not tell the Jews that they cannot be emancipated politically without radically emancipating themselves from Judaism, which is what Bauer tells them.'[386]

Some commentators have grudgingly conceded this point, but then sought to weaken the contrast with Bauer by suggesting that Marx's commitment to Jewish emancipation was in some way peculiarly reluctant. For example, he is described as supporting political emancipation, and as therefore having to admit that (for better or worse) political emancipation required removing legal discrimination against Jews.[387] Such accounts seem misleading. Whilst Marx disapproves of religious commitments of any kind, the evidence does not support the suggestion that he was a peculiarly grudging supporter of Jewish emancipation.

Others have reluctantly conceded this point, but then sought to weaken the contrast with Bauer by claiming that, emancipation apart, Marx endorsed Bauer's account of the character of Jews and Judaism.[388] This suggestion is simply mistaken.[389] In addition to their fundamental and non-trivial disagreement over Jewish emancipation, Bauer makes numerous

---

[383] This point is consistently obscured in Jeffrey S. Librett, *The Rhetoric of Cultural Dialogue: Jews and Germans from Moses Mendelssohn to Richard Wagner and Beyond* (Stanford CA, 2000) chapter 7.

[384] Marx to Arnold Ruge, 13 March 1843, *MEW* 27, p. 418; *MECW* 1, p. 400. See also Helmut Hirsch, 'Karl Marx und die Bittschriften für die Gleichberechtigung der Juden', *Archiv für Sozialgeschichte*, volume 8 (1968) pp. 229–45.

[385] Even this difference is sometimes obscured. Low, for example, claims that 'whatever their ulterior motives and ultimate purposes may have been, both Bauer and Marx obviously undercut the Jew's demand for emancipation'. Alfred D. Low, *Jews in the Eyes of the Germans: From the Enlightenment to Imperial Germany* (Philadelphia, 1979) p. 286.

[386] 'Zur Judenfrage' 361/160/226.

[387] See Carlebach, *Karl Marx and the Radical Critique of Judaism*, p. 165; and Wistrich, *Revolutionary Jews*, p. 38.

[388] Frankel maintains that, although they disagreed about emancipation, Marx accepted Bauer's 'factual judgements' concerning the Jews; and Wistrich suggests that 'according to Marx, there was nothing much wrong with Bauer's "critique of the Jewish religion" or with his description of the nature of the Jew to be emancipated'. See Jonathan Frankel, *Prophecy and Politics: Socialism, Nationalism and the Russian Jews, 1862–1917* (Cambridge, 1981) p. 18; and Robert S. Wistrich, *Socialism and the Jews: The Dilemmas of Assimilation in Germany and Austria-Hungary* (East Brunswick NJ, 1982) p. 20.

[389] The implausible suggestion that Marx was somehow a greater Jew-hater than Bauer also appears in the literature: Frankel claims that Marx's contempt for Jews is 'deeper perhaps than Bauer's'; Katz suggests that 'rather than soften Bauer's evaluations of Judaism and the Jewish character, Marx appears to sharpen them'; and Rose maintains that Marx expressed a Jew-hatred that was 'far more systematic in its theory than the other revolutionary efforts of Bauer and company'. See Frankel, *Prophecy and Politics*, p. 18; Katz, *From Prejudice to Destruction*, p. 170; and Rose, *German Question/Jewish Question*, p. 302.

claims about Jews or about Judaism on which Marx does not pass comment, and which there is no evidence that he endorses. This is scarcely
surprising given the different concerns of the two authors, but, as a result,
the claim that, emancipation apart, there was no difference between their
views should be rejected. Moreover, even if we limit their purported agreement to claims made by Bauer on which Marx expressed an opinion – apart
from the already noted disagreement about emancipation – this claim does
not withstand examination. A few additional examples will suffice here.
Whereas Bauer treats Judaism as a distinctly retrograde and abhorrent kind
of belief, and Jews as a distinctly retrograde and abhorrent kind of humanity,
Marx typically treats Judaism as a representative religion, and Jews as representative of individuals with religious commitments. Whereas Bauer offers
the remarkable characterisation of German Jews as less oppressed than the
Christian majority, Marx portrays German Jews as doubly oppressed, suffering not only (like all German subjects) from 'the general lack of political
emancipation', but also (unlike that majority) from 'the pronounced Christianity of the state'.[390] Whereas Bauer insisted on the non-historical nature
of the Jews, the young Marx endorsed Samuel Hirsch's view that the Jews
had not merely survived and changed but had also contributed to historical progress. In *Die heilige Familie*, noting Bauer's claim, made in response
to Hirsch, that the Jews were an 'eyesore', Marx remarks that 'something
which has been an eyesore to me from birth, as the Jews have been to the
Christian world, and which persists and develops with the eye is not an
ordinary sore, but a wonderful (*wunderbar*) one, one that really belongs to
my eye and must even contribute to a highly original development of my
eyesight'.[391]

So much for the characterisation of 'Zur Judenfrage' as an antisemitic
text. I turn now to consider whether the article provides any evidence of
'Jewish self-hatred' on Marx's part.

The concept of 'Jewish self-hatred' is widely used but its meaning is often
left unclarified.[392] In its original form it had psychopathological connotations of extravagant self-contempt. (The term was popularised by Theodor
Lessing's *Der jüdische Selbsthaß* (1930), which presented six case-studies of
individual self-hating Jews who were driven to suicide.[393]) However, more

---

[390] 'Zur Judenfrage' 349/148/213–14.   [391] *Die heilige Familie* 93/88.
[392] See the helpful discussion in Ritchie Robertson, *The 'Jewish Question' in German Literature,
1749–1939: Emancipation and Its Discontents* (Oxford, 1999) pp. 285ff.
[393] See Theodore Lessing, *Der jüdische Selbsthaß* (Munich, 1984); and Lawrence Baron, 'Theodor
Lessing: Between Jewish Self-Hatred and Zionism', *Leo Baeck Institute Year Book*, volume 26 (1981)
pp. 323–40.

recent usage has typically jettisoned those connotations, and frequently uses the term to connote what might be called 'Jewish antisemitism' (that is, to identify Jewish proponents of antisemitism).[394]

For either sense to apply here, Marx has to be considered Jewish. There are at least four senses in which – notwithstanding his baptism at the age of six and a half – Marx might be considered a Jew. First, he was a Jew according to the dominant interpretation of religious law (where matrilineal descent has – since Ezra – governed Jewish lineage), since he was the child of a Jewish mother (however we characterise his father, who converted to Christianity the year before Karl was born).[395] Second, Marx was a Jew according to self-description, in that he described himself as such.[396] For example, in correspondence with his uncle Lion Philips, Marx identifies himself as a Jew by descent, referring to Disraeli as a man coming 'from our common stock (*unser Stammgenosse*)'; and, in another letter to his uncle, referring ironically to the shock to 'our ancestral pride' delivered by Darwin's demonstration that all humankind are descended from the apes.[397] Third, Marx was a Jew according to the reactive criteria of attribution, in that he was routinely identified as such by both friends and enemies.[398] (The first published antisemitic attack on Marx appeared as early as 1850, from the pen of the journalist – and, in Engels's compelling description, 'first-class brawler' – Eduard Müller-Tellering.[399]) Fourth, Marx was a Jew by virtue of his multi-rabbinical background; his uncle, grandfather, and great-grandfather were rabbis in his native city of Trier, and the family

---

[394] See Gilman, *Jewish Self-Hatred*, p. 1.

[395] His mother (née Henriette Pressburg) – whose father, Isaac Pressburg, was a rabbi and businessman in Nijmegen (Holland) – delayed conversion until 1825.

[396] This is occasionally denied: 'never once', writes Clark, 'publicly or privately, did he proclaim, admit, state, defend, or just refer to himself as a Jew'. Joseph Clark, 'Marx and the Jews: Another View', *Dissent*, volume 28 (1981) p. 83.

[397] See, for example, Marx to Lion Philips, 29 November 1864, *MEW* 31, pp. 431–3; *MECW* 42, pp. 46–8; and Marx to Lion Philips, 25 June 1864, *MEW* 30, pp. 665–7; *MECW* 41, pp. 542–4. The first letter is sometimes (erroneously) cited as Marx's sole acknowledgement that he was of Jewish descent. See, for example, Isaiah Berlin, 'Benjamin Disraeli, Karl Marx and the Search for Identity', *Against the Current: Essays in the History of Ideas*, ed. Henry Hardy (Oxford, 1989) pp. 276–7. On Marx's Dutch relatives, see Werner Blumenberg, 'Ein Unbekanntes Kapitel aus Marx' Leben: Briefe an die holländischen Verwandten', *International Review of Social History*, volume 1 (1956) pp. 54–111.

[398] For the claim that 'the Jew is one whom other men consider a Jew', see Jean-Paul Sartre, *Anti-Semite and Jew* (New York, 1948) p. 68. For the suggestion that Jewish identity is largely preserved by Gentile hatred, see Spinoza's *Tractatus Theologico-Politicus* in *Spinoza's Political Works*, ed. A. G. Wernham (Oxford, 1958) p. 63.

[399] See Werner Blumenberg, 'Eduard von Müller-Tellering: Verfasser des ersten antisemitischen Pamphlets gegen Marx', *Bulletin of the International Institute for Social History*, volume 6 (1951) pp. 178–97; and Roman Rosdolsky, *Engels and the 'Non-Historic' Peoples: The National Question in the Revolution of 1848*, ed. John-Paul Himka (Glasgow, 1986) pp. 191–207.

genealogy includes a significant number of distinguished rabbis and Talmudic scholars.[400] The literature usually mentions two distinguished fifteenth- and sixteenth-century rabbis from Padua – Judah ben Eliezer Halevi Minz and Meir Katzenellenbogen – amongst his forebears. More recently Marx's paternal ancestry has even been traced back to Rashi, the acronym of the eleventh-century Solomon b. Isaac, a hugely important and influential rabbinical scholar and Bible exegete whose commentary on the Talmud is still read.[401] (Indeed, this rather understates his importance; his commentary is included with almost all printed editions of the Talmud, and the traditional way of studying the latter is with one finger on the talmudic text and one finger on Rashi's commentary.) On his maternal side, Marx's ancestors include not only a number of highly distinguished Court Jews, but perhaps also the sixteenth-century rabbi, talmudist, and kabbalist Judah Loew, known by the acronym Maharal, who was reputed to have created a homunculus, the Golem of Prague, out of soil (the *adamah* out of which God had made Adam and Lilith).[402]

That said, there seems little evidence of 'Jewish self-hatred', either in 'Zur Judenfrage' or elsewhere in the early writings. Adopting the original psychopathological usage of the term, there is no significant biographical or textual evidence – let alone the serious clinical or confessional evidence that would really be required – to suggest that the young Marx suffered from inordinate self-loathing on any grounds (including that of his Jewish identity).[403] Adopting the later non-psychopathological reading, since 'Zur Judenfrage' is not (on either of the two mooted definitions) an antisemitic text (see above) it cannot be evidence of Marx's purported 'Jewish antisemitism'.

Nevertheless, that Marx was in some relevant sense a Jew makes his appropriation of Gentile abuse in the second part of 'Die Judenfrage' rather more shocking to modern readers than would otherwise be the case. This reaction is understandable. However, Marx was far from unique in this regard. Points of comparison can, for example, be found in the contemporary writings of two of the young Marx's closest acquaintances – Heine and Moses

[400] See Monz, *Karl Marx*, p. 222.
[401] See Shlomo Barer, *The Doctors of Revolution: Nineteenth-Century Thinkers Who Changed the World* (London, 2000) chapter 29 and appendix.
[402] On Judah Loew, see Byron L. Sherwin, *Mystical Theology and Social Dissent: The Life and Works of Judah Loew of Prague* (Rutherford NC, 1982); and Byron L. Sherwin, *The Golem Legend: Origins and Implications* (Lanham MD, 1985).
[403] For Marx's supposed 'Jewish self-hatred', see Wistrich, *Revolutionary Jews*, chapter 1; Murray Wolfson, *Marx: Economist, Philosopher, Jew: Steps in the Development of a Doctrine* (London, 1982) chapter 5; and Gilman, *Jewish Self-Hatred*, pp. 188–208.

Hess – who shared his Jewish descent, radical politics, and Rhenish origins. Heine and Hess not only repeat themes from the Gentile abuse of Jews but also adopt the same linguistic extension as Marx.

Hess has been described accurately as a talented and decent man who, in the early 1840s, seemed likely to become the third member of the 'alliance' that Engels had formed with Marx.[404] He is now perhaps best known as the author of *Rom und Jerusalem* (1862), an idiosyncratic and disorganised work which established his claim to be considered as a prescient forerunner of Zionism.[405] Inspired by the example of Italian unification (and Josephine Hirsch), Hess argued that a Jewish 'national' redemption was both desirable and feasible.[406] Resettlement and statehood in Palestine were desirable as a way both of escaping the deep-seated hostility of Gentiles and of realising 'Mosaic, that is, socialist principles'.[407] It was feasible given the sympathy of Western powers (especially France), and the willing participation of *Ostjuden* (together with Sephardic Jews from Arabic-speaking countries). This interest in the fate of modern Jewry was also apparent in Hess's earliest writings, albeit that he had then come to very different conclusions. In *Die heilige Geschichte der Menschheit* (1837) and *Die europäische Triarchie* (1841), Hess insisted on the historical importance of Judaism at the same time as hesitating about its present and future role (equivocating between an endorsement of assimilation and an account of the 'ghost-like' character, incapable of death or resurrection, of contemporary Jewry which would seem to preclude it).[408] In the intervening period, however, Hess's views about Jews and Judaism underwent a complex and irregular development, not always illuminated by his own later attempts to characterise and account for it. Of particular interest, in the present context, are Hess's socialist writings from the early 1840s.

In some of these articles, and notwithstanding his own consistent support for Jewish emancipation, Hess incorporated motifs from the tradition of Gentile abuse into his social criticism. Perhaps most strikingly, he used the

---

[404] See Franz Mehring (ed.), *Aus dem literarischen Nachlass von Karl Marx, Friedrich Engels und Ferdinand Lassalle*, volume 2 (Stuttgart, 1913) p. 358.

[405] Isaiah Berlin describes Hess as having 'virtually invented' Zionism. Isaiah Berlin, *The Life and Opinions of Moses Hess* (Cambridge, 1959) p. 1. On Hess's life and work, see also Edmund Silberner, *Moses Hess: Geschichte seines Lebens* (Leiden, 1966); Shlomo Na'aman, *Emanzipation und Messianismus: Leben und Werk des Moses Hess* (Frankfurt am Main, 1982); and Shlomo Avineri, *Moses Hess: Prophet of Communism and Zionism* (New York, 1985).

[406] Josephine Hirsch (the sister of Hess's sister-in-law) was the anonymous grieving friend to whom the work is addressed. See Silberner, *Moses Hess*, p. 403.

[407] For this elision of Judaism and socialism, see *Rom und Jerusalem* 116/85.

[408] See *Die europäische Triarchie*, pp. 111–12; and *Die heilige Geschichte der Menschheit, Schriften*, p. 72.

idea of human sacrifice to link modern civil society with Judaism. Thus, in 'Philosophie der That', Hess identifies the Hebrew 'Jehovah' with the god Moloch, who demands human sacrifice.[409] This *'jüdischen Moloch-Jehova'*, he suggests, is the 'archetype *(Urtypus)*' of the bloody sacrifice which characterises the religious and political alienation of the modern world.[410] This extraordinary association of Judaism and human sacrifice is repeated in 'Über das Geldwesen' in the context of an extended parallel between human sacrifice in religion and the modern cult of money.[411] Modern economic greed and ancient ritual sacrifice, Hess suggests, are analogous denials of humanity. Importantly, however, the modern cult of money is not identified as a uniquely Jewish phenomenon. Instead, Hess adopts a linguistic extension and applies this motif from the tradition of Gentile abuse of Jews to the majority population; he refers to the 'modern Jewish-Christian world of shopkeepers *(der modernen jüdisch-christlichen Krämerwelt)*' as a 'prosaic *(prosaisch)*' realisation of the brutal 'cult of blood' found in ancient Judaism, in which money replaces blood (*'Das Geld is das soziale Blut'*).[412]

In linking civil society and Judaism through the idea of human sacrifice, Hess utilises, and could be seen as lending credibility to, one of the central elements of medieval Jew-hatred.[413] Moreover, in considering Hess's use of these motifs in his social criticism, it is important for modern readers to realise that the blood libel was of not merely historical interest in nineteenth-century Europe. The most recent of such allegations – the 'Damascus affair', in which several Jews 'confessed' under torture to the ritual murder of an Italian monk and his servant – had taken place in 1840.[414] In contemporary Germany, the blood libel had intellectual as well as populist advocates. For example, Georg Daumer and Friedrich Ghillany insisted that the God of the Jews before the Babylonian exile was the same deity as that of surrounding peoples (namely Moloch and Baal), and portrayed human sacrifice as having led an underground existence throughout Jewish history. The Damascus affair, they maintained, was simply the most recent of those periodic occasions on which ritual murder had broken cover.

---

[409] See Hess, *Schriften*, pp. 210–26.   [410] *Ibid.* p. 215.

[411] *Ibid.* pp. 329–48. For the (contested) influence of Hess's 'Über das Geldwesen' on 'Zur Judenfrage', see Silberner, *Moses Hess*, pp. 191–2; and Carlebach, *Karl Marx and the Radical Critique of Judaism*, pp. 110ff.

[412] Hess, *Schriften*, pp. 345.

[413] For the rise of the stereotype of Jews as involved in ritual murder and cannibalism, see Gavin I. Langmuir, *Toward a Definition of Antisemitism* (Berkeley, 1990) especially chapter 11.

[414] See Frankel, *The Damascus Affair*.

Heine's relation to Judaism and to Jews is a complex and much studied subject.[415] His portraits of historical and contemporary Jewry often reproduce Gentile stereotypes, albeit in complex, serious, and interesting ways. (Heine's rather conventional observations about *Ostjuden* constitute a possible exception. He reproduced both dominant clichés, namely that, relative to their western counterparts, *Ostjuden*, were not only dirtier and less educated, but also possessed greater integrity or authenticity.[416])

Perhaps most striking, given modern sensibilities, is Heine's enthusiastic use of derogatory stereotypes of the physical and bodily. His writings are, for example, full of Jewish noses. They are perhaps most prominent in his prose works. In *Die Bäder von Lucca*, for example, having dwelt at length on the noses of Gumpel and Hirsch, Heine suggests – the allusion is, of course, to conversion – that 'these long noses are a sort of uniform whereby Jehovah recognises his old bodyguards even when they have deserted'.[417] However, there are also examples in his poetry. Thus, when the eponymous ursine hero of *Atta Troll*, suffering from a fever, wakes up in a bedroom containing stuffed birds with elongated beaks he is reminded, in his delirium, of Hamburg (with its Jewish quarter).[418]

Perhaps more importantly, given both the topic of this chapter and his connections with the young Marx (see Chapter 2), Heine also links contemporary Jewry and commercial activity using the derogatory language of contemporary Gentile abuse. There are some stark examples in *Lutezia* (which originated in articles written for the *Augsburger Zeitung* in the 1840s). In the course of criticising the response of French Jews to the Damascus affair, for example, Heine remarks that the 'money power of the Jews is indeed great, but experience teaches us that their greed (*Geiz*) is still greater'.[419] In the context of this association (of greed and Jewry) Heine uses the same strategy of linguistic extension – taking a thread from the tradition of Gentile abuse of Jews and extending it to cover the majority population as well – that is found in the writings of Marx and Hess.[420] Thus, in *Lutezia*, Heine

---

[415] See, for example, William Rose, *Heinrich Heine: Two Studies of His Thought and Feeling* (Oxford, 1956) part 2; Ruth L. Jacobi, *Heinrich Heines jüdisches Erbe* (Bonn, 1978); and especially S. S. Prawer, *Heine's Jewish Comedy: A Study of His Portraits of Jews and Judaism* (Oxford, 1983).

[416] On the contemporary situation and perception of *Ostjuden*, see Steven E. Aschheim, *Brothers and Strangers: The East European Jew in German and German-Jewish Consciousness, 1800–1923* (Madison, 1982); and Jack Wertheimer, *Unwelcome Strangers: East European Jews in Imperial Germany* (Oxford, 1987).

[417] *Die Bäder von Lucca*, pp. 88–9. For the seriousness here, see Prawer, *Heine's Jewish Comedy*, pp. 132ff.

[418] See *Atta Troll* 64–9/463–6.   [419] *Lutezia* 1, p. 53.

[420] In this context, see also Ludwig Börne's essay 'Der Jude Shylock im *Kaufmann von Venedig*', *Sämtliche Schriften*, ed. Peter and Inge Rippmann, volume 1 (Düsseldorf, 1964) pp. 499–505; and Orlando Figes, 'Ludwig Börne and the Formation of a Radical Critique of Judaism', *Leo Baeck Institute Year Book*, volume 29 (1984) pp. 351–82.

claims that among French Jews '*as with other Frenchmen*, gold is the god of the time, and industry is the prevailing religion'.[421] The same extension appears elsewhere, not least in the context of observations about Hamburg, a city whose commercial centre and vibrant Jewish community evoke a double association in Heine's work ('huckstering' and the '*Dreckwall*'). Heine initially associates the Jews of Hamburg with this 'huckster world' whose stench he abhors, but is quick to implicate Christians in the same practices (both Jews and Christians, he observes, blame the smell on the canal).[422] Perhaps the starkest clarification of this strategy appears in an early letter to Christian Sethe, in which Heine explained: 'All Hamburgers I call Jews; those whom I call baptised to distinguish them from the circumcised are what the vulgar call Christians.'[423]

Such parallels between the contemporary writings of Heine, Hess, and Marx do not, of course, license any elision of the many and significant differences that also exist between these authors. In the present context, I note two specific contrasts between Marx, on the one hand, and Hess and Heine, on the other.

First, by comparison with Hess and Heine, and despite his distinguished family heritage, Marx's knowledge of, and interest in, both Judaism and Jewish history and culture appear very slight indeed. Hess received (albeit reluctantly) an orthodox Jewish education under the supervision of his grandfather in Bonn.[424] As an adult, Hess always maintained an eclectic but genuine interest in Jewish literature and history, developing a significant friendship with Heinrich Graetz. Hess promoted Graetz's work in France and provided him with materials for his history; whilst Graetz repeatedly attempted to persuade Hess to join him on a trip to Palestine.[425] (Interestingly, on a visit to the Carlsbad spa in 1876, Marx also met Graetz, and subsequently sent him some photographs and a copy of *Kapital* as a token of his 'great respect (*Hochachtung*) and friendship'.[426] Graetz clearly felt warmly towards Marx and his family, but was at something of a loss to know what he might send Marx in return.[427]) Heine, meanwhile, although

[421] *Lutezia* I, p. 53 (my emphasis).   [422] 'Tannhäuser' 60/353. See also 'Anno 1829'.

[423] Heine to Christian Sethe, 20 November 1816, *Säkularausgabe* volume 20 (Berlin, 1970), p. 22.

[424] See Silberner, *Moses Hess*, pp. 1–21; and Theodor Zlocisti, *Moses Hess: Vorkämpfer des Sozialismus und Zionismus, 1812–1875: eine Biographie*, second edition (Berlin, 1921) pp. 16–22. For his reluctance, see the diary excerpts in Wolfgang Mönke, *Neue Quellen zur Hess-Forschung* (Berlin, 1964).

[425] See Reuwen Michael, 'Graetz and Hess', *Leo Baeck Institute Year Book*, volume 9 (1964) pp. 91–121; and Edmund Silberner, 'Heinrich Graetz' Briefe an Moses Hess, 1861–1872', *Annali*, volume 4 (1961) pp. 374ff.

[426] Heinrich Graetz, *Tagebuch und Briefe*, ed. Reuven Michael (Tübingen, 1977) p. 336 n. 2.

[427] See *ibid.* pp. 336–7.

his family do not seem to have been observant, spent some time in a *heder* before receiving his secondary education in a Gentile Gymnasium. Although it is clear that Heine's knowledge of both Hebrew and Yiddish was not extensive, his interest in Jewish history, religion, and identity, continued – notwithstanding his conversion and occasional denials – in adulthood.

(Confronted by Marx's ignorance of, and lack of interest in, Jewish history and culture, some have sought out implicit affinities between Marx's work and certain Jewish traditions. For example, his writings have been portrayed as embodying such characteristic concerns of Jewish thought as a conception of humankind as driven by a need to improve the world, a 'midrashic' approach to texts, and a conception of liberation as a return from exile.[428] Such observations can have heuristic utility, but I am not persuaded that this interpretative perspective provides much new insight into Marx's work.)

Second, Marx's use in 'Zur Judenfrage' of some negative associations of Judaism and Jewish life is not balanced by clear and compelling evidence of more generous sentiments elsewhere in his work, say of the kind that can be found with ease in the writings of Heine and Hess. (One distinguished modern scholar could locate 'only one passage' in the entire Marx corpus which spoke of a group of Jews 'with a certain friendliness'.[429]) Hess's interest in the history and fate of European Jewry is reflected most obviously in his enthusiasm for a socialist programme of settlement in Palestine, but his later writings also embody a concern about the effects of acculturation on traditional patterns of Jewish solidarity, and, in that context, a deeply felt and simply expressed sympathy for religious orthodoxy, the Hebrew language, and the routines of Jewish family life.[430] Similarly, Heine's poetry and prose always reflect his genuine, if complex, enthusiasm for the Bible, Jewish history and legend, the customs and ritual of Judaism, Hebrew and

[428] See Dennis Fischman, *Political Discourse in Exile: Karl Marx and the Jewish Question* (Amherst NE, 1991).
[429] Edmund Silberner, 'Was Marx an Anti-Semite?', *Historia Judaica*, volume 11 (1949) pp. 40ff. The passage concerns the Jews of Jerusalem in an article for the *New York Tribune*, 15 April 1854. *MEW* 10, pp. 168–76; *MECW* 13, pp. 100–8. Henry Pachter portrays this article as 'one of the few where this most unsentimental writer rises to chords of moving lament'. Henry Pachter, 'Marx and the Jews', *Socialism in History: Political Essays of Henry Pachter*, ed. Stephen Eric Bronner (New York, 1984) p. 242. Note that Marx's remarks evince only a general human sympathy. See also Carlebach, *Karl Marx and the Radical Critique of Judaism*, chapter 19.
[430] See Hess, *Jüdische Schriften*. For the suggestion that Hess's life and work illuminate some modern dilemmas of Jewish identity, see Ken Koltun-Fromm, *Moses Hess and Modern Jewish Identity* (Bloomington IN, 2001).

Yiddish words, and, perhaps especially – a less complex enthusiasm this –
for the culinary joys of '*Kuggel*' and '*Schalet*'.[431]

I have been concerned in this chapter with the young Marx's account of
the character of the modern state, especially in 'Zur Judenfrage'. That this
account is developed in the course of a critical engagement with Bruno
Bauer, and through a series of sometimes strained and distracting analogies with Christianity, has not facilitated comprehension of Marx's views.
However, I maintain that some attention to that context and those religious
parallels can illuminate the argument of this rich but elusive text.

In his middle-period writings on 'the Jewish question', Bauer propounds
a derogatory view of the (exclusive and tenacious) nature of Jews, and
of their (exclusive, positive, and hypocritical) religion. He insists that the
essential nature of Jews is not only incompatible with the real freedom
which constitutes the subject and end of human history, but also makes
them unsuitable recipients of more familiar forms of contemporary emancipation. On Bauer's account, baptism offers Jews no escape from disadvantage, the exclusion of Jews from the privileges of the majority in the
Christian state is no wrong, and the conditions of citizenship in the modern
constitutional state are impossible for Jews to fulfil.

Marx used his disagreement with Bauer's writings on 'the Jewish question'
as a springboard from which to develop an account of the achievements and
limitations of political emancipation. In 'Zur Judenfrage', Marx identified
two claims as central to Bauer's rejection of Jewish emancipation. Suitably
reconstructed, these claims assert that meaningful liberty is impossible as
long as either individuals or the state retain a religious character.

Marx's rejection of the first of these claims appealed to empirical evidence as demonstrating that meaningful liberty – in the form of political
emancipation – was compatible with religious commitment. The example
of the most advanced contemporary American states clarified Marx's understanding of the characteristic form of political emancipation as a process

---

[431] 'Kuggel' is a noodle pudding which can be savoury or sweet (served hot on Friday night and cold
on Saturday). Heine judged it to have done more to preserve Jewishness than all the publications
of the *Verein für Cultur und Wissenschaft der Juden* put together. See Heine to Moses Moser, 14
December 1825, *Säkularausgabe*, volume 20, p. 227. 'Schalet' is the traditional Sabbath midday stew
(better known as cholent) which Heine refers to as 'kosher-type ambrosia . . . catered straight from
heaven'. 'Prinzessin Sabbat' 128/654.

whereby society separated out into a political and civil realm, and property and religion were relegated to the latter.

Marx's rejection of the second of these claims utilised a revisionist definition of the 'Christian' state as equivalent to the modern democratic state. Although this revisionist definition enables a swift rejection of Bauer's position – since, if the modern democratic state is 'Christian', then Bauer is obviously mistaken in suggesting that a state with a religious character cannot emancipate the Jews – the rationale for such a usage is initially unclear. I suggested that Marx was tempted by this idiosyncratic nomenclature, not only because it enabled him to indulge his enthusiasm for paradiastolary figures of speech, but also because he thought that a twofold parallel between Christianity and the modern state could provide significant insight into the achievements and limitations of political emancipation.

On this account, the achievement shared by Christianity and the modern state was that both acknowledged the value of community, a notion with several associations in Marx's early writings (including important links with equality and human nature). The limitation shared by Christianity and the modern state was that their embodiment of community was an inadequate one. In particular, Marx maintained that the modern social world is organised in such a way that the various defects of civil society are allowed to continue, to intensify, and to shape and dominate the state.

This understanding of the limitations of the modern state plays a significant role in Marx's rejection of Bauer's claim that it is the religious and egoistic nature of Jews which makes them ineligible as rights bearers in the modern state. Since the constitutional arrangements of modern states function, on Marx's account, to protect religion and egoism, Bauer's characterisation of the nature of Jews does not provide any reason for their exclusion from political life. Marx's critical examination of the constitutional self-understanding of modern states was portrayed, not as evidence of his hostility to moral rights, but rather as an attempt both to undermine Bauer's attack on Jewish emancipation, and to suggest that the model of citizenship embodied in, and protected by, the modern state is an impoverished one.

Finally, I suggested that the portrayal of 'Zur Judenfrage' as compelling evidence of either antisemitism or 'Jewish self-hatred' should be rejected. That said, Marx's incorporation of strands from the Gentile abuse of Jews into his wider social criticism – a practice also evident in the contemporaneous writings of Heine and Hess – should be seen, not only as falling short of modern sensibilities, but also as having strategic and critical failings of its own.

So much for the character of the modern state, and Marx's polemical assault on Bauer. I turn now, after an examination of the nature and influence of Feuerbach's writings, to Marx's account of the fate of the state in a future society characterised by extensive human flourishing.

CHAPTER 4

Human flourishing

In the early writings, Marx contrasts 'political emancipation' with what he calls 'human emancipation'. This comparison has two central elements: political emancipation is flawed but extant, whilst human emancipation, although it avoids the 'incompleteness and contradiction' of its political counterpart, is not yet realised in the world.[1]

The unrealised character of human emancipation underpins many of the interpretative difficulties with which the present chapter wrestles. That the young Marx was less certain of the social and political arrangements of the future than of the lineaments of the contemporary world is scarcely surprising. That, in the absence of such certainty, he offered so little by way of clear or considered speculation is rather more remarkable. (Clear and careful reflection is not, of course, incompatible with what is sometimes called 'ideal theory' – that is, theory concerned with questions of institutional design in a society which does not suffer from scarcity, injustice, and so on.[2]) Even measured by the standards of the early writings, Marx's account of human emancipation is abbreviated and opaque.

The final two chapters of this book pursue two closely related tasks. In the present chapter, I outline the young Marx's vision of human emancipation, attempting, in particular, to flesh out its elusive political dimension. In the following (and final) chapter, I examine the rationale for Marx's considered reluctance to say more about the contours of the society of the future.

There is an additional difficulty here. The little that is said about human emancipation is scattered throughout the early writings, and, as a result, Marx's views have to be pieced together from a series of fragments. Whereas the textual focus of the last two chapters was on a single work (the *Kritik* and 'Zur Judenfrage' respectively), these final two chapters are, of necessity, rather more wide-ranging.

---

[1] 'Zur Judenfrage' 361/160/226.
[2] For the notion of ideal theory, see John Rawls, *A Theory of Justice* (Oxford, 1971) pp. 8–9; and John Rawls, *Political Liberalism* (New York, 1993) p. 284.

That said, the present account of human emancipation does have a textual starting point and leitmotif. It might be thought of, somewhat figuratively, as an extended commentary on the oft-quoted final paragraph of the first part of 'Zur Judenfrage'.[3] In this guiding paragraph, Marx observes that human emancipation requires a reorganisation of society such that the individual becomes 'a *species-being* (*Gattungswesen*)' in 'his empirical life'.[4] In such a world, the 'real individual man (*wirkliche individuelle Mensch*)' seemingly 'resumes (*zurücknimmt*)' the 'abstract citizen (*abstrakten Staatsbürger*)' into himself, and social force is no longer separated from individuals in the form of '*political* force (*politischen Kraft*)'.[5] In this chapter, I am especially keen to discover what it might mean for an individual to become a 'species-being' in this regard, and what happens to the political dimension of social life in this transformation.

THE STRUCTURE OF HUMAN EMANCIPATION

Like many of the left-Hegelian terms of art which surface periodically in the early writings, the notion of 'species-being' manages to confuse modern readers and to generate conflicting commentary. That said, Marx's use of the term appears largely straightforward and intelligible. (I do not mean to suggest that the term has a single connotation which is adopted consistently throughout the early writings, but rather that, in most cases, it is possible to decipher Marx's meaning.)

In our guiding passage from 'Zur Judenfrage', a 'species-being' is an individual who has actualised – that is, developed and deployed – his essential capacities.[6] By essential capacities, I mean those capacities that characterise the species (across history and between cultures), and not those that might distinguish one person from another, or members of one kind of society or culture from members of another. Marx suggests that only an individual actualising these essential capacities can be said to have developed in a healthy and vigorous manner, and that only an individual who has developed in such a manner can be said to have flourished. At one point, Marx refers to this flourishing individual as 'the *true* man (*der wahre Mensch*)',

---

[3] The complete passage reads: 'Only when real, individual man resumes the abstract citizen into himself and as an individual man has become a *species-being* in his empirical life, his individual work and his individual relationships, only when man has recognised and organised his *forces propres* as *social forces* so that social force is no longer separated from him in the form of *political* force, only then will human emancipation be completed.' 'Zur Judenfrage' 370/168/234.
[4] *Ibid.*   [5] *Ibid.*   [6] See also *Manuskripte* 574/333/386.

using 'true' in the Hegelian sense to connote an entity that adequately expresses (is true to) its essential nature.[7]

Marx maintains that becoming a species-being is a difficult and demanding task. Human beings may possess these essential capacities universally, but they are extensively actualised – that is, developed and deployed by many individuals – only under certain historical conditions. In particular, as the previous chapter sought to demonstrate, Marx holds that the conditions for extensive human flourishing are not met in the modern social world. Human nature is said to find only a limited and contradictory expression in the political state, whilst the 'everyday' life of individuals takes place in civil society, a sphere whose organising principle is inimical to human flourishing. Indeed, the unrestrained individualism of civil society gives free rein not to 'the true man' but to what – in a typically unwieldy but enticing passage – the young Marx describes as 'man in his uncultivated, unsocial aspect, man in his contingent existence, man just as he is, man as he has been corrupted, lost to himself, sold, and exposed to the rule of inhuman conditions and elements by the entire organisation of our society – in a word, man who is not yet a *true species-being*'.[8]

It is the notion of becoming a species-being in the 'actual' rather than the 'ideal' world which provides the benchmark of human emancipation. Marx maintains that human emancipation will be 'completed' only when 'the *true* man' is found in 'empirical life', and not merely reflected in the pale and inadequate form of 'the *abstract citizen*' of the political state.[9] The emancipatory aspirations of the early writings revolve around this notion of a social world organised so as to allow individuals to develop and deploy their essential human capacities in everyday life.[10]

That Marx uses human nature as an evaluative standard – to define human emancipation and criticise the modern social world – is readily apparent. This constitutes what might be called the perfectionist thread in the early writings. Perfectionism is a moral standpoint which values the development and deployment of certain human capacities (for artistic expression, for example) apart from any pleasure or happiness that they might bring. (The name of this moral standpoint derives from the traditional characterisation of such capacities, whose promotion constitutes the morally good, as 'perfections' of human character.) Because it treats the development and deployment of these human capacities as good in

---

[7] 'Zur Judenfrage' 370/167/234. See also *ibid.* 366/164/231.   [8] *Ibid.* 360/159/226.
[9] *Ibid.* 370/168/234.   [10] See *Auszüge aus James Mill* 451/217/265.

themselves, irrespective of their hedonistic consequences, perfectionism is often characterised as an objective theory of the good.[11] Some modern scholars distinguish between broad perfectionism (which values certain characteristics of the individual) and narrow perfectionism (which values certain characteristics of the individual because they realise some aspect of human nature).[12] The perfectionist thread in the early writings would appear to belong to the latter variant.[13]

This characterisation of perfectionism as a 'thread' is intended to suggest that this is not the only moral framework that can be identified in the early writings. The temptation to portray Marx's work as uniform or systematic where it is not should be resisted. Nor do I mean to imply that the moral pluralism of these texts – in which, for example, perfectionist considerations sit alongside an occasionally Kantian vocabulary (see Chapter 3) – is a structured or consistent one. The moral dimension of the early writings may be central to his social and political thought, but the young Marx is scarcely to be considered a moral *theorist* of any significance.

Moreover, to characterise this thread as a perfectionist one is to say little about the substance of Marx's views. A perfectionist approach can take a wide variety of forms (one need only think of the number and diversity of authors, from Aristotle to Nietzsche, who have been characterised as perfectionists). Disagreements within this tradition concern, not least, the constitution of human nature, and consequently the various elements of a perfected human life.

It is, of course, Marx's account of human flourishing, and, in particular, his understanding of the fate of the state in a society characterised by human emancipation, which forms my central concern here. However, before turning to examine Marx's substantive account of human nature, I want to consider the work of Ludwig Feuerbach. The notion of 'species-being' is widely and rightly identified with Feuerbach. Moreover, of all the left-Hegelians, it is Feuerbach's influence on the young Marx that is usually adjudged the most pervasive and significant.

FEUERBACH'S CRITIQUE OF RELIGION AND PHILOSOPHY

Ludwig Feuerbach is not a well-known figure. However, it would be a mistake to categorise him, alongside Bauer, for example, as known to modern

---

[11] See Thomas Hurka, *Perfectionism* (Oxford, 1993) part 1.   [12] See *ibid.* p. 4.
[13] This might be regretted, not least by those who doubt that the appeal to human nature can allow for an intrinsic preference to be given to virtue over vice. See Thomas Hurka, *Virtue, Vice, and Value* (Oxford, 2001) p. vii.

readers mainly as one of the targets of Marx's polemic. Feuerbach is rather one of those thinkers whose fate is to be mentioned often but seldom read; a name frequently invoked in passing (in introductions to the philosophy of religion, in accounts of the roots of *Existenzphilosophie*, and in sketches of the transition from Hegel to Marx) but whose writings are usually not thought to merit much close or independent scrutiny. Feuerbach has been said to typify 'the great forerunners whose influence outstrips their work and consigns the work itself to oblivion'.[14] This might be regretted, since Feuerbach's writings contain much of interest.

Without too much distortion, Feuerbach's work can be divided into three chronological periods: early writings (1828–39), middle-period writings (1839–45), and later works (1845–72).

Feuerbach's early writings (1828–39) include three volumes on the history of philosophy – a survey of modern philosophy from Bacon to Spinoza (which contains discussions of Hobbes, Gassendi, Böhme, Descartes, Geulincx, and Malebranche), a monograph on Leibniz, and a study of Pierre Bayle – which were well-received in progressive Hegelian circles.[15] These works can be seen as foreshadowing some of Feuerbach's later concerns, but from within an explicit, if not uncritical, commitment to Hegelian idealism.[16] The overarching structure of these volumes was provided by a Hegelian model of the historical progress of ideas, in which the truth of absolute idealism slowly unfolded as the necessary result of the critical clash of ever more adequate philosophies, each of them transcending the weaknesses, and incorporating the achievements, of their predecessors. However, within that broadly Hegelian framework, Feuerbach also articulated questions of his own; developing an interest, for example, in what the most defensible kind of 'empiricism' might look like.[17] This period can be thought of as ending with Feuerbach's break with the Hegelian system, if not with every aspect of Hegelianism, in 'Zur Kritik der Hegelschen Philosophie' (1839). Absolute idealism was no longer treated as the benchmark against which the inadequacies of all previous philosophies could be measured, but was rather attacked as part of Feuerbach's rejection of all system-building. This is also the point at which Feuerbach was forced to abandon any realistic hope of a conventional academic career. (His identification as the author of *Gedanken über Tod und Unsterblichkeit* – an

---

[14] Georg Lukács, *Reviews and Articles from 'Die rote Fahne'* (London, 1983) p. 58.
[15] For the development of Feuerbach's early thought, see Marx W. Wartofsky, *Feuerbach* (Cambridge, 1977) pp. 28–134.
[16] For evidence of critical judgement, see the three 'doubts (*Zweifel*)' of 1827–8. 'Fragmente' 155–6/269–70.
[17] See, for example, the discussion of Bacon in Feuerbach, *Geschichte der neuern Philosophie*, pp. 50ff.

anonymous and irreverent rejection of the Christian notion of personal immortality – appears to have been a factor here.)

Feuerbach's middle-period writings (1839–45) include the best-known and most influential of his works. Amongst German radicals, the 'Vorläufige Thesen zur Reform[ation] der Philosophie' (1842) and the *Grundsätze der Philosophie der Zukunft* (1843) had considerable impact. However, it was *Das Wesen des Christentums* (1841) which became his most famous book, and which secured his wider European reputation. These middle-period works deal with three topics which Feuerbach thought of as interrelated: the critique of Christianity, the critique of speculative philosophy, and the development of a new philosophy of 'sensationalism'. The first two of these topics are dealt with more fully below. The proper characterisation of the third is a matter of dispute, and these middle-period writings have generated an interesting dichotomy amongst commentators. Feuerbach is interpreted either as advancing (largely inadequate) abstract arguments (of a familiar kind) in support of an outmoded philosophical position (some variety of naïve empiricism) or as engaged in a less conventional project, seeking to motivate his readers to adopt a different and non-philosophical standpoint from which to view the world.[18]

Feuerbach's later works (1845–72) had less of an impact on both contemporaries and posterity. They have typically been seen as largely predictable attempts to elaborate, defend, and develop the ideas of his middle-period writings. They can be divided usefully into two groups. The first of these comprises a series of attempts to rebut the charge that he had been too quick to generalise from the critique of Christianity to religion in general, and more especially that his anthropocentric focus was unable to account for religions of nature. These works included *Das Wesen der Religion* (1846), the *Vorlesungen über das Wesen der Religion* (delivered in Heidelberg between December 1848 and March 1851), and the *Theogonie* (1857). (Because this group of works includes several attempts to elaborate and defend his middle-period writings, I make occasional reference to them in what follows.) The second group of works – including *Spiritualismus und Sensualismus* (1857), and *Das Geheimnis des Opfers oder Der Mensch ist, was er ißt* (1862) – was concerned to develop Feuerbach's account of human dependency on nature. The most notorious of these pieces, 'Die Naturwissenschaft und die Revolution' (1850), contained his infamous punning claim that '*Man is what*

---

[18] See, for example, Eugene Kamenka, *The Philosophy of Ludwig Feuerbach* (London, 1970) pp. 93–4; and Daniel Brudney, *Marx's Attempt to Leave Philosophy* (Cambridge MA, 1998) chapters 1–2, respectively.

he eats (Der Mensch ist, was er ißt)'.[19] (Despite what might generously be described as his inexpert grasp of the natural sciences, and as a qualification to the generalisation above about the declining impact of Feuerbach's work, there is some evidence that these later writings had an influence on 'scientific materialists' such as Karl Vogt, Jacob Moleschott, Ludwig Büchner and Heinrich Czolbe.[20])

In the present context, it is certain aspects of Feuerbach's middle-period writings which are of particular relevance. More precisely, it is the two negative threads in Feuerbach's middle-period works, rather than the positive 'new philosophy', which provide the main subject of the present section. That is, I focus here on the critique of Christianity (which he often calls a critique of 'religion') and the critique of speculative philosophy (which he often calls a critique of 'philosophy'). Given Feuerbach's understanding of the relation between these subjects (outlined below), they can be treated in parallel. I begin, however, with Feuerbach's critique of Christianity in *Das Wesen des Christentums*; or rather, since that book contains a number of different themes rather than a single coherent argument, I begin with an account of its dominant thread.[21]

In *Das Wesen des Christentums*, Feuerbach seeks to provide a philosophical analysis of Christian religious experience. He distinguishes this focus from that of other contemporary critics of Christianity, including those (like Daumer) who offered a historical (rather than philosophical) account of Christianity, and those (like Bauer and Strauss) who were preoccupied with dogmatic theology (rather than religious experience).[22] Feuerbach's book is organised into two parts, prefaced by some (subsequently much anthologised) introductory remarks, in which he outlines the need for, and main conclusions of, his analysis, together with a defence of those conclusions against an obvious Christian rejoinder.

On Feuerbach's account, Christian religious consciousness requires philosophical analysis because its proper meaning is obscured to those who experience it; 'ignorance' of its real object is said to be a defining feature of

---

[19] Feuerbach, 'Naturwissenschaft', p. 367. For some adumbrations of the pun (including Brillat-Savarin's 'Dis-moi ce que tu manges, je te dirai qui tu es'), see Simon Rawidowicz, *Ludwig Feuerbachs Philosophie: Ursprung und Schicksal* (Berlin, 1964) p. 202; for a sympathetic discussion of the article, see Melvin Cherno, 'Feuerbach's "Man is what he eats": A Rectification', *Journal of the History of Ideas*, volume 24 (1963) pp. 397–406; and for an idiosyncratic modern appropriation of Feuerbach's remarks, see Ken Geach, *The Feuerbach Diet* (Garnant, n.d.).

[20] See Frederick Gregory, *Scientific Materialism in Nineteenth-Century Germany* (Dordrecht, 1977).

[21] For a careful attempt to delineate these threads, see Van A. Harvey, *Feuerbach and the Interpretation of Religion* (Cambridge, 1995) especially chapters 2–3. See also David Leopold, 'Review of Van A. Harvey', *The Bulletin of the Hegel Society of Great Britain*, no. 34 (1996) pp. 67–71.

[22] Feuerbach especially resented the latter association. See, for example, 'Zur Beurteilung'.

religion.[23] This opacity underpins Feuerbach's various characterisations of his own method.[24] Christianity is understood neither as literally true nor as perfectly transparent, but rather as having a hidden meaning which is in need of excavation.

The disarmingly simple conclusion of Feuerbach's excavatory analysis is that in Christianity individuals worship the predicates of human nature projected on to an ideal entity. The epigrammatic claim that 'theology is anthropology' reflects his conviction 'that there is no distinction between the *predicates* of the divine and human nature, and consequently, no distinction between the divine and human subject'.[25] (Feuerbach invokes the *Analytics* of Aristotle to justify this 'consequently'; it is because the predicates in question are not accidents 'but express the essence of the subject' that there is no distinction between subject and predicate.) The Christian God is a collection of essential human predicates, 'purified from the limits of the individual man', which are viewed as if they were the predicates of an objective being existing apart from humankind.[26] There are, in short, two elements to the relation between humankind and the Christian God; it is 'the relation of man to himself, or more correctly to his own nature . . . but a relation to it, viewed as a nature apart from his own'.[27] In this context, Feuerbach often writes of the 'truth' and 'falsity' of Christianity. The 'truth' of Christianity is that in religious consciousness human beings stand in a direct relation with their own nature, and the 'falsehood' of Christianity is that they do not recognise that nature as their own.[28] (Several complexities are glossed over in this summary account of Feuerbach's work. For example, it ignores an ambiguity in his account of the human characteristics which are projected on to the divine being, whereby God is described sometimes as an embodiment of human capacities and powers, and sometimes as a reflection of human hopes and fears.[29])

Feuerbach recognised that Christians might seek to accommodate his claim that the idea of God involves the projection of human predicates on to the divine subject, without conceding his claim that there is no disjunction between the human and the divine subjects.[30] Most obviously, Christians might argue that the anthropomorphic character of God reflects our own inability to grasp His nature except in human terms, and that this human limitation tells us nothing about God's real nature.

---

[23] *Wesen* 46/13.   [24] See *ibid.* 14/xiii and 20/xix.   [25] *Ibid.* 18/xvii.
[26] *Ibid.* 48/14. See also *ibid.* 268/153.   [27] *Ibid.* 48–49/14.   [28] *Ibid.* 334–5/197.
[29] Perhaps depending on the context, see Harvey, *Feuerbach and the Interpretation of Religion*, p. 70. See also Brudney, *Marx's Attempt to Leave Philosophy*, pp. 31ff.
[30] See *Wesen* 51/16.

Feuerbach's response engages with both the validity and the wider meaning of this putative Christian rejoinder. He maintains that it rests on a distinction, between how a thing is and how it appears to be, which is applicable only in cases where we possess some independent access to how things are in themselves.[31] Since, in the present instance, we assuredly lack such access, Feuerbach concludes that the Christian use of this distinction is 'unfounded and untenable'.[32] Moreover, he suggests that the wider meaning of this Christian rejoinder is a revealing one. The willingness to believe that God is very different from how He appears to be implies that 'unbelief' has already taken root, has already 'obtained the mastery of faith'.[33] Indeed, Feuerbach confidently predicts that this Christian response embodies a kind of unbelief about the predicates of God which – barring 'faint-heartedness' and 'intellectual imbecility' – will soon be followed by unbelief concerning the subject of those predicates.[34]

Feuerbach sought to reassure readers that this introductory summary of his anthropological reduction was grounded in more detailed research, and, more especially, that it was justified as well as elaborated by his efforts in the remainder of the book. These subsequent efforts take two directions, as Feuerbach attempts first to unpack the real meaning of particular elements of Christian religious experience, and then to expose the reflections of dogmatic theology on that religious detail.

These two different endeavours structure not only Feuerbach's distinction between the primary and derivative concerns of *Das Wesen des Christentums* but also the two-part organisation of the book itself.

In Part One of *Das Wesen des Christentums*, Feuerbach is concerned with Christian religious experience and describes his aim as a positive or constructive one. Feuerbach seeks to sift out 'real things' from the 'entrancing splendour of imagination and caprice'.[35] His discussion of the Christian doctrine of the Incarnation can provide an illustration.

Feuerbach insists that the Incarnation constitutes both the central doctrine of Christianity and compelling proof of its inherent anthropomorphic tendencies. On the Christian account, God became human for reasons of mercy, and, in particular, out of His compassion for human want and misery. God could have been so moved, Feuerbach suggests, only because 'what is human is not alien to him'.[36] (The allusion to Terence's dictum – 'nothing human is alien to me (*humani nihil a me alienum puto*)' – is surely

---

[31] Elsewhere, Feuerbach restricted use of the distinction to 'directly sensed' objects. See *Grundsätze* 271/10.
[32] See *Wesen* 51/16.   [33] *Ibid.* 53/17.   [34] *Ibid.*   [35] *Ibid.* 20/xix.   [36] *Ibid.* 109/54.

deliberate.[37]) The implicit assumption here is that compassion has a limited remit. As Feuerbach elsewhere explained: 'only a being itself actually
human can love man, at least in a manner satisfactory to, and appropriate
to, man'.[38] As a result, God's affection for humankind is said to reveal that
He has, 'if not an anatomical, yet a psychical human heart'.[39] The Incarnation, in other words, is a manifestation of the human nature of God,
since if He were not already human He would not have been affected by
our suffering.[40]

In Part Two of *Das Wesen des Christentums*, Feuerbach is concerned with
the abstract reflections of theology on Christian religious consciousness,
and describes his aim as a negative or destructive one. Theological reflection is said to depend on, and distort, Christian religious consciousness –
downplaying and denying its truth whilst providing an exaggerated, deliberate, and damaging insistence on its falsehood – and Feuerbach seeks to
expose its confusion and deceit.[41] His discussion of the theological account
of the nature of 'God in general' can provide an illustration.

Feuerbach emphasises the tensions and disparities (which he calls 'contradictions') between the God of religious consciousness and the God of
the theologians. The former is an 'individual' and 'personal' being with
human characteristics (He is just, merciful, good, and so on); whereas the
latter is a 'universal' and 'not . . . a personal' being whose characteristics are
'non-human and extra-human' (He is infinite, omniscient, self-subsistent,
and so on).[42] On Feuerbach's portrayal, this theological account of God
functions to promote the 'falsehood' of religion by emphasising the disparity between God and humankind. Whereas individuals can easily identify
with the 'personal' God of religious belief, the 'metaphysical' God of the
theologians remains alien to them.[43]

Feuerbach portrays theology as always striving to resist the tendency of
ordinary religious consciousness to identify the divine and the secular. In
its attempt to separate and distinguish God from humankind, theology
typically appeals to the doctrine of the 'unsearchableness' and 'incompre-
hensibility' of the divine nature.[44] When the ordinary Christian says that
God is 'love' or that God is 'understanding', the theologian is quick to
interject that these divine predicates are nonetheless 'essentially different'
from their human counterparts.[45] Theologians allow that God has 'such

[37] Terence, *Heauton Timorumenos*, I, i, 25. Feuerbach subsequently described this as the motto of
the new philosophy. See *Grundsätze* 337/70. Marx would later claim it as his 'favourite maxim'.
'Confession' 597/568.
[38] *Luther* 412/116.   [39] *Wesen* 112/55.   [40] See *ibid.* 102/50.   [41] See *ibid.* 338/199 and 335/197.
[42] *Ibid.* 359/213.   [43] *Ibid.* 62/25.   [44] *Ibid.* 360/214.   [45] *Ibid.* 370/221.

and such attributes' but insist that we have no knowledge of '*how* He has them'.[46] On Feuerbach's account, however, the divine predicates differ from their human equivalents only in that theology describes their operation in deliberately unfathomable ways (the process of divine creation, for example, is portrayed in a contrived and obfuscatory manner solely in order to distance it from human productive activity).[47]

This sketch of the structure and argument of *Das Wesen des Christentums*, whilst hopefully not inaccurate, does little to convey Feuerbach's understanding of the critical purpose and historical impact of his anthropological reduction. Feuerbach saw his work not simply as a contribution to a local sphere of knowledge, what might now be called the sociology of religion, but rather as a turning point in the development of humankind. This is likely to appear an extravagant and puzzling claim, not least because anthropological accounts of religion have a lengthy historical pedigree (as early as the fifth or sixth century BCE, Xenophanes of Colophon had observed that Ethiopian gods were snub-nosed and black, whereas Thracian gods had light blue eyes and red hair).[48] To make sense of Feuerbach's claim, some appreciation of his understanding of the relationship between Christianity and self-knowledge is needed.

Feuerbach thinks of self-knowledge (or 'self-consciousness') as something which human beings have historically lacked, but which they are driven by nature to acquire. The rationale behind this claim is unclear, but may rest on the view that human beings are only potentially selves, and that in order to actualise that potential (and attain full-blown selfhood) they require self-knowledge. Feuerbach's account of the latter follows the familiar Hegelian model according to which self-knowledge is necessarily the result of an indirect process. A subject can come to recognise and understand itself only in an encounter with something (apparently) other.

In the opening chapter of *Das Wesen des Christentums*, Feuerbach suggests that a wide variety of objects, both 'spiritual' and 'sensuous', could play the role of the 'other' in this process.[49] However, these remarks encouraged two misunderstandings of his position.

The first misunderstanding arose from Feuerbach's loose elaboration of this claim about 'sensuous' objects. When Feuerbach described the 'object of the subject' as being 'nothing else than the subject's own nature taken objectively', some readers understood him to be making a claim about

[46] *Ibid.* 365/217.   [47] See the discussion in *ibid.* 365/217ff.
[48] See Xenophanes, 'fragment 16', G. D. Kirk, J. E. Raven, and M. Schofield (eds.), *The Presocratic Philosophers: A Critical History and Selection of Texts*, second edition (Cambridge, 1983) pp. 168–9.
[49] *Wesen* 34/5.

the unreality of material entities.⁵⁰ Julius Müller, for example, accused Feuerbach of 'anthropocentric subjectivism', of a solipsism which dissolved the finite world into fictitious symbols of human consciousness.⁵¹ However, when Feuerbach wrote that even 'the moon, the sun, and the stars' call out to humankind, Γνῶθι σεαυτόν ('Know thyself'), he meant only to claim that it was our idea of such objects which spoke to us in this way.⁵² Feuerbach, in a reply to Müller, explained that his subject matter was not objects as such but human consciousness of them, and from the fact that objects 'in so far as man knows them' are 'mirrors of his essence (*Spiegel seines Wesens*)' no conclusions about the 'unreality' of the objects in themselves can be drawn.⁵³

The second misunderstanding arose from Feuerbach's remark about the variety of possible 'others'. Feuerbach appears to imply that religion is merely one of many vehicles of self-knowledge. However, such a view is hard to square with what might be called his considered account of the (foundational) role of religion. According to the latter, the advance of humankind to self-knowledge is impossible without religious progress. To emphasise the structural parallel with Hegel's metaphysics, we might say that for Feuerbach it is religion (rather than the creation and development of the world) that constitutes a necessary detour in the progress of humankind (rather than of the absolute) to self-knowledge.

Das Wesen des Christentums contains rather little about the structure of religious progress. There are some incidental remarks about the historical transfer of authority concerning standards of conduct from divine to human authorities. However, these suggestions remain largely unelaborated, and function mainly as an opportunity to rehearse Hegel's pejorative characterisation of Judaism as a 'positive' religion inevitably superseded by Christianity.⁵⁴

Feuerbach is less interested in the historical pattern of religious progress than in what he considers to be its culminating peak. Christianity occupies this unique position because of its insight into the human character of the divine. Religious forms constitute symbolic modes of human self-understanding, and an adequate account of human nature is said to appear for the first time in Christianity. (One of several alternative titles that Feuerbach considered for his best-known work was *Know Thyself* (*Erkenne dich*

⁵⁰ *Ibid.* 46/12.
⁵¹ See Erich Schneider, *Die Theologie und Feuerbachs Religionskritik: Die Reaktion der Theologie des 19. Jahrhunderts auf Ludwig Feuerbachs Religionskritik mit Ausblicken auf das 20. Jahrhundert und einem Anhang über Feuerbach* (Göttingen, 1972) pp. 42ff.
⁵² *Wesen* 34/5. ⁵³ See 'Beleuchtung einer theologischen Rezension', pp. 178–9.
⁵⁴ See *Wesen* 73–4/31–2.

selbst).[55]) However, in Christianity, this knowledge is obscured, thereby generating a need for its translation from symbolic to literal form. It is only with Feuerbach's deconstruction of Christianity in *Das Wesen des Christentums* that the self-knowledge of humankind is finally completed.

Accounts of Feuerbach's work often describe this anthropological reduction without adequately conveying its intended historical import. In Heine's *Atta Troll*, for example, the eponymous dancing bear, having taken his son solemnly aside to warn him against 'men like Feuerbach' who are 'preaching atheism', goes on to describe what the 'great creator' of the universe – *pace* these godless Germans – is actually like:

> Droben in dem Sternenzelte,
> Auf dem goldnen Herrscherstuhle,
> Weltregierend, majestätisch,
> Sitzt ein kolossaler Eisbär.
>
> Fleckenlos und schneeweiß glänzend
> Ist sein Pelz; es schmückt sein Haupt
> Ein Kron' von Diamanten,
> Die durch alle Himmel leuchtet.
>
> In the starry tent above us,
> On the golden throne of lordship,
> Ruling all the world, majestic,
> Sits a polar bear, a titan.
>
> Spotless and snow-white and shining
> Is his fur; upon his head
> Is a sparkling crown of diamonds
> That illuminates all the heavens.[56]

Atta Troll is, of course, implicitly invoking the 'anthropological' reduction of religion at the same time as he is ostensibly denying it. However, although these verses illustrate Heine's satirical brilliance, they might also be said to obscure Feuerbach's point. The anthropological reduction of *Das Wesen des Christentums* does not involve the projection of familiar predicates on to an ideal entity; rather, in deconstructing Christianity, we discover (for the first time) who we really are. This is why Feuerbach could think of his own work in such seemingly extravagant terms, as constituting a 'historical turning point (*Wendepunkt der Geschichte*)'.[57]

Feuerbach claims to possess a positive attitude towards religion. He sought not to destroy Christianity but rather to liberate its content from

---

[55] See Feuerbach to Otto Wigand, 5 and 16 January 1841, *Gesammelte Werke* 18, pp. 47, 56.
[56] Heine, *Atta Troll* 30–1/436.   [57] *Wesen* 443/270.

otherworldly forms.[58] This self-understanding explains his (idiosyncratic) denial that he was an atheist. Since Feuerbach affirmed the non-existence of God, he is conventionally, and not unreasonably, thought of as an atheist. However, Feuerbach insists that, properly understood, atheism involves the denial not only of the existence of God as subject but also of those predicates traditionally associated with divinity. 'Hence', Feuerbach contends, 'he alone is the true atheist to whom the predicates of the Divine Being – for example, love, wisdom, justice – are nothing; not he to whom merely the subject of those predicates is nothing.'[59]

Feuerbach did not seek to deny the divine predicates but rather to establish their presence in everyday human life. However, what this might actually involve is far from transparent. Not least, the manner in which Feuerbach broached this claim in the closing paragraph of *Das Wesen des Christentums* generated considerable contemporary confusion. Announcing that the 'profoundest secrets' lay in 'common everyday things', Feuerbach bemoaned the fact that these 'real mysteries' are typically ignored in favour of the 'imaginary, illusory ones' of Christianity.[60] He called for a spiritual re-evaluation of everyday life, in order 'to vindicate to common things an uncommon significance, *to life, as such, a religious import*'.[61] Marriage, friendship, the 'well-being of every man', he continues, should be considered as 'sacred *in and by themselves*'.[62] Indeed, Feuerbach suggests that eating and drinking – which are said to constitute the real content of the Christian sacraments – should be treated as a 'religious act', before concluding his remarks with 'Amen'.[63] Such comments, and especially the religious language in which they were framed, prompted two distinct interpretative responses.

In the first place, they encouraged the suspicion amongst his left-Hegelian contemporaries that Feuerbach harboured a vestigial religiosity. The most significant and sustained version of this charge was propounded by Max Stirner in *Der Einzige und sein Eigentum*.[64] However, a briefer (and more frivolous) example can be found in *Der Triumph des Glaubens* (the epic poem written by Engels and Edgar Bauer).

---

[58] See B. M. G. Reardon, *Religious Thought in the Nineteenth Century: Illustrated From Writings of the Period* (Cambridge, 1966) p. 7; and Paul Ricoeur, 'The Critique of Religion', *The Philosophy of Paul Ricoeur: An Anthology of his Work*, ed. Charles E. Reagan and David Stewart (Boston, 1978) p. 217.
[59] *Wesen* 58/21.   [60] *Ibid.* 452/276.   [61] *Ibid.* 454/278.   [62] *Ibid.* 445/271.
[63] *Ibid.* 453/277–8.
[64] See David Leopold, 'Introduction', Max Stirner, *The Ego and Its Own*, ed. David Leopold (Cambridge, 1995) pp. xixff.

Es ist, hilf Sankt Johann! – der grause *Feuerbach*.
Er rast und springet nicht, er schwebet in den Lüften,
Ein grauses Meteor, umwallt von Höllendüften.
In seiner einen Hand den blinkenden Pokal,
Und in der anderen des Brotes labend Mahl,
Sitzt bis zum Nabel er in einem Muschelbecken,
Den neuen Gottesdienst der Frechen zu entdecken.
Das Fressen, Saufen und das Baden, sagt er frei,
Daß dies die Wahrheit nur der Sakramente sei.

Help us, Saint John, it's *Feuerbach* of dreadful name!
He neither raves nor bounds, but hovers in mid-air,
An awful meteor girt by hellish vapours there.
In the one hand he holds outstretched the cup that shines,
And in the other one, the bread loaf that sustains,
He sits up to his navel in a sea shell basin,
Trying to find a new church service for the brazen.
Guzzling, boozing, bathing, firmly he maintains,
Are all the truth the holy sacrament contains.[65]

Feuerbach is portrayed here as a half-hearted atheist still concerned with spirituality (he 'hovers in mid-air'), whose remarks about the sacraments are parodied as an attempt to update Christianity for a secular age (to discover 'a new church service for the brazen').

In addition, Feuerbach's concluding remarks encouraged subsequent commentators to understand him as demanding a spiritual reinterpretation, rather than a practical transformation, of the existing social order. Feuerbach's work, it was said, lacked a social and political dimension. (This interpretation is contested in the following section, but I turn first to outline Feuerbach's account of speculative philosophy.)

Feuerbach's account of Christianity provides the framework within which his critique of speculative philosophy is usefully situated. (Feuerbach occasionally characterises speculative philosophy as a broad historical tradition – originating with Spinoza, revived by Schelling, and perfected by Hegel – but more often treats it as synonymous with its perfection in the work of Hegel. I will follow his dominant usage here.)

Attempts to understand Feuerbach's developing intellectual project are not helped by the formal changes in his work following *Das Wesen des Christentums*.[66] The arguments of these subsequent texts – not least, the

---

[65] *Triumph* 302/337. In the second edition, Feuerbach defended his remarks. See *Wesen* 15/xiv.
[66] These changes were motivated by Feuerbach's conviction that 'simplicity' was a distinguishing characteristic of the new philosophy. See 'Vorläufige Thesen' 251/162. This conviction was reflected

'Vorläufige Thesen' and the *Grundsätze* – are often obscured by the adoption of a fragmentary apothegmatic structure, ambiguous terminology, and excessive use of aphoristic sentence inversion. Reflecting on the precision and clarity of these middle-period writings, Feuerbach's French translator has laconically observed that in approaching them it is necessary 'to renounce the idea that Feuerbach attributed to each word *a univocal meaning*'.[67] Feuerbach's ambition seems to have been to mark the innovative content of his new philosophy by adopting an equally pioneering form. However, these texts typically lack the fine detail of the earlier critique of Christianity and proceed largely by assertion, as if it were sufficient to point towards, rather than argue for, a philosophical standpoint opposed to speculative idealism.

Feuerbach views speculative philosophy as analogous to Christian theology, representing, as one commentator has admirably put it, 'the continuation of theology by other means'.[68] Feuerbach provides both a conceptual and a historical account of the relation between these two modes of understanding.

Feuerbach's conceptual account echoes Hegel's own interpretation of the relation between religion and philosophy. Christian theology and speculative philosophy are judged to have the same content, but speculation is said to possess the greater conceptual rigour and to remain hostile to Christianity's sensual imagery.[69] In the 'Vorläufige Thesen', for example, Feuerbach characterises the speculative claim that 'reality is posited by the idea' as 'the *rational* expression' of the theological doctrine 'that nature is created by God'.[70] Similarly, in the *Grundsätze*, the supposed presuppositionlessness of the Hegelian system, its purported 'lack of premise and beginning', is portrayed simply as a philosophical variant of the 'aseity of the divine being'.[71]

The main conceptual parallel between speculation and Christianity concerns the 'secret' of their concealed relationship with the finite and empirical world.[72] In *Das Wesen des Christentums*, Feuerbach adopts a physiological

in successive editions (1841, 1843, and 1849) of *Das Wesen des Christentums*, in which Latin citations were removed or translated, more quotations and examples were introduced, and words with Latin roots were exchanged for German ones ('*Objekt*' becomes '*Gegenstand*', for example). Other changes to the text may have reflected developments in Feuerbach's substantive views. See Francis Schuessler-Fiorenza, 'Feuerbach's Interpretation of Religion and Christianity', *The Philosophical Forum*, volume 15, no. 2 (Winter 1979–80) pp. 161–81.
[67] Louis Althusser, 'Note du traducteur', Ludwig Feuerbach, *Manifestes philosophiques: Textes choisis, 1839–1845* (Paris, 1973) p. 7.
[68] The neat Clausewitzian allusion is from Wartofsky, *Feuerbach*, p. 349.
[69] See *Grundsätze* 266/6.   [70] 'Vorläufige Thesen' 258/167.   [71] *Grundsätze* 281/18.
[72] *Ibid.* 300/36.

metaphor in order to capture the twofold movement at the heart of Christianity. Just as in the circulatory system 'the action of the arteries drives the blood into the extremities, and the action of the veins brings it back again', so in religion there is a 'perpetual systole and diastole'.[73] In the 'Vorläufige Thesen', these two stages of religious construction are characterised in terms of a process of separation and restoration; whereby Christianity 'divides and alienates the human being in order then to re-identify the alienated essence with the human being'.[74]

The first stage (of 'systole') concerns the origin of the Christian God, in which 'man propels his own nature from himself'.[75] Officially, of course, God has no origin; as Feuerbach remarks, 'God alone is the being who acts of himself'.[76] However, the real origin of the idea of God lies in the projection of human predicates on to an imaginary subject. This stage is characterised as one of 'separation'; a stage in which human nature is separated from, and 'placed outside' of, humankind.[77]

The second stage (of 'diastole') concerns the recovery of these previously relinquished predicates, in which the religious individual retrieves his 'rejected nature'.[78] This is accomplished when the individual makes the well-being of humankind the mainspring of his actions.[79] Since God has a 'profound interest' in human well-being, when religious individuals act in order to promote His purposes they thereby act to promote the 'moral and eternal salvation' of humankind (albeit, for Feuerbach, in an indirect and unsatisfactory manner).[80] This stage is also characterised as one of 'restoration', in which human predicates are re-appropriated as the motivating force of finite individuals.[81]

On Feuerbach's account, this two-stage process of separation and restoration is not unique to Christianity. It is duplicated in speculative philosophy.

The first stage (of separation) concerns the origin of Hegel's categorical system; the source of the various 'determinations, forms, categories, or however one wishes to refer to it' that make up the underlying structure of the absolute.[82] For Hegel these categories are, in some sense, prior to, and independent of, humankind. But Feuerbach insists that they constitute a hypostatisation of human thinking, since the various determinations of the speculative system – 'quality, quantity, measure, essence, chemism, mechanism, organism', and so on – are simply categories developed by humankind in order to make sense of the empirical world.[83]

[73] *Wesen* 73/31.　[74] 'Vorläufige Thesen' 246/158.　[75] *Wesen* 73/31.　[76] *Ibid.*
[77] 'Vorläufige Thesen' 246/158.　[78] *Wesen* 73/31.　[79] *Ibid.*　[80] *Ibid.* 72/30.
[81] 'Vorläufige Thesen' 246/158.　[82] *Ibid.* 252/162.　[83] *Ibid.* 245/158.

The second stage (of restoration) concerns the speculative reinstatement of the world. The categories of speculation are said to produce and govern (the necessary elements of) the social and natural worlds. The finite and empirical, previously identified by Feuerbach as the hidden source of the Hegelian logic, is thus restored as the product and creature of the speculative categories. Feuerbach emphatically rejects Hegel's 'a priori' or 'speculative' model of knowledge, in which 'an archetype precedes the objects and creates them', in favour of an 'a posteriori' or 'empirical' account, in which human knowledge 'follows the objects as their copy'.[84]

In elaborating the 'secret' of speculative construction, Feuerbach draws several additional parallels between Hegelianism and Christianity. Two examples will suffice here.

The first concerns the 'double-counting' that is said to occur in both Christianity and speculation. On the Christian account, God created the finite world out of nothing, a feat possible, Feuerbach suggests, only if all the determinations of that world were already, in some form, contained in God. In short, 'we have everything twice in theology', since entities must have been in God '*in abstracto*' before they appear on earth '*in concreto*'.[85] The same double counting, he suggests, appears in the speculative account: 'We also have everything *twice* in the Hegelian philosophy'.[86] Every (necessary) thing exists first 'as an object of logic' before reappearing 'as an object of the philosophies of nature and of spirit'.[87]

The second example concerns the 'inversion' of the finite and empirical that occurs in both Christianity and speculation. The real source of the speculative and theological entities is presented, in the self-understandings of Hegelianism and Christianity, as their somewhat mysterious product.[88] Both speculation and theology thus exemplify what Feuerbach characterises as the 'distorted procedure' of going from the 'abstract' to the 'concrete', from the 'ideal' to the 'real'. Such a procedure, he insists, can never reveal 'the *true, objective* reality' but only provide 'the *realisation of their own abstractions*'.[89]

Feuerbach acknowledges that speculative and theological procedures are often presented as revealing some deep mystery. The articulation of 'what is such as it is not' not only '*falsely* and *distortedly* articulated what truly is', but does this in a way which '*appears profound*'.[90] In comparison, Feuerbach concedes that his own direct appeal to the empirical and finite might appear shallow. The articulation of 'what is *such as it is*' that lies at the heart of

---

[84] *Grundsätze* 278/15.   [85] 'Vorläufige Thesen' 245/158.   [86] *Ibid.*   [87] *Ibid.*
[88] See *ibid.* 249/160.   [89] *Ibid.* 251/161.   [90] *Ibid.* 251/162.

his new philosophy may have '*truthfully* articulated what truly is', but does this in a way which could appear '*superficial*'.[91] Feuerbach sought to resist this appearance in two ways: not only through his successive attempts to deconstruct the supposed mysteries of Christianity and speculation, but also by repeatedly promoting '*simplicity*' and '*determinacy*' as virtues which are synonymous with '*truthfulness*'.[92]

For all these structural similarities, speculative philosophy and Christianity remain parallel rather than identical modes. Feuerbach emphasises two differences between Christianity and speculation.

The first of these concerns the nature of the divine entity. Hegelianism makes an apparently simple substitution, replacing the Christian God with reason. However, in effecting this switch, the objectification of human nature is replaced by the objectification of *part* of human nature. Both theology and speculative philosophy make a '*transcendent*' divinity out of human characteristics. However, whereas Christianity makes a God out of the 'essence of the human being', speculation makes its divinity out of the 'thinking of the human being', out of rationality.[93] Speculative reason thus embodies only a fragment of human nature, 'a faculty torn from the totality of the real human being and isolated for itself'.[94]

(At least, this is the claim advanced in these middle-period writings. In his later works, Feuerbach was more willing to concede that Christianity might not represent 'the whole human essence' but only '*a part* of man, torn out of the whole', namely the elements of 'spirit or soul'.[95] However, the significance of this concession is not to be underestimated. Once Christianity is seen to offer only a partial account of human nature, its role as the culminating point of religious progress is undermined. As a result, Feuerbach's Hegelian account of the historical significance of his anthropological reduction appears to be displaced, in his later writings, by rather more conventional work in what might be called the sociology of religion.)

The second of these differences concerns the relation between the divine entity and the finite world. The Christian God is an 'otherworldly' one, standing in an external relation to the world.[96] In contrast, the Hegelian absolute stands in an internal or immanent relation to the finite.[97] In short, 'what lies in the other world for religion lies in this world for philosophy'.[98] (This immanentism reminded Feuerbach of Neoplatonism, and provides the context of his epigrammatic quip that 'Hegel is not the "German or

---

[91] *Ibid.* [92] *Ibid.* [93] *Ibid.* 246/158. [94] *Grundsätze* 334/67. [95] *Vorlesungen* 287/256.
[96] *Grundsätze* 266/5–6. [97] See 'Vorläufige Thesen' 243/156. [98] *Grundsätze* 266/5.

Christian Aristotle" – he is the German Proclus'.[99]) Moreover, the Christian divinity is already ('in itself, by nature') a being 'detached and liberated from sensation and matter'.[100] In contrast, the Hegelian absolute has to battle through a progression of historical stages in order to liberate itself from the sensuous and material other. The speculative God 'himself must undertake this labour and, like the heroes of paganism, fight through virtue for his divinity'.[101] Only at the end of the historical process does the Hegelian absolute achieve what the Christian God possessed from the beginning.

Feuerbach also puts forward a historical account of the relation between speculative philosophy and Christianity. In 'Nothwendigkeit einer Reform der Philosophie', he describes human history as a succession of chronological epochs distinguished from each other on the basis of 'religious changes'.[102] The contemporary world, on this account, is situated on the 'threshold of a new age'.[103] From that vantage point, modern philosophy is identified as belonging to the period of 'the decline and fall' of Christianity, with speculative philosophy, in particular, being associated with the last stages of that era – the stages of 'inner decay'.[104] Feuerbach is not to be understood as making a contingent historical observation about when this intellectual tradition happened to originate, but rather as claiming that the rise of speculative philosophy was a reflection of, and response to, the terminal decline of Christianity. Hegel had sought to defend Christianity by concealing its 'contradictions' behind a speculative reformulation of its content. However, on Feuerbach's account, this attempt to obscure the emerging tension between a particular religious foundation and the march of historical progress was doomed to failure. Speculation, which ostensibly seeks to 'affirm' Christianity, inevitably ends up 'negating' it.[105]

To illustrate this claim, Feuerbach compares the Christian and speculative accounts of God against the two criteria of consistency and religious truth. Consistency is defined as respecting the principle that 'where the consciousness of God is, there is the being of God'. Religious truth is said to consist in recognising the identity of divine and human predicates.[106]

According to the conventional Christian account, both the 'being' and the 'consciousness' of God are indifferent to, and independent of, humankind. Feuerbach judges this Christian account to be consistent but wholly mistaken. In comparison, the speculative account of God embodies a clear advance, in that it views God as dependent on humankind (as the

---

[99] *Ibid.* 311/47. Hegel had been described as the 'German Aristotle' in a well-known review of the *Phänomenologie* by his former student K. F. Bachmann.
[100] *Ibid.* 295/32.   [101] *Ibid.* 296/32.   [102] 'Nothwendigkeit' 216/146.
[103] *Ibid.* 215–6/145.   [104] *Ibid.* 217/147.   [105] See *ibid.*   [106] *Wesen* 385/230.

vehicle of His self-consciousness). Feuerbach portrays this denial that God is capable of consciousness independent of human consciousness as identifying precisely that which Christianity separated, namely the divine and human predicates.[107] However, the Hegelian recognition that God is not 'free and independent' of humankind does not extend to God's 'being'.[108] Speculative philosophy therefore fails to respect the principle of consistency, and is accordingly judged a contradictory and unsatisfactory 'half measure'.[109]

Historically speaking, speculation can be said to have attempted to defend Christianity by making a concession to the truth of religion. However, in acknowledging only the identity of divine and human 'consciousness' – and not the identity of divine and human 'being' – it introduced a contradictory element into its account of the relation between God and humankind. The result is a counterproductive defence of Christianity, since speculation thereby opens the door to an account which can resolve that contradiction without sacrificing the (limited) advance of speculation towards the truth of religion. That account, of course, is Feuerbach's own. His insistence that theology is anthropology satisfies not only the criteria of consistency but also the criteria of truth by binding divine and human predicates together in 'a true, self-satisfying identity'.[110]

FEUERBACH AND POLITICS

The subject of the present section may appear an unlikely one, since modern commentators typically maintain that an antithetical relationship exists between Feuerbach and political concerns. Feuerbach is variously portrayed as 'basically apolitical',[111] as 'notoriously apathetic in the political arena',[112] as having a 'distaste' for politics,[113] as 'little interested' in practical issues and 'even less in political ones',[114] as 'never interested in the relation between philosophy and politics and society',[115] as having analysed religion without ever 'discussing the state',[116] and so on.

[107] See *ibid.* 378/226. [108] *Ibid.* 378/227. [109] *Ibid.* 386/231. [110] *Ibid.* 385/231.
[111] André Liebich, *Between Ideology and Utopia: The Politics and Philosophy of August Cieszkowski* (Dordrecht, 1979) p. 323 n. 44. See also William J. Brazil, *The Young Hegelians* (New Haven, 1970) p. 77.
[112] Gregory, *Scientific Materialism*, p. 190. [113] Wartofsky, *Feuerbach*, p. 396.
[114] Nicholas Lobkowicz, *Theory and Practice: History of a Concept from Aristotle to Marx* (Notre Dame IN, 1967) p. 250.
[115] Harold Mah, *The End of Philosophy, the Origin of 'Ideology': Karl Marx and the Crisis of the Young Hegelians* (Berkeley, 1987) p. 6.
[116] Paul Thomas, *Karl Marx and the Anarchists* (London, 1980) p. 135.

These characterisations include not only claims about the subject matter of Feuerbach's writings but also some element of biographical comment. The latter appears misguided. Even a cursory inspection reveals Feuerbach's lifelong engagement with social and political concerns. It may be helpful to rehearse a few of those biographical details here.

Feuerbach's early adulthood was marked by his sympathy for, and association with, some of the more radical elements of the *Burschenschaften*. (The *Burschenschaften* were clandestine student organisations devoted to a unified Germany and, less clearly and consistently, to a democratic constitution.[117]) For example, as a teenager Feuerbach had made a pilgrimage to the grave of the 'brave' Karl Sand, sending his mother a cutting of grass from the burial site.[118] (Sand was a somewhat unbalanced member of the *Schwarzen*, the more radical – and less enthusiastically duelling and drinking – wing of the *Burschenschaften*, who was executed for the murder of the reactionary journalist and playwright August von Kotzebue.) As a graduate student Feuerbach was required to make several formal depositions denying membership of any secret organisation, but remained the object of official suspicion and was continually dogged – in the words of his father, the distinguished liberal jurist, Anselm Feuerbach – by 'the attacks and persecutions of spies'.[119] For example, Feuerbach's university transfer from Heidelberg to Berlin was delayed by a police investigation into his involvement with a radical group led by Karl Follen. As a result of that investigation, Feuerbach's brother Karl – a brilliant young mathematician – was arrested and spent fourteen months in prison, during which he twice attempted suicide.[120] (Out of prison, Karl suffered bouts of mental illness, and, after a period living as a recluse, died in 1834.[121]) Feuerbach himself came to see his own subsequent exclusion from academic life as inevitable at

117 On the post-Karlsbad *Burschenschaften*, see Roland Ray Lutz Jr, 'The German Revolutionary Student Movement, 1819–33', *Central European History*, volume 4 (1971) pp. 215–41.

118 See Feuerbach to Wilhelmine Feuerbach, 22 October 1820, *Gesammelte Werke* 17, p. 9.

119 Anselm Feuerbach to Feuerbach, 15 August 1824, *Gesammelte Werke* 17, p. 51. Anselm Feuerbach was best known for his reform of the Bavarian Penal Code, but his criminological writings also include an account of Kaspar Hauser (whom he befriended and protected). Lawrence Stepelevich has published three of Feuerbach's sworn statements in *The Philosophical Forum*, volume 8, no. 2–4 (1978) pp. 28–30.

120 Karl's proof of a theorem in Euclidean geometry (the nine-point circle of a triangle) is still known as 'Feuerbach's theorem'.

121 See Laura Guggenbuhl, 'Karl Wilhelm Feuerbach', Charles Coulston Gillispie (ed.), *The Dictionary of Scientific Biography* (New York, 1971) pp. 601–2; and Feuerbach, 'Paul Johann Anselm von Feuerbach und seine Söhne', pp. 329–30. On Follen, see Karl H. Wegert, 'The Genesis of Youthful Radicalism: Hesse-Nassau, 1806–1819', *Central European History*, volume 10 (1977) pp. 183–205; and Leonard Krieger, *The German Idea of Freedom: History of a Political Tradition* (Chicago, 1972) pp. 266ff.

a time when public life was 'poisoned and befouled', and the price of a university post was 'political servility and religious obscurantism'.[122] Indeed, Feuerbach would describe the rural isolation of Bruckberg, in which his best-known works were composed, as 'a moral necessity'.[123] However, the sleepiness of his *Biedermeier* retreat should not be exaggerated: Feuerbach maintained connections with political radicals (for example, he remained friends with Arnold Ruge), his work continued to be censored (for example, *Das Wesen des Christentums* was proscribed in Austria, and his contribution to the so-called 'Leo-Hegelsche Streit' was banned after two instalments), and he remained subject to police surveillance and harassment (for example, his home was raided by the authorities in 1842 after it was discovered that Hermann Kriege had been staying there). In 1848, inspired by news of revolutionary Paris, Feuerbach left rural Bavaria for Frankfurt, then the centre of revolutionary events in Germany.[124] In circumstances of revolutionary 'turmoil', he insisted, individuals have a duty to abandon everything for 'politics'.[125] Like many left-liberals, Feuerbach quickly became disillusioned with the National Assembly and associated with the 'republican or democratic' forces outside the parliament; he was, for example, a member of the Democratic Congress held in June.[126] After the defeat of the revolution, Feuerbach occasionally despaired at the short-term prospects for democratic change in Germany, but he never abandoned his political interests.[127] In later life, he corresponded with leaders of the left-liberal *Fortschrittspartei* in Prussia, read Marx's *Kapital*, showed interest in the question of women's suffrage, and, two years before his death, joined what would become the *Sozialdemokratische Partei Deutschlands*.[128]

These scattered biographical details would seem to cast doubt on the description of Feuerbach as apolitical, uninterested in politics, and so on. Rather, they reveal a consistent interest in politics, an interest which is also

[122] *Vorlesungen* 9/3.
[123] Feuerbach to Christian Kapp, 18 May 1844, *Gesammelte Werke* 18, p. 353. See also *Vorlesungen* 9/2.
[124] See Feuerbach to Otto Wigand, 3 March 1848, *Gesammelte Werke* 19, p. 145. See also Feuerbach to Bertha Feuerbach, 30 June 1848, *Gesammelte Werke* 19, pp. 166–8.
[125] *Vorlesungen* 7/1.
[126] See Feuerbach to Bertha Feuerbach, 30 June 1848, *Gesammelte Werke* 19, pp. 166–8, and Feuerbach to Bertha Feuerbach, 6 June 1848, *Gesammelte Werke* 19, pp. 156–8. Feuerbach saw Robert Blum's defeat – over the issue of executive power – as the moment when the National Assembly 're-established the old era'. Feuerbach to Bertha Feuerbach, 30 June 1848, *Gesammelte Werke* 19, p. 167. See also Feuerbach to Otto Wigand, 5 June 1848, *Gesammelte Werke* 19, pp. 155–6.
[127] See Feuerbach to Bertha Feuerbach, 6 June 1848, *Gesammelte Werke* 19, p. 157. See also Feuerbach to Otto Wigand, 28 September 1848, *Gesammelte Werke* 19, p. 184.
[128] On Marx's 'great critique of political economy' see Feuerbach's letter to Friedrich Kapp, 11 April 1868, *Briefe*, letter 336. See also Marx to Engels, 25 September 1869, *MEW* 32, pp. 371–2; *MECW* 43, p. 354. On Feuerbach and the SPD see Rawidowicz, *Ludwig Feuerbachs Philosophie*, p. 316.

apparent in Feuerbach's writings, not least in his middle-period critiques of Christianity and philosophy.

It is widely recognised that Feuerbach's middle-period writings are pre-occupied with the problem of alienation.[129] His aim in these works is to overcome the inappropriate separation of individuals from their essential human nature, a separation which lies at the heart of Christianity and which he explicitly identifies as a source of harm and distress.[130] However, the character of this preoccupation is often misunderstood.

In attempting to establish this claim, the distinction between 'objective' and 'subjective' accounts of alienation is again of use. Alienation is said to be subjective when it consists in the presence (or absence) of certain beliefs or feelings. For example, individuals are sometimes characterised as (subjectively) alienated when (negatively) they do not feel at home in the modern social world or when (positively) they feel estranged from that world. In contrast, objective alienation can be discussed in terms which make no reference to the beliefs or feelings of individuals. For example, individuals are sometimes characterised as (objectively) alienated when they are unable to develop and deploy their essential human capacities, whether or not they experience that lack of self-realisation as a loss.

Much of the literature follows what I shall call the cognitive interpretation of Feuerbach's work. On this cognitive interpretation, Feuerbach's preoccupation with the problem of alienation is acknowledged, but he is portrayed as offering a subjective account of both the nature of, and the solution to, alienation. The alienation of modern individuals is said to consist in their holding false beliefs about God, in particular their misidentifying the projection of their own essential predicates as an objective being. Commentators variously claim, for example, that Feuerbach maintains that alienation '*consists* in a condition of false consciousness', that is, in individuals holding false beliefs about the world,[131] and that alienation was 'equated' in his work 'with some mistaken form of consciousness'.[132] This alienation is overcome, on the cognitive interpretation, by changing those false beliefs for correct ones (in particular, by replacing a literal belief in Christianity with Feuerbach's anthropological reduction). Commentators variously claim, for example, that for Feuerbach alienation was to be overcome '*at the level of conceptualisation*' (that is, he did not believe that alienation needed

[129] For a dissenting view, see Richard Schacht, *Alienation* (London, 1971) p. 69 n. 5.
[130] 'Every separation of beings essentially allied is painful (*Jede Trennung zusammengehörender Wesen ist schmerzlich*)'. *Wesen* 313/183. See also *ibid.* 310/181.
[131] Allen W. Wood, *Karl Marx* (London, 1981) p. 13.
[132] David Conway, *A Farewell to Marx. An Outline and Appraisal of His Theories* (London, 1987) p. 34.

to be overcome 'practically and socially' but rather required a solution 'at the level of consciousness'),[133] that, on Feuerbach's account, alienation 'requires a mere adjustment of consciousness for its rectification',[134] that his viewpoint had no consequences for 'actual, practical alienation',[135] that alienation 'is surmounted by a cognitive act',[136] that only our 'understanding' and not 'social reality' required transformation,[137] and so on.

The cognitive reading of Feuerbach is a tempting one.[138] It reflects and reinforces some widely held views about Feuerbach's life, writings, and intellectual context: it is consistent with the view of Feuerbach as personally uninterested in social and political change, it offers an explanation of his emphasis (especially in *Das Wesen des Christentums*) on the self-knowledge of humankind, and it promises a tidy account of Feuerbach's relation to some of his contemporaries (Marx, for example, can be portrayed as breaking with Feuerbach's subjective account of alienation). However, as will be apparent, none of these considerations is decisive: this 'apolitical' account of Feuerbach's life appears mistaken (see above), alternative explanations of this emphasis on self-knowledge are possible (see below), and tidiness is an inadequate substitute for accuracy.

The cognitive account recognises Feuerbach's preoccupation with the problem of alienation, but it ignores the practical dimensions of that concern. Feuerbach not only characterises his own work as having a therapeutic goal – healing the painful separation at the heart of alienation – but also explicitly identifies that goal as synonymous with practical, as opposed to purely theoretical, concerns.[139] Indeed, the very 'purpose (*Zweck*)' of *Das Wesen des Christentums* is described as a '*therapeutic* or *practical* (*therapeutischer oder praktischer*)' one.[140]

The cognitive interpretation typically makes two errors. The first is a failure to recognise that Feuerbach's account of alienation has an objective (as well as a subjective) dimension.

Consider, in this context, Feuerbach's widespread, but little noticed, insistence that 'human sacrifice' belongs to the 'very idea' of Christianity.[141]

[133] Thomas, *Karl Marx and the Anarchists*, pp. 101, 71, 138.
[134] Paul Thomas, 'Karl Marx and Max Stirner', *Political Theory*, volume 3, no. 2 (1975) p. 162.
[135] István Mészáros, *Marx's Theory of Alienation* (London, 1970) p. 84. See also *ibid.* p. 236.
[136] Robert C. Tucker, *Philosophy and Myth*, second edition (Cambridge, 1972) p. 91.
[137] Nicholas Lash, *A Matter of Hope: A Theologian's Reflections on the Thought of Karl Marx* (London, 1981) p. 60.
[138] Marx's own comments sometimes encourage this interpretation. See, for example, *Die deutsche Ideologie* 42/58. However, see also *ibid.* 42–3/38–9.
[139] See, for example, 'Beziehung' 429/82.
[140] *Wesen* 8/. This passage is one of several omitted from George Eliot's English translation.
[141] *Ibid.* 596/330.

The most implausible thread in this claim about human sacrifice involves Feuerbach's apparent willingness to swallow Daumer's antisemitic account of the relation between Judaism and early Christianity.[142] (Not the least striking element in Daumer's secularised version of the blood libel is his historical claim that the cult of Moloch had been passed by Jews to the early Christian communities. According to Daumer, Jesus and his disciples, except for Judas, were followers of Moloch; indeed, the Last Supper is said to have been a cannibalistic meal.)

Feuerbach acknowledged that Christian sacrifice no longer took a literal form in the modern social world, but he insists that the scale and significance of its non-literal forms should not be underestimated.[143] Simply put, the cost of Christian belief is the sacrifice, the practical denial or repression, of essential human characteristics. Feuerbach often describes this non-literal notion of sacrifice in terms of a relationship between the sacred and the secular, whereby anything gained by the one is lost by the other. 'To enrich God', he writes, 'man must become poor; that God may be all, man must be nothing.'[144] The reasoning here is not obvious, but may reflect the thought that affirmation, at least in this context, has the characteristics of a positional good (a good whose value depends on the amount of it that one has in comparison with others). 'To affirm God', Feuerbach maintains, 'is to negate man; to honour God is to scorn man; to praise God is to revile man.'[145] Whatever its rationale, one consequence of this relationship is that religious belief has a practical cost to humankind. 'The glory of God', Feuerbach insists, 'rests only on the lowliness of man, divine blessedness only on human misery, divine wisdom only on human folly, divine power only on human weakness.'[146]

This notion of Christian self-sacrifice provided Feuerbach with a flexible, if somewhat elusive, vocabulary for discussing objective forms of alienation. Consider, for example, Feuerbach's treatment of sexuality as an 'essential' human need which is denied or repressed by Christianity.[147] Outside of a loving (heterosexual) relationship, he maintains that a person is incomplete, 'is only part of a being'.[148] In contrast, Christianity views the individual as

[142] See, for example, *ibid.* 597/330–1. Feuerbach broke with the 'sick' Daumer in 1844. See Feuerbach to Schibich, 21 October 1851, *Gesammelte Werke* 19, pp. 321–5. See also Feuerbach, 'Über den Marienkultus'. On Daumer, see Karlhans Kluncker, *Georg Friedrich Daumer: Leben und Werk 1800–1875* (Bonn, 1984); and Paul Lawrence Rose, *German Question/Jewish Question: Revolutionary Antisemitism from Kant to Wagner* (Princeton, 1992) pp. 47–8, 251–62.
[143] *Wesen* 433–4/262. Literal sacrifice, Feuerbach later speculated, might be said to survive in the judicial executions of contemporary Christian states. See *Vorlesungen* 370/328.
[144] *Wesen* 65/26.   [145] *Luther* 354/33.   [146] *Ibid.*   [147] *Wesen* 291/168. See also *ibid.* 434/263.
[148] *Ibid.* 291/167.

perfect 'by himself'.[149] The human 'sexual instinct' thus runs counter to the austere and ascetic Christian ideal – the 'principle of sexual love', Feuerbach claims, 'is excluded from heaven as an earthly, worldly principle' – and the individual believer 'must therefore deny this instinct' in this world.[150] This repression of an essential human need is reflected in both the beliefs and the behaviour of Christians. It is, for example, apparent in the privileged ethical status attributed (especially by Catholicism) to virginity, and in the view of marriage as a concession to the weakness of the flesh (Christianity is said to sanction marriage 'not in order to hallow and satisfy the flesh, but to restrict the flesh, to repress it, to kill it').[151] It is also reflected in both individual behaviour (the turning away in 'mock modesty' from a painting or sculpture of a naked angel) and in social and political arrangements (the contemporary repression, by 'legal force' and social pressure, of public expressions of sensuality).[152]

This repression of essential human characteristics can never be entirely successful. The propensity of human nature to actualise itself is a strong one, apparent even in the form of repression. Feuerbach suggests, for example, that the greater the Christian denial of the sexual instinct, the more that human sexuality finds surrogate expression in the sensuous content of particular Christian beliefs. The historical association between the rise of monasticism and the cult of the Virgin Mary is said to confirm that 'the more the sensual tendencies are renounced, the more sensual is the God to whom they are sacrificed'.[153]

Perhaps the most important example of self-abnegation concerns the Christian notion of virtue, which Feuerbach describes as based on 'the idea of compensating sacrifice'; that is, the idea that individuals should sacrifice themselves to God because He sacrificed Himself for them.[154] Feuerbach maintains that the sacrifice required by Christian virtue is the repression of human nature. The more that the individual subjugates his essential nature the greater the resulting merit (the 'greater the abnegation, the greater is the virtue').[155]

Feuerbach identifies this denial of human nature as responsible for the Christian indifference towards moral duties.[156] He distinguishes between obligations of faith (which are concerned with 'duties to God') and obligations of morality (which are concerned with 'duties towards man').[157]

[149] *Ibid.*   [150] *Ibid.* 287/165 and 291/167.
[151] *Ibid.* 548/313. See also *ibid.* 286/165. Feuerbach allows that other religions attribute a 'religious' significance to marriage. See *ibid.* 286/165 and 292/168.
[152] *Ibid.* 550–1/314.   [153] *Ibid.* 65–6/26.   [154] *Ibid.* 433/262.
[155] *Ibid.* 434/263.   [156] See *ibid.* 431/261.   [157] *Ibid.* 429/260.

Christians do not completely ignore the latter, but, whenever these two sets of duties conflict, they always rank the former first ('by so much higher are duties towards God than duties towards man').[158] What Feuerbach calls the Christian 'indifference' to morality consists in this readiness to sacrifice morality to faith, and to subordinate duties to humankind to duties to God.[159] (This indifference is scarcely surprising since, for Christians, the small matter of personal salvation depends on 'faith' alone, and not 'on the fulfilment of common human duties'.[160])

This Christian indifference to moral duties appears in a variety of contexts. Energies which ought to be devoted 'to life, to humankind', are lavished instead on a being 'who wants nothing'.[161] For example, Feuerbach suggests that Christianity prevents people from adequately discharging obligations of gratitude.[162] Christians are often 'grateful to God' but 'unthankful to man', even for those benefits rendered by other individuals at some personal cost.[163] Elsewhere, he gives the example of parental obligations, asking rhetorically, 'how can you expect me to love and honour *them*' (that is, my parents) when they 'are only agents of God?'[164] Do you thank the servant, he elaborates, 'who brings you a gift in the name of his master?'[165]

More dramatically, Feuerbach suggests, that 'all the horrors of Christian religious history' are the result of this indifference.[166] Christianity subordinates morality to faith, and faith is characterised by 'narrowness, partiality, and intolerance'.[167] Christian faith is said to anathematise all those actions and dispositions which accord with 'love, humanity, reason'.[168] The results, he remarks, with a cautious eye to the censorship, are both catastrophic and well known. Christian faith 'necessarily' passes into hatred, just as hatred, in turn, inevitably passes into persecution.[169] The claim is a stark one. These historical crimes do not represent some contingent deformation of religious belief, but rather reflect the moral bankruptcy at the heart of Christianity.[170]

I now turn to the second of the two errors typically made by the cognitive interpretation, namely the failure to recognise that, for Feuerbach, overcoming contemporary alienation requires a change in the world (and not merely in our understanding of that world).

In the *Grundsätze*, Feuerbach acknowledges that there are individuals who seek to overthrow subjective forms of human estrangement (to 'persecute the theoretical negation of Christianity') without attempting to overthrow objective forms of human estrangement (whilst letting 'the actual

---

[158] *Ibid.*   [159] See also 'Beziehung' 440/90.   [160] *Wesen* 430/261.   [161] *Ibid.* 446/272.
[162] *Ibid.* 447/272.   [163] *Ibid.* 446/272.   [164] *Merkwürdige Äußerungen* 424/125.
[165] *Ibid.*   [166] *Wesen* 426/257–8.   [167] *Ibid.* 426/258.
[168] *Ibid.* 427/257.   [169] *Ibid.* 429/260.   [170] See *ibid.* 426/257.

negations of Christianity, in which the modern era abounds, stand as they are').[171] However, he describes this stance only in order to reject it. Indeed, Feuerbach characterises this neglect of practical change as a 'ridiculous (*lächerlich*)' position to hold.[172] Attempting to understand why anyone might subscribe to such a risible standpoint, he refers to the 'shortsightedness and complacency' of those who recognise only the 'necessity' of 'changes and revolutions' in the past, and ignore or (worse still) resist the pressing contemporary need for social change.[173]

Nor is this an isolated endorsement of the need for practical change. In the second edition of *Das Wesen des Christentums*, recognising that his philosophical reputation had been built on a rejection of 'idealism' in metaphysics and epistemology, Feuerbach observes that he remained nonetheless an 'idealist' in one particular realm, namely 'in the region of *practical* philosophy'.[174] This striking self-description, repeated in the 'Vorläufige Thesen', reflects Feuerbach's conviction that the social and political are realms in which 'practical change' was demanded by both 'right' and 'reason'.[175]

The extent and character of this commitment to social and political reform are not often appreciated. Feuerbach was reluctant to say much about his understanding of the transition to, and character of, the unalienated society of the future. His reluctance to discuss such issues seems to have several sources. It flows, in part, from a genuine uncertainty about the contours of that world. For all his 'faith in the historical future', Feuerbach was not confident of anything other than the very broad outline of social progress.[176] The possibility of thinking and acting 'in a pure and human fashion' would be 'granted only to future generations', and Feuerbach believed that he and his contemporaries could have only the faintest intimation of the contours of such a life.[177] In addition, Feuerbach's reticence reflected a view about the appropriate priorities of contemporary social criticism. In the *Grundsätze*, he identifies a division of labour between the positive task of describing the unestranged humankind of the future ('man as such') and the negative task of removing the 'mud' in which existing individuals are encrusted.[178] His own energies, he insists, were fully occupied by this latter task (the 'unsavoury work of cleansing').[179] Finally, this reticence reflected something of his own character and the political context in which he worked. Feuerbach was a cautious individual, who,

---

[171] *Grundsätze* 288/25.   [172] *Ibid.*
[173] *Ibid.* 289/25. See also *Wesen* 15/xiv and 'Vorläufige Thesen' 251/162.   [174] *Wesen* 15/xiv.
[175] 'Vorläufige Thesen' 252/162.   [176] *Wesen* 15/xiv.
[177] *Grundsätze* 264/3. See also *Vorlesungen* 315/281.   [178] *Grundsätze* 264–5/3.   [179] *Ibid.* 265/3.

despite the censorship and police surveillance, was keen to maintain both his public voice and personal liberty, without recourse to exile. His discussion of social and political issues was, as a result, typically circumspect and occasionally coded.

We can divide that reluctant and cryptic comment into two parts: Feuerbach's understanding of the character of the unalienated society of the future; and his understanding of the transition to that unalienated society of the future. I begin with the latter.

Feuerbach's account of the *transition* to the unalienated society of the future turns on the need for a change in human understanding. However, this emphasis comes about, not – as the cognitive reading would have it – because of a conviction that practical reforms are redundant, but rather because Feuerbach sees a change in individual beliefs as a precondition for social and political progress.

In *Das Wesen des Christentums*, Feuerbach described himself as aiming 'simply to destroy an illusion', but insisted that this particular illusion is 'profoundly injurious in its effects on humankind'.[180] Feuerbach returned to this self-description in his reply to criticisms of his position made by Max Stirner. Feuerbach explained that his own preoccupation with religious illusion was the result of his conviction that it is religious illusion which supports both other illusions and other (non-illusory) types of constraint. Feuerbach describes the illusion of 'God as subject' as 'humanity's primary illusion, primary prejudice, primary constraint', and insists that 'all illusions, all prejudices, all unnatural constraints' depend on it for their survival.[181] In devoting his time and energies so completely 'to the dissolution of the primary illusion', Feuerbach was not only seeking a theoretical liberation but aiming simultaneously to dissolve all the 'constraints derived from it'.[182] The same explanation is rehearsed in the 1846 foreword to his *Sämtliche Werke*, in which Feuerbach responds to the objection, made by an impatient younger generation, that his writings were too concerned with religion at the expense of social and political change.[183] Feuerbach insists that there is a connection between religious belief and practical constraints on human flourishing, a connection which this new generation neglected at their peril. Simply put, the injustice, inequality, poverty, and unfreedom of the contemporary world were a 'necessary consequence' of the belief in the 'illusory, fantastic, heavenly' form of humankind.[184] Far from denying the necessity of overthrowing these other evils, Feuerbach insists that it

[180] *Wesen* 450/274.   [181] 'Beziehung' 429/82.   [182] *Ibid.* See also *ibid.* 427/81.
[183] 'Vorwort [zu *Sämtliche Werke*]', p. 189.   [184] *Ibid.*

is precisely that necessity which provides the rationale for his critique of Christianity. To undermine belief in the Christian God is to undermine the most important barrier to social and political reform.[185]

Feuerbach's understanding of the actual mechanisms whereby religious illusions sustain the practical 'limitations' of the contemporary world is not always clear. However, he does give some account of how Christianity might operate in a specific case, namely in order to inhibit 'the basic drive of contemporary humankind' towards 'political freedom'.[186] There are two distinct threads, each associated with different variants of Christianity, in Feuerbach's explanation of this antithesis between Christian beliefs and political progress.

The first thread in Feuerbach's explanation appeals to the hierarchical and inegalitarian character of Christianity (predominent in its Catholic variants). Feuerbach maintains that the power of 'earthly majesty', that is, of absolutist monarchy, depends on the widespread acceptance of the belief that 'the person of majesty is an entirely different sort of being' to ordinary subjects.[187] The main support of such a belief, he suggests, is the widespread acceptance of the idea of 'heavenly majesty'.[188] Those who have grown up with the 'idea of a Father in Heaven' find it hard to conceive of a human society 'without a prince'.[189] From this starting point, Feuerbach reasons that if he can get contemporaries to abandon their belief in a God who stands above and apart from humankind, then it will deal a fatal blow to the inegalitarian belief that sustains absolutism – namely that humankind contains some individuals who stand above and apart from the rest. With the realisation that the person of the monarch 'is just as good' and 'no better' than any other, the institution of monarchy would lose its rationale and 'majesty' before vanishing into 'nothing'.[190]

The second thread in Feuerbach's explanation appeals to the consolatory and otherworldly character of Christianity (predominent in its Protestant variants). Unlike heathens, Christians were interested only in the heavenly life and 'had no interest either in the natural or the political world'.[191] As a result, they have proved all too willing to sacrifice what they regard as 'transitory welfare and life to eternal welfare and life, perishable goods to imperishable goods, limited and finite joy to infinite and immeasurable and endless joy'.[192] In particular, the Christian notion of heaven func- tioned as a repository of otherwise earthbound aspirations; the belief in 'a better life in heaven' drained away belief 'in a better life on earth' and

---

[185] See 'Beziehung' 429/82.   [186] 'Nothwendigkeit' 218/148.   [187] 'Beziehung' 428/82.
[188] *Ibid.* See also *Vorlesungen* 157/138.   [189] *Vorlesungen* 115/100–1.   [190] 'Beziehung' 428/82.
[191] *Vorlesungen* 274/245.   [192] *Luther* 412/116.

thereby undermined the 'striving to attain such a life'.[193] Thus the otherworldly realisation of the egalitarianism of the political republic (in the Christian heaven) hindered its earthly progress (by compensating for its earthly absence). In the Christian religion, Feuerbach suggests, 'you have your republic in heaven and you do not need one here'.[194] Only when that heavenly consolation was removed, he reasoned, would there be a sufficient motivation for establishing an earthly republic.[195]

With his own anthropological reduction, Feuerbach thereby hoped to deal a fatal blow to the absolutist state. By undermining Christianity, he saw himself as weakening both the inegalitarian beliefs that sustained absolutism and the otherworldly consolations that sublimated the striving for a political republic. Feuerbach was convinced that once his contemporaries had renounced 'a God who is other than man', a 'transformation of politics' would be ushered in.[196]

I turn now to consider Feuerbach's understanding of the character of the unalienated future society. Its formal structure is reasonably clear. Feuerbach appears committed to an account of historical progress as both reflecting, and being driven by, the progressive realisation of human nature. According to this model – characterised by one commentator as an 'anthropological teleology'– historical epochs form an identifiable progression from less adequate to more adequate embodiments of human nature.[197] History culminates in a social world in which essential human attributes are fully realised.

This formal account reveals little about the content of that unalienated future. However, scattered observations in Feuerbach's work suggest that individual character, social relations, cultural life, and political institutions would all be transformed once the dichotomy between 'the here and the beyond' was overcome.[198]

Feuerbach's comparison between the typical member of contemporary society and the representative individual of the future contrasts a collection of fractured components with an integrated whole. Contemporary individuals are said to 'live in discord', separated from their essential human capacities.[199] In contrast, once religion no longer prevented the 'harmony' between the actions and the underlying nature of humankind, individuals

[193] *Vorlesungen* 315/281. See also *Luther* 390/84.   [194] 'Nothwendigkeit' 222/152.   [195] See *ibid.*
[196] *Ibid.* 219/149.
[197] Hans Blumenburg, *Die Legitimität der Neuzeit*, second edition (Frankfurt am Main, 1988) p. 520. See also *Gedanken* 286/83.
[198] 'Fragmente' 159/273.   [199] 'Nothwendigkeit' 219/149.

would become 'complete and whole'.[200] For the first time, people would have what Feuerbach calls an 'undivided soul'.[201]

Feuerbach also contrasts contemporary social relations with those of the unalienated future. The subordination of morality to faith which characterises the Christian world, is said to be reflected in the egoism and intolerance that governs existing relationships between individuals. In contrast, the 'highest and first law' of unalienated social relations would be the 'love of man to man'.[202] Feuerbach's official tripartite account of human nature identified 'reason, will, and affection (*die Vernunft, der Wille, das Herz*)' as the essential human characteristics.[203] The affective element of human nature, he suggests, would find its full expression in social relations based on 'love'.[204] What Feuerbach means by love is not always very clear. In places, he identifies love with selflessness.[205] More often, however, love is described in terms of a willingness to promote the interests of others.[206] This emphasis on mutual concern may underpin Feuerbach's enthusiasm for the Stoics and their insistence 'that man was not born for his own sake, but for the sake of others, i.e., for love'.[207]

At one point, this emphasis on mutual concern led Feuerbach to characterise himself as a 'communist'.[208] This self-description was initially welcomed by radical contemporaries as a political conversion. For example, in an article (written for an English Owenite audience) on the progress of communism on the Continent, Engels reported that Feuerbach ('the most eminent philosophical genius in Germany at the present time') had recently announced 'that Communism was only a necessary consequence of the principles he had proclaimed'.[209] However, it soon emerged that Feuerbach's use of this new and still fluid term was intended, not to indicate a new ideological commitment – endorsing some form of common ownership, for example – but simply as a potentially confusing (and quickly abandoned) shorthand for the mutual concern that he also called 'love'.[210]

Feuerbach also believed that the future reconciliation of individuals with their own essential nature would lead to a cultural renaissance. He boldly prophesied that the sublation of Christianity would inaugurate a new era of

---

[200] *Vorlesungen* 241/214.   [201] 'Nothwendigkeit' 219/149.   [202] *Wesen* 444/271.
[203] See *ibid.* 30–1/3.   [204] *Grundsätze* 319/54.   [205] See, for example, *Luther* 398/95.
[206] See, for example, 'Fragmente' 180/295.
[207] *Wesen* 440/267. Possibly an echo of Cicero, *De Officiis*, I.22.
[208] 'Beziehung' 441/91. See also Feuerbach to Otto Wigand, 8–16 November 1847, *Gesammelte Werke* 19, p. 137; and Feuerbach to Friedrich Kapp, 15 October 1844, *Gesammelte Werke* 18, p. 398.
[209] 'Rapid Progress', pp. 235–6. See also Engels to Marx, 22 February–7 March 1845, *MEW* 27, p. 20; *MECW* 38, p. 22; and Alex Callinicos, *Marxism and Philosophy* (Oxford, 1983) p. 32.
[210] See 'Fragmente' 180/295 and 'Beziehung' 432–3/85.

poetry and art, surpassing all its predecessors in 'energy, depth, and fire'.[211]
In an attempt to explain the contrast between the Greek mastery of the
plastic arts and the failure of Christian art, Feuerbach suggests that this
Greek superiority was grounded in their polytheism and idolatry. It was
because the ancients took the human form as '*unconditionally* and *unre-
servedly* the highest', as the form of their divinity, that their sculpture had
remained as yet unsurpassed.[212] In contrast, Christians had proved incapable of producing artistic works adequate to the objects of their worship.
Art can present only what is true and unequivocal, and Christianity rests
on an equivocation (namely that Christ is both human and not-human).[213]
However, Feuerbach confidently predicts that once the recognition that 'the
human is the divine' became widespread, the tyranny of Greece would be
overthrown.[214] Genuine art, he insists, arises from the conviction 'that the
life of this life is true life'.[215] As a result, otherworldly beliefs are incapable
of true poetry; the source of 'lyrical fire' is human pain, a pain which is
diminished and undermined by otherworldly beliefs.[216]

The political dimension of the unalienated society of the future is not
yet apparent. It is certain that political life should be reorganised in accordance with human nature. As the third-person form of his reply to Max
Stirner has it: 'Feuerbach does not make morality into a measuring stick
for man, but rather man the measure of morality: good is what is fit for
man, suitable; bad, objectionable, what contradicts him.'[217] However, the
political arrangements which, in Feuerbach's judgement, would embody
that formal moral standard are not yet clear.

In the *Vorselungen*, Feuerbach compares his own position with that of
Aristotle. (Feuerbach has in mind Aristotle's apparent endorsement of the
rule of a single superior individual, if one could be found, in the remarks on
the ideal polis that close Book III of the *Politics*.) Feuerbach sees Aristotle's
general approach – in treating conformity with human nature as the criteria
for the best form of government – as peerless, but begs to differ about the
political conclusions that follow from applying that principle. 'I protest
and maintain', he explains, 'that the republic, the democratic republic is
the form of government which reason must recognise to be consonant with
human nature and therefore best.'[218] This break with Aristotle's conclusions

---

[211] 'Vorläufige Thesen' 248/160.   [212] *Ibid.* 248/159.
[213] There is an echo here of Heine's preference for 'Hellene' sensuality over 'Nazarene' repression. See,
in this context, Margaret A. Rose, *Marx's Lost Aesthetic: Karl Marx and the Visual Arts* (Cambridge,
1984) chapters 1–2.
[214] 'Vorläufige Thesen' 248/160.   [215] *Ibid.* 247/159.   [216] *Ibid.* 248/160.
[217] 'Beziehung' 440/91.   [218] *Vorlesungen* 380/336.

rests on Feuerbach's identification of the impulse to 'political freedom' as the 'basic drive of contemporary humankind'.[219] Human nature, he insists, includes 'an instinct for an active participation in the affairs of the state, an instinct demanding the abolition of political hierarchy'.[220]

Feuerbach maintains that this practical instinct can only be fully realised in a political republic, although he concedes that a constitutional monarchy might, in certain historical contexts, including contemporary German conditions, be the most 'practical' or 'suitable' form of government.[221] However, a 'monarchy attenuated by democracy or democratic institutions' could never be judged the best form of government.[222] Constitutional monarchy was 'a hybrid system' plagued by 'contradiction, indecision, and pusillanimity' as a result of the two competing powers ('prince and people') which 'govern or dispute the government'.[223] Progress requires that a constitutional monarchy be replaced eventually by the 'true and complete democracy' of a political republic.[224]

In the more cautious and coded language of the early 1840s, Feuerbach explained the transformation of political life that progress required by means of an extended analogy with the Reformation. The analogy associates Catholicism with hierarchy and Protestantism with egalitarianism. Catholicism is said to demand, in its religious form, that a pope stand above the community of believers and, in its political form, that a monarch stand above the community of citizens. Feuerbach suggests that whilst the Reformation had destroyed religious Catholicism it had left political Catholicism intact.[225] The challenge of the present age was to achieve in the 'field of politics' what the Reformation had achieved in the 'field of religion' (namely the destruction of hierarchy).[226] Only the political republic would give adequate expression to the human instinct for active participation in a non-hierarchical state ('an instinct demanding the negation of political Catholicism').[227]

Of course, on Feuerbach's account, the collapse of absolute monarchy would follow, more or less automatically, from the abandonment of the Christian beliefs that sustained it. Once the 'religious content' of Christianity had been successfully 'exposed', he insists, 'political republicanism' would 'naturally' follow.[228] In this way, amongst others, Feuerbach was occasionally tempted to identify himself as a second Luther, whose critique

---

[219] 'Nothwendigkeit' 218/148.
[220] *Ibid.* 221/151. Feuerbach later suggested that republics have an affinity with the 'egalitarianism' of nature in general. See *Vorlesungen* 155–7/137–9.
[221] *Vorlesungen* 380/336.   [222] *Ibid.* 168/149.   [223] *Ibid.* 180/159.   [224] *Ibid.* 168/149.
[225] 'Nothwendigkeit' 221/151.   [226] *Ibid.*   [227] *Ibid.*   [228] *Ibid.* 222/152.

of Christianity would finally complete the Reformation and inaugurate a truly modern age.

<h3 style="text-align:center">FEUERBACH AND MARX</h3>

The period 1843–5, which provides the chronological framework of the present volume, is rightly portrayed as the high-water mark of Feuerbach's influence on Marx. The language, subject matter, and substantive content of the early writings all bear the impress of Feuerbach's work. The recent description of the young Marx as 'no more than an *avant-garde* Feuerbachian' may be a provocative exaggeration but it is not without foundation.[229] (At the time, Max Stirner advanced the same plausible overstatement, treating the young Marx as a minor disciple of Feuerbach.[230])

A comprehensive account of the relation between these two authors is well beyond the scope of this section.[231] My comments here are constrained by space, my chosen chronological remit, and the major concerns of this particular chapter. Within those parameters, I briefly consider some issues of familiarity (Marx's knowledge of Feuerbach's work), of affinity (Marx's intellectual proximity to Feuerbach's work), and of acknowledgement (Marx's own judgement of Feuerbach's work).

I start with the most straightforward of these three issues, namely familiarity. Simply put, the young Marx's knowledge of Feuerbach's output is extensive and well established. The early writings are full of references to the best-known of Feuerbach's middle-period texts; *Das Wesen des Christentums*, *Das Wesen des Glaubens im Sinne Luthers*, the 'Vorläufige Thesen', and the *Grundsätze* are all regularly mentioned. Marx was also acquainted with some of Feuerbach's less well-known writings from this period, including his 1840 review of Karl Bayer's book on 'ethical spirit'.[232] Nor does this exhaust the young Marx's knowledge of the Feuerbach corpus. He had also read some of the earlier writings. For example, in preparing his doctoral thesis, Marx had made use of Feuerbach's *Geschichte der neuern Philosophie von Bacon von Verulam bis Benedikt Spinoza*.[233]

---

[229] Louis Althusser, *For Marx* (London, 1969) p. 46.

[230] See Stirner, *Der Einzige* 192/158.

[231] Book-length treatments include Klaus Erich Bockmuhl, *Leiblichkeit und Gesellschaft: Studien zur Religionskritik und Anthropologie im Frühwerk von Ludwig Feuerbach und Karl Marx* (Göttingen, 1961); and Werner Schuffenhauer, *Feuerbach und der Junge Marx: Zur Entstehungsgeschichte der Marxistischen Weltanschauung* (Berlin, 1965).

[232] For Feuerbach's review, see *Gesammelte Werke* 9, pp. 82–99. For Marx's familiarity, see Marx to Ruge, 10 February 1842, *MEW* 27, p. 395; *MECW* 1, p. 381.

[233] See *Differenz* 59/94. See also Warren Breckman, *Marx, the Young Hegelians, and the Origins of Radical Social Theory* (Cambridge, 1999) pp. 266ff.

Of all these works, it was perhaps the 'Vorläufige Thesen' and the *Grundsätze* which had the greatest impact on the young Marx.[234] This is not to suggest that he was uninterested in, or uninfluenced by, Feuerbach's critique of religion – and it was certainly *Das Wesen des Christentums* that secured Feuerbach's wider European reputation – merely that it was the critique of speculative philosophy which established the latter's theoretical stature in Marx's own mind.[235]

Turning to the second (and less straightforward) issue of affinity, it will already be apparent that Feuerbachian threads appear throughout the early writings. Three main affinities are especially striking. They concern the young Marx's account of Christianity, of speculative philosophy, and of scientific method. First, many of Marx's claims about Christianity and religion provide a direct echo of (elements of) Feuerbach's standpoint. In the 'Kritik: Einleitung', for example, Marx not only insists that '*man makes religion, religion does not make man*', but also goes on to endorse the view that the detour of religion constitutes a stage in the developing 'self-knowledge' of humankind.[236] Second, Marx's basic account of speculative philosophy – as involving a distinctive and recurring pattern of inversion whereby the empirical is transformed into the speculative and the speculative is then transformed into the empirical – also broadly follows Feuerbach's own analysis of the systole and diastole of Hegelianism. Third, some of the young Marx's remarks about the appropriate scientific method mirror Feuerbach's own comments. For example, Marx's claim, in the *Manuskripte*, that sense perception 'must be the basis of all science' parallels Feuerbach's own account of the sensuous and empirical as the necessary starting point for scientific knowledge.[237]

These particular affinities will not be discussed further here. Given the remit of this chapter, I want rather to consider some additional and less remarked-upon connections between Feuerbach's middle-period writings (especially his critique of Christianity and speculative philosophy) and the young Marx's account of human flourishing. My account of the latter is developed more fully in the second half of this chapter. However, two striking affinities might be anticipated here. First, there is a foundational similarity in that Feuerbach and Marx share the view that social and political

---

[234] See, for example, *Manuskripte* 468/232/281 and 569/327/380. See also David McLellan, *The Young Hegelians and Karl Marx* (London, 1969) pp. 95ff.

[235] Both *Das Wesen des Christentums* and *Das Wesen des Glaubens im Sinne Luthers* are mentioned favourably in Marx to Feuerbach, 11 August 1844, *MEW* 27, pp. 425, 428; *MECW* 3, pp. 354, 357.

[236] 'Kritik: Einleitung' 378/175/244.

[237] *Manuskripte* 543/303/355. See also Feuerbach, 'Über den "Anfang der Philosophie"' 145/137–8.

relations ought to reflect perfectionist considerations. Thus Marx's appeal to the flourishing of human nature as the benchmark by which emancipation might be measured (and modern society criticised) has affinities with Feuerbach's own naturalistic account of social and political life. Second, there is some substantive overlap in their respective models of human nature. Marx's philosophical anthropology seems much richer than Feuerbach's tripartite account of human nature (with its effusive invocation of 'love'). However, both authors can be said to see the realisation of community – itself grounded in some notion of mutual concern – as central to human flourishing.

How much significance should be placed on these two additional affinities, however, is not certain. Both perfectionism and an account of community as central to human flourishing can be found in other authors with whom Marx was familiar (most obviously Aristotle). In such circumstances, one might hesitate to move from carefully qualified claims about the affinities between Feuerbach and Marx to emphatic assertions regarding the influence of the former on the latter.

It is also important to distinguish between such broad foundational affinities and the use to which they are subsequently put. In this context, special attention should be drawn to a substantive disparity in the political views of Feuerbach and Marx. Throughout the 1840s, Feuerbach's political ideal remained the modern state, the kind of secular republic which was to be found in America (both the land of the 'future' and a country that he considered moving to).[238] This was, of course, precisely the form of political community which Marx had already criticised at length for offering only a limited and contradictory form of emancipation. The young Marx may have used Feuerbach's account of the achievements and failings of Christianity in order to elaborate his own understanding of the achievements and failings of the modern state, but there is no evidence that Feuerbach shared that critical assessment of the modern polity. (There are, of course, other political differences between the two authors – their views about private property or proletarian agency, for example – but these fall outside the remit of the present chapter.)

The third of my comparative issues concerns acknowledgement (the young Marx's own assessment of Feuerbach's work). Marx is not usually thought of as a charitable reader of the work of others, but the most striking feature of the remarks about Feuerbach contained in the early writings

---

[238] On emigration, see Feuerbach to Friedrich Kapp, 3 March 1850, *Gesammelte Werke*, volume 19, p. 227.

is their warm and ungrudging nature. I have mentioned previously (see Chapter 2) some examples of the enthusiasm for Feuerbach's writings in the *Manuskripte* – where Marx recommends that Feuerbach be hailed for both 'the extent of his achievement' and 'the quiet simplicity' with which he presents his conclusions to the wider world – but this generous measure of praise also appears in Marx's published work.[239] In *Die heilige Familie*, for example, Feuerbach is distinguished from Bauer (and his entourage) on the grounds that only the former has 'disclosed real mysteries'.[240] Indeed, the book as a whole is identified by its authors as a defence of 'real humanism' – a label whose Feuerbachian connotations would have been readily apparent to its contemporary audience – against the attacks of Bauerian 'critical criticism'.[241] When, in later life, Marx obtained a copy of *Die heilige Familie* (see Chapter 1), he wrote to Engels recording his surprise that it contained nothing that they should be ashamed of, although he conceded that, from his present vantage point, its 'cult of Feuerbach' created a 'humorous impression'.[242] The young Marx also expressed this enthusiasm for Feuerbach's work in his somewhat earnest correspondence with the author himself. In one letter, Marx praises *Das Wesen des Glaubens im Sinne Luthers* and the *Grundsätze* (despite their slimness) as more important than 'the whole of contemporary German literature put together', before reassuring Feuerbach 'of the great respect and – if I may use the word – love, which I feel for you'.[243]

Elsewhere, the young Marx identifies several threads in Feuerbach's 'real theoretical revolution' as especially deserving of praise.[244] Interestingly, these correspond to the three main affinities identified above involving Feuerbach's accounts of Christianity, of speculative philosophy, and of scientific method. Marx praises Feuerbach for having largely completed the critique of religion in Germany. It was Feuerbach, Marx notes, who had recognised that in the 'fantastic reality of heaven' man finds nothing 'but the reflection of himself'.[245] In addition, Feuerbach is heralded as 'the true

---

[239] *Manuskripte* 569/328/381. See also *ibid.* 468/232/281.   [240] *Die heilige Familie* 58/56.
[241] *Ibid.* 7/7. Marx notified Feuerbach that he intended to publish 'a small booklet' criticising Bauer's *Allgemeine Literatur-Zeitung*, a journal containing 'much covert polemic against you'. Marx to Feuerbach, 11 August 1844, *MEW* 27, p. 427; *MECW* 3, p. 356.
[242] Marx to Engels, 24 April 1867, *MEW* 31, p. 290; *MECW* 42, p. 360.
[243] Marx to Feuerbach, 11 August 1844, *MEW* 27, p. 425; *MECW* 3, p. 354. As a token of that respect and love, Marx included a copy of his 'Kritik: Einleitung'.
[244] *Manuskripte* 468/232/281.
[245] 'Kritik: Einleitung' 378/175/243. Feuerbach is not named, but it is his views which are clearly being paraphrased. Note also Marx's comments on Feuerbach's insight into the Incarnation and Trinity in *Die heilige Familie* 58/56.

conqueror of the old philosophy'.[246] In particular, he is said to have been the
first to grasp (and demonstrate) that the Hegelian philosophy was a form of
'speculative and mystical empiricism'.[247] Finally, Feuerbach is credited with
some insight into the correct scientific method. He is said, for example,
to have appreciated that the starting point for investigation must be (in
some sense) empirical, that science must begin with 'the positive, that is
sensuously ascertained'.[248]

None of these elements in Marx's account of Feuerbach's achievement
concerns the society of the future (the primary subject of the present chapter). However, that is precisely the issue raised by perhaps the most striking
of the bouquets in Marx's effusive letter to the author. In this missive,
and in addition to his other achievements, Marx credits Feuerbach with
having (intentionally or not) provided 'a philosophical basis (*philosophische
Grundlage*) for socialism (*Sozialismus*)'.[249]

I do not want to exaggerate the significance of this striking – but isolated
and scarcely transparent – remark. The meaning of 'socialism' in both
Marx's early writings and the wider intellectual culture was far from being
either precise or fixed at this time.[250] In addition, it might be a mistake
to place too much weight on this kind of personal correspondence from a
youthful admirer to 'the most eminent philosophical genius in Germany'
(to use Engels' contemporaneous description).[251] However, I am reluctant
to dismiss Marx's claim, either as wholly unclear, or as a piece of empty
ephebic enthusiasm.

By way of elaboration, the young Marx goes on to commend Feuerbach for having made the 'unity of man with man (*Einheit der Menschen
mit den Menschen*)' the essential principle of his theory, a principle whose
wider meaning, Marx observes, the 'communists (*Kommunisten*)' have

[246] *Manuskripte* 569/328/381.
[247] *Die heilige Familie* 41/39. Note also Marx's comments regarding the religious character of speculative philosophy in *Manuskripte* 569/328/381.
[248] *Manuskripte* 570/329/382. See also *ibid.* 543/303/355.
[249] Marx to Feuerbach, 11 August 1844, *MEW* 27, p. 425; *MECW* 3, p. 354.
[250] On the shifting meaning of socialism and communism, see Wolfgang Schieder, 'Sozialis-mus', *Geschichtliche Grundbegriffe: Historisches Lexikon zur politische-sozialen Sprache in Deutsch-land*, ed. Otto Brunner, Werner Conze, and Reinhart Koselleck, volume 5 (Stuttgart, 1984) pp. 923–96; Wolfgang Schieder, 'Kommunismus', *Geschichtliche Grundbegriffe*, ed. Brunner, Conze, and Koselleck, volume 3 (Stuttgart, 1982) pp. 455–529; and Jacques Grandjonc, *Communisme/Kommunismus/Communism: Origine et développement international de la terminolo-gie communautaire pré-marxiste des utopistes aux neo-babouvistes, 1785–1842*, volume 1: *Historique*, volume 2: *Pièces justificatives* (Trier, 1989).
[251] 'Rapid Progress' 235–6. See also Engels to Marx, 22 February–7 March 1845, *MEW* 27, p. 20; *MECW* 38, p. 22; and Callinicos, *Marxism and Philosophy*, p. 32.

immediately understood.[252] Marx's striking remark is perhaps best understood as suggesting that Feuerbach had not only rightly built his social theory on perfectionist foundations, but also appreciated that community, grounded in mutual concern, was central to human flourishing. In this way, the young Marx might be said to have acknowledged the two additional affinities that were identified above.

In this generous appraisal of Feuerbach's achievement, there is no reference to the latter's view of the specifically political arrangements of the good society. On the present account, which identifies a significant gulf between the two authors on this issue, this omission is scarcely surprising. Feuerbach and Marx share both a foundational view (that social and political relations ought to reflect narrow perfectionist considerations) and a substantive element in their models of human nature (identifying community, grounded in mutual concern, as central to human flourishing). However, they build very different social and political conclusions around these basic affinities. Not least, throughout the 1840s, Feuerbach's political ideal remained the secular modern state which Marx had already criticised for offering only a limited and contradictory form of emancipation.

(Some readers may wonder why I have not drawn on 'Luther als Schiedsrichter zwischen Strauss und Feuerbach' as evidence of Marx's assessment of Feuerbach. This anonymous article was first published in Ruge's *Anekdota* in 1843, and was attributed to Marx by David Ryazanov. Its appearance in some older editions of the young Marx's writings still leads secondary sources to treat its attribution as uncontroversial.[253] However, I am persuaded that Ryazanov's attribution is mistaken, and note that the best modern editions of Marx concur in that judgement.[254])

MARX AND HUMAN NATURE

I turn now to consider the perfectionist thread in the writings of the young Marx in a little more detail. I begin with his substantive account of human nature.

---

[252] Marx to Feuerbach, 11 August 1844, *MEW* 27, p. 425; *MECW* 3, p. 354. See also *Manuskripte* 570/328/381; and Feuerbach, *Grundsätze* 339–40/72.

[253] For example, the article appears in *MEW* 1, pp. 26–7; and *Writings of the Young Marx on Philosophy and Society*, ed. L. D. Easton and K. H. Guddat (Garden City NY, 1967). Marx's authorship is presupposed, for example, in Brudney, *Marx's Attempt to Leave Philosophy*, pp. xviii, 98.

[254] For the case against Ryazanov's attribution, and in favour of Feuerbach's authorship, see Hans-Martin Sass, 'Feuerbach statt Marx: Zur Verfasserschaft des Aufsatzes "Luther als Schiedsrichter zwischen Strauss und Feuerbach"', *International Review of Social History*, volume 12 (1967) pp. 108–19. The editors of *MECW* summarily report that the case against Marx's authorship is now 'proved'. 'Preface', *MECW* 1, p. xxxiii.

Two issues typically dominate modern discussions of Marx and human nature, namely his attitude towards the universality of human nature (that is, the existence of aspects of human nature which are constant across history and between cultures) and his account of the *differentia specifica* of the human species (that is, those features which distinguish human beings from other animals). In the present section, I offer only brief observations on these topics – together with a justification of that brevity – before turning to consider Marx's substantive treatment of human nature.

Marx's attitude towards the universality of human nature is easily summarised. He holds that human nature has both constant and mutable elements; that is, he maintains that human beings are characterised not only by universal qualities, constant across history and between cultures, but also by variable qualities, reflecting historical and cultural diversity. Marx would later refer to the former as 'human nature in general' and the latter as 'human nature as modified in each epoch'.[255]

This brief statement of his views involves a rejection of the long-lived but puzzling claim that, for Marx, human nature has no universal elements. The latter interpretation, which I shall call the historicist account of Marx's views, has many proponents.[256] However, it no longer has an unchallenged dominance in the literature, it is hard to square with the relevant textual evidence, and it has been persuasively challenged by others.[257] The chronological remit of the present work also provides a reason for largely ignoring the historicist reading. Adherents of the latter crucially locate Marx's rejection of the universality of human nature from 1845 onwards (he is often portrayed as announcing that changed view in the so-called 'Thesen über Feuerbach').[258] The (sometimes implicit) guiding assumption here is that Marx's theory of history, whose emergent form can be detected in *Die*

---

[255] *Kapital* 637/605.
[256] For endorsements of the historicist reading, see Van A. Harvey, 'Ludwig Feuerbach and Karl Marx', Ninian Smart, John Clayton, Patrick Sherry, and Steven T. Katz (eds.), *Nineteenth Century Religious Thought in the West*, volume 1 (Cambridge, 1985) p. 292; Sidney Hook, *From Hegel to Marx: Studies in the Intellectual Development of Karl Marx* (London, 1936) p. 74; and Vernon Venable, *Human Nature* (London, 1946) p. 22.
[257] For rebuttals of the historicist reading, see John McMurtry, *The Structure of Marx's World View* (Princeton, 1978) chapter 1; Norman Geras, *Marx and Human Nature. Refutation of a Legend* (London, 1983); and W. Peter Archibald, *Marx and the Missing Link: 'Human Nature'* (London, 1989) part 3.
[258] See, for example, Wal Suchting, 'Marx's *Theses on Feuerbach*: Notes Towards a Commentary (With a New Translation)', John Mepham and David-Hillel Ruben (eds.), *Issues in Marxist Philosophy*, volume 2: *Materialism* (Brighton, 1979) p. 19; and Joseph Margolis, 'Praxis and Meaning: Marx's Species-Being and Aristotle's Political Animal', George E. McCarthy (ed.), *Marx and Aristotle: Nineteenth-Century German Social Theory and Classical Antiquity* (Lanham MD, 1992) pp. 332–3. For a definitive rejoinder, see Geras, *Marx and Human Nature*.

deutsche Ideologie, somehow conflicted with, and subsequently displaced, claims about the universality of human nature.[259] My assumption that the young Marx subscribed to a concept of universal human nature should therefore not prove contentious, even to those who claim – in my view, mistakenly – that Marx subsequently adopted a historicist view of these matters. (For reasons of economy, I refer henceforth to 'human nature' when I mean the universal elements of human nature.)

Marx's account of the *differentia specifica* of humankind may be harder to identify but it is similarly marginal to the present study. Commentators have identified a wide variety of potential candidates for the role of *differentia specifica* in Marx's writings. These include consciousness, intentionality, language, co-operation, tool use, tool-making, productive activity, creative intelligence, and projective consciousness.[260] This list is remarkable in two respects. The number and variety of candidates on offer might suggest that Marx's views on this subject are not as clear as they might be. In addition, many of these candidates would appear vulnerable to the claims of modern ethological literature. Simply put, that literature typically lacks Marx's confidence that, as he would remark in *Kapital*, 'the worst architect' is easily distinguished from 'the best of bees'.[261] Fortunately, the clarity and plausibility of Marx's views on this issue do not bear on the concerns of the present study.

This may appear a surprising assertion, since the young Marx occasionally appears to link his views about human flourishing (an issue with which I am very much concerned in the present chapter) with his views about the *differentia specifica* of the human species (an issue which I intend largely to ignore). In particular, Marx may have thought that the truth of a particular claim about the *differentia specifica* of the species (namely that humankind alone engages in productive activity) would provide support for his account of human flourishing (which identifies fulfilling work as central to the good life for humankind). However, this connection, between the *differentia specifica* of the species and the importance of any particular aspect of human flourishing, appears mistaken. It is hard to see why the importance to humankind of fulfilling work, for example, would be

[259] The claim that Marx's philosophical anthropology is antithetical to the theory of history is rejected by those who maintain that the latter presupposes the former, and by those who maintain that the latter is independent of the former. See McMurtry, *The Structure of Marx's World View*, pp. 19–20; and G. A. Cohen, *History, Labour, and Freedom: Themes From Marx* (Oxford, 1988) chapters 5, 8, and 9 respectively.

[260] See Jon Elster, *Making Sense of Marx* (Cambridge, 1985) pp. 62ff.; and McMurtry, *The Structure of Marx's World-View*, pp. 21ff.

[261] *Kapital* 193/188.

diminished by the discovery of another species – say from another solar system – which engaged systematically in productive activity (that is, by the discovery that productive activity was not the *differentia specifica* of the human species). The present chapter is concerned with Marx's account of human flourishing, and since, whatever he may himself have thought, that account is neither dependent on, nor supported by, his account of the *differentia specifica*, the latter will not be discussed further.

I turn instead to the young Marx's substantive account of human nature, and, in particular, to his account of the conditions for human flourishing. Much of the evidence that I will consider here appears in an indirect manner, as part of Marx's discussion of needs. Since the connection between human needs and human flourishing may not be obvious, I begin with some formal remarks.

The concept of 'need' is concerned with the things that one cannot do without, with the things that are necessary.[262] It must, in principle, be possible to explain what makes those things necessary, that is, what they are needed *for*. Statements of need, it is sometimes said, are of the form '*A* needs *z* in order to φ'.

In the present context, it is Marx's account of non-volitional needs which is of particular interest. What makes a need 'non-volitional' is that its end-state (the 'in order to φ') is, in principle, independent of any desires, wants, and preferences (I use these terms interchangeably) that an individual might have. For example, the claim 'children need vitamin D in order to avoid rickets' refers to a non-volitional need. These needs are 'in principle' independent of such desires because, although a non-volitional need for some thing can be, and often is, accompanied by a desire for that thing, this is not a necessary feature of such a need. Individuals do not lose their non-volitional need for a thing if they happen not to desire it. Non-volitional needs are, as a result, sometimes described as objectively valuable in that satisfying them is valuable independent of our (actual or ideal) desires.

Accounts of non-volitional needs can be divided into more or less demanding varieties. Two contrasting examples – from amongst a wider range of possibilities – should indicate what I have in mind here. What I shall call *restricted* non-volitional accounts specify that needs are what human beings require in order to survive or avoid harm.[263] In contrast, what I shall call *expansive* non-volitional accounts specify that needs are

[262] See Harry G. Frankfurt, *The Importance of What We Care About: Philosophical Essays* (Cambridge, 1988) p. 106.
[263] See, for example, Joel Feinberg, *Social Philosophy* (Englewood Cliffs NJ, 1973) p. 111.

what human beings require in order to flourish.[264] These expansive accounts provide a more demanding list of conditions since for an entity to flourish it must typically do better than merely survive or avoid harm. In order to flourish, an entity must do well.

The exegetical suggestion advanced here is that the young Marx utilises an expansive non-volitional account of needs from which it is possible to reconstruct something of his model of human flourishing. The test of this suggestion is whether it helps to make sense of Marx's substantive remarks about human needs. However, I also note that this suggestion appears consistent with (some of) the young Marx's comments on the form of human needs. For example, in a difficult and convoluted passage about human nature in the *Manuskripte*, Marx characterises the dependency of individuals on certain natural objects as a 'need' in those cases where those objects are 'indispensable' for 'the exercise and confirmation' of the 'essential powers' of human beings.[265] That is, he suggests that human beings can be said to 'need' an object when it is necessary for human flourishing. Marx happily acknowledges that it is not only human beings which have needs of this kind. For example, he discusses the human need for food in the same terms as the need of plants for sunlight; sustenance for the individual, like sunlight for the plant, is said to be 'an indispensable object which confirms its life'.[266] Moreover, Marx maintains that for both the human and the plant, the object is 'indispensable' to 'the expression of its essential nature (*Wesensäußerung*)' whether or not that need is 'acknowledged'.[267]

I turn now to the substantive account of the conditions for human flourishing that can be recovered from Marx's scattered remarks (especially in the *Manuskripte* and the *Auszüge aus James Mill*). It is a raw and varied list, and, in order to give it some shape, I will collate these conditions for human flourishing under two broad headings: basic physical needs and less basic social needs.

The young Marx's advocacy of basic physical needs is not usually thought to constitute a distinctive part of his account of human flourishing. References to these needs are made largely in passing, and Marx appears to acknowledge the derivative and conventional nature of his account. At one point, for example, he adds an 'etc.' after mentioning a few such needs, as if he were inviting the reader to continue a familiar and uncontentious list unaided.[268]

---

[264] See, for example, G. E. M. Anscombe, 'Modern Moral Philosophy', *Philosophy*, volume 33 (1958) p. 7.
[265] *Manuskripte* 578/336/389–90.   [266] *Ibid.* 578/336/390.   [267] *Ibid.*
[268] See *ibid.* 515/275/327–8.

That said, a reasonably extensive list of basic physical needs can be reconstructed from his comments. Marx refers to a human need for sustenance (he talks about 'eating, drinking' and, more generally, 'nourishment'),[269] for warmth and shelter (he lists 'heating' and 'clothing' as well as a 'dwelling'),[270] for certain climatic conditions (he mentions both 'light' and 'air'),[271] for physical exercise (the need 'to move about' and the need for 'physical exercise'),[272] for basic hygiene ('the simplest animal cleanliness'),[273] and for reproduction and (heterosexual) sexual activity (he writes of 'procreation' and describes sexual relationships between women and men as characteristic of the 'species').[274]

Notwithstanding their minimal and (broadly) uncontroversial character, Marx notes that these basic physical needs are not always met in the modern social world. Indeed, he claims that they are not even met in the most economically advanced parts of that world. For example, the need for light and air is not satisfied by 'the pestilential atmosphere of English basement dwellings', and the need for clothing is scarcely fulfilled by 'the fantastic rags in which the English poor are clothed'.[275] More generally, Marx suggests that, as far as the satisfaction of basic physical needs is concerned, the 'savage' and the 'animal' may do rather better than the inhabitants of the 'little Ireland' which can be found in any of the larger industrial towns of France and England.[276]

As this last remark confirms, these basic physical needs may be shared with (non-human) animals. This does not, on Marx's account, make those needs any less 'human'. However, he does express concern about social conditions in which individuals have no other aim than to satisfy basic physical needs. In particular, he claims that the individual who, as a result of poverty, is 'burdened' by basic physical needs is not only likely to neglect more refined sensibilities (such a person 'has no sense of the finest of plays') but is also likely to satisfy those basic needs in the 'crudest' of forms. Marx observes that 'it would be hard to say' how a starving man satisfying his hunger differed from an animal eating.[277] In such circumstances, he remarks, the individual is reduced to 'nothing more than an animal'.[278]

By comparison with basic physical needs, what I am calling less basic social needs are both more demanding to satisfy and less widely recognised. These less basic social needs can be divided into two groups: those which are *not* often thought to constitute a distinctive part of Marx's account of human flourishing, and those which *are* often thought of in that way.

[269] *Ibid.* 514–15/275/327–8.   [270] *Ibid.* 514/275/328.   [271] *Ibid.* 548/308/359.
[272] *Ibid.* 548–9/308–9/360.   [273] *Ibid.* 548/308/359.
[274] *Ibid.* 514–5/275/327 and 'Zur Judenfrage' 375/172/239.   [275] 'Kritische Randglossen' 396/193/406.
[276] *Manuskripte* 548/308/360.   [277] *Ibid.* 542/302/353.   [278] *Ibid.* 515/275/327.

The first group of less basic social needs – those which are not often thought to constitute a distinctive part of Marx's account of human flourishing – might initially appear curious. Not least, some members of this group, such as 'book-buying', look insufficiently universal to be identified amongst the necessary conditions of human flourishing.[279] However, Marx's comments are best read as listing historically and culturally specific examples of needs which are themselves universal. The need to buy books, on this account, would simply represent one particular historical and cultural form that a more universal need for intellectual stimulation or improvement might take.

A reasonably extensive account of these less basic social needs can be compiled from the early writings. The young Marx refers to a human need for recreation (to 'go drinking', to 'go dancing', to 'fence', to 'sing'),[280] for culture (to 'go to the theatre'),[281] for education and intellectual exercise (to 'think', to 'theorise', to 'buy books', to engage in 'learning'),[282] for artistic expression (to 'paint'),[283] for emotional fulfilment (to 'love'),[284] and for aesthetic pleasure (Marx identifies 'a musical ear, an eye for the beauty of form' as among our essential human capacities and powers).[285]

The second group of less basic social needs – those which are often thought to constitute a distinctive part of Marx's account of human flourishing – includes the need for fulfilling work and the need for meaningful community.

The young Marx is widely (and rightly) associated with the claim that self-realisation in work is a central element in human flourishing. Not all work, of course, provides the right conditions for self-realisation. Indeed, Marx identifies the productive activity which is most characteristic of the modern social world as responsible for forming 'stunted monsters' rather than creative and fulfilled human beings.[286] (In the remarks that follow, I use 'work' or 'productive activity' to refer to the generic activity, and 'labour', 'modern labour', or 'alienated labour' to refer to the form that this activity usually takes in the modern social world.[287])

The precise features of modern labour which make it so detrimental to human flourishing are not obvious. The young Marx suggests a number of

---

[279] See *ibid.* 549/309/361.   [280] *Ibid.*   [281] *Ibid.*
[282] *Ibid.* Note also Marx's enthusiasm for the 'craving for knowledge' evidenced in the nascent labour movement. *Die heilige Familie* 89/84.
[283] *Manuskripte* 549/309/361.   [284] *Ibid.*   [285] *Ibid.* 541/301/353.
[286] 'Kritische Randglossen' 396/193/406. For similarly forceful language, see *Auszüge aus James Mill* 455/220/269.
[287] See C. J. Arthur, *Dialectics of Labour: Marx and his Relation to Hegel* (Oxford, 1986) pp. 12–19. The terminological distinction remains useful even if its attribution to the young Marx is far from certain.

candidates without always clarifying the relation between them. Moreover, the number and variety of these putative conditions for labour inimical to self-realisation are easily underestimated, not only as a result of Marx's failure to distinguish clearly between them, but also because many commentators reduce his account to the much-quoted four conditions of alienated labour listed in the *Manuskripte* (according to which modern labour separates the individual from his product, from his productive activity, from other individuals, and from his own nature).

The first of these four well-known conditions concerns the relation between the modern worker and his product. In the modern social world, Marx claims, the product of the worker's labour confronts him 'as an alien object that has power over him'.[288] This represents an early invocation of the idea of fetishism – that is, the idea of individuals creating objects which are endowed with powers which (in some sense) they lack – which is central to Marx's later critique of political economy.[289] The modern worker is said to have bestowed 'life' on an object which now 'confronts him as hostile and alien'.[290] As the young Marx elucidates, 'our own product has stood up on its hind legs against us: it had seemed to be our property, but in reality we are its property'.[291] That the object in question does not inherently possess this power is of little comfort. This phenomenon of fetishism is already treated in the early writings as a distinguishing feature of the modern social world. The 'rule of the person over the person' which is said to have typified earlier historical epochs has been replaced in the modern social world by the 'rule of the *thing* over the *person*, the product over the producer'.[292]

The second of these conditions concerns the relation of the modern worker, not to his product, but to the process or activity by which that product is created. Marx maintains that in the very act of production the modern worker relates 'to his own activity as something which is alien and does not belong to him'.[293] Not least, it becomes a wholly '*accidental* and *unimportant*' matter whether the 'activity' of working 'involves the fulfilment of his [the worker's] personality, the realisation of his natural talents and spiritual goals'.[294] Modern labour, for Marx, typically fails to actualise these various creative potentials of the individual. Productive activity, which has the potential to be empowering and creative, is experienced instead as 'impotence' and 'emasculation'.[295]

[288] *Manuskripte* 515/275/327.
[289] See G. A. Cohen, *Karl Marx's Theory of History: A Defence* (Oxford, 1978) chapter 5.
[290] *Manuskripte* 512/272/324.   [291] *Auszüge aus James Mill* 461/227/276.
[292] *Ibid.* 455/221/270. For a later, and better-known, injunction of this idea, see *Kapital* 86/83.
[293] *Manuskripte* 515/275/327.   [294] *Auszüge aus James Mill* 454/220/269.
[295] *Manuskripte* 515/275/327.

The third of these conditions concerns the relation between the modern worker and other individuals. In terms of a distinction which is drawn in the *Auszüge aus James Mill*, the issue here is not one of 'self-estrangement (*Selbstentfremdung*)', that is, the separation between an individual and his own nature, but rather one of 'mutual estrangement (*wechselseitigen Entfremdung*)', that is, the separation between individuals.[296] This '*estrangement of man from man*' is reflected in the way that each individual 'regards the other' as simply a means to his own ends.[297] In the modern social world, concern for others is said to survive predominantly in the pale and inadequate form of a calculation about the effect those others might have on our own narrow self-interest. Elaborating this point, Marx observes that, in the modern social world, although your essential nature might generate a need for the product of my labour, your need establishes no power 'no rights of *possession* (*Eigentum*)' over my product.[298] Indeed, your needs, far from giving you some claim to my product, typically become a means 'whereby I acquire power over you'.[299] The young Marx would seem to view the failure of the modern social world to treat essential human needs as generating moral claims on the property of others as a matter of regret.

The fourth of these conditions concerns the relation between the modern worker and human nature (that is, concerns the issue of 'self-estrangement' rather than 'mutual estrangement').[300] For Marx, the human need for self-realisation in productive activity is degraded once work becomes a means to survival only. When productive activity is merely a means for the satisfaction of the worker's basic needs, 'his *human* essence' is made into 'a means for his physical existence'.[301] In such circumstances, Marx describes the individual as 'estranged from his own essence'.[302] The character of modern labour, he maintains, turns the essential nature of the worker into something '*alien*'.[303]

This fourfold account of alienated labour – as separating the individual from his product, from his productive activity, from other individuals, and from his own nature – is not transparent.[304] However, in the present context, further elaboration of the young Marx's account would be otiose. I turn instead to some additional features of labour detrimental to human

[296] *Auszüge aus James Mill* 456/222/270.   [297] *Manuskripte* 517–18/277–8/330.
[298] *Auszüge aus James Mill* 460/225/275.   [299] *Ibid.*
[300] *Ibid.* 456/222/270.   [301] *Manuskripte* 517/277/329.   [302] *Auszüge aus James Mill* 455/220/269.
[303] *Manuskripte* 517/277/329.
[304] Consider, for example, the various interpretations of Marx's apparent attempt in the *Manuskripte* to 'derive' the other three dimensions from alienated productive activity. See, for example, Mészáros, *Marx's Theory of Alienation*, pp. 78ff.; Isidor Wallimann, *Estrangement: Marx's Conception of Human Nature and the Division of Labour* (Westport CN, 1981) pp. 31ff.; and John Maguire, *Marx's Paris Writings: An Analysis* (Dublin, 1972) pp. 67ff.

flourishing which are often neglected in the literature. This neglect is a matter of regret, since these additional features are an integral part of Marx's account of the contemporary degradation of work and its accompanying transformation of the modern worker into 'a *mentally* and physically *dehumanised* being'.[305]

Four of these additional features might be mentioned here. The first is 'overwork', that is the amount of time that the modern worker has to spend engaged in productive activity.[306] The young Marx's main concern here is with the consequences, rather than the nature, of overwork. He insists, in particular, that overwork shortens lives, resulting in the 'early death' of workers.[307] The second is the 'more and more one-sided' development of the worker.[308] These remarks are often read as a simple-minded attack on specialisation, but are perhaps better understood as a condemnation of a lack of variety in activity. (It is the repetitiveness of labour, the 'monotony' of the modern factory system, which Marx censures.[309]) The third is the machine-like ('mechanical') character of labour.[310] This machine-like character concerns the mental as well as the physical demands of modern labour, not least the absence of judgement and control as the worker is 'depressed both intellectually and physically to the level of a machine'.[311] The fourth is the stupidity (the 'idiocy and cretinism') that results from the organisation of work in the modern social world.[312] It is readily apparent that Marx is not referring to formal intelligence here (regarding academic standards, for example), but rather the neglect of mental skills in productive activity.

This account of the young Marx's understanding of alienated labour is far from exhaustive. However, it does illustrate the heterogeneous and unsystematic character of his remarks. Productive activity in the modern social world separates the individual from his product, from his productive activity, from other individuals, and from his own nature. In addition, it creates workers that are overworked, one-sided, machine-like, and intellectually stunted.

In addition to a (negative) account of the nature of alienated labour in the modern social world, the young Marx also provides a (positive) glimpse of what unalienated labour might look like. The *Auszüge aus James Mill* is an especially rich text in this regard. It offers a rare illustration of Marx

[305] *Manuskripte* 524/284/336.   [306] 'Kritische Randglossen' 396/193/406.
[307] *Manuskripte* 474/238/285.
[308] *Ibid.* 474/238/286. See also *ibid.* 513/273/325 and *ibid.* 524/284/336.
[309] 'Kritische Randglossen' 396/193/406.   [310] *Ibid.*
[311] *Manuskripte* 474/237–8/285. See also *Auszüge aus James Mill* 455/220/269.
[312] *Manuskripte* 513/273/326.

venturing to discuss future possibilities directly and in (a little) detail. 'Let us suppose', he writes, 'that we had produced as human beings.'[313] Unusually, Marx uses the first person (plural and singular) to characterise the position of the unalienated worker (perhaps reflecting a tendency on his part to identify the potential fulfilment of productive activity with his own experience of the satisfactions of creative intellectual endeavour).

Marx's account of unalienated production is highly compressed and not easily understood. However, it makes some sense to read his remarks as providing the non-alienated alternatives to the four dimensions of alienated labour outlined in the *Manuskripte*. (So construed, these remarks might be thought to confirm the overlapping relationship between these texts broached in Chapter 2.)

The first dimension of non-alienated work concerns the relation between the worker and his product. Marx makes two main points. He claims that in self-realising work my 'personality' would be made 'objective' in my product, that is, my creations would embody my talents and abilities in a '*sensuous perceptible*' form.[314] In addition, Marx suggests that I would enjoy ('experience an individual pleasure') contemplating that feature of the objects that I produce.[315]

The second dimension of non-alienated work concerns the relation of the worker to the process or activity by which that product is created. Again Marx makes two main points. He claims that I would have demonstrated my 'individuality' in the productive process, that is, have expressed my talents and abilities in the activity of work. As a result, fulfilling productive activity is said to be 'authentic' or 'true' to the character of the worker.[316] In addition, productive activity would no longer be an activity that 'I loathe'.[317] The implicit (and not implausible) connection between these claims is that human beings are assumed to enjoy the activity of self-realisation in work. In fulfilling work, I would have 'enjoyed the *expression* of my own individual life'.[318]

The third dimension of non-alienated work concerns the relation between the worker and other individuals. One aspect of this concerns the worker's attitude to others. In this context, Marx claims that I would gain '*immediate* satisfaction' from your use or enjoyment of my product.[319] This satisfaction arises from the 'knowledge' of having produced an object 'corresponding to the needs of another human being'.[320] I take pleasure in having provided for your ends, and not, for example, from the anticipation

[313] *Auszüge aus James Mill* 462/227/277.   [314] *Ibid.*   [315] *Ibid.*   [316] *Ibid.* 463/228/278.
[317] *Ibid.*   [318] *Ibid.* 462/227/277.   [319] *Ibid.* 462/228/277.   [320] *Ibid.*

of some future benefit that I think might accrue to me as a result of having
done so. Another aspect of this relation is your attitude to me. The essential
role that I play in the satisfaction of your needs and in the 'completion' of
your essential nature is something that is understood and 'acknowledged' by
you.[321] I would find myself treated, not only reflectively but also emotion-
ally – 'in your thoughts and your love' – as 'an essential part of yourself'.[322]
The picture here is probably best understood as one of mutuality rather
than intimacy, but, even with this qualification, the existence of strong
affective bonds between individuals is unquestionably central to the young
Marx's vision of human flourishing.

The fourth dimension of non-alienated work concerns the relation
between the worker and human nature. It is the basic capacities and powers of humankind, and not merely the talents and abilities of particular
individuals, which find expression in the activity and result of production.
Indeed, the young Marx maintains that the process and products of creation are just so many reflections of '*human nature*'.[323] However, there is an
additional aspect to this relation. Since the products of unalienated labour
satisfy human needs, I can also be said to have 'created an object corresponding to the need of another man's essential nature'.[324] Your humanity
is thereby both expressed and fulfilled in the consumption of what I produce. In satisfying your needs, I can be described as 'the *mediator*' between
'you and the species', that is, as the element which unites other individuals
with their own essential nature.[325] This is clearly a significant and controversial claim. The young Marx insists that individuals need each other in
order to be fully human. That I play this essential role in the affirmation
of your essential nature is, he suggests, confirmation of the 'communal'
character of human nature.[326]

A ZŌON POLITIKON

The need for community is the second less basic social need whose advocacy is often thought to constitute a distinctive element in Marx's account
of human flourishing. This need is central to the concerns of this chapter, but unfortunately Marx offers only the briefest characterisation of it.
Despite the difficult and contested nature of the concept of community,
the early writings offer only a passing and uncertain elaboration of its
meaning.

[321] *Ibid.*   [322] *Ibid.*   [323] *Ibid.*   [324] *Ibid.*   [325] *Ibid.*   [326] *Ibid.* 463/228/278.

Some initial purchase on the concept can be obtained by considering the familiar contrast between community and association.[327] An association is usually characterised as a contractual (or quasi-contractual) grouping formed for the purpose of advancing the self-regarding interests of the individuals who compose it. In contrast, a community might be described as a group of individuals who share values and a way of life, identify with the group and its practices, and recognise each other as members.[328] This distinction is useful, and the model of community that it propounds would seem to respect much ordinary usage.

However, as previously noted, the early writings contain a conception of community which is rather more demanding than this basic model. The young Marx's notion of community requires, in addition, that some (imprecisely specified) equality obtains between individuals, and that individuals operate with a genuine (and not merely instrumental or self-regarding) concern for others.[329] This latter idea requires something more than individuals receiving the reciprocal benefits of co-operation (a model of community that Marx associates with political economy).[330] It is not enough that you happen to benefit from my (self-regarding) actions, rather I must act (in part) in order to help you fulfil your needs.[331]

The young Marx maintains that the modern social world fails to provide an environment in which a community of the right kind can flourish. (Hereafter, when I refer to 'community' I will mean 'community of the right kind'.) However, he does not consider community to be wholly absent from the modern social world. There are at least two contexts in which community is prefigured in the contemporary world: it finds some limited and inadequate expression at the level of the modern state (see Chapter 3), and it is manifested in a few small pockets of civil society. Consider, in this latter context, Marx's observations concerning the gatherings of French socialist workers that he witnessed in Paris.[332] Marx maintains that the social

[327] The distinction between 'Gemeinschaft' and 'Gesellschaft' is associated with Ferdinand Tönnies, but had a lengthy history in German social thought (most immediately in the work of Otto von Gierke and Theodor Mommsen).
[328] See the 'ordinary concept' of community outlined in Andrew Mason, *Community, Solidarity and Belonging: Levels of Community and their Normative Significance* (Cambridge, 2000) pp. 20–7.
[329] See, for example, 'Zur Judenfrage' 366/164/230.
[330] See Marx's comments on Smith and de Tracy in *Auszüge aus James Mill* 451/217/266.
[331] See *Manuskripte* 516/276/328 and *Auszüge aus James Mill* 463/228/278. On the relation between reciprocity and community, see Michael Taylor, *Community, Anarchy and Liberty* (Cambridge, 1982) pp. 28–33.
[332] See Marx to Feuerbach, 11 August 1844, *MEW* 27, p. 426; *MECW* 3, p. 355. See also Schuffenhauer, *Feuerbach und der Junge Marx*, chapter 4; and J. Grandjonc, *Marx et les communistes allemands à Paris: 1844* (Paris, 1974) chapter 3.

The Young Karl Marx

interaction ('company, association, conversation') that formed part of membership in these groups was not treated as a 'means' to some individual goal ('smoking, eating and drinking, etc.'), but had rather become the 'purpose (*Zweck*)' of their membership in those groups.[333] The 'immediate aim' of these communist workers when they first gathered together may have been 'instruction, propaganda, etc.', but they simultaneously acquired 'a new need – the need for society', and, as a result, what first 'appears as a means has become an end'.[334] The contrast here is, of course, with the attitude – widespread in the modern social world – according to which membership of a group is thought of as valuable only because, and to the extent that, it is a means to some self-regarding interest.[335] In the social interaction of radicalised workers, the young Marx rhapsodises, 'the brotherhood of man (*die Brüderlichkeit der Menschen*)' is not a hollow phrase, it is a reality, and the nobility of man shines forth upon us from their work-worn figures'.[336]

Marx characterises the connections between human nature and community in a variety of ways. Perhaps most strikingly, he refers to the individual as 'a communal being (*Gemeinwesen*)', and as having a 'communal' nature.[337] For Marx, to live in a society which is not a community is accordingly to be estranged (to that degree) from one's own nature. The claim that a particular society is a 'caricature of a *true community*', he maintains, is 'identical' to the statement 'that *man* is estranged from himself'.[338]

There are two central elements to this relation between the 'true man' and community. Community is both a condition for, and a product of, human flourishing.

First, Marx maintains that living in a community is a *condition* for being a 'species-being', a necessary requirement for successfully developing and deploying the essential capacities of humankind. In short, individuals can only flourish in a community. An individual who is not a member of a community is necessarily 'a being estranged from himself' since his communal nature remains unsatisfied.[339] The significance of this separation of the individual from his own nature is not to be underestimated. By comparison with other kinds of isolation, the isolation from human nature is described by Marx as 'far-reaching, unbearable, terrible and contradictory'.[340] A person who is not a member of a community lives what Marx is prepared to characterise as 'a dehumanised life'.[341]

[333] *Manuskripte* 553–4/313/365. [334] *Ibid.* 553/313/365. [335] See, for example, *ibid.* 516/276/328.
[336] *Ibid.* 554/313/365. [337] See, for example, 'Zur Judenfrage' 355/154/220 and *Kritik* 284/80/147.
[338] *Auszüge aus James Mill* 451/217/265. [339] *Ibid.*
[340] 'Kritische Randglossen' 408/205/419. [341] *Ibid.*

Second, Marx maintains that a community would also be the *product* of human nature, that is, result from the actualisation of human nature. 'Humankind', Marx claims, 'by activating their own essence, produce, create this human community.'[342] The community that results from such activity would not be some 'abstract, universal power standing over against the solitary individual' (like the modern state) but rather an expression of 'the essence of every individual, his own activity, his own life, his own spirit'.[343]

In this context, it is hard to resist an analogy between Marx and Aristotle. Such comparisons are not, of course, entirely new. Indeed, there is a developing body of literature linking both their moral views and (what is often called) their social ontology.[344] However, the analogy offered here is a less familiar one. It concerns what I shall call an Aristotelian account of politics and human nature. (The adjective is intended to denote an account which has a clear and close connection with what we know of Aristotle's view of politics and human nature, and which proceeds by reference to his work, but which also omits some significant aspects of his account, for example, concerning which persons count as full members of the political community.[345])

This point of comparison might seem unlikely. After all, these two authors are often said to hold 'strikingly different' views of these matters; Marx's account of politics, as a realm of estrangement which a fully liberated society could do without, is sharply contrasted with Aristotle's understanding of political life as essential to human flourishing.[346] However, on the interpretation offered here, matters are not so straightforward.

More than any other thinker, Aristotle is associated with what is sometimes called a naturalistic understanding of politics, in that he assigns a central role to the concept of nature in his examination and assessment of social and political life.[347] In particular, Aristotle is associated with the two claims that human beings are by nature 'political animals', and that the state is a natural entity.

[342] *Auszüge aus James Mill* 451/217/265. [343] *Ibid.*
[344] On morality, see, for example, Alan Gilbert, 'Marx's Moral Realism: Eudaimonism and Moral Progress', Terence Ball and James Farr (eds.), *After Marx* (Cambridge, 1984) pp. 154–81; and Richard W. Miller, 'Marx and Aristotle: A Kind of Consequentialism', *Canadian Journal of Philosophy*, supplementary volume 7 (1981) pp. 323–52. On social ontology, see, for example, G. E. M. Ste Croix, *The Class Struggle in the Ancient Greek World: From the Archaic Age to the Arab Conquests* (London, 1981) p. 69ff.; and Scott Meikle, *Essentialism in the Thought of Karl Marx* (London, 1985).
[345] Not least, it omits Aristotle's account of women and of 'natural' slaves.
[346] Richard Robinson, 'Introduction', Aristotle, *Politics Books III and IV* (Oxford, 1995) pp. vii–xxx.
[347] See Fred D. Miller Jr, *Nature, Justice, and Rights in Aristotle's 'Politics'* (Oxford, 1995) chapter 2.

The first of these central Aristotelian claims can be broken down into two parts: the description of human beings as 'political animals', and the description of them as such 'by nature'.[348] Both of these claims require elaboration.

There are two main competing interpretations of Aristotle's concept of a political animal. On what might be called the narrower reading, the term denotes a 'city-state-dwelling' creature. (In *Kapital*, Marx refers to this as the 'strict' sense of Aristotle's definition.[349]) This reading is narrow in that neither barbarians nor moderns would be political animals in this sense. Such an interpretation has its attractions. It succeeds, for example, in emphasising the etymological connection between *'politikon zoon'* and *'polis'* to which Aristotle is often thought to appeal in the *Politics*. However, this narrower reading fits uneasily with other parts of that text. For example, at one point, Aristotle makes a quantitative comparison, describing human beings as 'more (*mallon*) of a political animal' than bees and other gregarious creatures.[350] If these other creatures are 'political animals', albeit to a lesser degree than human beings, then – since these creatures are not, in any meaningful sense, 'city-state-dwellers' – there must be a usage here which the narrower interpretation fails to capture.[351]

This broader usage is elaborated in a striking passage from the *History of Animals*. Having divided animals that live in large groups (as opposed to animals that are solitary or that are both solitary and herding) into non-political and political categories, Aristotle explicitly identifies human beings, bees, wasps, ants, and cranes as 'political animals'.[352] According to this broader usage, political animals are those that engage in complex forms of co-operation in pursuit of the common good of their community.[353] (The inclusion of cranes is perhaps more puzzling to modern readers than that of bees, wasps, and ants. It would seem to result from some distinctive Greek views about the complex and hierarchical division of labour that cranes

---

[348] Kullmann identifies seven passages in the Aristotelian corpus referring to political animals. See Wolfgang Kullmann, 'Man as a Political Animal in Aristotle', David Keyt and Fred D. Miller Jr, (eds.), *A Companion to Aristotle's 'Politics'* (Oxford, 1991) pp. 94–117. See also David J. Depew, 'Humans and Other Political Animals in Aristotle's *History of Animals*', *Phronesis*, volume 40 (1995) pp. 156–81; and especially John M. Cooper, 'Political Animals and Civic Friendship', *Reason and Emotion: Essays on Ancient Moral Psychology and Ethical Theory* (Princeton, 1999) pp. 356–77.

[349] *Kapital* 346 n. 13/331 n. 4.   [350] *Politics* 1253a7–9.

[351] For an attempt to acknowledge this usage and maintain the connection with the polis, see Richard Kraut, *Aristotle: Political Philosophy* (Oxford, 2002) p. 250.

[352] *History of Animals* 488a9–10.

[353] See Cooper, 'Political Animals and Civic Friendship', pp. 358ff. For an account of this broader usage as 'metaphorical', see R. G. Mulgan, *Aristotle's Political Theory: An Introduction for Students of Political Theory* (Oxford, 1977) p. 24.

operate, especially when migrating.[354]) The Greek city-state – at least on Aristotle's own account – involves a high degree of such co-operation, but it would not necessarily be the only form that this might take.

In describing human beings as political animals 'by nature', Aristotle is claiming that complex co-operation in pursuit of the common good (embodied, for example, in the polis) reflects the kind of creatures that we are, involving, as it does, the natural capacities and tendencies that individuals possess. Human beings not only have innate capacities which potentially facilitate this kind of co-operation (such as language and a sense of justice), they also have an 'instinct (*hormē*)' to actualise those capacities and thereby attain a community of the right kind.[355]

For Aristotle, there is a connection between the innate disposition that we have to form political communities and the role that such communities play in human flourishing. Human beings can *exist* outside of a political community but they cannot *flourish* or be perfected outside of it (an individual lacking a need for society must famously be 'either a beast or a god').[356] On Aristotle's teleological account, it is because life in a political community is a necessary condition of human flourishing that nature endows human beings with such a strong disposition to form them – nature, he insists, 'makes nothing in vain'.[357] (I take Aristotle to mean that nature forms a coherent and rule-governed system, not that nature is a conscious creator.)

The second of these central Aristotelian claims is that the political community is natural or exists by nature. There is widespread consensus about the viewpoint that Aristotle's proposition was designed to rebut, namely the view of those (especially the Sophists) who held that the state existed only by convention.[358] However, there is surprisingly little agreement regarding the viewpoint he means to endorse.

On one interpretation, it is assumed that in order to exist 'by nature' the state must be a self-moving entity, or have an internal principle of change directing its growth (the state, in other words, must be a natural substance of the type discussed in the *Physics*).[359] However, although some of what Aristotle says may suggest this interpretation, he never describes the state

[354] Aristotle discusses the intelligent and co-operative behaviour of cranes in *History of Animals* 614b18–26. See also D'Arcy Wentworth Thompson, *A Glossary of Greek Birds*, new edition (Oxford, 1936) pp. 71–2; and J. E. Pollard, *Birds in Greek Life and Myth* (London, 1977) pp. 83–4.

[355] *Politics* 1253a29–30.   [356] *Ibid.* 1253a29.   [357] *Ibid.* 1253a9–10.

[358] On the Sophists, see W. K. C. Guthrie, *A History of Greek Philosophy*, volume 3, part 1: *The Sophists* (Cambridge, 1969); and G. B. Kerferd, *The Sophistic Movement* (Cambridge, 1981).

[359] See, for example, Ernest Barker, *The Political Thought of Plato and Aristotle* (New York, 1965) p. 281; and Stephen R. L. Clark, *Aristotle's Man: Speculations in Aristotelian Anthropology* (Oxford, 1975) pp. 102–4.

in precisely this way. Moreover, this reading seems in tension with other elements of the *Politics*. For example, Aristotle happily acknowledges that political communities are brought into being by the artifice of a lawgiver, and artefacts (on his own account) lack an internal cause.[360] Both of these considerations provide good reasons for doubting this first interpretation.

Fortunately, an alternative account of what it means for the state to be a natural entity can be found in Aristotle's writings.[361] In the *Physics*, he appears to distinguish between natural substances which 'have a nature' and other entities which are, or exist, 'by nature or according to nature'.[362] (Swallows' nests and spiders' webs might be examples of the latter.[363]) In order to be classified as existing by, or according to, nature, an entity must be a necessary condition for the promotion of the ends of a natural substance, and its existence must be (in part) the result of the natural impulse of such a substance. On this account, Aristotle's claim that the state is a natural entity must be understood in the context of human characteristics and goals. The state exists, not according to its own inner principles of change, but for the sake of human flourishing. The state is not only a product of the natural impulse of humankind to live in a particular way, but also has as its purpose the promotion of human flourishing. As a result, it fulfils the two conditions for existing by, or according to, nature. (On this account, there is no insurmountable difficulty in acknowledging the causal importance of lawgivers in the historical emergence of states; these are simply occasions, of an entirely familiar kind, on which art can be said to co-operate with nature.)

Both of these central Aristotelian claims find a positive echo in the early writings. First, in a society which properly reflects the kinds of creature we are, the young Marx holds that individuals would engage in complex co-operation in pursuit of the common good; that is, he views human beings as political animals in the relevant sense. Politics and human nature are intimately related in the early writings. At one point in the *Kritik*, for example, Marx takes issue with a remark in Hegel's *Rechtsphilosophie* concerning the merely contingent and external relation that exists between

---

[360] *Politics*, 1325b40–1326a5. Keyt identifies the 'contradiction' between the claim that the state is natural and the claim that the role of the lawgiver is fundamental as 'a blunder at the very root of Aristotle's political philosophy'. David Keyt, 'Three Basic Theorems in Aristotle's *Politics*', Keyt and Miller, *A Companion to Aristotle's 'Politics'*, p. 118.

[361] See Stephen Everson, 'Aristotle on the Foundations of the State', *Political Studies*, volume 36 (1988) pp. 89–101; and Miller, *Nature, Justice, and Rights in Aristotle's 'Politics'*, pp. 40–5.

[362] *Physics* 192b30–36. See also Bernard Yack, *The Problems of a Political Animal: Community, Justice, and Conflict in Aristotelian Political Thought* (Berkeley, 1993) pp. 91–2; and Sarah Waterlow, *Nature, Change, and Agency in Aristotle's 'Physics'* (Oxford, 1982) p. 50.

[363] See *Physics* 199a7–8, and 199a29–30.

political office and individual human beings in the rational or modern state. He understands Hegel as denying that there is a '*vinculum substantiale*' (an 'essential link') between human nature and political arrangements, and accuses him of forgetting that 'the affairs of state' are expressions ('the modes of action and existence') of human nature.[364] (It is, of course, Marx's own position rather than his Hegel scholarship which is at issue here.) Second, Marx maintains that a community of the right kind is not only a product of, but also a condition for, the actualisation of essential human capacities (that is, that the state is a natural entity). Like Aristotle, the young Marx sees membership of a community as essential to human flourishing. In the *Kritik*, for example, Marx insists that the capacity to discern and act on common interests belongs to humankind in general (and is not restricted, for example, to the class of Hegelian civil servants). The individual who is excluded from developing and exercising such capacities not only lives 'outside of the state', but is also, and as a result, cut off 'from himself'.[365]

HUMAN FLOURISHING

I have suggested that the young Marx's account of human flourishing can be reconstructed, in part, from his expansive understanding of non-volitional human needs. In order to flourish, the essential capacities of the individual must have developed in a healthy and vigorous manner. This is possible only in a society which satisfies not only basic physical needs (for sustenance, warmth and shelter, certain climatic conditions, physical exercise, basic hygiene, procreation and sexual activity) but also less basic social needs, both those that are *not* often thought of as a distinctive part of Marx's account (for recreation, culture, intellectual stimulation, artistic expression, emotional satisfaction, and aesthetic pleasure) and those that *are* often thought of in this way (for fulfilling work and meaningful community).

Such a summary list of human needs invites additional comment. I will limit myself here to some observations concerning its omissions (whether the list excludes important needs), its emphasis (whether the list neglects important needs), and its extravagance (whether the list is too demanding).

As regards omissions (that is, the exclusion of important needs), there seems no good reason either to regard this list as complete or to think that Marx regarded it as such. I do not mean to imply that he would have viewed all putative additions favourably, only that I can find no suggestion that

---

[364] *Kritik* 222/21/77–8.   [365] *Ibid.* 253/51/112.

the young Marx thought of his scattered remarks on human flourishing as providing a comprehensive enumeration of its component parts.

As regards emphasis (that is, the neglect of important needs), matters are perhaps more complicated. I might tentatively suggest that, whatever its other failings, this list avoids the bias of some other well-known accounts of human flourishing. Consider, for example, the overemphasis on the virtues of contemplation that is often said to mar Aristotle's account of the good life in the *Nicomachean Ethics*.[366] Others, however, have been more critical.

In particular, Marx's philosophical anthropology has been described as suffering 'severely from one-sidedness'.[367] Whilst keen to emphasise the creative side of human nature (the development and exercise of individual talents and abilities), Marx is said to have neglected 'a whole domain of human need and aspiration', namely the need for, and interest in, unhyphenated 'self definition'. Unhyphenated self definition refers to our need to be defined by, or located in, something larger than ourselves.[368] One indication of this insufficient emphasis is said to be that this neglect is carried over into, and accordingly corrupts, Marx's vision of future society. In particular, although community (in that vision) is treated as a condition for the actualisation of individual talents and abilities, it is said to be treated only 'as a *means*' to that independently specified goal.[369]

This broad criticism is not implausible. Marx's work is undoubtedly characterised by a passionate enthusiasm for the creative dimensions of human nature; for example, he identifies 'hebetude (*Hebetismus*)' as an example of an inhuman condition.[370] However, I am not persuaded by the brute charge that Marx *neglects* the need for unhyphenated self definition. In part, my doubt here is a formal one, namely that to neglect something is to fail to emphasise it sufficiently, and I am unclear about the benchmark of 'sufficiency' that is being used. (Matters are not helped when, at one point, the charge that Marx 'neglects' the need for self definition is conflated with the charge that Marx 'overlooks' the need for self definition.[371] I take it that to 'overlook' some thing is to fail to notice it, to disregard or ignore it, and not simply to fail to give it 'due emphasis'.) There is also a substantive concern here. The indication of this neglect is said to be that membership of a community is viewed as being of only instrumental value, as a means for the development of individual talents and abilities. However, on the account presented here, the young Marx would appear to be innocent of

---

[366] For a discussion and (partial) defence of Aristotle, see Anthony Kenny, *Aristotle on the Perfect Life* (Oxford, 1992) chapters 7–8.
[367] Cohen, *History, Labour, and Freedom*, p. 137.   [368] *Ibid.*   [369] *Ibid.* p. 143.
[370] *Die heilige Familie* 44/42.   [371] Cohen, *History, Labour, and Freedom*, p. 154.

this charge.[372] In the early writings, not only is Marx clear about the human need to be located as a member of a community of a particular sort (a social embodiment of the need for 'self definition'), but he also persistently rails against the modern social world for treating community as a mere means to individual ends. Marx maintains that in a properly human society – whose relationships are, in this respect, prefigured by the gatherings of socialist workers that he witnessed in Paris – community would become one of the purposes of association. The view that 'the essential bond' joining individuals to each other is to be understood as something 'inessential', as a mere means to the satisfaction of individual interests, is explicitly identified as a product of a situation where the communal aspects of human nature are underdeveloped or frustrated.[373]

(Note that I maintain only that the young Marx recognises the need for unhyphenated self definition, and not that his mechanisms for satisfying that need will strike everyone as satisfactory. There exists, of course, a persistent modern scepticism about the assumption that a need for 'determinate embodiment' can be met by identifying as human beings. However, this is to raise a rather different complaint – which I do not address here – concerning the means that Marx proposes for satisfying a human need that he does recognise.)

As regards extravagance (that is, whether this list of needs is too demanding), it is apparent that Marx invokes an exacting vision of human flourishing. Not least, he provides a standard by which not only the modern social world but also all known societies fall short. However, I am reluctant to characterise this vision of human emancipation as too demanding, that is, as hopelessly unrealistic about the limits of human perfectibility. In particular, I can find little evidence that Marx saw human emancipation as overcoming *all* the possible sources of discontent, frustration, conflict, anxiety and so on, to which individuals are liable. The reason for briefly considering, if only to reject, what might be called the 'paradisiacal' reading of human emancipation is that it is occasionally advanced in the literature. Marx has been described, for example, as offering the prospect of 'a society of perfect unity, in which all human aspirations would be fulfilled, and all values reconciled'.[374] The account of human emancipation outlined in the

---

[372] Not merely, as a footnote concession has it, 'less guilty' of that charge. *Ibid.* p. 138 n. 7.

[373] *Auszüge aus James Mill* 451/217/266.

[374] Leszek Kolakowski, *Main Currents of Marxism: Its Rise, Growth, and Dissolution*, volume 3: *The Breakdown* (Oxford, 1978) p. 523. See also J. L. Talmon, *Political Messianism: The Romantic Phase* (London, 1960) pp. 201ff; Lash, *A Matter of Hope*, chapter 18; and Alvin W. Gouldner, *The Dialectic of Ideology and Technology: The Origins, Grammar, and Future of Ideology* (London, 1976) p. 76.

present chapter scarcely merits such a description. A society which satisfied the human needs identified above is not necessarily a society in which all difficulties and limitations have disappeared, still less a society in which any aspiration can be fulfilled.[375] By comparison with the paradisiacal account, and risking the suggestion of paradox, the young Marx's vision of a rational and humane future might be described as a modestly demanding one.

There is one well-known passage in the early writings – described by one commentator as 'a dazzling vision of universal harmony' – which might be thought to lend support to the paradisiacal reading of human emancipation.[376] In these much-quoted remarks from the *Manuskripte*, Marx describes communism as 'the *genuine* resolution (*wahrhafte Auflösung*) of the conflict between man and nature, and between man and man, the true resolution (*wahre Auflösung*) of the conflict between existence and being, between objectification and self-affirmation (*Vergegenständlichung und Selbstbestätigung*), between freedom and necessity, between individual and species. It is the solution of the riddle of history and knows itself to be the solution.'[377] A number of points might be made about this particular Famous Quotation. First, the meaning of this characterisation of communism as the 'true resolution' of these various conflicts is opaque. There is certainly no obvious licence for equating this 'true resolution' with the various elements of the paradisiacal interpretation. The 'true resolution' of the conflict between individuals, for example, might involve the elimination, not of all conflicts between human beings, but only of those conflicts whose elimination is feasible and desirable. Communist society might, for example, avoid class conflict and yet still contain rejected lovers. Second, the passage does not explicitly indicate the young Marx's attitude to the communism which it describes. Marx appears (although this is contested by some) to be less dismissive of this form of communism than of the 'wholly crude and unthinking variety' which he had discussed earlier.[378] However, it is not obvious that he identifies wholesale with *any* of the varieties of communism discussed in the *Manuskripte*.[379] This is a

---

[375] See also, in this context, G. A. Cohen, 'Isaiah's Marx, and Mine', Edna Ullmann-Margalit and Avishai Margalit (eds.), *Isaiah Berlin: A Celebration* (London, 1991) pp. 122–3.

[376] Krishan Kumar, *Utopia and Anti-Utopia in Modern Times* (Oxford, 1987) p. 62. See also Helmut Gollwitzer, *The Christian Faith and the Marxist Criticism of Religion* (Edinburgh, 1970) pp. 73ff.

[377] *Manuskripte* 536/296–7/348.

[378] *Ibid.* 534/294/346. Avineri, for example, sees not two models of communism – criticised and endorsed, respectively – but rather an adumbration of the two historical stages of communism identified by the later Marx. See Shlomo Avineri, *The Social and Political Thought of Karl Marx* (Cambridge, 1969) p. 223–4.

[379] See, for example, Seigel's discussion of Marx's denial that communism is 'the goal of human development'. Jerrold Seigel, *Marx's Fate: The Shape of a Life* (Princeton, 1978) p. 132.

text in which Marx is still thinking through his understanding of, and attitude towards, the various forms of contemporary socialism with which he
was familiarising himself. Third, this is an isolated and contested passage
from an unpublished notebook. In whatever way it is interpreted, it scarcely
licenses a more general conclusion about the meaning of human emancipation in the early writings. In short, this opaque passage provides insufficient
authority for introducing into the young Marx's account of human emancipation ideas which are patently implausible and find no textual support
elsewhere.

In order to sustain the claim that there is a political dimension to the young
Marx's account of human flourishing it might be thought insufficient to
demonstrate that there is some (more or less idiosyncratic) Aristotelian sense
in which the 'true man' can be characterised as a political animal. The more
sceptical are likely to want to see the institutional and sociological detail –
the kinds of offices, the nature of decision-making, the distribution of
power, and so on – that characterise the political arrangements intended to
replace the modern state. Yet even a clearer understanding of his account of
human nature, of the kind which I have sought to provide above, offers little
insight into Marx's view of the institutional arrangements which would best
facilitate human flourishing.

Nor is this merely a question of delivering on a wayward interpretative
claim, concerning the existence of a political dimension to Marx's account of
human emancipation. There is a more general problem here. To insist that
the social world should be organised in such a way as to allow human flourishing is to say little about what such a world might actually look like. Not
least, such a condition might be fleshed out in a variety of competing ways
(depending on further assumptions and facts about the world). Indeed,
there seems little reason to think that any account of human nature –
at least any account developed at this level of generality – mandates a
specific set of institutional arrangements. Moreover, without some more
concrete sense of such arrangements, it remains difficult to respond to, and
engage with, Marx's vision of human emancipation.

The early writings offer scant guidance to the institutional dimensions of
future society. Marx provides a relatively clear critical account of modern
political life but only the most passing observations about what might
replace it. For reasons discussed below (see Chapter 5), he forswore any
attempt to describe the social and political arrangements of the future in any

detail. In this regard, the most that can be extracted from the early writings (and especially from the *Kritik*) are three quasi-institutional threads.

The first of these three quasi-institutional threads concerns the extent and character of participation in political life. This was, of course, one of the affinities, identified by the young Marx, between the Hegelian *Rechts-philosophie* and the modern political state (see Chapter 2).

As far as the *extent* of participation in political life is concerned, both modern and Hegelian states are said to concede a principle only to back away from its full implementation. On the one hand, these states recognise the need for, and legitimacy of, the participation of ordinary citizens in collective decision-making; on the other, they seek to limit and control the extent of that involvement. Both states are prepared to let 'the people' in, but only in a limited manner, in what Marx refers to as a 'trussed and dressed (*zubereiten*)' form.[380]

The result is a tension between the theory and practice of citizenship. On the one hand, participation in the modern state is judged to be something 'essential to' and 'proceeding from' the very nature of citizenship.[381] The young Marx has no quarrel with this theoretical claim. Indeed, he treats the connection between citizenship and participation as a conceptually neces-sary one, insisting that we cannot assert of '*real* members of the state' that 'they *ought* to participate in the affairs of the state'.[382] That assertion could only be made about 'those subjects who *want* and *ought* to be members of the state, but *are not* in reality'.[383] However, on Marx's account, if subjects do not actually participate in the state, by 'deliberating and deciding' ques-tions concerning the common good, then they are not '*real* members' of the state.[384] On the other hand, the practical political arrangements of the modern state are such that citizens participate only 'for a moment', typically in the infrequent and indirect selection of representatives.[385] Participation takes the form of a 'single and temporary' political act.[386]

As far as the *character* of participation is concerned, Marx maintains that when modern citizens do participate, rather than being motivated genuinely by the common good, they are concerned typically only with their own particular interests. This generates a second tension between the theory and practice of modern political life. When they participate, individuals are supposed to treat matters of common concern 'as if they were their own'.[387] That is, citizens are thought to be motivated by, and to aim at, the common good. However, political participation in the modern

---

[380] *Kritik* 273/70/134.   [381] *Ibid.* 263/60/124.   [382] *Ibid.* 323/118/188.   [383] *Ibid.*
[384] *Ibid.*   [385] *Ibid.* 263/60/124.   [386] *Ibid.* 317/112/181.   [387] *Ibid.* 263/60/124.

social world is not only fleeting but also exceptional, in that it bears no relation to the rest of the lives of individual citizens. Political participation for the individual citizen is something 'sensational' (Marx refers to it as a 'moment of *ecstasy*').[388] As a result, the expectation (in theory) concerning the motivation and direction of the involvement of citizens is destined to be disappointed (in practice).

Marx maintains that the actions of members of modern civil society are inevitably 'rooted in their private standpoint and their private interests'.[389] The daily activity of the class of private citizens, he writes, is neither 'determined by', nor has 'as its end', the common good.[390] In order to acquire a genuine concern for the common good, this class of private citizens would have to 'abandon what it is'; in short, it would have to renounce its overwhelming concern with private interests and embrace that 'part of its being which not only has nothing in common with, but indeed is opposed to, its real civil existence'.[391] In several places – playing on the familiar association of politics and Christianity – Marx refers to this putative requirement as involving a 'thoroughgoing transubstantiation' (that is, a radical conversion which he considers impossible).[392] The 'truth of the matter' is that modern individuals are overwhelmingly concerned with 'private interests', and Marx evidently doubts that the common good can result from the infrequent participation of an agency 'which does not possess any special knowledge of the universal interest and whose actual content is an opposing interest'.[393]

The modern state is, for Marx, an advance on its predecessors precisely because 'the people *begins* to participate in the state'.[394] However, it is important not to confuse the beginning of a process with its full development. Modern political participation suffers, in particular, from a twofold limitation: there is too little of it, and it is governed by the wrong spirit. The involvement of private citizens in determining the common good is something 'exceptional (*ausnahmsweisen*)' in two senses: it is infrequent and it is unrelated to their everyday existence.[395] In a society where the common good is presumed to emerge largely without 'the interference of the people' – that is, without the regular participation of individuals committed to the interests of the community as a whole – citizenship is adjudged to be a pale and inadequate affair.[396]

Marx identifies these two tensions between the theory and practice of modern political life as an ironic counter-example to the Hegelian

[388] *Ibid.* 317/112/181.   [389] *Ibid.* 266/63/127.   [390] *Ibid.* 280/76/142.   [391] *Ibid.* 281/77/143.
[392] *Ibid.* 280/77/143.   [393] *Ibid.* 266/63/127.   [394] *Ibid.* 270/66/131.
[395] *Ibid.* 276/73/138.   [396] *Ibid.* 265/62/125.

claim that 'the rational is actual'.[397] Marx makes the (chiastic and opaque) suggestion that, in the modern state, reality 'shows itself to be the contrary of what it asserts, and asserts the contrary of what it is'.[398] It is readily apparent that his complaint here is not with the theoretical assertion but with its inadequate realisation in the modern social world. In what Marx calls, with another nod to Hegel and the irrationality of the modern social world, 'a really rational state' – that is, in the political community required by human emancipation – these two limitations would be overcome.[399] Individuals would not only take a greater share in deliberating and deciding matters of general interest, but would also participate as members of a community with a genuine concern for the common good (rather than as private individuals keen to advance their own narrow and particular interests).

The second of these three quasi-institutional threads concerns the administration of the political community. For Marx, the account of bureaucracy in the *Philosophie des Rechts* not only revealed Hegel's personal predilections (including an uncritical faith in the civil service), but also provided an 'empirical description' of the institution as it 'exists in reality' in the modern state.[400] (Unlike post-Weberian sociologists of organisation, both Hegel and Marx limit their conception of bureaucracy to the state administration.) Marx's various remarks embrace, on the one hand, the spirit and failings of the modern bureaucratic power, and, on the other, the alternatives to such an administration in the political community required by human emancipation.

The young Marx possesses a sceptical interest in what might be called the modern bureaucratic ethos. He offers a critical description of that spirit as organised around a 'hierarchy of knowledge', in which the upper echelons of the civil service credulously attribute to the lower an 'insight into particulars', at the same time as the lower echelons of the civil service credulously attribute to the upper an insight into the common good.[401] This mutual deception is said to form a self-contained structure, 'a magic circle from which no-one can escape', operating according to the various norms of 'secrecy', 'passive obedience', and 'careerism'.[402]

Marx's primary objection to modern bureaucracy, however, concerns not its ethos, but its practical failure to live up to its theoretical billing. Modern bureaucracy advertises its concern with the common good but fails to operate in accordance with that objective. Marx describes the coincidence

[397] See *Philosophie des Rechts* ¶12.   [398] *Kritik* 266/63/127.   [399] *Ibid.* 322/116/186.
[400] *Ibid.* 247/45/106.   [401] *Ibid.* 249/46–7/108.   [402] *Ibid.* 249/47/108.

which is presumed (in theory) to exist between bureaucratic interests and 'universal' interests as an 'imagined identity'.[403] In practice, the bureaucracy captures the sphere of politics, a sphere which is ostensibly concerned with the common good, and uses it as a vehicle for the pursuit of its own particular interests. Marx maintains that in the modern bureaucracy 'the *interest of the state* becomes a *particular* private purpose opposed to other private purposes'.[404] In short, the political state effectively becomes the '*private property*' of the bureaucratic class.[405] (It is therefore accurate to describe Marx's earliest account of bureaucracy as challenging the association of bureaucracy with the common good, but mistaken to suggest that the young Marx saw modern bureaucracy as simply serving the interests of the economically dominant class.[406])

In the political community required by human emancipation the common good would be the responsibility of all and would not operate as the special concern of a separate and privileged group. In such a context, Marx refers to the 'supersession (*Aufhebung*)' of the bureaucracy.[407] What this 'supersession' might involve, however, is neither clear nor uncontentious.

Marx's remarks do not, I think, suggest a world in which there are no longer any administrative functions left to discharge, but rather a society in which any remaining administrative functions – the co-ordination and execution of policy, for instance – are no longer the preserve of a separate and privileged group. Thus, at one point in the *Kritik*, he seizes on a description of the civil service in the *Philosophie des Rechts*, as executing decisions made elsewhere, as having an implication that Hegel resists, namely that the entire 'hierarchy of knowledge' could be abandoned, and executive functions could be 'carried out wholly' by ordinary members of civil society.[408] (The precarious nature of this implication will be obvious, but it nonetheless reveals something of the young Marx's own vision.)

The young Marx does not explain what this appropriation of bureaucratic functions might involve. However, his comments on Hegel's endorsement of a bureaucracy open to all on the basis of 'knowledge' and 'proof of ability' assessed through examinations provide some elaboration of his own views.[409] (The historical context here is, of course, Hegel's opposition to

[403] *Ibid.* 250/48/109.   [404] *Ibid.*   [405] *Ibid.* 249/47/108.
[406] For a reading of the *Kritik* combining both elements, see David Beetham, *Bureaucracy* (Milton Keynes, 1987) p. 75.
[407] *Kritik* 250/48/109.   [408] *Ibid.* 252/50/111.
[409] *Philosophie des Rechts* §291. Note that there remains a role for selection by the monarch, since examinations were expected to produce a surfeit of otherwise equally well-qualified candidates. See *ibid.* §292; and Marx's comments in *Kritik* 253–4/51/113.

the Prussian tradition of restricting positions in the higher civil service to the nobility.)

Marx does not underestimate the significance – in this bureaucratic context, at least – of Hegel's rejection of the link between birth and office.[410] However, he objects that Hegel's alternative method of selection (namely competitive examinations) would both reproduce the undesirable bureaucratic ethos and fail to tackle the basic problem with the modern bureaucracy. Marx's elaboration of these objections utilises his well-rehearsed analogy between Christianity and the modern state. Competitive examinations, Marx suggests, do not overcome the (secretive and hierarchical) ethos of the bureaucracy, but simply function as a 'baptism' into that mentality.[411] In addition, Hegel's proposed change to the conditions for entry into the hierarchy ignores the fact that 'the hierarchical organisation is itself the *principal abuse*'.[412] An examination, no matter how competitive, offers only an equal opportunity for a few to join the elite; it does not end the power and isolation of that group. As Marx elaborates, from the fact that every Catholic 'has the opportunity of becoming a priest (i.e. of turning his back on the laity and the world)', it does not follow that 'the priesthood ceases to be a power remote from Catholics'.[413]

Marx's alternative vision, of common interests becoming the concern of all citizens, suggests – in his own mind, at least – the example of the ancient world. In a passing jibe at Hegel's bureaucratic enthusiasms, Marx offers the sardonic remark: 'It is not recorded that Greek and Roman statesman ever took examinations. But then what is a Roman statesman compared to a Prussian civil servant?'[414] As with the ancient world, Marx implies, so also in the political community that would replace the modern state, the 'knowledge' and 'proof of ability', to use Hegel's own criteria, required to exercise administrative responsibilities would be those possessed by ordinary citizens.[415] However, unlike the ancient world, in the political community required by human emancipation the class of citizens concerned with the common good would be 'really universal', that is, would include all subjects.[416] In contrast, contemporary citizens of the modern state are merely provided with the opportunity for some of them to abandon civil society and join the 'universal class' of civil servants (thereby further confirming that the classes of civil society do not embody a concern for the common

[410] See *Kritik* 252/50/111. In other contexts – including, of course, his defence of hereditary monarchy – Hegel maintains the need for such links. See Marx's scornful remarks in *ibid.* 299/95/162.
[411] *Ibid.* 253/51/112.   [412] *Ibid.* 255/52/114.   [413] *Ibid.* 253/50/112.
[414] *Ibid.* 253/51/113. See also M. I. Finley, *Politics in the Ancient World* (Cambridge, 1983) chapter 4.
[415] *Philosophie des Rechts* §291.   [416] *Kritik* 253/50/112.

good).[417] Indeed, Marx observes wryly that in a genuinely 'rational' state it would make more sense to provide examinations for a 'cobbler' (who needs skills that ordinary citizens lack) than for an 'executive civil servant' (who does not).[418]

The young Marx's references to both the ancient world and the continued existence of executive civil servants in 'a really rational state' offer further confirmation that his vision is not of all administrative tasks disappearing, but rather of those tasks no longer being the preserve of an isolated elite. Marx accepts that, when it comes to executing decisions concerning the common good, it may make sense to have some individuals 'act for the others'.[419] He considers it 'obvious', for example, that the execution of a 'specific' decision cannot be 'performed by *all people individually*'.[420] However, he rejects the notion that devotion to the common good is the 'permanent function' of a particular class.[421] For Marx, the capacity to discern the common good and the ability to act on such considerations is more universal than both Hegel and the modern state would allow. The administration of the political community required by human emancipation would reflect and utilise that wider understanding of, and devotion to, the common good.

The third and last of these three quasi-institutional threads concerns the legislative dimension of the political community required by human emancipation. Marx's remarks on this topic are particularly abbreviated, but two elements can be identified – a critique of modern representative practices and an endorsement of some idea of popular delegacy.

In his account of the political structures of the modern social world, the young Marx emphasises the divide between ordinary citizens and their political representatives. He maintains that the modern 'separation' of the political state from civil society is reflected in 'a separation of the deputies from their electors'.[422] Marx is critical of this separation, in which 'society simply deputes elements of itself to become its political existence'.[423] In the *Kritik*, he suggests that there is a twofold 'contradiction (*Widersprüche*)' in this relationship between representatives and ordinary citizens.[424] (As before, these 'contradictions' involve a tension between the theory and the practice of modern representative institutions.)

The first ('formal') 'contradiction' concerns the relationship between representatives and ordinary citizens. Representatives in the modern political state 'should be *deputies* but they are *not*'.[425] In theory, representatives

[417] See *ibid.* [418] *Ibid.* 253/51/112. [419] *Ibid.* 323/118/188.
[420] *Ibid.* [421] *Ibid.* 274/71/136. [422] *Ibid.* 329/123/193.
[423] *Ibid.* [424] *Ibid.* 332/128/197. [425] *Ibid.* 329/123/194.

are bound to their electorate, but, in practice, this connection is too brief and infrequent to act as a meaningful constraint. Political representatives are 'formally' authorised in elections but, once elected, they can act independently of their electorate for significant periods of time. As a result, Marx maintains, they subsequently '*cease* to be *authorised*'.[426] Meaningful authorisation is something that political representatives in the modern state possess only fleetingly (in the exceptional moment of election).

The second ('material') 'contradiction' concerns the relationship between representatives and the common good. Marx observes that, in the modern state, representatives are in theory motivated by consideration of '*public* affairs' but in practice work to advance '*particular* interests'.[427] He characterises this 'contradiction' as running between, on the one hand, 'the object of representation (*das Objekt der Vertretung*)', which consists of 'the universal interest', and, on the other, 'the substance of representation (*der Stoff der Vertretung*)' which consists of 'particular' interests.[428] In the modern social world, Marx maintains that it is particular interests which govern the 'spirit' of the representatives.[429]

In short, there is a twofold conflict between the theory and practice of modern representative institutions. In theory, modern representatives are said to be, and to describe themselves as, both servants of the people and guardians of the common good. In reality, Marx claims that they are neither. Modern representatives are at once unconstrained by their electors and preoccupied with the pursuit of private interests.

Although critical of the modern representative state, the young Marx resists a simplistic appeal to direct democracy. He is willing, not only to characterise indirect electoral practices in a positive way, but also to accept that the feasibility of direct democracy is constrained by the size of political communities. At least, that is the apparent implication of two passages from the *Kritik*.

In the first of these passages, Marx considers Hegel's contrast between entitlement by birth and the purported 'hazards' of election (the context here is Hegel's defence of the direct participation of the owners of entailed estates in the estates-assembly). Marx treats the idea that 'a particular race of men' should have a natural right to the 'highest dignity' of political office as absurd.[430] There is no 'immediate coincidence' between 'the *birth of an individual*' and the individual '*embodiment of a particular social position or function*', and he concludes that only convention could have established any

[426] *Ibid.*   [427] *Ibid.*   [428] *Ibid.* 332/128/197.
[429] *Ibid.*   [430] *Ibid.* 310/105/173.

subsequent connection (between birth and office).[431] However, it is Marx's further comments which are of particular interest here. He maintains that it is the selection of legislators by the 'physical accident of birth', and not the use of elections, which really merits being described as 'hazardous'.[432] In this context, Marx offers a positive characterisation of indirect electoral practices as 'the conscious product of the trust of the citizenry'.[433]

In the second of these passages, Marx considers Hegel's insistence that the 'fluctuating' elements of civil society could enter the legislature 'only by means of *deputies*'.[434] The 'essential' reason for this limitation concerns the conflict between the nature of civil society and the nature of the state. Hegel maintains that, because the members of civil society are dominated by private concerns, they are ill-equipped to participate directly in the legislature. Marx agrees with Hegel's characterisation of the motivation of ordinary citizens but questions whether the use of representatives provides a solution to this difficulty. On Marx's account, the use of representatives is an implausible remedy because representatives (like ordinary citizens) are similarly preoccupied with private concerns. It is Marx's further comment which is of particular interest here. He notes that Hegel has a supplementary, and merely 'external', reason for insisting on indirect participation. That reason concerns the '*multiplicity*' of these 'fluctuating' elements.[435] Given the 'external' nature of this consideration, Marx remarks that there is no need to rebut it.[436] Some care is needed here. An 'external' reason, for Hegel, is not a consideration which has little weight, but rather a consideration whose weight is a contingent matter to be determined empirically. In short, the young Marx appears to accept that the number of citizens may restrict the feasibility of 'deliberating and deciding on political matters of general concern' in a direct manner.[437] As he subsequently remarks, this 'external', merely 'numerical', consideration may yet turn out to be 'the best argument against the direct participation of all' in legislative activity.[438]

In short, the young Marx appears to be both critical of modern representative institutions and wary of a simplistic appeal to direct democracy. His preferences, in this context, are perhaps suggested by his earlier complaint about the relationship between modern representatives and their electorate. Marx's basic objection was that 'the deputies of civil society are a society which is not connected to its electors by any "instruction" or commission'.[439] What he seeks is an alternative in which deputies are

---

[431] *Ibid.* 310/105/174.   [432] *Ibid.*   [433] *Ibid.*
[434] *Ibid.* 317/112/181.   [435] *Ibid.* See also *Philosophie des Rechts* §308.
[436] *Kritik* 317/112/181.   [437] *Ibid.* 322/116/186.   [438] *Ibid.*   [439] *Ibid.* 329/123/194.

both meaningfully authorised by ordinary citizens and motivated by the common good. However, apart from this passing suggestion of connecting electorate and deputies by some 'instruction' or 'commission', Marx's views on these matters remain obscure and unelaborated.[440]

It is no part of my ambition to suggest that the young Marx's account of the political dimension of human flourishing is a detailed or developed one. However, I have maintained that three quasi-institutional threads can be recovered from the early writings. Marx's fragmentary vision of the future includes a more extensive participation in political life by citizens concerned with the common good, appropriation by those citizens of administrative tasks previously the preserve of a separate and privileged bureaucracy, and the possible replacement of representative democracy by some kind of popular delegacy. Given the echoes of Aristotle identified in Marx's account of the connections between politics and human nature (see above), and the possible influence of Machiavelli and Rousseau on Marx's use of various parallels between Christianity and the modern state (see Chapter 3), it is perhaps no surprise to discover, at this institutional level, these additional (albeit faint) echoes of the political tradition of civic republicanism.[441]

<h2>THE END OF POLITICS</h2>

My efforts to uncover the political dimensions of Marx's vision of human flourishing will strike some readers as fundamentally misguided. After all, Marx is often said to have rejected politics, in the sense that he excluded it from the arrangements that would replace the modern social world. 'The claim that Marx makes', insists one commentator, 'is that once things are set up aright, politics will no longer be needed.'[442] On this 'redundancy' account of the future role of politics, my interpretative difficulties here might be thought to arise not from Marx's reticence in describing future society but from the signal absence of a political dimension to his account of human flourishing.

The redundancy interpretation of the early writings typically makes two interpretative claims. The first of these claims concerns the fate of politics and the state, concepts which Marx sometimes treats as inexorably intertwined. (I report, rather than endorse, this occasional identification

[440] *Ibid.*
[441] Recent accounts include Philip Pettit, *Republicanism* (Oxford, 1997); and Martin van Gelderen and Quentin Skinner (eds.), *Republicanism: A Shared European Heritage*, 2 volumes (Cambridge, 2005).
[442] Allan Megill, *Karl Marx: The Burden of Reason (Why Marx Rejected Politics and the Market)* (Lanham MD, 2002) p. 58.

of politics with the state; there might instead be advantages in treating the state as one form that political organisation can take.) Marx is said to have insisted that human emancipation requires the 'abolition' or 'withering away' or 'disappearance' of the state and politics. The second of these claims concerns the means by which this result would be accomplished. The young Marx is said to have subscribed – at least, in the *Kritik* – to the surprising view that this 'abolition' or 'withering away' or 'disappearance' of the state would be brought about by the achievement of universal suffrage.

Before engaging with the two elements of this redundancy interpretation, some account of the young Marx's usage is required. It is important to note that he uses the term 'state' in both broader and narrower senses. (These two senses overlap in one significant respect. Both of them identify the characteristic political form of the modern social world as a 'state'. However, they differ in whether that term is to be extended to cover the political arrangements of other past and future epochs.)

Adopting the broader usage, Marx is happy to refer to other political forms, in addition to the modern state, as 'states'. Thus, for example, in 'Zur Judenfrage', he describes the pre-modern absolutist polity as the 'Christian-Germanic state (*christlich-germanischen Staat*)';[443] and, in the *Kritik*, he refers to the 'states' of both the ancient Greek world and (pre-Classical) Asiatic despotisms.[444] At times, the young Marx is even willing to extend this broader usage of 'state' to the political dimensions of a future society which facilitates human flourishing. In this sense, he refers to the existence of a 'true state (*wahren Staat*)' and a 'rational state (*vernünftigen Staat*)'.[445]

Adopting the narrower usage, however, Marx treats the 'state' as synonymous with the modern or political state, as if outside of the modern social world there were no such entity.[446] For example, in 'Zur Judenfrage', he maintains that there is 'no state as such (*kein Staat als Staat*)' in contemporary Germany (when he means only that there is no modern 'political' state);[447] in the same text, he also describes the Christian state of the Middle Ages as a 'non-state (*Nichtstaat*)' (as opposed to a distinct form of the state);[448] and asserts that the 'real state (*wirklichen Staat*)' is a creation of the modern social world.[449]

---

[443] 'Zur Judenfrage' 359/158/224.   [444] *Kritik* 234/32/91.   [445] *Ibid.* 253/50–1/112.
[446] For recent denials that, properly speaking, there were ancient or medieval states, see Andrew Vincent, *Theories of the State* (Oxford, 1987) p. 10; Christopher W. Morris, *An Essay on the Modern State* (Cambridge, 1998) p. 17; and Gianfranco Poggi, *The State: Its Nature, Development and Prospects* (Stanford CA, 1990) p. 25.
[447] 'Zur Judenfrage' 351/150/216.   [448] *Ibid.* 357/156/222.   [449] *Ibid.* 368/166/232.

In what follows, I try to distinguish clearly between these broader and narrower usages. I use the term 'state' to refer to the generic concept of the state, and the terms 'political state', 'modern state', or 'abstract state' to refer to the state which is a feature of the modern social world. In addition, I use the term 'political community' (rather than state) to refer to the future political arrangements required by human flourishing. I adopt the latter usage in order to differentiate sharply between two of the entities involved in the present discussion (namely the abstract state of the modern social world and the future political community that human emancipation requires). I do not adopt this usage in order to suggest that the political community required by human emancipation is not, in some perfectly familiar generic sense, a state. (For example, on the account offered here, the political community required by human emancipation would seem to include a set of institutions, operating in a given geographical territory, defining and implementing certain collectively binding decisions.)

I turn now to the first element of the redundancy interpretation of the early writings. Marx is frequently said to have insisted that human emancipation requires the abolition, or withering away, or disappearance of the state and politics. Commentators variously claim that Marx demands 'the abolition of the state',[450] that the state 'withers away' in future society,[451] that human emancipation requires that 'the state disappears',[452] that he thought that the state would become 'superfluous',[453] and so on. It will be readily apparent that these various formulations have different connotations. For example, as regards the willed character and time-scale of any such change, it would seem that 'abolition' suggests, as 'withering away' does not, a deliberate and immediate termination. However, in order to avoid taking a view on such issues, I will utilise what is intended as a more neutral formulation and refer only to the 'disappearance' of the state. I will assume that it is the broad sense of the state which is at issue here. On the redundancy account, Marx is portrayed, not as propounding the prosaic claim that human emancipation requires that a particular set of political institutions be replaced by a different set of political institutions – just as the feudal state was replaced by the modern political state – but the more remarkable suggestion that the state as such disappears, that political

[450] Joseph O'Malley, 'Introduction', Karl Marx, *Critique of Hegel's 'Philosophy of Right'*, ed. Joseph O'Malley (Cambridge, 1970) p. lxiii.

[451] Andrew Levine, *The End of the State* (London, 1987) p. 14. Engels famously insists that 'the state is not "abolished (*abgeschafft*)", it dies out (*er stirbt ab*)'. *Anti-Dühring* 262/268.

[452] Avineri, *The Social and Political Thought of Karl Marx*, p. 36. See also David McLellan, *Marx Before Marxism* (London, 1970) p. 115.

[453] Avineri, *The Social and Political Thought of Karl Marx*, p. 38.

institutions in general 'will cease to exist' in the future society.[454] This reading of the redundancy claim is presumably confirmed by the suggestion,
advanced by some of these commentators, that Marx's 'vision of a stateless
future' is shared by the anarchist tradition.[455]

However, despite the popularity of the redundancy interpretation, the
textual support for this first claim is slight. Consider three passages from
the early writings often said to support this interpretation. The first comes
from the *Kritik*, in which Marx refers to a world (a 'true democracy') where
'universality' exists throughout society, and not merely in a separate and
limited sphere. 'In modern times', he writes, 'the French have understood
this to mean that the *political state disappears* (*der politische Staat untergehe*)
in a true democracy (*wahren Demokratie*).'[456] Note that Marx is not making
a claim here about the state as such, but refers here only to the 'political
state' that is a central feature of the modern social world. Moreover, the
disappearance of this political state is said to take place in a 'democracy',
a description which might be thought to imply the continuing existence
of political arrangements of some sort (namely democratic ones). In addition, the passage in question identifies this 'disappearance' claim with 'the
French' and not (explicitly) as a view which Marx himself endorses. Finally,
'disappears' is not the only possible translation here; '*untergehen*' – which
typically means to sink or go down, as when the sun sets (or, more figuratively, in the case of a person, to drown or go under) – connotes not
so much ceasing to exist as ceasing to be visible or distinct. The second
passage, also from the *Kritik*, refers to electoral reform in the '*abstract political state (abstrakten politischen Staats)*' being 'equivalent to a demand for
its *dissolution* (*Auflösung*) and this in turn implies the *dissolution of civil
society*'.[457] Note again that Marx refers only to the 'abstract political state'
and not to the dissolution of the state as such. In addition, 'dissolution' –
an entirely appropriate translation of '*Auflösung*' – might suggest not the
simple disappearance of the relevant entities so much as the overcoming
of their separateness (dissolution can, of course, connote the process by
which one thing becomes incorporated into another). The third passage is
from an untitled note from the young Marx's excerpt notebooks, referred
to by modern editors – somewhat grandiosely but not inaccurately – as the
'Draft Plan for a Work on the Modern State'. It comprises a list of nine
brief points, the last of which reads (in its entirety): 'Suffrage, the fight for
the *abolition* (*Aufhebung*) of the state and bourgeois society.'[458] Note that

---

[454] Christine Sypnowich, *The Concept of Socialist Law* (Oxford, 1990) p. 1.
[455] Levine, *The End of the State*, p. 9.   [456] *Kritik* 232/30/88.
[457] *Ibid.* 327/120/191.   [458] 'Draft Plan' 537/666.

in linking the state with 'bourgeois' society, the implication of this passage is (again) that the state whose 'abolition' is sought is not the state *per se* but rather the modern political state (an implication also acknowledged in the editorial title given to these notes). Moreover, the note refers to the '*Aufhebung*' of the state, and this term does not, of course, connote disappearance as such; an entity which is '*aufgehoben*' does not simply cease to exist, but is also preserved and elevated.

In short, this textual evidence from the early writings provides inadequate support for the first element in the redundancy account. Cast in that role, these quotations share a central weakness. The redundancy account requires that the state as such disappears in the society of the future, whereas the young Marx says only that human emancipation requires that a particular form of state is replaced.

The second element in the redundancy account of the early writings concerns the means by which the disappearance of the state is to be accomplished. The young Marx is said to have held – at least in the *Kritik* – the remarkable view that the disappearance of the state would be brought about by universal suffrage. (For some commentators this is evidence of Marx's contemporary attachment to radical bourgeois democratic solutions, thereby confirming the status of the *Kritik* as an immature and soon abandoned work.[459]) Once again, the precise formulations differ, with commentators variously portraying Marx as believing that 'the instituting' of universal suffrage will result in the 'dissolution' of the state,[460] that the disappearance of the state is 'brought about' by 'universal suffrage' (that 'the act of the state in granting universal suffrage will be its last act as a state'),[461] that 'universal suffrage would lead to the dissolution of the state',[462] and so on.

This strikes me as a wholly unlikely interpretation of the *Kritik*. On the one hand, Marx clearly portrays the modern representative state as an integral part of the limitations of the contemporary social world (see Chapter 2), and, on the other, he is said to have held that the introduction of universal suffrage would overcome these limitations. There is an obvious tension between these two claims, since, on Marx's own account, the modern representative state is paradigmatically based on universal suffrage (see Chapter 3).

[459] See, for example, Auguste Cornu, *Karl Marx et Friedrich Engels: Leur vie et leur œuvre*, volume 2: *Du libéralisme démocratique au communisme la 'Gazette Rhénane': Les 'Annales franco-allemandes' 1842–1844* (Paris, 1958) p. 215.

[460] Megill, *Karl Marx*, p. 100.   [461] Avineri, *The Social and Political Thought of Karl Marx*, pp. 36–7.

[462] David McLellan, *Karl Marx: His Life and Thought* (London, 1973) p. 75.

The textual basis for this account of universal suffrage is, however, a tenuous one. It consists of two of the passages already considered, neither of which provides it with clear support. The first passage – according to which, in recent times, the French have held that the political state '*disappears* in a true democracy' – supports the reading in question only if we assume that 'a true democracy' and a representative democracy involving universal suffrage are one and the same.[463] However, the passage itself gives no licence for such an assumption, and the text as a whole provides every reason for rejecting it. (On the account offered here, the phrase 'true democracy' refers to the political arrangements that would replace the modern state.) The second passage does mention electoral reform (if not universal suffrage), but is no more supportive of this strand in the redundancy interpretation. In the context of some remarks about the suffrage movement in France and England, Marx notes that '*electoral reform* in the *abstract political state* is the equivalent to a demand for its *dissolution*'.[464] The main difficulty for the redundancy interpretation is that this quotation does not claim that this dissolution is accomplished by electoral reform, but only that electoral reform embodies a 'demand (*Forderung*)' for such a dissolution.[465] The demand for something is not, of course, to be equated with the satisfaction of that demand. Indeed, suitably paraphrased, the remarks in question might suggest that the contemporary demand for greater participation can be understood as an implicit request to dissolve the modern representative state (since, on Marx's account, participation in the latter is severely limited). This alternative reading is consistent with the present account of the early writings and offers no support for the second element of the redundancy interpretation.

Having rejected the redundancy interpretation – which claims both that the state as such disappears in the society of the future and that this disappearance will somehow result from the introduction of universal suffrage – I now turn to what the young Marx does claim about the fate of politics. As the textual evidence already considered confirms, it is the 'abstract' character of the state, and not the state as such, that disappears in future society. That said, precisely what this might involve is rather less clear.

In an earlier account of this important but elusive notion, I identified two senses in which the modern state might be characterised as 'abstract'

[463] *Kritik* 232/30/88.   [464] *Ibid.* 327/121/191.
[465] *Ibid.* Annette Jolin and Joseph O'Malley have 'advances' here, although *MEGA*② gives '*Forderung*' (not '*Förderung*'). See Marx, *Critique of Hegel's 'Philosophy of Right*', ed. O'Malley, p. 121; and *MEGA*② 1, 2, p. 131.

(see Chapter 2). First, the modern state is 'abstract' in that it forms a *separate* realm, antagonistic to civil society, with its own distinct organising principle (concern for the common good). Second, the modern state is abstract in that it is *remote* from the everyday life and influence of ordinary citizens.

In the political community required by human emancipation both of these 'abstract' characteristics would disappear. First, once individuals become 'species-beings' in their everyday lives, the characteristically modern antagonism between civil and political life would no longer exist. These areas of life would no longer be grounded in different and conflicting principles. Economic life, for example, would now be marked, not by an unmitigated egoism, but rather (in part) by a concern for others.[466] Second, the remoteness of the political community, its distance from the everyday life and influence of ordinary citizens, would be mitigated by the quasi-institutional threads already discussed. These faint echoes of the tradition of civic republicanism (the more extensive participation in political life by citizens concerned with the common good, the appropriation by those citizens of administrative tasks previously the preserve of a separate and privileged bureaucracy, and the possible replacement of representative democracy by a some kind of popular delegacy) would function to bridge the gap between individuals and the political community.

At this point, it is perhaps pertinent to recall the textual starting point and leitmotif of this chapter. In that well-known passage from 'Zur Judenfrage', Marx described human emancipation as requiring a reorganisation of society such that the individual would became a 'species-being' in 'his empirical life'.[467] One dimension of that reorganisation would be that 'social force' is no longer separated from the individual 'in the form of *political* force'.[468] On the present account – according to which 'political' is often used as a synonym of 'abstract' in the early writings – the young Marx should be understood as claiming, not that the state as such ceases to exist, but only that the political community no longer takes an 'abstract' form.

Other commentators, however, have understood this passage from 'Zur Judenfrage' very differently. Perhaps most strikingly, it has been identified as containing a 'soteriological myth' which forms an important bridge between Marx's writings and the totalitarian communism of the twentieth century.[469] In its best-known form, this alternative reading offers both an

[466] Marx writes of turning 'the political society into the real one'. *Kritik* 324/118/188.
[467] 'Zur Judenfrage' 370/168/234.   [468] *Ibid.*
[469] Leszek Kolakowski, 'The Myth of Human Self-Identity: Unity of Civil and Political Society in Socialist Thought', Leszek Kolakowski and Stuart Hampshire (eds.), *The Socialist Idea: A Reappraisal*

exegetical account of the early writings, and a historical account of the connection between those works and totalitarian communism. Given the remit of the present volume, it is the exegetical rather than the historical account which is of interest here.[470] The exegetical account claims that the young Marx was infatuated with the prospect of 'the perfect unity of social life'.[471] Central to this vision of perfect unity is the idea that individual interests would no longer conflict (either with each other or with the common good) in the society of the future.[472] As a result, Marx imagined that political power, which we might understand as paradigmatically concerned with the resolution of such conflicts, would become 'unnecessary' in such a society.[473]

This reading of the early writings seems problematic in a number of ways. I have already argued that, on Marx's account, political power does not become 'unnecessary' in the society of the future, but rather loses its 'abstract' character. In addition, I can find little evidence to suggest that Marx envisages the society of the future to be characterised by this perfect harmony between interests.[474] Marx's modestly extravagant account of human flourishing leaves plenty of scope for individual interests to conflict, and for individual interests to conflict with the common good (see above). He may require community – together with its various connotations (equality and concern for others) – to be actualised in everyday life, but it does not follow that the society of the future would have no other dimensions, or no remaining conflicts.

It is perhaps helpful to recall that Marx considered the 'abstract' character of the state to be a uniquely modern phenomenon, which did not exist in the ancient and feudal worlds (see Chapter 2). However, there is no evidence that he thought of that earlier 'unity' of civil and political life as precluding the existence of individual interests, the existence of conflict between individual interests, or the existence of conflict between individual

(London, 1974) p. 18. For discussion, see Stuart Hampshire, 'Unity Between Civil and Political Society: Reply to Leszek Kolakowski', Kolakowski and Hampshire, *The Socialist Idea*, pp. 36–44; Russell Keat, 'Liberal Rights and Socialism', Keith Graham (ed.), *Contemporary Political Philosophy: Radical Studies* (Cambridge, 1982) pp. 59–82; and Timothy O'Hagan, *The End of Law?* (Oxford, 1984) chapter 3.

[470] Kolakowski's historical account portrays the young Marx's idea of 'perfect unity' as central to his malign influence on the socialist movement and the course of history. Since any attempt to realise that vision of harmony was bound to fail – because conflicts of interests are, on any plausible account of material abundance, an ineradicable part of the human condition – it was only in a caricatured form (namely, of an artificial unity imposed by coercion from above) that the vision could ever be put into practice.

[471] Kolakowski, 'The Myth of Human Self-Identity', p. 34.   [472] *Ibid.* p. 33.   [473] *Ibid.*

[474] See David Archard, 'The Marxist Ethic of Self-Realization: Individuality and Community', J. D. G. Evans (ed.), *Moral Philosophy and Contemporary Problems* (Cambridge, 1987) pp. 19–34.

interests and the common good.[475] Nor, from the fact that 'civil life' in some
pre-modern societies had 'a *directly political* character', does it follow that
there was no distinction between the private and the public at that time.[476]
Accordingly, we would seem to require a good reason to assume that any
future 'unity' would preclude the existence of either conflicts of interest
or a 'private' dimension to life. The relevant textual evidence (considered
earlier in this chapter) seems to provide no such justification.

Of course, much remains unclear about the political dimension of the
young Marx's vision of human emancipation. Moreover, at some point, it
seems probable that continued scrutiny of the early writings, reading the
texts 'over and over again', will generate only diminishing returns.[477] In
those circumstances, an alternative strategy for fleshing out Marx's views
might appear tempting, namely the identification of antecedents of, and
possible influences on, this dimension of the early writings. Such an alternative strategy might promise to clarify not only the background but also
the structure and content of Marx's (fragmentary and otherwise obscure)
account.

In the remainder of this chapter, I consider two leading candidates for
this role of forerunner. The writings of Rousseau and of Saint-Simon are
often thought to illuminate Marx's understanding of the political dimension of human emancipation. In comparing these authors with the young
Marx, I consider issues of affinity (Marx's intellectual proximity to their
work), issues of familiarity (Marx's knowledge of their work), and issues of
acknowledgement (Marx's own judgement of their work).

MARX AND ROUSSEAU

Comparisons between Rousseau and Marx in the literature are many and
varied.[478] Indeed, there is a striking asymmetry between the widespread

---

[475] Consider, for example, Marx's account of feudal corporations ('Zur Judenfrage' 368/166/232), and
of the origins of the English Poor Laws ('Kritische Randglossen' 397/194/407ff.).

[476] 'Zur Judenfrage' 368/165/232.

[477] John Plamenatz, *Man and Society: A Critical Examination of Some Important Social and Political
Theories from Machiavelli to Marx*, volume I (London, 1963) p. x. Plamenatz's exhortation (to read the
texts 'over and over again') is famously criticised in Quentin Skinner, 'Meaning and Understanding
in the History of Ideas', James Tully (ed.), *Meaning and Context: Quentin Skinner and His Critics*
(Cambridge, 1988) p. 52.

[478] Significant discussions include Galvano della Volpe, *Rousseau and Marx, and Other Writings*
(London, 1978); Jean-Louis Lecercle, 'Rousseau et Marx', R. A. Leigh (ed.), *Rousseau After Two
Hundred Years: Proceedings of the Cambridge Bicentennial Colloquium* (Cambridge, 1982) pp. 67–79;
and Robert Wokler, 'Rousseau and Marx', David Miller and Larry Siedentop (eds.), *The Nature of
Political Theory* (Oxford, 1983) pp. 219–46.

agreement that there is an affinity between the two authors and the thorough absence of agreement about its character. Commentators have, for example, variously suggested that 'the whole of Marx's thought' is 'nothing but an elaboration' of Rousseau's insight into social dependency,[479] that the 'philosophical' framework of Marx's work is wholly dependent on Rousseau,[480] that both authors are preoccupied with the dehumanising effects of certain property relations,[481] that they both propound 'dialectical' conceptions of history (according to which the advancement of equality required an interim increase of inequality),[482] that they share a 'historical anthropology' (viewing the emergence of labour as marking the separation of humankind from the natural world),[483] that their theories of distributive justice are essentially congruent,[484] that Marx's 'political theory' stands in a relation of 'essential dependence' to that of Rousseau,[485] and so on. Given that the affinity between these two authors is said to be so remarkable, those of a sceptical cast of mind might wonder that there is not more consensus about its precise character.

Given the remit of this chapter, it is the last of these suggestions that I want to examine here, namely the claim – made by Lucio Colletti – that Marx's 'political theory' stands in a relation of 'essential dependence' to that of Rousseau.[486] Marx's early writings are said to be informed by a perspective which shows the need for the 'ultimate suppression' of the state, and whose two central elements consist in a critical analysis of parliamentarianism and a 'counter-theory' of popular delegation.[487] This perspective is portrayed as especially dependent on the writings of Rousseau. 'It is Rousseau', we are told, 'to whom the critique of parliamentarianism, the theory of popular delegacy and even the idea of the state's disappearance can all be traced back.'[488]

[479] Arthur M. Melzer, *The Natural Goodness of Man: On the System of Rousseau's Thought* (Chicago, 1990) p. 73 n. 6.
[480] Nathan Rotenstreich, 'Between Rousseau and Marx', *Philosophy and Phenomenological Research*, volume 9 (1949) pp. 717–19.
[481] See N. J. H. Dent, *A Rousseau Dictionary* (Oxford, 1992) p. 22.
[482] See Engels, *Anti-Dühring* 19/21 and 130/130. See also Marshall Berman, *The Politics of Authenticity: Radical Individualism and the Emergence of Modern Society* (London, 1971) part 3.
[483] Asher Horowitz, *Rousseau, Nature, and History* (Toronto, 1987) p. 75.
[484] Della Volpe, *Rousseau and Marx*, pp. 87ff.
[485] Lucio Colletti, *From Rousseau to Lenin: Studies in Ideology and Society* (New York, 1974) p. 185.
[486] *Ibid.*
[487] Lucio Colletti, 'Introduction', Karl Marx, *Early Writings* (London, 1975) p. 45.
[488] *Ibid.* p. 46. The work of Andrew Levine should also be mentioned in this context. Levine maintains that Rousseau implicitly 'discovered' a republic of ends (an association of persons and not a state) which would subsequently be elaborated and explicitly identified by Kant, and whose historical possibility would be demonstrated later still by Marx. See Levine, *The End of the State*; and Andrew Levine, *The General Will: Rousseau, Marx, Communism* (Cambridge, 1993) chapter 8.

As should be apparent, I am sympathetic to the broad thrust of this reading. Indeed, I have already drawn attention to Marx's critique of representation, to his apparent endorsement of the idea of an 'instruction' or 'commission', and to some of the wider republican themes echoed in the institutional fragments of the early writings. That said, I am slightly uneasy with some of the formulations advanced here. I do not doubt the existence of a political affinity between Marx and Rousseau, but recommend some caution regarding both its precise character and the emphasis that it should properly receive.

As regards its precise character, consider the subtly inflated description that is used in the comparison under consideration. The overlap in question concerns certain aspects of the relationship between political community and government, but is described as concerning the 'political theory' – albeit in the 'strict sense' – of Marx and Rousseau.[489] The parenthesised qualification is crucial but hardly transparent; a reader could easily miss the circumscribed character of the affinity here. Subtle inflation can also be discerned in the description of Marx's passing remark in the *Kritik* about an instruction or commission as a 'counter-theory' (to representative forms of democracy), a description which might suggest a degree of clarity and coherence that the text in question does not support.[490]

As regards appropriate emphasis, consider the effect of focusing only on this rather specific affinity. Neglecting to look at other aspects of the relation between two authors – including, of course, dissimilarities – can encourage a misleading impression. In the present case, the affinities between these two authors are perhaps less striking once one adjusts the point of comparison. Marx's essential 'dependency' on Rousseau can begin to appear rather less 'complete' once one either steps back to consider some broader features of Rousseau's political thought or moves closer to consider the institutional details of his account. Both the congruence here and its partial subversion require some elaboration.

Some relevant aspects of Rousseau's work can be introduced by considering his contested relationship with the dominant contractarian tradition within modern natural law theory (represented by the work of Grotius, Pufendorf, Barbeyrac, Burlamaqui, and others).[491] These writers typically portrayed the movement from a natural to a political state in terms of a double contract: the *pactum associationis*, a voluntary agreement whereby

[489] Colletti, *From Rousseau to Lenin*, p. 185.   [490] Colletti, 'Introduction', p. 45.
[491] For contrasting accounts of Rousseau's relation to natural law, see C. E. Vaughan (ed.), *The Political Writings of Jean-Jacques Rousseau*, volume 1 (Cambridge, 1915) pp. 423ff.; and Robert Derathé, *Jean-Jacques Rousseau et la science politique de son temps* (Paris, 1950) chapter 10.

a multitude of individuals emerged from the state of nature to form a political community, and the *pactum subjectionis*, a voluntary agreement whereby that political community submitted to the authority of the chosen magistrate(s). This second contract transferred sovereignty from people to magistracy, and completed the transformation of independent individuals into the subjects of a newly created sovereign.

Rousseau's critical response to this contractarian tradition includes both a redefinition of sovereignty and a description of government as a revocable commission. Most obviously, Rousseau rejects the legitimacy of the *pactum subjectionis*. He associates sovereignty and liberty, and – utilising the Lockean argument that one cannot enslave oneself by consent (possibly drawn from Barbeyrac's commentaries rather than from Locke himself) – rejects the claim that transfers of liberty can be morally legitimate.[492] In addition, Rousseau maintains that the creation of government occurs not as a transfer of sovereignty but as 'absolutely nothing but a commission' that the sovereign can limit, modify, and take back.[493] In short, Rousseau advocates a popular sovereign composed of 'the people' to which the government is accountable as a body of 'simple officers' entrusted only with the execution of the laws.[494]

The most obvious affinity here is that both Rousseau and the young Marx offer a critique of representation and endorse the idea of government as a 'commission'. However, the limited nature of this overlap is made more apparent once the focus of comparison between the two authors is widened. Three examples of these (wider) disparities will have to suffice.

First, although both authors are critical of the type of individual character engendered by modern civilisation, their respective accounts of the relation between human nature and the good society would appear to diverge. Whereas the young Marx's vision of human emancipation is grounded in the development and deployment of our essential human capacities, Rousseau's republicanism involves the 'denaturing' of humankind (as the right institutions correct the proclivities of individuals as they have been formed by nature and civilisation). In short, although an ideal of character is central to Rousseau's virtuous republic, he does not seem to identify that ideal with the actualisation of human nature. (In terms of the distinction referred to earlier, Rousseau should perhaps be considered a 'broad' rather than a 'narrow' perfectionist). In the *Contrat social*, the solutions to the

[492] See *Discours sur l'origine de l'inégalité* 183/58. On Barbeyrac, see Derathé, *Rousseau et la science politique de son temps*, pp. 89ff; and Helena Rosenblatt, *Rousseau and Geneva: From the 'First Discourse' to the 'Social Contract' 1749–1762* (Cambridge, 1997) pp. 93ff.
[493] *Contrat social* 396/167.   [494] *Ibid.*

problems of social order are found in artifice and not in nature (which, it would appear, has singularly failed to equip humankind for life in society).[495]

Second, whereas the young Marx thinks of the good society as the cumulative result of historical development, Rousseau thinks of its arrival as a wholly exceptional hiatus in the course of history. For Rousseau, as one modern commentator has pertinently observed, history 'does not redeem humankind', indeed only 'an irruption into history can effect the transformation needed if human beings are to be united in true community'.[496] This view both reflects and reinforces Rousseau's wider pessimism about the fate of those who live in civilisation (a pessimism which Marx clearly does not share).

Third, the young Marx's moral cosmopolitanism contrasts with Rousseau's views on patriotism. Both authors sought to replace the narrow egoism and *amour propre* of modern individuals with some kind of mutualism. That is, they both sought to establish social relations where both the harms suffered by others and the benefits which accrued to them might be experienced as if they were (in part) our own. However, for Rousseau, these ties can never be extended much beyond the limits of '*patrie*', of nation and country.[497] Rousseau does not deny that human beings possess common interests, but he seems to doubt whether these wider interests can ever motivate us.[498] Our loyalties, it would appear, are inevitably local.[499]

That a change in the point of comparison can draw attention to the limited extent and significance of the overlap between these two authors is confirmed by tightening (rather than widening) the focus on Rousseau's work. Three examples of these (narrower) disparities will have to suffice.

First, it is not clear that Rousseau and Marx agree on the composition of the sovereign. In the contest between opposing models of sovereignty, the young Marx's sympathies are clearly with the sovereignty 'of the people'.[500] Thus far, he aligns himself with Rousseau. However, whereas for Marx the people consist of the entire adult population – political emancipation is adequately realised only in the most advanced of American states – Rousseau's

[495] See Maurizio Viroli, *Jean-Jacques Rousseau and the 'Well-Ordered Society'* (Cambridge, 1988) chapter 2.
[496] David Gauthier, 'The Politics of Redemption', *Moral Dealing: Contract, Ethics, and Reason* (Ithaca NY, 1990) p. 95. See also Judith N. Shklar, *Men and Citizens: A Study of Rousseau's Social Theory* (Cambridge, 1969) chapter 1.
[497] Even then, only in small republics and not large nations. See *Rousseau juge de Jean-Jacques* 935/213.
[498] See Timothy O'Hagan, *Rousseau* (London, 1999) pp. 157–61.
[499] Consider Rousseau's claim that the moment a citizen has no fatherland 'he is no more; if not dead, he is worse-off than if he were dead'. *Considérations sur le gouvernement de Pologne* 966/19.
[500] See *Kritik* 229–30/28/86.

conception of the people sometimes appears to be a more restricted one. It is not simply that Rousseau regrets the contemporary confusion between citizens (that is, 'participants in the sovereign authority') and subjects (that is, those who are 'subject to the laws of the state'), but that he seems happy to accept rather narrow limits on the size of the former group.[501] It is pertinent to recall his enthusiasm for the political models of Geneva (where only two of the five political orders were citizens)[502] and of Rome (where the people are judged as sovereign 'in law and in fact' despite the highly inegalitarian voting system of the *comitia centuriata*).[503] Rousseau says little to suggest that this restricted account of citizenship represents some kind of tactical compromise on his part, as opposed to being an integral part of his political thought.[504] Modern enthusiasts for Rousseau may baulk at the (historically unsurprising) suggestion, but it would seem that the young Marx has the more inclusive conception of citizenship.

Second, the two authors do not seem to share an understanding of the remit and character of government. Rousseau insists that the government can neither represent the sovereign nor legislate.[505] In contrast, the young Marx appears to understand the legitimate remit of government as encompassing legislation and, although he denies that an individual can *constitute* sovereignty, he happily allows a single person to act as a 'representative and symbol' of it.[506] (Rousseau, of course, is not prepared to countenance either possibility.) Moreover, there are few signs in Rousseau's work of Marx's intimation of an executive of ordinary citizens (recall the latter's account of bureaucracy). Rousseau's governmental preference is for 'elective aristocracy', an institutional arrangement which presupposes some inequality of wealth in order that the administration of public affairs can 'be generally confided' to a small and stable minority of citizens with the financial independence to 'devote all their time' to it.[507]

Third, Rousseau and Marx may have different attitudes towards political participation. Marx's enthusiasm for the participation of ordinary citizens, and his complaint that the modern state represents only the beginnings of

[501] *Contrat social* 361/139.
[502] At the beginning of the eighteenth century, some 1,500 males out of a Genevan population of 18,500 were citizens. Rosenblatt, *Rousseau and Geneva*, p. 18. For an acknowledgement that Geneva provided his political model, see *Lettres écrites de la montagne* 809/234.
[503] *Contrat social* 449/207. Rome remained the 'best government that ever existed'. *Lettres écrites de la montagne* 809/233. On the *comitia*, see E. S. Staveley, *Greek and Roman Voting and Elections* (London, 1972) chapter 6; and C. Nicolet, *The World of the Citizen in Republican Rome* (London, 1980) chapter 7, especially pp. 246ff.
[504] See David Rosenfeld, 'Rousseau's Unanimous Contract and the Doctrine of Popular Sovereignty', *History of Political Thought*, volume 8 (1987) pp. 83–110.
[505] See *Contrat social* 368/145.   [506] *Kritik* 229/28/85.   [507] *Contrat social* 408/176.

what would be possible and desirable in this regard, are not unquestionably shared by Rousseau. For Rousseau, the primary role of the sovereign is to deter the corruption of the government, or rather, since that corruption is inevitable, to delay it. However, his comments on the amount and kind of civic participation that this role requires can surprise modern readers (even apart from the issue, raised above, of who gets to be a citizen). In the *Contrat social*, Rousseau indicates that the sovereign may meet only infrequently, since the commands of the government can pass for those of the sovereign ('so long as the sovereign, being free to oppose them, does not do so').[508] In addition, when the sovereign does convene, Rousseau would prefer citizens not to discuss and deliberate, but rather each to consult his own interior reason before announcing their judgement.[509] Moreover, the sovereign has no right to convene at its own initiative,[510] to nominate magistrates,[511] or to initiate legislation.[512]

My purpose in raising these apparent disparities is not to undermine the parallels between Rousseau and Marx that were identified above, concerning the critique of representation and the idea of government as a 'commission'. They are rather intended as a caution against characterising those specific parallels in over-expansive terms. It seems to me that this admonition is not sufficiently observed in the comparison under consideration. In short, claims about the young Marx's 'enormous debt' to Rousseau may need to be scaled down.[513] The picture I have tried to paint in the present work – of some more limited debt to the older and broader republican tradition of which Rousseau was a (crucial but not always representative) part – might offer a suitable replacement.

I turn now to consider the issue of Marx's familiarity with Rousseau's work. In sifting the evidence here, it soon emerges that many commentators suffer a double disappointment. We can be certain only that Marx had read a small proportion of the great Genevan's literary output. Moreover, the little that he had (certainly) read consists of what one might – somewhat mischievously – call the wrong works. In particular, there is no conclusive evidence that Marx had read anything other than the *Contrat social* and the *Encyclopédie* article on '*L'économie politique*'.[514] These are the 'wrong works' for many commentators because they do not include the *Discours sur l'origine de l'inégalité*, a book which has been characterised, anachronistically but revealingly, as 'the most Marxist of all Rousseau's works'.[515] Marx would need to have been familiar with this latter text if many of the

508 *Ibid.* 369/145.   509 See *ibid.* 371/147.   510 See *ibid.* 426/190.   511 See *ibid.* 442/202.
512 See *ibid.* 430/192.   513 Colletti, *From Rousseau to Lenin*, p. 179.
514 Wokler, 'Rousseau and Marx', p. 224.   515 *Ibid.*

comparisons in the literature – concerning their respective conceptions of history, property, distributive justice, and so on – were genuinely to reveal Rousseau's influence.

However, this double disappointment need not weigh too heavily here. After all, it is not possible to draw the precise limits of Marx's reading with certainty. He was, for example, undoubtedly aware of Rousseau's *Considérations sur le gouvernement de Pologne*, and it is certainly possible to find passages in Marx's work which suggest familiarity with the *Discours sur l'origine de l'inégalité*.[516] More importantly, '*L'économie politique*' and the *Contrat social* are not the 'wrong' writings for everyone. Indeed, given the limited parallel endorsed here, the relevant evidence might generate a double satisfaction. Marx had not only read the 'right' works but had also done so with impeccable timing. In particular, he had read and made notes from the *Contrat social* at around the same time as he was writing the *Kritik* and immediately before starting work on 'Zur Judenfrage'.

(Marx's notes on Rousseau have survived and it may be helpful to describe them briefly here. The second Kreuznach notebook contains some 103 excerpts from an undistinguished French language edition of the *Contrat social* published in London in 1782.[517] Scattered amongst them are a few short parenthetical sentences of Marx's own, none of which is substantive. The excerpts which he made appear designed to capture the main points in Rousseau's argument rather than revealing any distinctive concerns on Marx's own part. For example, they include notes on the conventional nature of the legitimate state, the inalienability of sovereignty, the distinction between sovereign and government, and the impossibility of representing the sovereign. Amongst the omissions are Rousseau's discussion of punishment and of population. The only significant exception to this pattern concerns the range of Marx's coverage. The number of excerpts tails off noticeably towards the end of the *Contrat social*. In particular, there are only two excerpts from Book IV, and these appear under Marx's heading for Book III. As a result, there are some important topics, including Rousseau's discussion of civil religion, on which the young Marx made no excerpts.)

Finally, I turn to consider briefly the issue of acknowledgement. Marx's work contains relatively few explicit references to Rousseau. One commentator calculates twenty-two, often passing, mentions of Rousseau in

[516] *Considérations sur le gouvernement de Pologne* is mentioned in 'Die moralisierende Kritik' 353/334; and the *Discours sur l'origine de l'inégalité* is suggested by 'Kritik der Gothaer Programms' 16/82.
[517] See *MEGA②*, 4, 2, pp. 91–101.

the entire Marx-Engels corpus.[518] That particular headcount almost certainly constitutes a slight underestimate, but the essential point – that Marx's references to Rousseau are both few and insubstantial – is a sound one.

These explicit references are not wholly negative. The portrayal of Marx as 'disparaging Rousseau and disavowing any intellectual debt to him' is misleading.[519] The reality, as some commentators have recognised, is 'more complicated'.[520] That said, Marx's remarks about Rousseau certainly suggest no great insight into, or appreciation of, the latter's work. Those remarks have been described accurately as 'on the whole unflattering and unperceptive'.[521]

In the early 1840s, Marx appears to think of Rousseau in the context of two larger traditions. Rousseau appears – in the company of Machiavelli, Hobbes, and Spinoza – as a member of the first generation of modern political theorists who 'began to regard the state through human eyes', arguing from reason and experience rather than from theological premises.[522] In addition, Rousseau appears – in the company of Voltaire, Condorcet, and Montesquieu – as an intellectual precursor of the bourgeois republic established by the French Revolution.[523]

Where the young Marx comments directly on Rousseau's writings, the results are not impressive. In 'Zur Judenfrage', for example, Marx glosses a quotation from the *Contrat social* as demonstrating Rousseau's failure to appreciate that there are social as well as political conditions for human emancipation. It is, at best, a clumsy and inaccurate remark. In that very text, Rousseau demonstrates a clear and considered interest in the social, cultural, and economic prerequisites for a virtuous republic (specifying that it requires a small population, cultural malleability, no extreme inequalities of wealth, and so on).[524]

Confronted with this minimal and unimpressive engagement with Rousseau, commentators exhibit differing degrees of discomfort. 'One point that is embarrassing and hard to explain in this whole affair', remarks one, 'is that in spite of the fact of his debt to Rousseau, Marx never gave

[518] Wokler, 'Rousseau and Marx', p. 221. Wokler had previously ventured an even lower estimate ('about a dozen'). See Robert Wokler, 'Discussion [of Jean-Louis Lecercle]', R. A. Leigh (ed.), *Rousseau After Two Hundred Years: Proceedings of the Cambridge Bicentennial Colloquium* (Cambridge, 1982) p. 81.
[519] Levine, *The End of the State*, p. 13.   [520] Lecercle, 'Rousseau et Marx', p. 67.
[521] John Plamenatz, *Karl Marx's Philosophy of Man* (Oxford, 1975) p. 60.
[522] 'Der leitende Artikel' 103/201 and 104/202.   [523] *Ibid.*
[524] Dumont refers to Marx's 'complete miscomprehension' of Rousseau's views at this point. Louis Dumont, *From Mandeville to Marx: The Genesis and Triumph of Economic Ideology* (Chicago, 1977) p. 125.

any indication of being remotely aware of it.'[525] Typically, the greater the
affinities that commentators identify between the two authors, the more
profound their disquiet at Marx's failure to acknowledge Rousseau's influence and insight. Marx's clumsy and inaccurate comment in 'Zur Judenfrage' is found especially embarrassing because it appears in a work which
some have judged 'literally inconceivable without Rousseau'.[526] It is the
appearance of such great affinity and such signal absence of understanding
within the same short text which is thought to require comment.

However, if the affinity between Marx and Rousseau is – as I have maintained – of a lesser scale and significance than sometimes claimed, then
this lack of appreciation becomes rather less remarkable. Moreover, in failing to understand and appreciate the distinctive and complex character
of Rousseau's social and political thought, Marx reflects a deafness that
was not unusual amongst his German contemporaries. The reduction of
Rousseau's role to that of an intellectual forerunner of the French Revolution – of either the Terror or the bourgeois republic – was especially
widespread.[527] (Indeed, Arnold Ruge managed to combine both adumbratory roles, portraying Rousseau as the inspirer of both those who defend
'political freedom' and those who 'have drunk from the bloody ditch of
revolution'.[528])

MARX AND SAINT-SIMON

Given the hostility towards utopian socialism that Marx is often said to
display (see Chapter 5), his writings might be expected to show few signs
of its influence. Yet most commentators agree that Marx's vision of future
society bears the clear impress of the utopian socialist tradition. Indeed,
it has been claimed that 'very nearly everything' that Marx wrote about
the concrete shape of the society of the future 'is based on earlier utopian
writings'.[529]

[525] Colletti, *From Rousseau to Lenin*, p. 187.   [526] *Ibid.* p. 189.
[527] For Rousseau and the French Revolution, see Gordon H. McNeil, 'The Cult of Rousseau and the French Revolution', *Journal of the History of Ideas*, volume 50 (1945) pp. 197–212; Joan McDonald, *Rousseau and the French Revolution: 1762–1791* (London, 1965); and Carol Blum, *Rousseau and the Republic of Virtue: The Language of Politics in the French Revolution* (Ithaca NY, 1986). (Blum's account of Rousseau's pantheonisation is especially recommended.)
[528] Ruge, 'Selbstkritik' 110/256.
[529] Eric J. Hobsbawm, 'Marx, Engels and Pre-Marxian Socialism', Eric J. Hobsbawm (ed.), *The History of Marxism*, volume 1: *Marxism in Marx's Day* (Bloomington IN, 1982) p. 9. See also Vincent Geoghegan, 'Marxism and Utopianism', Gordon Beauchamp, Kenneth Roemer, and Nicholas D. Smith (eds.), *Utopian Studies 1* (Lanham MD, 1987) p. 41.

Even those sceptical of such a broad assertion might be sympathetic to the suggestion that Marx's account of the political dimension of human emancipation owes much to utopian socialism. After all, the influence of Saint-Simon on this aspect of Marx's work is widely asserted in the literature, and Saint-Simon is routinely, if not unproblematically, identified as a utopian socialist (not least by Marx himself). It is said, for example, that Saint-Simon's writings contain 'a clear anticipation of the Marxian conception of the withering away of the state' and that Marx 'indisputably owed a significant debt to him',[530] that 'it was from Saint-Simon' that Marx 'derived the idea that the government of men must be replaced by the administration of things',[531] that 'almost all' of Marx's 'not strictly economic' ideas, and especially the so-called 'abolition of the state', are to be found 'in embryo' in the work of Saint-Simon,[532] and so on. It can seem that where some commentators see nothing but Rousseau, others see nothing but Saint-Simon.

Despite the distinguished provenance of some of these claims, these purported affinities are scarcely beyond doubt. Even a rudimentary sketch of his political thought reveals a considerable gulf between the work of Saint-Simon and that of the young Marx.[533]

The social theory of Saint-Simon is founded upon a psychological model of humankind. He claimed to have identified a universal human drive to seek power which, in the industrial future, would be deflected away from its immoral and destructive expression in the historical conflict between individuals into a co-operative victory over the natural world. Saint-Simon viewed human nature as having a tripartite structure, with one of three basic capacities (emotive, rational, and motor) being dominant within each individual. The social structure of the new industrial order would be differentiated according to these dominant capacities, into classes of '*artistes*' (including writers, painters, and musicians), '*savants*' (scientists), and '*industriels*' (including both wage labourers and owners of capital).[534] This class structure was deemed functional both to individual fulfilment

---

[530] Patrick Gardiner, 'Saint-Simon', Paul Edwards (ed.), *The Encyclopedia of Philosophy*, volume 7 (New York, 1967) pp. 276–7.

[531] Keith Taylor, 'Introduction', Saint-Simon, *Selected Writings on Science, Industry, and Social Organization (1802–1825)*, ed. Keith Taylor (London, 1975) p. 5.

[532] Engels, *Anti-Dühring* 241/247 and 272–3/278.

[533] For less rudimentary accounts of Saint-Simon and Saint-Simonianism, see Frank E. Manuel, *The New World of Henri Saint-Simon* (Cambridge MA, 1956); George G. Iggers, *The Cult of Authority: The Political Philosophy of the Saint-Simonians*, second edition (The Hague, 1970); and Robert B. Carlisle, *The Proffered Crown: Saint-Simonism and the Doctrine of Hope* (Baltimore, 1987).

[534] On Saint-Simon's changing view of scientists, see Frank E. Manuel, 'Henri Saint-Simon on the Role of the Scientist', *Freedom From History and Other Untimely Essays* (London, 1972) pp. 205–18.

('every citizen must naturally tend to confine himself to the role for which he is most suited') and to the social goal of production (which required the invention, examination, and execution of useful projects).[535] However, the greatest achievement of the new industrial regime was that it would solve the problem of social order. Saint-Simon was convinced that the threat of social upheaval, of which he had a prodigious horror, would dissipate once the reorientation of society around production had taken place. Once the population had acquired 'a taste for work', Saint-Simon believed, 'every tendency towards disorder' would be eliminated.[536]

More generally, Saint-Simon held that the solution to the most pressing social ills lay in the reorganisation of society under a new industrial hierarchy. He sought to shift power from the landed aristocracy to the most competent and 'productive' members of the new industrial society. ('Industry' was broadly defined as all the 'productive' parts of the economy; it included commerce and finance as well as manufacture.)

The social structure of the '*nouveau monde saint-simonian*' was to be hierarchical and meritocratic. Positions of responsibility would go to the most gifted, and rewards would reflect the contribution of the individual (and his capital) to productivity. In the context of the surfeit of new social theories in nineteenth-century France, this was scarcely an egalitarian or radical vision. Saint-Simon's aim was not to overturn the social pyramid but to replace the '*oisifs*' (the idlers) at its apex with leading manufacturers and bankers.[537] The contemporary appeal of this vision to talented and ambitious students at the Ecole polytechnique should come as no surprise.[538]

The organisation of sectional interests within this industrial hierarchy was to be discouraged. Saint-Simon urged workers, in particular, to refrain from establishing independent organisations to promote their own interests (whether politically or through strikes), and recommended that they submit to the greater wisdom of the leading industrialists and the 'administration' that the latter should rightly direct. In order to establish and maintain this proletarian submission, Saint-Simon argued, the use of religion and art as means of social control would prove vital.[539]

---

[535] *Deuxième extrait*, Oeuvres 2, p. 199; 'Taylor', p. 209.
[536] *De l'organisation sociale*, Oeuvres 5, p. 126; 'Taylor', p. 265.
[537] See Jean Dautry (ed.), *Saint-Simon: Textes choisis* (Paris, 1951) p. 113.
[538] See F. A. Hayek, *The Counter-Revolution of Science: Studies in the Abuse of Reason* (Indianapolis, 1979) pp. 185ff.
[539] On art as a means of social control, see Ralph P. Locke, *Music, Musicians, and the Saint-Simonians* (Chicago, 1986) chapters 3–4.

Saint-Simon was especially impressed by the effect of religion on individual behaviour, and by the ways in which, reorganised variously as the
'religion of Newton' or the 'new Christianity', it might promote the moral
duty 'to employ one's time and means in useful work' to the less enlight-
ened.[540] (This sociological view of religion has been identified as one of his
several debts to the Catholic counter-revolution.[541]) Saint-Simon recommended a network of spiritual authorities who would ensure the smooth
functioning of industrial society through the use of rhetoric, music, and
imagery, directing the ardour of the faithful (through 'feelings of terror or
joy') towards productive activity and away from disorder and idleness.[542]
Saint-Simon commissioned, as both an example and an inspiration, the
'Premier Chant des industriels' from Claude-Joseph Rouget de Lisle (better
known as the author and composer of the 'Marseillaise'), one representative
stanza of which celebrates the prominent woollen manufacturer Guillaume
Ternaux for his principled act of 'civil courage' in refusing the feudal title
of baron.[543]

The political arrangements deemed appropriate to this new industrial
order were those most favourable to production. Saint-Simon sought, not
to reduce the gulf between rulers and ruled, but rather to use 'temporal'
power to redirect human energies in a more benign direction. He occasionally identified a variant of parliamentary arrangements as the political form
which, 'reason' and 'experience' had revealed, best fulfilled that condition.[544]
However, these recommendations did little to promote the participation
of ordinary subjects; members of Saint-Simon's proposed European parliament, for example, were to be independently wealthy, to be selected by
professional bodies, and to serve for terms of ten years. Moreover, such
arrangements were intended to form only a transitional regime, which
would be replaced, in time, by a tri-cameral system structured according to the demands of production (with chambers devoted to the 'invention', 'examination', and 'execution' of industrial projects).[545] That said,
Saint-Simon considered the question of state forms to be of secondary
importance.[546] He predicted that government in the new industrial society

[540] *Le parti national, Oeuvres* 2, p. 204; 'Taylor', p. 190.
[541] For Saint-Simon's debts to de Bonald, de Maistre, and others, see Mary Pickering, *August Comte: An Intellectual Biography*, volume 1 (Cambridge, 1993) pp. 73ff.
[542] *Nouveau christianisme, Oeuvres* 3, p. 160; 'Taylor', p. 300.
[543] The score and lyrics are reproduced in Locke, *Music, Musicians, and the Saint-Simonians*, Appendix A.
[544] See *De la réorganisation de la société européenne, Oeuvres* 1, p. 182; 'Markham', p. 39. See also *De la réorganisation de la société européenne, Oeuvres* 1, book 1, chapter 5.
[545] See, for example, *Esquisse du nouveau système politique, Oeuvres* 2, pp. 46ff.; 'Taylor', pp. 201ff.
[546] See *Vues sur la propriété et la législation, Oeuvres* 2, p. 81; 'Taylor', p. 171.

would soon transmogrify into a much reduced 'administrative' structure whose only role would be to facilitate production.[547] Since the reorientation of society around production would have solved the problem of social order, there would no longer remain any need for a permanent army or police force.[548] His belief in natural inequality and the specialised nature of collective decision-making led Saint-Simon to assign 'temporal power' in this new social order to those he judged most competent to exercise such a role, namely the most successful members of the industrial class.[549] This would enable there to be 'as little' government 'as possible' and for that government to be conducted 'as cheaply as possible'; leading *'industriels'*, he surmised, would not only be strongly motivated to minimise the costs and extent of any government interference, but also possess the right talents to accomplish those aims.[550]

Saint-Simon ridiculed the notion that all should participate in 'public affairs' as an indication of the backward nature of contemporary political thought; it was, he suggested, as absurd as the idea that all are equally equipped 'to make discoveries in chemistry'.[551] Popular sovereignty, he maintained, was a 'dogma' which had no place in industrial society.[552] Once politics had become a positive science, the idea of political participation as the 'natural right' of all citizens would disappear. Politics would survive merely as 'the science of production', concerned solely with the administration of the new industrial order.[553] The criteria of political competence would become 'clear and fixed' and the 'cultivation of politics would be entrusted to a special class'.[554]

This brief sketch suggests few affinities with the young Marx's account of the political community that would replace the modern state (let alone with his broader social and political thought). Saint-Simon had an inegalitarian view of humankind, and did not associate community and human flourishing. Moreover, he was hostile to greater political participation, saw administrative tasks as the legitimate preserve of a specialist elite, and was hostile to any form of democracy. In short, on closer inspection, the much-vaunted affinity between the fate of politics in Marx and Saint-Simon's respective visions of future society would seem to evaporate.

[547] *Lettres de Henri Saint-Simon à un Américain, Oeuvres* 1, p. 168; 'Taylor', p. 165.
[548] *De l'organisation sociale, Oeuvres* 5, pp. 128–9; 'Taylor', p. 266.
[549] See, for example, *Le parti national, Oeuvres* 2, pp. 201–2; 'Taylor', p. 189.
[550] *Déclaration de principes, Oeuvres* 1, p. 132; 'Taylor', p. 159.
[551] *Du système industriel, Oeuvres* 3, pp. 16–17; 'Taylor', p. 230.
[552] *Du système industriel, Oeuvres* 3, p. 209; 'Ionescu', p. 160.
[553] *Lettres de Henri Saint-Simon à un Américain, Oeuvres* 1, p. 188; 'Taylor', p. 168.
[554] See *Du système industriel, Oeuvres* 3, p. 17; 'Taylor', p. 230.

The issue of familiarity also creates problems for those who would link Saint-Simon with Marx's early writings. There is no clear evidence of Marx having read Saint-Simonian literature before he moved to Paris, and no evidence of his having read that body of work with much care prior to starting work on *Die deutsche Ideologie*.[555] The significance of this timing is that it largely postdates the early writings as defined here. If the account of human flourishing contained in the early writings were to have been influenced significantly by Saint-Simon, Marx would have had to have been exposed to the latter's work somewhat earlier and rather more extensively than appears to have been the case.

Some commentators claim that Saint-Simon must have exercised an earlier and *indirect* influence on Marx. The channels of this purported influence vary. At times, the source suggested is a general one, namely the 'early wave of Saint-Simonian enthusiasm' in Germany.[556] Elsewhere, a more particular conduit is proposed; Ludwig von Westphalen, Marx's father-in-law, or Eduard Gans, one of Marx's teachers at the University of Berlin, are favourite candidates.[557] (Heine would be another potential source, although the timing and precise nature of his attraction to Saint-Simonian ideas make this a less likely link.[558]) There seems no reason to deny the very possibility of influence here, but I remain sceptical. Marx would have been thirteen or fourteen years old during the heyday of German interest in Saint-Simonianism, and at that time the doctrine in question was viewed by contemporaries with 'alarm', not enthusiasm, as 'absurd and potentially mischievous'.[559] The more particular conduits are also problematic. Not least, before they could be described as plausible rather than speculative, the relevant connections would have to be traced in much greater detail than has so far been attempted in the literature. Moreover, these indirect accounts offer a solution to a problem – how could an author have influenced Marx before we can be sure that he had read his work? – which does not exist for my own reading. On the account presented here, there is no affinity in need of an explanation.

---

[555] See especially the passages (written c. April 1846) exposing Karl Grün's ignorance of the Saint-Simonians. *Die deutsche Ideologie* 480–98/493–510.

[556] Hayek, *The Counter-Revolution of Science*, pp. 306–7.

[557] See, for example, O'Malley, 'Introduction', p. xix; and Werner Blumenberg, *Karl Marx: An Illustrated Biography* (London, 1972) pp. 44–6, respectively.

[558] By the early 1840s Heine's enthusiasm for the sensualistic pantheism of the Saint-Simonians had long passed. See Nigel Reeves, *Heinrich Heine: Poetry and Politics* (Oxford, 1974) pp. 76–86; Georg G. Iggers, 'Heine and the Saint-Simonians: A Re-examination', *Comparative Literature*, volume 10 (1958) pp. 289–308; and E. M. Butler, *The Saint-Simonian Religion in Germany: A Study of the Young German Movement* (Cambridge, 1926) part 3.

[559] Butler, *The Saint-Simonian Religion in Germany*, pp. 63–4.

Finally, the young Marx's acknowledgement of Saint-Simon offers little encouragement to those who would seek to link the two authors. The early writings contain only a few references to Saint-Simon or his followers. Saint-Simon is identified as one of a number of thinkers who identified 'movable property' (rather than land) as the true source of wealth, and his followers are criticised both for misunderstanding the credit system and for conflating the productive power of humankind with present-day industry. There is no mention of Saint-Simon's views either of politics or of the state.[560]

In short, the evidence that I have sketched does not provide a secure or convincing foundation on which to establish strong claims about the influence of Saint-Simon on the young Marx's account of the political dimensions of human flourishing. The content of their respective writings, considered alongside Marx's lack of familiarity with, and scant acknowledgement of, Saint-Simon's work offers little hope to those who would emphasise the possible links here.

A (BRIEF) DIGEST

In the present chapter, I have sought to elucidate the fragmentary and opaque account of human emancipation which is contained in the early writings. The young Marx calls for a reorganisation of society such that the 'true man' – the individual who has actualised (that is, developed and deployed) his essential human capacities – is found in everyday life, and not merely reflected in the pale and inadequate form of the abstract political state.

Although the subject matter, language, and substantive content of the early writings show the pervasive influence of Feuerbach, I suggested that the latter's influence on the young Marx's account of the political community of the future remains a modest one. Despite sharing both a narrow perfectionism and an appreciation of the communal dimension of human nature, their political ideals would seem to stand at some distance from each other.

The perfectionist thread of the early writings can be fleshed out by considering Marx's account of the conditions for human flourishing. This requires a society which satisfies not only the basic physical needs of the individual (for sustenance, warmth and shelter, certain climatic conditions,

---

[560] For Saint-Simon, see *Manuskripte* 528/288/340; *ibid.* 534/294/345; *Die heilige Familie* 32/31; and 'Library' p. 667. For the Saint-Simonians, see *Auszüge aus James Mill* 448/214/263; *Die heilige Familie* 52/50; and 'Draft Article on Friedrich List', pp. 282–3.

physical exercise, basic hygiene, procreation and sexual activity) but also
the less basic social needs of the individual, both those that are *not* typically thought of as a distinctive part of Marx's account (for recreation,
culture, intellectual stimulation, artistic expression, emotional satisfaction,
and aesthetic pleasure) and those that *are* typically thought of in this way
(for fulfilling work and meaningful community). I have denied that this
account of human flourishing is (necessarily) complete, one-sided, or hopelessly extravagant.

There are two senses in which the young Marx's account of human
flourishing might be said to have a political dimension. First, there is an
Aristotelian sense according to which the 'true man' is a political animal,
in that Marx understands the complex co-operation in pursuit of the common good (which characterises community) as both a condition for, and a
product of, human flourishing. Second, there are some faint institutional
elements in the young Marx's account of the political dimension of future
society. In particular, he appears committed to a more extensive participation in political life by citizens concerned for the common good, the
appropriation by those citizens of administrative tasks previously the preserve of a separate and privileged bureaucracy, and the possible replacement
of representative democracy by some kind of popular delegacy. These fragmentary echoes of the tradition of civic republicanism form part of a vision
in which politics does not disappear, but rather loses its abstract character.

Finally, in an attempt to elucidate Marx's account of the political dimension of human emancipation, I examined some of the antecedents and
influences suggested in the literature. In this context, I could find no significant affinities between Saint-Simon and the young Marx, and only a
rather narrow parallel with Rousseau – a critique of representation and the
suggestion of government as a 'commission' – which it would be wrong to
characterise in too expansive a manner.

My excursus into possible antecedents and influences, whilst it may
have illuminated aspects of Marx's work, cannot be said to have made his
remarks on this topic look much less fragmentary and opaque. I turn now
to consider Marx's evident failure to be embarrassed by the unelaborated
character of his account of the society of the future.

CHAPTER 5

Epilogue

Following some preliminary observations about my subject matter (in Chapter 1), the three central chapters of this book have been concerned with what I have referred to, somewhat schematically, as the young Marx's account of the emergence, character, and replacement of the modern state. In Chapter 2, I traced a significant shift in the young Marx's critical interests, away from the extant and anachronistic German polity, towards the modern state whose essential contours he saw reflected in the work of Hegel. Whilst highly critical of Hegel's absolute idealism, Marx was prepared to credit the *Philosophie des Rechts* with considerable empirical insight into both the structure of the modern social world and the main forms of alienation which disfigured it. In Chapter 3, I sought to show how Marx developed his understanding of political emancipation in the course of a critical engagement with Bauer's antisemitism. Whilst crediting the modern state with an acknowledgement of the value of community (and thereby of an important aspect of human nature), Marx saw its realisation of community as both limited (having a restricted extent) and 'contradictory' (as ultimately being shaped and dominated by the defects of civil society). Finally, in Chapter 4, I considered the young Marx's vision of human emancipation – that is, of a world organised so as to make extensive human flourishing possible – by way of an account of Feuerbach. Whilst it is undoubtedly suggestive, for example, in its elaboration of certain non-volitional needs, I described the young Marx's account of a society in which humankind would flourish as opaque and problematic. Not least, he was seen to have failed to clarify the institutional elements of the political community required by human emancipation (beyond a few faint echoes of the republican tradition in political thought).

   The present chapter takes the young Marx's striking neglect of the institutional forms of human emancipation as given, and reflects on the intentional character of that omission. After all, Marx did not simply forget to

279

portray future developments in any detail; his unwillingness, in this regard, was neither accidental nor a matter of regret for him. Not only was Marx reluctant to engage with what might be called the problems of socialist design; he also had a justification (of sorts) for this reluctance. Marx's justification – and the more general relation between his early writings and utopianism – form the subject of these concluding reflections.

DEFINITIONAL PRELIMINARIES

Utopia, with its various cognates, is a slippery term.[1] The neologism was, of course, coined by Thomas More as the name of the fictional island discovered, and enthusiastically recommended, by the equally fictional Raphael Hythloday. More added a Latin ending to a combination of a Greek adverb for 'not' (*ou*) and a Greek noun for 'place' (*topos*). The resulting word for 'nowhere' was explicitly linked with the notion of a 'happy' or 'fortunate' (*eu*) place – not least in the poem (by the island's laureate) which was included in the prefatory materials for *Utopia* (1516) – to produce the additional connotation of a good society which does not (yet) exist.[2] The word spawned many neologistic imitators, and its additional connotations rapidly multiplied. One result of this proliferation of meanings, over several hundred years, is that the characteristics which make any body of work utopian remain moot.[3]

Discussion of the relation between Marx and utopianism is often preoccupied with the question of whether Marx's own work is utopian. This would seem to depend, in part, on the definition of utopianism that is adopted. A narrow definition – for example, limiting utopianism to the writing of texts which possess a particular literary form – might exclude Marx from the genre.[4] In contrast, a much broader definition – for

[1] See Lucian Hölscher, 'Utopie', *Geschichtliche Grundbegriffe: Historisches Lexikon zur politische-sozialen Sprache in Deutschland*, ed. Otto Brunner, Werner Conze, and Reinhart Koselleck, volume 6 (Stuttgart, 1990) pp. 733–88. For some definitions and typologies, see J. C. Davis, *Utopia and the Ideal Society* (Cambridge, 1981) chapter 1; Ruth Levitas, *The Concept of Utopia* (London, 1990) introduction and chapter 8; and Lyman Tower Sargent, 'The Three Faces of Utopianism Revisited', *Utopian Studies*, volume 5 (1994) pp. 1–37.
[2] See Thomas More, *Yale Edition of the Complete Works of St Thomas More*, ed. S. J. Surtz and J. H. Dexter (New Haven, 1965) volume 4: *Utopia*, p. 21.
[3] Some of its linguistic progeny have proved more popular than others ('dystopia' has stuck, for example, better then 'practopia', 'euchronia', and 'eupsychia').
[4] See, for example, the definition of utopia as 'an imaginary country described in a work of fiction'. A. L. Morton, *The English Utopia* (London, 1952) p. 10.

example, identifying utopianism with the envisioning of improved social arrangements – would certainly have to include him.[5]

No attempt will be made here to arbitrate between these and other conflicting usages. However, there is one familiar sense in which Marx spoke of other writers being utopian and according to which it would be inappropriate to characterise his own work as such. It is in this sense that the word will be used here. (I leave open the question of whether there are other senses in which Marx uses the word, and other senses according to which it might be appropriate to characterise his own work as utopian.[6])

Marx associated utopianism with an enthusiasm for the drawing up of 'fantastic pictures and plans of a new society'.[7] This association is a plausible and familiar one. Indeed, the willingness to offer a detailed description of a good society that does not (yet) exist is frequently identified as a defining feature of utopianism.[8] In noting the 'enthusiasm' and 'willingness' of utopians in this regard, I mean to suggest that they consider the provision of such descriptions as an entirely legitimate, even necessary, endeavour. In referring to the 'detail' of utopian descriptions, I mean to emphasise their comprehensive and involved character, and not to imply that these descriptions of future social arrangements are always complete or rigorous (still less persuasive). This detail is often a source of both the charm and the speculative appearance of utopian writings. (Fourier, for example, does not merely assert that labour has the potential to become a source of happiness; he provides a precise hourly breakdown of the daily productive activities of representative 'Harmonians' at different times of the year.[9])

This enthusiasm for blueprints (the various plans, models, and templates of a possible future society) characterises the work of utopian theorists and

---

[5] See, for example, the definition of utopia as 'the expression of the desire for a better way of being'. Levitas, *The Concept of Utopia*, p. 8. Expansive definitions predominate in recent 'utopist' literature, reflecting, in part, the influence of Ernst Bloch, who portrayed the utopian impulse as extending to 'all human activities'. Ernst Bloch, *The Principle of Hope* (Oxford, 1986) volume 2, p. 624.

[6] See, for example, Abram L. Harris, 'Utopian Elements in Marx's Thought', *Ethics*, volume 60 (1950) pp. 79–99; Andrew Altman, 'Is Marxism Utopian?', *Philosophy and Social Criticism*, volume 8 (1981) pp. 387–403; and Darren Webb, *Marx, Marxism and Utopia* (Aldershot, 2000) chapters 2–3.

[7] *Erster Entwurf* 557/499.

[8] See, for example, the definition of utopia as 'a nonexistent society described in considerable detail'. Lyman Tower Sargent, 'Utopian Traditions: Themes and Variations', Roland Schaer, Gregory Claeys, and Lyman Tower Sargent (eds.), *Utopia: The Search for the Ideal Society in the Western World* (New York, 2000) p. 15.

[9] See the account of 'Lucas' and 'Mondor' in Charles Fourier, *Oeuvres complètes de Charles Fourier*, volume 6: *Le Nouveau Monde industriel et sociétaire* (Paris, 1845) pp. 67–8.

is (intentionally) absent from Marx's own writings. It would, of course, be a mistake to imply that Marx offers no intimation whatsoever of the future social order whose emergence he envisaged. However, Marx is as reluctant as the utopians are eager to offer a detailed description of that future. As the previous chapter has illustrated, whilst it is possible to uncover the broad contours of Marx's vision of the future, this kind of utopian enthusiasm and detail is singularly absent.

I now turn from these definitional difficulties to consider some problems of evidence. The only form of utopianism that Marx considers at any length is utopian socialism, and his view of the former has largely to be reconstructed from his remarks regarding the latter. Moreover, most of these comments are made in passing, in discussions of other subjects, and in unpublished work; there is no single text or even sustained passage in which he pulls together his thoughts on these topics. There is a further difficulty here. Whilst the early writings provide more evidence of Marx's attitude towards utopianism than one might expect, in order to illuminate that evidence I have also needed to make some reference to later work. In these occasional forays beyond the early writings, I use material from the 1840s wherever possible. That wider spread of evidence suggests a surprising degree of consistency in Marx's considered view of utopianism, which I hope, in turn, licenses its use.[10]

MARX'S (QUALIFIED) APPROVAL OF UTOPIANISM

Marx is often portrayed as having a fierce and unqualified hostility towards utopianism: his opposition to utopianism is portrayed as 'total and unwavering',[11] his references to utopianism are characterised as 'invariably critical',[12] he is described as having 'contemptuously' dismissed utopian forms,[13] he is said to have possessed an 'aggressive' attitude towards the utopian socialists,[14] to have 'never ceased to scorn' their work,[15] and so on. In what follows, I reject these relentlessly negative characterisations of

---

[10] For an account which discusses the full chronological range of Marx's work, see David Leopold, 'The Structure of Marx and Engels' Considered Account of Utopian Socialism', *History of Political Thought*, volume 26 (2005) pp. 443–66.

[11] Webb, *Marx, Marxism and Utopia*, p. 1.

[12] Nicholas Lash, *A Matter of Hope: A Theologian's Reflections on the Thought of Karl Marx* (London, 1981) p. 235.

[13] Kerry S. Walters, *The Sane Society Ideal in Modern Utopianism* (Lewiston NY, 1988) p. 12.

[14] Avner Cohen, 'Marx and the Abolition of the Abolition of Labour', *Utopian Studies*, volume 6 (1995) p. 40.

[15] Robert C. Tucker, *Philosophy and Myth in Karl Marx* (Cambridge, 1972) p. 201.

Marx's attitude towards utopianism, before describing and commenting on his (qualified) rejection of the same.[16]

The early writings may not contain a lengthy or sustained engagement with utopian socialism; however, not all of what the young Marx says can be characterised as relentlessly negative. For example, in a series of introductory remarks to a little-known article on suicide, Marx writes positively about both the form and the content of Fourier's work. (In 'Peuchet: von Selbstmord', Marx's brief introductory comments on French criticism are followed by some lengthy and freely rendered excerpts from Jacques Peuchet's posthumous memoirs, which included a large amount of empirical material on social problems garnered when he was custodian of the Paris police archives.) Marx identifies Fourier as an example of a tradition of French criticism whose 'great merit' was to have 'shown up the contradictions and unnaturalness of modern life'.[17] Moreover, Marx continues, Fourier accomplishes this in a manner which evinces 'the warmth of life itself, broadness of view, refined subtlety, and bold originality of spirit'.[18]

Further evidence of positive elements in his attitude towards utopianism is suggested by one of the young Marx's earliest practical projects. In the first half of 1845, he planned, together with Engels (and Hess), the publication of a series of foreign (French and English) socialist writings in German translation with a general introduction and commentaries on each author.[19] (The timing is not certain, but Marx's list of authors and groups for possible inclusion appears in a notebook next to material which can be dated March 1845.) According to the plan sketched by Marx, this 'Library of the Best Foreign Socialist Writers' was to have included works by Charles Fourier, Robert Owen, and Henri de Saint-Simon (as well as Etienne Cabet, and others).[20] As Engels explained, the intention was to open the series with the founding fathers of utopian socialism, on the grounds that the best of their works had 'most to offer the Germans and are closest to our

---

[16] On Marx and utopianism, see also Steven Lukes, 'Marxism and Utopianism', Peter Alexander and Roger Gill (eds.), *Utopias* (London, 1984) pp. 153–67; Vincent Geoghegan, *Utopianism and Marxism* (London, 1987) chapter 2; Webb, *Marx, Marxism, and Utopia*; and G. A. Cohen, *If You're an Egalitarian, How Come You're So Rich?* (Cambridge MA, 2000) chapters 3–4.

[17] 'Peuchet: vom Selbstmord' 77/597.   [18] *Ibid.*

[19] See Hess's letter to Marx, 17 May 1846, Moses Hess, *Briefwechsel* (The Hague, 1959) p. 154. See also Zvi Rosen, 'The Attitude of Hess to French Socialism', *Philosophical Forum*, volume 8 (1978) pp. 310–22; and Zvi Rosen, *Moses Hess und Karl Marx: Ein Beitrag zur Enstehung der Marxschen Theorie* (Hamburg, 1983) pp. 52ff.

[20] See 'Library' p. 667. A subsequent note in the same notebook appears to add three names – Campanella, Lamennais, and Thompson (presumably William Thompson) – to the original list.

principles'.[21] Difficulties in getting a German publisher for this kind of material eventually led to the abandonment of the project, but there is every indication that Marx endorsed this positive assessment of the educative value and intellectual standpoint of the works of the utopian socialists.[22] (Only Engels' translation of 'Ein Fragment Fouriers über den Handel' – in which, having outlined the thirty-six crimes of trade, Fourier indulged his enthusiasm for typology yet further by enumerating all thirty-six sub-varieties of the crime of bankruptcy – appeared in print.)

This is not, of course, to deny that, alongside such approbation, the young Marx also offers some negative, and more often quoted, remarks. In the 'Briefwechsel von 1843', for example, Marx distances himself from aspects of the utopian programme. He insists that, in order to influence contemporaries, political practice must engage with their concerns and not simply confront them with a 'ready-made' utopia such as the *Voyage en Icarie* (Cabet's best-known work).[23] It is necessary, Marx continues, to abandon the view that the 'key to all riddles' lies in the writing desks of intellectuals, and that 'the stupid, uninitiated world had only to wait around for the roasted pigeons (*die gebratenen Tauben*) of absolute knowledge to fly into its open mouth'.[24] (The allusion to Cockaigne – or, more properly, *Schlaraffenland*, its German variant – is surely deliberate.[25])

However, it does not follow that Marx's attitude towards utopian socialism is an ambiguous or contradictory one. That characterisation might suggest that he praises and castigates utopianism in disparate and conflicting ways. In fact, there is an underlying structure to Marx's remarks, which helps to make sense of judgements which otherwise might appear to conflict. In order to reveal that structure, two distinctions are required (both of which appear in, as well as illuminate, Marx's comments on utopianism).

---

[21] Engels to Marx, 17 March 1845, *MEW* 27, p. 24; *MECW* 38, p. 27. Marx's letters to Engels in this period have not survived.

[22] Some hope of realising the project continued into 1847. See Andreas Gottschalk to Marx, 5 November 1847, Herwig Förder, Martin Hundt, Jefin Kandel, and Sofia Lewiowa (eds.), *Der Bund der Kommunisten: Dokumente und Materialen*, volume 1: *1836–1849* (Berlin, 1983) p. 608.

[23] 'Briefwechsel von 1843' 345/143/208. On Cabet, see Christopher H. Johnson, *Utopian Communism in France: Cabet and the Icarians, 1839–1851* (Ithaca NY, 1974); Leslie J. Roberts, 'Etienne Cabet and his *Voyage en Icarie* (1840)', *Utopian Studies*, volume 2 (1991) pp. 77–94; and Robert P. Sutton, *Les Icariens: The Utopian Dream in Europe and America* (Urbana IL, 1994) chapters 1–7.

[24] 'Briefwechsel von 1843' 344/142/207.

[25] Local variants of Cockaigne are found across Europe (and America). For English versions, see Morton, *The English Utopia*, chapter 2 and appendix (Morton's rendering of a fourteenth-century poetic example has a certain charm, even to those of us who cannot rhyme any better: 'And the larks that are so couth/Fly right down into man's mouth'); medieval Dutch versions (the Flemish *Luilekkerland* may be familiar from Bruegel's painting of the same name) are discussed in Herman Pleij, *Dreaming of Cockaigne* (New York, 2001); and for the German *Schlaraffenland*, see Lucian Hölscher, 'Utopie', pp. 734ff.

The first of these distinctions is a chronological one. It differentiates between, on the one hand, the original generation of utopian socialists, and, on the other, their successors, disciples, and epigones. Marx usually identifies the founding triumvirate as Fourier, Owen, and Saint-Simon. (It is not implausible to think of these three as belonging to the same generation. They not only form an age cohort – that is, a group born within certain dates – but also share a certain historical identity.[26]) The second and subsequent generations include Cabet, as well as assorted contemporary Fourierists, Owenites, and Saint-Simonians. The degree of approbation contained in Marx's comments parallels this chronological distinction. He is typically quite generous about the original creators of these utopian systems, and quite critical of their successors and imitators.[27]

Examples of this distinction, and of its associated levels of approval, can be found throughout Marx's work in the 1840s. In *Die deutsche Ideologie*, he maintains that it would be wrong to dismiss the original generation of utopian socialists out of hand given the 'undeveloped' historical circumstances in which they lived, circumstances in which their various writings typically had a 'propaganda value' which they now lack.[28] The general principle involved here is stated more explicitly in the *Manifest der kommunistischen Partei*, namely that the merits of utopian socialism are in 'inverse proportion to historical development'.[29] In accordance with this principle, the *Manifest* ranks these different generations of utopians against a scale of historical progression, noting that 'although the originators of these systems were, in many respects, revolutionary', their myriad modern imitators (all with their own 'duodecimo editions of the New Jerusalem') have 'in every case, formed mere reactionary sects'.[30]

The second of these distinctions is concerned with the object, the subject matter, of utopian writings. It differentiates between, on the one hand, the 'systematic' dimension of the work of the utopian socialists (that is, those

---

[26] Marx was, of course, much younger, and Owen was the only member of this original triumvirate whom he encountered directly. Marx heard Owen lecture on the occasion of the latter's eightieth birthday; reporting that 'despite his *idées fixes*, the old man was ironical and endearing'. Marx to Engels, 21 May 1851, *MEW* 27, p. 263; *MECW* 38, p. 360.

[27] Not least, Marx saw this first generation as – in certain respects – forerunners of his own views. For example, he describes utopianism as bearing within itself 'the seeds of critical and materialist socialism'. Marx to Friedrich Sorge, 19 October 1877, *MEW* 34, p. 303; *MECW* 45, p. 284.

[28] *Die deutsche Ideologie* 448/461.

[29] *Manifest* 491/516. Those anxious about co-authored works might note that Marx was largely responsible for the final version. See Terrell Carver, *Marx and Engels: The Intellectual Relationship* (Brighton, 1983) pp. 78–94.

[30] *Manifest* 491/516.

positive elements which describe the ideal society of the future) and, on the other, the 'critical' dimension of their work (that is, those negative elements which describe faults with present civilisation). Particular elements of utopian design might have both systematic and critical dimensions, but these two functions are, in principle, distinct. For example, Fourier's description of work in a phalanx not only describes how individuals might one day live but also highlights failings in the contemporary organisation of labour. This second distinction, like the first, is associated with a difference in the degree of approbation. Simply put, Marx is typically more enthusiastic about the 'critical' than about the 'systematic' elements of the writings of the utopian socialists.

Examples of this second distinction, and its associated levels of approval, can also be found throughout Marx's work in the 1840s. In the already quoted article on suicide, for example, it is Fourier's 'criticism' of existing society, and not his system-building, which is praised for having illuminated 'the contradictions and unnaturalness of modern life'.[31] In *Die deutsche Ideologie*, Marx remarks that it would be regrettable if his German contemporaries were to judge Cabet by his 'system' alone, and thereby fail to take into account his political activity and 'polemical writings' as well.[32] In the same text, Marx criticises Karl Grün, in particular, for concentrating on the 'system' rather than on 'the critical side' of Fourier's work, since it is the 'critical side' of Fourier which represents his 'most important contribution'.[33] Finally, in the *Manifest*, it is the 'critical element' of utopian literature, as distinct from its 'fantastic pictures of future society', which is acclaimed as being 'full of the most valuable materials for the enlightenment of the working class'.[34]

In highlighting this second distinction, I do not mean to suggest that Marx, whilst warm to the social criticism of the utopian socialists, is relentlessly critical of their system-building. My claim is rather that Marx is more approving of their 'criticism' than of their 'systems'. Note that, on occasion, Marx also wrote positive things about the systems of the utopian socialists. In *Die deutsche Ideologie*, for example, the claim of the 'true socialists' that *all* systems are 'dogmatic and dictatorial' is dismissed as getting us nowhere.[35] The systems of the utopian socialists are identified as possessing a number of merits. For example, these systems may be of historical interest, providing an authentic reflection of 'the needs of the time in which they arose',

---

[31] 'Peuchet: vom Selbstmord' 77/597. See also *Die heilige Familie* 88/84 and 207–8/196.
[32] *Die deutsche Ideologie* 448/461.   [33] *Ibid.* 498/510.   [34] *Manifest* 490–1/515–16.
[35] *Die deutsche Ideologie* 449/462.

or they may have aesthetic value (Fourier's 'system', in particular, is said to exhibit a 'vein of true poetry').[36]

(Discussion of the young Engels' rather more extensive comments on utopian socialism falls beyond the remit of this volume.[37] However, I shall not resist quoting one of his positive remarks about the value of utopian systems. In the introduction to 'Ein Fragment Fouriers über den Handel', Engels rehearses the by now familiar complaint that German contemporaries – and, in particular, the 'true socialists' – had picked up on Fourier's 'schematic plans of future society, the *social systems*', whilst simultaneously ignoring his '*criticism of existing society*'.[38] Consequently, Engels notes, they had drawn attention to the 'worst' and not the 'best' aspects of Fourier's work.[39] However, Engels suggests that, given the 'wit and humour' with which Fourier criticised existing social relations, the wilder excesses and 'cosmological fantasies' of his system can readily be forgiven.[40] Even the 'eccentricities' of Fourier's system, Engels continues, were the 'products of genius'.[41] Referring to the notorious seas of lemonade and the antilions which populate Fourier's writings, Engels remarks that he preferred to believe in 'all these stories' than in the Hegelian 'identity of being and nothing'.[42] 'French nonsense', he writes, 'is at least cheerful (*lustig*), whereas German nonsense is gloomy and profound (*morose und tiefsinnig*)', adding, in a memorable aperçu, that in the dour Teutonic realm of the absolute 'there is no lemonade at all'.)[43]

---

[36] *Ibid.* 449/462 and 448/461. For Renaissance utopias as a source of historical information, see Miriam Eliav-Feldon, *Realistic Utopias: The Ideal Imaginary Societies of the Renaissance, 1516–1630* (Oxford, 1982).

[37] In the early 1840s, Engels was – relative to Marx – perhaps more informed and enthusiastic about utopian socialism. See, for example, 'Kommunistischen Ansiedlungen' and 'Progress of Social Reform on the Continent'.

[38] 'Fourier' 605/614.   [39] *Ibid.*

[40] *Ibid.* 606/615. Fourier's followers often downplayed the more extravagant aspects of his work, including his views on cosmology, metempsychosis, and 'universal analogy'.

[41] *Ibid.* 607/642.

[42] *Ibid.* 605/615. Fourier maintained that once the evils of civilisation were overcome, the resulting changes to the global climate would result in 'boreal citric acid' entering the oceans, and combining with the salt water to give the sea the flavour of (a particular kind of) lemonade (known as 'aigresel'). See Fourier, *Oeuvres complètes de Charles Fourier*, volume 1: *Théorie des quatres mouvements et des destinées générales* (Paris, 1841) p. 66; and Charles Fourier, *The Theory of the Four Movements*, ed. Gareth Stedman Jones and Ian Patterson (Cambridge, 1996) p. 50. Fourier also held that dangerous animals would become transformed into docile and obedient servants of humankind. The 'antilion' would carry passengers in comfort (comparable to carriages with suspension) at speeds up to twenty-five miles an hour. (Sadly less well known are the anti-hippopotamuses which would pull boats along rivers, the anti-sharks which would help fishermen track down fish, and the anti-whales which would come to the aid of becalmed vessels.) See Fourier, *Théorie de l'unité universelle*, pp. 254–5.

[43] 'Fourier' 605–6/615.

In short, the characterisation of Marx's attitude towards utopianism as relentlessly negative is inaccurate. Scattered throughout his work, and alongside more critical remarks, there are numerous acknowledgements of the achievements of utopian socialism. Moreover, there is a structure to these apparently disparate judgements. Marx thinks more highly of the first generation of utopian socialists than he does of their successors, and he thinks more highly of the critical dimension of utopian writings than he does of their system-building.

MARX'S (QUALIFIED) DISAPPROVAL OF UTOPIANISM

To put the matter in this way is, of course, to acknowledge that approval is not the whole story. Accordingly, I now provide a more detailed account of, and some critical engagement with, the young Marx's (qualified) disapproval of utopian socialism.

The structure of these negative comments mirrors Marx's qualified approval of utopian socialism. In general, Marx thinks less highly of subsequent generations than he does of the founding generation of utopian socialism, and he thinks less highly of the 'systematic' than of the 'critical' dimensions of the writings of utopian socialists. However, the reasons underlying that (qualified) disapproval remain to be elaborated.

The rationale for the greater degree of hostility that Marx expresses towards later generations of utopians than towards earlier ones revolves around a notion of culpability. Marx does not consider the founding fathers of utopian socialism to be free from error – for example, concerning the nature of, and transition to, socialism – but he does view them (unlike their successors) as lacking responsibility for these erroneous beliefs. The intellectual formation of this first generation of utopian socialists, Marx maintains, took place at a time when both the material conditions of modern society and the agency capable of transforming those conditions were underdeveloped and not yet readily apparent.[44] As a result, these writers' understandings of the nature of, and transition to, any future society were bound to suffer. Their misunderstandings, we might say, were unavoidable and, as such, they themselves remain blameless. In contrast, although later generations of utopians do not (necessarily) make more or greater errors

---

[44] Marx would later describe this as a period 'in which the working class themselves were neither sufficiently trained and organised by the march of capitalist society itself to enter as historical agents upon the world's stage, nor were the material conditions of their emancipation sufficiently matured in the old world itself'. *Erster Entwurf* 557/499.

than their forebears, Marx considers them responsible for those errors in a way that their predecessors were not.

In the *Manifest*, the approach of the utopian socialists to the transition to socialism is criticised. For examples, utopians are portrayed as underestimating the role of proletarian agency, substituting in its place appeals to both 'society at large' and 'the force of example' (small-scale experiments funded by the 'purses of the bourgeoisie') as the means by which socialism might come about.[45] However, for the first generation of utopians such errors and misunderstandings are judged unavoidable. The futility of universal appeals and small-scale experimentation was not yet apparent, and the emerging proletariat, 'as yet in its infancy', appeared to contemporaries as 'the most suffering class' rather than as an independent collective agent capable of 'historical initiative'.[46] However, once those historical conditions had changed, there remained no excuse for clinging to the mistaken strategies and limited understanding of an earlier period. (Marx rehearses this reasoning in a much later article, adding an elucidatory analogy with progress in the natural sciences. Referring to Fourier, Owen, and Saint-Simon, Marx insists that 'we cannot repudiate these patriarchs of socialism, just as chemists cannot repudiate their forebears the alchemists'; however, he adds that it would be nonetheless 'inexcusable' if we, in changed historical circumstances, were to repeat their 'mistakes'.[47])

The rationale behind the young Marx's greater hostility towards utopian 'systems' over utopian 'criticism' is not only less clear than that behind his greater hostility towards later as opposed to earlier generations of utopian socialists, but also less straightforward than it might initially appear. It would be easy to assume that, in order to achieve their goals, socialists need not only detailed and persuasive accounts of the failings of contemporary society, but also detailed and persuasive accounts of what any future socialist alternative might look like. Marx's relative enthusiasm for the 'critical' over the 'systematic' dimension of utopian socialism might then follow from the view that utopian accounts of the failings of modern society are more accurate or plausible than utopian accounts of what any future socialism will look like. However, on closer inspection, this is not Marx's position.

There is a significant asymmetry in Marx's view of these matters. On the one hand, he sees a need for a detailed and persuasive account of what is wrong with modern society and acknowledges that utopian socialists have something to contribute to that account. In *Die heilige Familie*, for example,

---

[45] *Manifest* 491/516. See also Marx to Engels, 20 June 1866, *MEW* 31, p. 229; *MECW* 42, p. 287.
[46] *Manifest* 490/515.   [47] 'L'indifferenza in materia politica' 301/394.

there is a reference to Fourier's 'masterly characterisation' of contemporary marriage.[48] On the other hand, Marx appears to reject the assumption that we need detailed and persuasive accounts of what socialism might look like. When it comes to issues of socialist design, Marx criticises the utopian socialists, not primarily for the inadequacy and implausibility of their blueprints, but for supposing that we need blueprints at all. This seems to me to be a remarkable view to hold, and in the remainder of this section I not only provide some evidence for attributing this claim – that blueprints are redundant – to the young Marx, but also seek to understand why he might have held it.[49]

In the 'Briefwechsel von 1843', the young Marx contrasts his own approach with that of the utopians. This is a short and problematic text but two threads in this contrast can be distinguished. In the present context, the significance of these different threads is that although one of them would seem to make blueprints redundant, the other does not. (The letters published under this title were between Ruge, on the one hand, and Marx, Feuerbach, and Bakunin, on the other.[50] This exchange of correspondence functioned as a dialogic and rather unfocused mission statement for the *Deutsch-Französische Jahrbücher*. The resulting text is problematic, not least because of the uncertain extent to which the original letters were heavily edited for publication by Ruge.)

In the first of these threads, Marx engages with the question of how one might successfully motivate people to change, in certain fundamental ways, the social world in which they live. He avers that one must start from existing attitudes and circumstances, and not simply propose solutions from a standpoint which has no connection with these views and that context.[51] The latter approach is explicitly associated with that of the utopian socialists. Whereas utopians oppose the world as it is with their 'ready-made system', such as the *Voyage en Icarie*, Marx advocates engaging with contemporary German religious and political views 'as they

---

[48] *Die heilige Familie* 208/196.

[49] My reflection on these matters has been much influenced by Cohen, *If You're an Egalitarian*, chapters 3–4.

[50] *MEGA②* 1, 2, pp. 471–89, contains all the letters (the authors are identified by initial only). 'B' is very occasionally identified as Karl Ludwig Bernays; however, I have seen no evidence supporting this view, and note that the conventional identification of 'B' is accepted by Bakunin scholars and confirmed by Ruge's correspondence. See Bakunin, *Sobranie sochinenii I pisem 1828–76* (Moscow, 1934–5) volume 3, pp. 213–14; and Ruge to Julius Fröbel, 19 December 1843, quoted in *MEGA②* 1, 2, p. 939.

[51] There is a faint adumbration here of Michael Walzer's distinction between internal and external criticism. See Michael Walzer, *Interpretation and Social Criticism* (Cambridge MA, 1987) especially chapter 2.

are', thereby avoiding the utopian tendency to 'confront the world with new doctrinaire principles and proclaim: here is the truth, on your knees before it!'[52] This contrast, whilst not developed in any systematic way, is clear enough. Note, in particular, that this first thread does not make blueprints unnecessary. It may well place constraints on the kinds of blueprints that are required and on how they are used – requiring, for example, blueprints which respect the limitations of particular historical circumstances, and which engage with, rather than impose upon, existing concerns – but it does not make blueprints redundant.

In the second of these threads, Marx draws a rather different contrast between his own approach and the utopian one. Whereas the utopians try to 'anticipate (*antizipieren*)' the new world – this is identified (explicitly) as one source of their doctrinaire tendencies – Marx's own project involves an attempt to 'discover (*finden*)' the new world in the old.[53] This is not a transparent contrast. However, in the present context, Marx's characterisation of his own methodology is significant. If the new world is to be found in the old – provided, no doubt, that the old world is sufficiently developed and that one looks at it in the right way – this can only be because it is already there to be found. Moreover, if the new world is already there to be discovered, then it does not need to be designed or created. Blueprints, in short, are unnecessary. This broad picture is confirmed elsewhere in the same text. In order to inaugurate a new social order, Marx claims, humankind does not need to begin 'any *new* work'; all that is required is that 'its old work' is brought to completion.[54] The proper role of political practice is accordingly not to proffer designs for the future but to help bring existing struggles to their fulfilment. Blueprints appear to be redundant because the solutions to the social and political problems of humankind are immanent in the historical process. Many years later, it was this rejection of utopian design that Marx recollected when, as part of an acerbic and awkward émigré polemic, he looked back at his attempts, with Engels, Wilhelm Wolff, and others, to influence the political practice of the League of the Just – later the Communist League – during his exile in Paris. Marx recalled that they had sought to persuade their reluctant contemporaries 'that it was not a matter of putting some utopian system into effect, but of conscious participation in the historical process revolutionising society before our very eyes'.[55]

This view of the historical process is confirmed by the young Marx's otherwise puzzling response to Ruge's pessimistic account (his 'breathtaking

---

[52] 'Briefwechsel von 1843' 345/144/208.   [53] *Ibid.* 344/142/207.
[54] *Ibid.* 346/144/209.   [55] *Herr Vogt* (1860) 439/79.

funeral dirge') of social and political conditions in Germany.[56] Whilst
emphasising that he did not underestimate the scale of contemporary obstacles to social change, Marx insists that he has 'no doubt' that these
obstacles can be overcome.[57] The rationale behind this striking confidence
is summarised in the extraordinarily sanguine claim that 'whatever is necessary comes to pass (*was notwendig ist, das fügt sich*)'.[58] The young Marx
seems to reject a view of the historical process as setting humankind problems to which individuals have to invent solutions, in favour of a view
of the historical process as providing its own solutions (which individuals
would be motivated to identify and help bring into life). In a revealing and
familiar metaphor, he refers to the new world which has yet to see the light
of day as 'the fruit which the present now bears within its womb (*welches
die Gegenwart in ihrem Schoße trägt*)'.[59]

This obstetric metaphor is, of course, familiar from Marx's later work.[60]
What is not always appreciated is that the metaphor, and its attendant
baggage, appear in the early writings, and that it underpins his (qualified)
disapproval of utopianism. The young Marx's insistence that there is little
to learn from utopian blueprints for a future society is the product, not of a
belief that we can come up with better proposals, but rather of a conviction
that such plans are unnecessary.[61] The role of historical midwives, to pursue
the obstetric theme, is to deliver and not to design the contents of wombs.

Marx's belief that solutions to the problems of socialist design are immanent in the historical process is usually thought to have Hegelian origins[62]
(although this view, that the outcome of the redemptive process is fixed in
all its details, has also been identified as having more ancient roots).[63] Hegel,
is not, of course, concerned with questions of *socialist* design. However, he
does provide a historical model in which humankind acts as a vehicle for
the actualisation of a developmental plan which they have not themselves
designed. Hegel holds that the finite world is both produced and governed

[56] 'Briefwechsel von 1843' 338/134/200.   [57] *Ibid.* 343/142/206.   [58] *Ibid.*
[59] *Ibid.* 343/141/206.
[60] For example, Marx would later describe the proletariat as having 'no ideals to realise, but to set free
    elements of the new society with which the old collapsing bourgeois society itself is pregnant'. *Der
    Bürgerkrieg in Frankreich* 343/335.
[61] For a contrasting account, see Webb, *Marx, Marxism and Utopia*, p. 79.
[62] See, for example, Perry Anderson, *Arguments Within English Marxism* (London, 1976) p. 170; William
    A. Galston, *Justice and the Human Good* (Chicago, 1980) p. 23; and Cohen, *If You're an Egalitarian*,
    p. 57.
[63] In *Paths in Utopia* (first published in Hebrew in 1946), Martin Buber identified two modes of escha-
    tological thinking – the 'prophetic' (originating in ancient Israel) and the 'apocalyptic' (originating
    in ancient Persia) – as having influenced utopian socialism and Marxism, respectively. In the apoca-
    lyptic, but not the prophetic, mode, the structures of redemption are predetermined in all its detail.
    See Martin Buber, *Paths in Utopia* (London, 1949) pp. 10–11.

by a categorical system (see Chapter 2). However, there is an initial lack of fit between this categorical system and its embodiment, and this imperfect fit drives historical development onwards. Humankind is seen as a vehicle for the developmental plan which is immanent in the sensible world, and the essential structure of our historical development is said to be a product of the purposeful striving of that plan towards actualisation. There are some important, and occasionally neglected, features of this account. For example, since humankind is essential to the actualisation of reason and, in playing this role, we fulfil our own interests, it would be a mistake to think of human beings as simply the 'means' which happen to be used by some external purpose.[64] However, the concept is not a human product, and history is properly understood as 'the unfolding of God's nature'.[65] Contemplating the role of human agency in that 'unfolding', Hegel distinguishes between, on the one hand, those whom he calls 'adventurers' who pursue 'ideals' of their own invention which are in conflict with present circumstances, and, on the other, those world-historical individuals (such as Alexander, Caesar, and Napoleon) who draw their energy from 'that hidden spirit whose hour is near but which still lies beneath the surface'.[66] The principles realised by world-historical individuals, Hegel explains, are not of 'their own invention' but are rather 'already inwardly present' in the world.[67]

THE NECESSITY OF BLUEPRINTS

Whatever its origins, the young Marx's denial of the need for solutions to problems of socialist design appears misguided and unfortunate.

I can find no persuasive justification in the early writings for this rejection of the need for blueprints. Hegel's reasons for holding that successful political agency limits itself to delivering the solutions to social problems that are immanent in the historical process may be extravagant and hard to accept, but they are also identifiable and possess a certain coherence. However, even if it were thought that an alternative (secular and non-metaphysical) theory of history might, in principle, be able to underwrite a parallel view of the role of human agency, the early writings contain no such alternative account. The young Marx appears to have held this restricted account of the remit of human agency – limited to delivering a solution that it did

---

[64] See, for example, Hegel's discussion of the (Kantian) distinction between 'internal' and 'external' teleology, *Enzyklopädie* §205A.
[65] *Vernunft* 48/42.   [66] *Ibid.* 97/83.   [67] *Ibid.* 98/83.

not invent – without subscribing to a theory of history which might justify it.[68]

The young Marx's rejection of the need for blueprints is also unreasonable. It seems to require a confidence in the historical process which was perhaps widely felt in nineteenth-century Europe, but which is now considerably harder to sustain. In the wake of what has been plausibly characterised as 'the *morally* worst century of human history', the belief that solutions to the social problems that face humankind need only to be delivered and not designed no longer seems a reasonable one.[69] For most of us, confidence in the possibility of such solutions is hard enough; an assured belief in their immanence in the historical process is unthinkable.

Finally, the idea that the new society is to be found in the old appears to be a dangerous one. It encourages a lack of attention to questions of design, to consideration of what this new society should look like. In the present context, this weakness is reflected in the opacities and obscurities of the young Marx's account of human emancipation (and, perhaps more strikingly, in his evident failure to be embarrassed by these features of his work).[70] The dangers here, of course, are not merely theoretical. The failure to clarify ends, and the social and political arrangements that might embody them, can have serious practical consequences. As one author has wisely observed, unless we write recipes for the cookshops of the future 'there's no reason to think we'll get food that we like'.[71] (The allusion is to the 'Afterword' to the second edition of *Kapital*, where Marx says that he has confined himself to 'the mere critical analysis of actual facts' instead of writing recipes 'for the cookshops of the future'.[72]) The historical experience of the twentieth century has surely magnified, rather than reduced, such concerns.

These brief reflections have been concerned to explain the young Marx's failure to elaborate his vision of human emancipation. Marx's qualified disapproval of utopianism, and, in particular, his rejection of the need for blueprints, resulted from his problematic conviction that the solutions to social problems were immanent in the historical process. I have suggested

---

[68] This is merely to allow that some theory of history might justify such an account, not to suggest that historical materialism does so.

[69] Joseph Raz, *Value, Respect, and Attachment* (Cambridge, 2001) p. 10. For a survey of some twentieth-century events widely thought to have undermined confidence in moral progress, see Jonathan Glover, *Humanity: A Moral History of the Twentieth Century* (London, 1999).

[70] Plamenatz remarks: 'It is as if [Marx] were pointing with one hand in the direction in which he wanted men to go, and with the other were throwing dust in their eyes.' John Plamenatz, *Karl Marx's Philosophy of Man* (Oxford, 1975) p. 472.

[71] Cohen, *If You're an Egalitarian*, p. 77.   [72] *Kapital* 25/17.

that this belief lacks a theoretical justification, it is hard for us to share, and it has practical dangers.[73]

In the introductory remarks with which this book began, I noted the suggestive but opaque character of the early writings. I explained that it was precisely these characteristics which had motivated me to write the present volume. In attempting to understand works which I found interesting but unclear, I hoped to reach a sounder judgement of their worth. I would not want my emphatic rejection of his position on this question of socialist design to give a misleading impression of my wider judgement of the work of the young Marx.

In the first place, there are many aspects of the early writings on which my verdict would be more favourable. Such a formulation may seem overly cautious. However, both the range and the nature of topics broached in the early writings militate against a simple summary evaluation.

The young Marx's account of the emergence of the modern state (discussed in Chapter 2) includes a wide-ranging and powerful critique of Hegel's metaphysics (covering the epistemological status of the Hegelian categories, the speculative attitude towards the empirical world, the purported link between the concept and its realisation, the nature of speculative explanation, and the Hegelian identity of God and the world); a historically sensitive sketch of the distinctive features of the modern social world (covering the character of, and separation between, the antagonistic spheres of civil and political society); an evocative account of two of the main forms of alienation which disfigure that world (the 'atomism' of modern civil society, and the 'abstract' character of the modern state); and a nuanced and appreciative assessment of Hegel's empirical acumen (as grasping both the essential character and the flaws of the modern social world).

The young Marx's account of the character of the modern state (discussed in Chapter 3) includes a robust appreciation of the recognition of community in that state (community being a complex notion in the early writings, with important connections to equality and human nature); a persuasive critique of the 'incomplete' and 'contradictory' character of modern political life (according to which the unrestrained individualism of civil society

---

[73] The positive case for utopianism is beyond the remit of the present work. However, for some tentative remarks, in a different context, see my 'Introduction' to William Morris, *News From Nowhere*, ed. David Leopold (Oxford, 2003) pp. xxx–xxxi.

comes to shape and dominate the sphere of the common good); a striking moral condemnation of certain endemic features of the modern social
world (including its tendency to promote 'objectification' and to violate the
Kantian principle that persons should not be treated only as means); and
a subtle account of the constitutional self-understanding of modern states
(as implicitly condoning the corruption of the common good by narrow
and particularistic interests).

The young Marx's account of the replacement of the modern state (discussed in Chapter 4) includes a seductive call for the reorganisation of
society such that the 'true man' – the individual who has developed and
deployed his essential human capacities – is found in everyday life (not
merely reflected in the pale and inadequate form of the abstract political
state); a modestly demanding account of human flourishing as requiring a society that satisfies both the basic physical needs (for sustenance,
warmth and shelter, certain climatic conditions, physical exercise, basic
hygiene, procreation and sexual activity) and the less basic social needs (for
recreation, culture, intellectual stimulation, artistic expression, emotional
satisfaction, aesthetic pleasure, fulfilling work and meaningful community) of individuals; a striking (and broadly Aristotelian) picture of the
complex co-operation (in pursuit of the common good) which characterises the political community of the future as both a condition for, and
a product of, human flourishing; and a fragmentary but evocative echo of
a civic republican vision in which politics does not disappear but rather
loses its abstract character (the faint institutional threads of this vision
include extensive participation in political life by citizens concerned for the
common good, the appropriation by those citizens of administrative tasks
previously the preserve of a separate and privileged bureaucracy, and the
possible replacement of representative democracy by some kind of popular
delegacy).

It is hard to imagine any serious consideration of these issues resulting
in a simple overall verdict, not only because of the number and variety
of topics here, but also because the truth of these matters is complex and
contested. Moreover, a brute summary of the topics on which the young
Marx held 'correct' views might do violence to the spirit in which this book
is written. It seems certain that we learn from the 'mighty dead' in various
and complex ways. Not least, we may learn from them even when their
treatment of issues is mistaken or confused in some respect. (Indeed, I am
tempted to suggest that one of the defining features of the 'mighty dead' is
that identifying and reflecting on their errors and opacities can be genuinely
enlightening.) For example, I have criticised the young Marx for rejecting

the need to engage with problems of socialist design, but that conclusion emerged only from a serious engagement with his views on utopianism.

In my opening remarks, I spoke of a new generation of readers who no longer feel obliged to swallow (or spew out) Marx whole. This book was written with those readers in mind. It was driven by the conviction that the young Marx's various discussions of the fate of individuals in contemporary civil society, of the achievements and failings of modern political life, and of the (as yet unrealised) possibilities of human flourishing are full of insight and illumination. The early writings provide the fascinating and uncommon spectacle of a powerful and imaginative intellect engaging with a series of important and complex issues that remain relevant to contemporary readers. There are a myriad ways in which we might learn from such an encounter, provided that we approach it with an open and critical mind.

Bibliographical note

This Bibliographical Note expands the short form of reference used above for works by Marx and some other authors.

(A) BRUNO BAUER

Über die Prinzipien des Schönen: References (divided by a forward slash) are to *Über die Prinzipien des Schönen: De pulchri principiis: Eine Preisschrift*, edited by Douglas Moggach and Winfried Schultze (Berlin, 1996), and 'On the Principles of the Beautiful', Douglas Moggach, *The Philosophy and Politics of Bruno Bauer* (Cambridge, 2003), pp. 188–212, respectively.

Posaune: References (divided by a forward slash) are to *Die Posaune des jüngsten Gerichts über Hegel, den Atheisten und Antichristen: Ein Ultimatum* (Leipzig, 1841), and *The Trumpet of the Last Judgement Against Hegel the Atheist and Antichrist: An Ultimatum*, edited and translated by Lawrence S. Stepelevich (Lewiston NY, 1989), respectively.

'Letter to Arnold Ruge (19 October 1841)': References are to 'Letter to Arnold Ruge (19 October 1841)', translated by Lawrence S. Stepelevich, *The Philosophical Forum*, volume 8, nos. 2–4 (1978), pp. 121–5.

Die Judenfrage: References (divided by a forward slash) are to *Die Judenfrage* (Brunswick, 1843), and *The Jewish Problem*, translated by Helen Lederer (typescript dated 1958 and held by the Hebrew Union College – Jewish Institute of Religion, Cincinnati, Ohio), respectively.

'Fähigkeit': References (divided by a forward slash) are to 'Die Fähigkeit der heutigen Juden und Christen, frei zu werden', *Feldzüge der reinen Kritik* (Frankfurt am Main, 1968), pp. 175–95, and 'The Capacity of Present-Day Jews and Christians to Become Free', translated by Michael P. Malloy, *The Philosophical Forum*, volume 8, nos. 2–4 (1978), pp. 135–49, respectively.

Das entdeckte Christenthum: References are to *Das entdeckte Christenthum in Vormärz: Bruno Bauers Kampf gegen Religion und Christenthum und Erstausgabe seiner Kampfschrift*, edited by Ernst Barnikol (Jena, 1927).

Briefwechsel: References are to *Briefwechsel zwischen Bruno Bauer und Edgar Bauer während der Jahre 1832–1842 aus Bonn und Berlin* (Aalen, 1969). Facsimile reprint of first edition published in 1844.

Das Judenthum in der Fremde: References are to *Das Judenthum in der Fremde: Separat-Abdruck aus dem Wagener'schen Staats- und Gesellschaftslexicon* (Berlin, 1863).

'The Present Position of the Jews': References are to 'The Present Position of the Jews', *New York Daily Tribune*, Monday 7 June 1852, p. 5.

Russland und das Germanentum: References are to (excerpt from) *Russland und das Germanentum, Die Hegelsche Linke*, edited by Karl Löwith (Stuttgart, 1962).

Christus und die Cäsaren: References are to *Christus und die Cäsaren: Der Ursprung des Christenthums aus dem römischen Griechenthum* (Berlin, 1877).

(B) FRIEDRICH ENGELS

'Progress of Social Reform': References are to 'Progress of Social Reform on the Continent', *MECW*, volume 3, pp. 392–408.

'Briefe aus London': References (divided by a forward slash) are to 'Briefe aus London', *MEW*, volume 1, pp. 468–79, and 'Letters From London', *MECW*, volume 3, pp. 379–91, respectively.

'Kommunistischen Ansiedlungen': References (divided by a forward slash) are to 'Beschreibung der in neuerer Zeit entstandenen und noch bestehenden kommunistischen Ansiedlungen', *MEW*, volume 2, pp. 521–35, and 'Description of Recently Founded Communist Colonies Still in Existence', *MECW*, volume 4, pp. 214–28, respectively.

'Rapid Progress': References are to 'Rapid Progress of Communism in Germany', *MECW*, volume 4, pp. 229–42.

'Fourier': References (divided by a forward slash) are to 'Ein Fragment Fouriers über den Handel', *MEW*, volume 2, pp. 604–10, and 'A Fragment of Fourier's on Trade', *MECW*, volume 4, pp. 613–44, respectively.

Anti-Dühring: References (divided by a forward slash) are to *Herrn Eugen Dührings Umwälzung der Wissenschaft*, *MEW*, volume 20, pp. 3–303, and *Herr Eugene Dühring's Revolution in Science*, *MECW*, volume 25, pp. 5–309, respectively.

'Bruno Bauer und das Urchristentum': References (divided by a forward slash) are to 'Bruno Bauer und das Urchristentum', *MEW*, volume 19, pp. 297–305, and 'Bruno Bauer and Early Christianity', *MECW*, volume 24, pp. 427–35, respectively.

'How Not to Translate Marx': References are to 'How Not to Translate Marx', *MECW*, volume 26, pp. 335–40.

(C) FRIEDRICH ENGELS AND EDGAR BAUER

Triumph: References (divided by a forward slash) are to *Die frech bedräute, jedoch wunderbar befreite Bibel. Oder: Der Triumph des Glaubens. Das ist: Schreckliche, jedoch wahrhafte und erkleckliche Historia von dem weiland Licentiaten Bruno Bauer: wie selbiger vom Teufel verführet, vom reinen Glauben abgefallen, Oberteufel geworden und endlich kräftiglich entsetzet ist. Christliches Heldengedicht in vier Gesängen*, *MEW*, Ergänzungsband, volume 2, pp. 283–316, and *The Insolently Threatened, Yet Miraculously Rescued Bible. Or: The Triumph of Faith. To Wit, The Terrible Yet True and Salutary History of the Erstwhile Licentiate Bruno Bauer; How the Same, Seduced by the Devil, Fallen From the True Faith, Became Chief Devil, and Was Well and Truly Ousted in the End. A Christian Epic in Four Cantos*, *MECW*, volume 2, pp. 313–51, respectively.

(D) LUDWIG FEUERBACH

Gedanken: References (divided by a forward slash) are to *Gedanken über Tod und Unsterblichkeit, aus den Papieren eines Denkers, nebst Anhang theologisch-satyrischer Xenien, hrsg. von einem seiner Freunde, Gesammelte Werke*, volume 1, pp. 175–515, and *Thoughts on Death and Immortality: From the Papers of a Thinker, Along with an Appendix of Theological-Satirical Epigrams, Edited by One of his Friends*, edited and translated by James A. Massey (Berkeley, 1980), respectively.

Geschichte der neuern Philosophie: References are to *Geschichte der neuern Philosophie von Bacon von Verulam bis Benedict Spinoza, Gesammelte Werke*, volume 2.

'Zur Kritik': References (divided by a forward slash) are to 'Zur Kritik der Hegelschen Philosophie', *Gesammelte Werke*, volume 9, pp. 16–62, and 'Towards a Critique of Hegelian Philosophy', translated by Zawar Hanfi, *The Young Hegelians: An Anthology*, edited by Lawrence S. Stepelevich (Cambridge, 1983), pp. 95–128, respectively.

Wesen: References (divided by a forward slash) are to *Das Wesen des Christentums*, *Gesammelte Werke*, volume 5, and *The Essence of Christianity*, translated by George Eliot (New York, 1957), respectively.

'Über den "Anfang der Philosophie"': References (divided by a forward slash) are to 'Einige Bemerkungen über den "Anfang der Philosophie" von Dr J. F. Reiff', *Gesammelte Werke*, volume 9, pp. 143–53, and 'Several Comments on "The Beginning of Philosophy" by Dr J. F. Reiff', *The Fiery Brook: Selected Writings of Ludwig Feuerbach*, edited and translated by Zawar Hanfi (New York, 1972), pp. 135–44, respectively.

'Nothwendigkeit': References (divided by a forward slash) are to 'Nothwendigkeit einer reform der Philosophie', *Sämtliche Werke* (Stuttgart, 1960–4), volume 2, pp. 215–22, and 'The Necessity of a Reform of Philosophy', *The Fiery Brook: Selected Writings of Ludwig Feuerbach*, edited and translated by Zawar Hanfi (New York, 1972), pp. 145–52, respectively.

'Über den Marienkultus': References are to 'Über den Marienkultus', *Gesammelte Werke*, volume 9, pp. 156–76.

'Zur Beurteilung': References are to 'Zur Beurteilung der Schrift *Das Wesen des Christentums*', *Gesammelte Werke*, volume 9, pp. 229–42.

'Beleuchtung einer theologischen Rezension': References are to 'Beleuchtung einer theologischen Rezension über "Das Wesen des Christentums" (Replik)', *Gesammelte Werke*, volume 9, pp. 177–228.

Grundsätze: References (divided by a forward slash) are to *Grundsätze der Philosophie der Zukunft*, *Gesammelte Werke*, volume 9, pp. 264–341, and *Principles of the Philosophy of the Future*, translated by Manfred H. Vogel (Indianapolis, 1986), respectively.

'Vorläufige Thesen': References (divided by a forward slash) are to 'Vorläufige Thesen zur Reform[ation] der Philosophie', *Gesammelte Werke*, volume 9, pp. 243–63, and 'Provisional Theses for the Reform[ation] of Philosophy', translated by Daniel Dahlstrom, *The Young Hegelians: An Anthology*, edited by Lawrence S. Stepelevich (Cambridge, 1983), pp. 95–128, respectively.

Luther: References (divided by a forward slash) are to *Das Wesen des Glaubens im Sinne Luthers: Ein Beitrag zum 'Wesen des Christentums'*, *Gesammelte Werke*, volume 9, pp. 353–412, and *The Essence of Faith According to Luther: A Supplement to 'The Essence of Christianity'*, translated by Melvin Cherno (New York, 1967), pp. 31–117, respectively.

'Merkwürdige Äußerungen': References (divided by a forward slash) are to 'Merkwürdige Äußerungen Luthers nebst Glossen', *Gesammelte Werke*, volume 9, pp. 420–6, and 'Comments Upon Some Remarkable Statements by Luther', translated by Melvin Cherno, *The Essence of Faith According to Luther* (New York, 1967), pp. 119–27, respectively.

'Beziehung': References (divided by a forward slash) are to 'Über das "Wesen des Christentums" in Beziehung auf Stirners "Der Einzige und sein Eigentum" (Replik)', *Gesammelte Werke*, volume 9, pp. 427–41, and 'On *The Essence of Christianity* in Relation to Stirner's *The Ego and Its Own* (Reply)', translated by Frederick Gordon, *The Philosophical Forum*, volume 8, nos. 2–4 (1978), pp. 81–91, respectively.

'Vorwort [zu *Sämtliche Werke*]': References are to 'Vorwort [zu L. Feuerbach: *Sämtliche Werke*, Bd I]', *Gesammelte Werke*, volume 10, pp. 181–90.

'Fragmente': References (divided by a forward slash) are to 'Fragmente zur Charakteristik meines philosophischen curriculum vitae', *Gesammelte Werke*, volume 10, pp. 151–80, and 'Fragments Concerning the Characteristics of My Philosophical Curriculum Vitae', *The Fiery Brook: Selected Writings of Ludwig Feuerbach*, edited and translated by Zawar Hanfi (New York, 1972), pp. 265–96, respectively.

'Paul Johann Anselm von Feuerbach und seine Söhne': References are to 'Paul Johann Anselm von Feuerbach und seine Söhne', *Gesammelte Werke*, volume 10, pp. 324–32.

'Naturwissenschaft': References are to 'Die Naturwissenschaft und die Revolution', *Gesammelte Werke*, volume 10, pp. 347–68.

Vorlesungen: References (divided by a forward slash) are to *Vorlesungen über das Wesen der Religion*, *Gesammelte Werke*, volume 6, and *Lectures on the Essence of Religion*, translated by Ralph Manheim (New York, 1967), respectively.

Briefe: References are to (letter number in) *Ausgewählte Briefe von und an Ludwig Feuerbach*, edited by Wilhelm Bolin (Leipzig, 1904).

Gesammelte Werke: References are to *Gesammelte Werke*, edited by Werner Schuffenhauer, 21 volumes (Berlin, 1967–2003). References are to volume and page number.

(E) G. W. F HEGEL

'Der Geist des Christentums': References are to 'Der Geist des Christentums und sein Schicksal', *Werke*, volume 1, pp. 274–418.

'Krug': References are to 'Wie der gemeine Menschenverstand die Philosophie nehme, – dargestellt an den Werken des Herrn Krug', *Werke*, volume 2, pp. 188–207.

Logik: References (divided by a forward slash) are to *Wissenschaft der Logik*, parts I and II, *Werke*, volumes 5 and 6, and *Hegel's Science of Logic*, translated by A. V. Miller (London, 1969), respectively.

Phänomenologie: References (divided by a forward slash) are to *Phänomenologie des Geistes*, *Werke*, volume 3, and *Phenomenology of Spirit*, translated by A. V. Miller with analysis of the text and foreword by J. N. Findlay (Oxford, 1977), respectively.

Philosophie des Rechts: References (divided by a forward slash) are to *Grundlinien der Philosophie des Rechts*, *Werke*, volume 7, and *Elements of the Philosophy of Right*, edited and introduced by Allen W. Wood, translated by H. B. Nisbet (Cambridge, 1991), respectively. References are to sections (§); an 'A' indicates Hegel's 'Remarks (*Anmerkungen*)'; a 'Z' indicates editorial 'Additions (*Zusätzen*)'. References beginning with a paragraph mark (¶) followed by a number indicate a paragraph in the 'Preface' of the text.

Enzyklopädie: References (divided by a forward slash) are to *Enzyklopädie der philosophischen Wissenschaft im Grundrisse*, *Werke*, volumes 8–10, and (the relevant volume of) *The Encyclopedia Logic, Part 1 of the Encyclopedia of Philosophical Sciences with the Zusätze*, translated by T. F. Geraets, W. A. Suchting, and H. S. Harris (Indianapolis, 1991); *Hegel's Philosophy of Nature*, being part 2 of the *Encyclopaedia of the Philosophical Sciences*, translated by A. V. Miller (Oxford, 1970); or *Hegel's Philosophy of Mind*, being part 3 of the *Encyclopaedia of the Philosophical*

Sciences, translated by William Wallace and A. V. Miller (Oxford, 1971), respectively. References are to sections (§); a 'Z' indicates editorial 'Additions (*Zusätzen*)'.

Vorlesungen über die Geschichte der Philosophie: References (divided by a forward slash) are to *Vorlesungen über die Geschichte der Philosophie*, *Werke*, volumes 18–20, and *Lectures on the History of Philosophy*, translated by E. S Haldane and F. Simson, 3 volumes (London, 1892), respectively.

Vorlesungen über die Philosophie der Religion: References (divided by a forward slash) are to *Vorlesungen über die Philosophie der Religion*, part 1: *Einleitung, Der Begriff der Religion* (Hamburg, 1983), and *Lectures on the Philosophy of Religion*, volume 1: *Introduction and the Concept of Religion*, translated by R. F. Brown, P. C. Hodgson, and J. M. Stewart, with the assistance of J. P. Fitzer and H. S. Harris (Berkeley, 1984), respectively.

Vernunft: References (divided by a forward slash) are to *Die Vernunft in der Geschichte*, edited by J. Hoffmeister (Hamburg, 1955), and *Lectures on the Philosophy of World History. Introduction: Reason in History*, translated by H. B. Nisbet with an introduction by Duncan Forbes (Cambridge, 1975), respectively.

Werke: References are to *Werke in zwanzig Bänden*, edited by Eva Moldenhauer and Karl Markus Michel, third edition (Frankfurt am Main, 1993–6). References are to volume and page number.

(F) HEINRICH HEINE

Die Bäder von Lucca: References are to *Die Bäder von Lucca*, *Historische-kritische Gesamtausgabe der Werke* (*Düsseldorfer Ausgabe*), volume 7, part 1 (Hamburg, 1986), pp. 81–152.

Kahldorf: References are to *Einleitung zu 'Kahldorf über den Adel'*, *Historische-kritische Gesamtausgabe der Werke* (*Düsseldorfer Ausgabe*), volume 11 (Hamburg, 1978), pp. 134–45.

Geschichte: References are to *Zur Geschichte der Religion und Philosophie in Deutschland*, *Historische-kritische Gesamtausgabe der Werke* (*Düsseldorfer Ausgabe*), volume 8, part 1 (Hamburg, 1979), pp. 9–120.

'Tannhäuser': References (divided by a forward slash) are to 'Der Tannhäuser: Ein Legende', *Historische-kritische Gesamtausgabe der Werke* (*Düsseldorfer Ausgabe*), volume 2 (Hamburg, 1983), pp. 53–60, and 'Tannhäuser: A Legend', *The Complete Poems of Heinrich Heine: A Modern English Version by Hal Draper* (Oxford, 1982), pp. 348–53, respectively.

'Anno 1829': References (divided by a forward slash) are to 'Anno 1829', *Historische-kritische Gesamtausgabe der Werke* (*Düsseldorfer Ausgabe*), volume 2 (Hamburg, 1983), pp. 79–80, and 'Anno 1829', *The Complete Poems of Heinrich Heine: A Modern English Version by Hal Draper* (Oxford, 1982), pp. 368–9, respectively.

Atta Troll: References (divided by a forward slash) are to *Atta Troll: Ein Sommernachtstraum*, *Historische-kritische Gesamtausgabe der Werke* (*Düsseldorfer Ausgabe*), volume 4 (Hamburg, 1985), pp. 13–87, and *Atta Troll: A Summer Night's Dream, The Complete Poems of Heinrich Heine: A Modern English Version by Hal Draper* (Oxford, 1982), pp. 419–80, respectively.

Deutschland: References (divided by a forward slash) are to *Deutschland: Ein Wintermärchen, Historische-kritische Gesamtausgabe der Werke (Düsseldorfer Ausgabe)*, volume 4 (Hamburg, 1985), pp. 89–157, and *Germany: A Winter's Tale, The Complete Poems of Heinrich Heine: A Modern English Version by Hal Draper* (Oxford, 1982), pp. 481–536, respectively.

Lutezia 1: References are to *Lutezia 1 [Lutetia 1], Historische-kritische Gesamtausgabe der Werke (Düsseldorfer Ausgabe)*, volume 13, part 1 (Hamburg, 1988).

Lutezia 2: References are to *Lutezia 2 [Lutetia 2], Historische-kritische Gesamtausgabe der Werke (Düsseldorfer Ausgabe)*, volume 14, part 1 (Hamburg, 1990).

'Prinzessin Sabbat': References (divided by a forward slash) are to 'Prinzessin Sabbat', *Historische-kritische Gesamtausgabe der Werke (Düsseldorfer Ausgabe)*, volume 3 (Hamburg, 1992), pp. 125–9, and 'Princess Sabbath', *The Complete Poems of Heinrich Heine: A Modern English Version by Hal Draper* (Oxford, 1982), pp. 651–5, respectively.

Briefe: References are to *Briefe*, edited by Friedrich Hirth, 6 volumes (Mainz, 1950–1). References are to volume and page number.

Säkularausgabe: References are to *Heinrich Heine: Säkularausgabe*, projected 30 volumes (Berlin and Paris, 1970–). References are to volume and page number.

(G) MOSES HESS

Die europäische Triarchie: References are to *Die europäische Triarchie* (Leipzig, 1841). (Facsimile edition, Amsterdam, 1971.)

Rom und Jerusalem: References (divided by a forward slash) are to *Rom und Jerusalem: Die letzte Nationalitätsfrage* (Leipzig, 1862), and *Rome and Jerusalem*, translated by Rabbi Maurice J. Bloom (New York, 1958), respectively.

Schriften: References are to *Philosophische und sozialistische Schriften, 1837–1850*, edited with an introduction by Auguste Cornu and Wolfgang Mönke (Berlin, 1961).

Jüdische Schriften: References are to *Jüdische Schriften*, edited by Theodor Zlocisti (Berlin, 1905).

(H) KARL MARX

Hefte zur epikureischen, stoischen und skeptischen Philosophie: References (divided by a forward slash) are to *Hefte zur epikureischen, stoischen und skeptischen Philosophie*, *MEW, Ergänzungsband*, volume 1, pp. 13–255, and *Notebooks on Epicurean, Stoic, and Sceptic Philosophy*, *MECW*, volume 1, pp. 403–509, respectively.

Differenz: References (divided by a forward slash) are to *Differenz der demokritischen und epikureischen Naturphilosophie (Doktordissertation)*, *MEW*, *Ergänzungsband*, volume 1, pp. 257–373, and *Difference Between the Democritean and Epicurean Philosophy of Nature (Doctoral Dissertation)*, *MECW*, volume 1, pp. 25–105, respectively.

'Der leitende Artikel': References (divided by a forward slash) are to 'Der leitende Artikel in Nr. 179 der *Kölnischen Zeitung*, *MEW*, volume 1, pp. 86–104, and 'The Leading Article in No. 179 of the *Kölnische Zeitung*', *MECW*, volume 1, pp. 184–202, respectively.

'Briefwechsel von 1843': References (divided by a forward slash) are to 'Briefe aus den *Deutsch-Französischen Jahrbüchern*', *MEW*, volume 1, pp. 337–46; 'Letters From the *Deutsch-Französische Jahrbücher*', *MECW*, volume 3, pp. 133–45; and 'Letters from the *Franco-German Yearbooks*', *EW*, pp. 199–209, respectively. (Note that *MEW* and *MECW* include only Marx's contributions, whilst *MEGA①* and *MEGA②* contain all the programmatic correspondence.)

Kritik: References (divided by a forward slash) are to *Kritik des Hegelschen Staatsrechts*, *MEW*, volume 1, pp. 201–333; 'Contribution to the Critique of Hegel's Philosophy of Law', *MECW*, volume 3, pp. 3–129; and 'Critique of Hegel's Doctrine of State', *EW*, pp. 57–198, respectively.

'Zur Judenfrage': References (divided by a forward slash) are to 'Zur Judenfrage', *MEW*, volume 1, pp. 347–77; 'On the Jewish Question', *MECW*, volume 3, pp. 146–74; and 'On the Jewish Question', *EW*, pp. 211–41, respectively.

'Kritik: Einleitung': References (divided by a forward slash) are to 'Zur Kritik der Hegelschen Rechtsphilosophie: Einleitung', *MEW*, volume 1, pp. 378–91; 'Contribution to the Critique of Hegel's Philosophy of Law: Introduction', *MECW*, volume 3, pp. 175–87; and 'Critique of Hegel's Philosophy of Right: Introduction', *EW*, pp. 243–57, respectively.

'Kritische Randglossen': References (divided by a forward slash) are to 'Kritische Randglossen zu dem Artikel "Der König von Preussen und die Sozialreform: Von einem Preussen"', *MEW*, volume 1, pp. 392–409; 'Critical Marginal Notes on the Article "The King of Prussia and Social Reform: By A Prussian"', *MECW*, volume 3, pp. 189–206; and 'Critical Notes on the King of Prussia and Social Reform', *EW*, pp. 401–20, respectively.

Manuskripte: References (divided by a forward slash) are to *Ökonomisch-philosophische Manuskripte aus dem Jahre 1844*, *MEW*, *Ergänzungsband*, volume 1, pp. 465–588; *Economic and Philosophic Manuscripts of 1844*, *MECW*, volume 3, pp. 229–346; and *Economic and Philosophical Manuscripts*, *EW*, pp. 279–400, respectively.

'Auszüge aus James Mill': References (divided by a forward slash) are to 'Auszüge aus James Mills Buch "Elémens d'économie politique"', *MEW*, *Ergänzungsband*, volume 1, pp. 443–63; 'Comments on James Mill, *Elémens d'économie* politique', *MECW*, volume 3, pp. 211–28; and 'Excerpts from James Mill's Elements of Political

Economy', *EW*, pp. 259–78, respectively. (Note that *MECW* omits some quotations from Mill.)

'Draft Plan': References (divided by a forward slash) are to 'Die bürgerliche Gesellschaft und die kommunistische Revolution', *MEW*, volume 3, p. 537, and 'Draft Plan for a Work on the Modern State', *MECW*, volume 4, p. 666, respectively.

'Library': References are to 'Plan of the "Library of the Best Foreign Socialist Writers"', *MECW*, volume 4, p. 667. (Not in *MEW*.)

'Peuchet: vom Selbstmord': References (divided by a forward slash) are to 'Peuchet: vom Selbstmord', *Marx on Suicide*, edited by Eric A. Plaut and Kevin Anderson, (Evanston, 1999), pp. 77–101, and 'Peuchet: On Suicide'; *MECW*, volume 4, pp. 597–612, respectively.

'Draft Article on Friedrich List': References are to 'Draft of an Article on Friedrich List's *Das nationale System der politischen Ökonomie*', *MECW*, volume 4, pp. 265–93. (Not in *MEW*.)

'Die moralisierende Kritik': References (divided by a forward slash) are to 'Die moralisierende Kritik und die kritisierende Moral: Beitrag zur deutschen Kulturgeschichte gegen Karl Heinzen', *MEW*, volume 4, pp. 331–59, and 'Moralising Criticism and Critical Morality: A Contribution to German Cultural History Contra Karl Heinzen'; *MECW*, volume 6, pp. 312–40, respectively.

Misère de la philosophie: References (divided by a forward slash) are to *Das Elend der Philosophie: Antwort auf Proudhons "Philosophie des Elends"*, *MEW*, volume 4, pp. 63–182, and *The Poverty of Philosophy: A Reply to the Philosophy of Poverty by M. Proudhon*, *MECW*, volume 6, pp. 105–212, respectively.

'Die Taten des Hauses Hohenzollern': References (divided by a forward slash) are to 'Die Taten des Hauses Hohenzollern', *MEW*, volume 6, pp. 477–80, and 'The Deeds of the House of Hohenzollern', *MECW*, volume 9, pp. 418–22, respectively.

Die achtzehnte Brumaire: References (divided by a forward slash) are to *Die achtzehnte Brumaire des Louis Bonaparte*, *MEW*, volume 8, pp. 111–207, and *The Eighteenth Brumaire of Louis Bonaparte*, *MECW*, volume 11, pp. 99–197, respectively.

'Bauer's Pamphlets': References are to 'B. Bauer's Pamphlets on the Collision with Russia', *MECW*, volume 15, pp. 181–93. (Not in *MEW*.)

'1859 Vorwort': References (divided by a forward slash) are to *Zur Kritik der politischen Ökonomie*, *MEW*, volume 13, pp. 7–11, and *Contribution to the Critique of Political Economy*, *MECW*, volume 29, pp. 261–5, respectively.

Herr Vogt: References (divided by a forward slash) are to *Herr Vogt*, *MEW*, volume 14, pp. 381–686, and *Herr Vogt*, *MECW*, volume 17, pp. 21–329, respectively.

'Confession': References (divided by a forward slash) are to 'Bekenntnissen', *MEW*, volume 31, p. 597, and 'Confession', *MECW*, volume 42, pp. 567–8, respectively.

Kapital: References (divided by a forward slash) are to *Das Kapital: Kritik der politischen Ökonomie*, Erster Band, Buch 1: *Der Produktionsprozeß des Kapitals*, *MEW*, volume 23, and *Capital: Critique of Political Economy*, volume 1, Book 1: *The Process of Production of Capital*, *MECW*, volume 35, respectively.

Erster Entwurf: References (divided by a forward slash) are to *Erster Entwurf zum 'Bürgerkrieg in Frankreich'*, *MEW*, volume 17, pp. 493–571, and *First Draft of 'The Civil War in France'*, *MECW*, volume 22, pp. 437–514, respectively.

Der Bürgerkrieg in Frankreich: References (divided by a forward slash) are to *Der Bürgerkrieg in Frankreich*, *MEW*, volume 17, pp. 313–65, and *The Civil War in France*, *MECW*, volume 22, pp. 307–55, respectively.

'L'indifferenza in materia politica': References (divided by a forward slash) are to 'Der Politische Indifferentismus', *MEW*, volume 18, pp. 299–304, and 'Political Indifferentism', *MECW*, volume 23, pp. 392–7, respectively.

'Kritik der Gothaer Programms': References (divided by a forward slash) are to 'Randglossen zum Programm der deutschen Arbeiterpartei', *MEW*, volume 19, pp. 15–32, and 'Marginal Notes on the Programme of the German Worker's Party', *MECW*, volume 24, pp. 75–99, respectively.

EW: References are to Karl Marx, *Early Writings*, translated by Rodney Livingstone and Gregor Benton (London, 1975).

(I) KARL MARX AND FRIEDRICH ENGELS

Die heilige Familie: References (divided by a forward slash) are to *Die heilige Familie, oder Kritik der kritischen Kritik: Gegen Bruno Bauer und Konsorten*, *MEW*, volume 2, pp. 3–223, and *The Holy Family, or Critique of Critical Criticism: Against Bruno Bauer & Co.*, *MECW*, volume 4, pp. 3–211, respectively.

Die deutsche Ideologie: References (divided by a forward slash) are to *Die deutsche Ideologie: Kritik der neuesten deutschen Philosophie in ihren Repräsentanten Feuerbach, B. Bauer und Stirner, und des deutschen Sozialismus in seinen verschiedenen Propheten*, *MEW*, volume 3, pp. 9–530, and *The German Ideology: Critique of the Latest German Philosophy as Exemplified by its Representatives Feuerbach, B. Bauer and Stirner, and of German Socialism as Exemplified by its Various Prophets*, *MECW*, volume 5, pp. 19–539, respectively.

Manifest: References (divided by a forward slash) are to *Manifest der kommunistischen Partei*, *MEW*, volume 4, pp. 459–493, and *Manifesto of the Communist Party*, *MECW*, volume 6, pp. 477–519, respectively.

MEGA①: References are to *Karl Marx-Friedrich Engels-Historische-kritische Gesamtausgabe: Werke, Schriften, Briefe*, Marx-Engels-Institute (Moscow), 12 volumes (of projected 42) completed (Frankfurt am Main and Berlin, 1927–32, 1935). References are to series, volume, and page number.

MEW: References are to *Karl Marx-Friedrich Engels-Werke*, Institut für Marxismus-Leninismus beim Zentralkomitee der Sozialistischen Einheitspartei Deutschlands,

39 volumes plus 'Ergänzungsbanden' (Berlin, 1957–68). References are to volume and page number.

MECW: References are to Karl Marx and Friedrich Engels, *Collected Works*, 50 volumes (Moscow, London, and New York, 1975–2005). References are to volume and page number.

MEGA②: References are to *Karl Marx/Friedrich Engels/Gesamtausgabe*. This ongoing edition was initially edited by the Institut für Marxismus-Leninismus beim Zentralkomitee der Kommunistischen Partei der Sowjetunion und vom Institut für Marxismus-Leninismus beim Zentralkomitee der Sozialistischen Einheitspartei Deutschlands, and published in Berlin by Dietz Verlag (1975–98). It is now edited by the Internationale Marx-Engels Stiftung (IMES) and published in Berlin by Akademie Verlag (1998–). References are to series, volume, and page number.

(J) JEAN-JACQUES ROUSSEAU

Discours sur l'origine de l'inégalité: References (divided by a forward slash) are to *Discours sur l'origine et les fondements de l'inégalité parmi les hommes, Oeuvres complètes*, volume 3: *Les écrits politique* (Paris, 1964), pp. 111–237, and *Collected Writings of Rousseau*, volume 3: *Discourse on the Origins of Inequality (Second Discourse), Polemics, and Political Economy* (Hanover NH, 1992), pp. 1–95, respectively.

Contrat social: References (divided by a forward slash) are to *Du contrat social, Oeuvres complètes*, volume 3: *Les écrits politiques* (Paris, 1964), pp. 349–470, and *Collected Writings of Rousseau*, volume 4: *Social Contract, Discourse on the Virtue Most Necessary for a Hero, Political Fragments, and Geneva Manuscripts* (Hanover NH, 1994), pp. 127–224, respectively.

'Lettres à Usteri': References are to two letters from Rousseau to Leonard Usteri, 30 April 1763 and 18 July 1763, *Political Writings*, edited by C. E. Vaughan (Cambridge, 1915), volume 2, pp. 166–8.

'L'économie politique': References are to *Discours sur l'économie politique* (1755), *Oeuvres complètes*, volume 3: *Les écrits politiques* (Paris, 1964), pp. 241–78.

Lettres écrites de la montagne: References are to *Lettres écrites de la montagne, Oeuvres complètes*, volume 3: *Les écrits politiques* (Paris, 1964), pp. 685–897, and *Collected Writings of Rousseau*, volume 9: *Letter to Beaumont, Letters Written from the Mountain, and Related Writings* (Hanover NH, 2001), pp. 131–306, respectively.

Rousseau juge de Jean-Jacques: References are to *Rousseau juge de Jean-Jacques, Oeuvres complètes*, volume 1: *Les Confessions: Autres textes autobiographiques* (Paris, 1959), pp. 657–989, and *Collected Writings of Rousseau*, volume 1: *Rousseau Judge of Jean-Jacques: Dialogues* (Hanover NH, 1990), respectively.

Considérations sur le gouvernement de Pologne: References (divided by a forward slash) are to *Considérations sur le gouvernement de Pologne, Oeuvres complètes*, volume 3:

Les écrits politiques (Paris, 1964), pp. 953–1041, and *The Government of Poland* (Indianapolis, 1985), respectively.

(K) ARNOLD RUGE

Briefwechsel: References are to *Briefwechsel und Tagebuchblätter aus den Jahren 1825–80*, edited by Paul Nerrlich, 2 volumes (Berlin, 1886).

'Rechtsphilosophie': References (divided by a forward slash) are to (the column number of) 'Die Hegelshe Rechtsphilosophie und die Politik unserer Zeit', *Deutsche Jahrbücher*, volumes 189 and 190 (August 1842), and 'Hegel's *Philosophy of Right* and the Politics of our Times', translated by James A. Massey, *The Young Hegelians*, edited by Lawrence S. Stepelevich (Cambridge, 1983), pp. 211–36, respectively.

'Selbstkritik': References (divided by a forward slash) are to 'Selbstkritik des Liberalismus', *Sämtliche Werke* (Mannheim, 1847), volume 4, pp. 76–116, and 'A Self-Critique of Liberalism', translated by James A. Massey, *The Young Hegelians*, edited by Lawrence S. Stepelevich (Cambridge, 1983), pp. 237–59, respectively.

(L) SAINT-SIMON

Oeuvres: References are to *Oeuvres de Claude-Henri de Saint-Simon*, 6 volumes (Paris, 1966).

'Ionescu': References are to *The Political Thought of Saint-Simon*, translated by Valence Ionescu (Oxford, 1976).

'Markham': References are to *Selected Writings*, translated by F. M. H. Markham (Oxford, 1952).

'Taylor': References are to *Selected Writings on Science, Industry, and Social Organization (1802–1825)*, translated by Keith Taylor (London, 1975).

(M) MAX STIRNER

Der Einzige: References (divided by a forward slash) are to *Der Einzige und sein Eigentum*, with an afterword by Ahlrich Meyer (Stuttgart, 1972), and *The Ego and Its Own*, translated by Steven T. Byington, edited with an introduction by David Leopold (Cambridge, 1995), respectively.

(N) DAVID FRIEDRICH STRAUSS

Das Leben Jesu: References are to *Das Leben Jesu, kritisch bearbeitet*, 2 volumes (Tübingen, 1835–6).

Streitschriften: References are to *Streitschriften zur Vertheidigung meiner Schrift über das Leben Jesu und zur Charakteristik der gegenwärtigen Theologie* (Tübingen, 1837).

Index

IDEAS IN CONTEXT

Edited by QUENTIN SKINNER and JAMES TULLY

LaVergne, TN USA
19 August 2009

155174LV00003B/20/P